Kawasaki ZX600
(Ninja ZX-6 & ZZ-R600)
Fours Owners Workshop Manual

by Mike Stubblefield and John H Haynes
Member of the Guild of Motoring Writers

Models covered:

Kawasaki ZX600D (Ninja ZX-6). 599cc. (US 1990 to 1993)
Kawasaki ZX600D (ZZ-R600). 599cc. (UK 1990 to 1993)
Kawasaki ZX600E (Ninja ZX-6). 599cc. (US 1993 to 1995)
Kawasaki ZX600E (ZZ-R600). 599cc. (UK 1993 to 1995)

ABCDE
FGHIJ
KLMNO
PQRST

Haynes Publishing
Sparkford Nr Yeovil
Somerset BA22 7JJ England

Haynes North America, Inc
861 Lawrence Drive
Newbury Park
California 91320 USA

Acknowledgments

Our thanks to Kawasaki Motors (UK), Ltd. for permission to reproduce certain illustrations used in this manual. We would also like to thank NGK Spark Plugs (UK) Ltd for supplying the color spark plug condition photos and the Avon Rubber Company for supplying information on tire fitting.

A book in the Haynes Owners Workshop Manual Series

Printed by J. H. Haynes & Co. Ltd., Sparkford, Nr Yeovil, Somerset BA22 7JJ, England

ISBN 1 56392 146 4

Library of Congress Catalog Card Number 95-80976

British Library Cataloguing in Publication Data
A catalogue record for this book is available from the British Library

We take great pride in the accuracy of information given in this manual, but motorcycle manufacturers make alterations and design changes during the production run of a particular motorcycle of which they do not inform us. No liability can be accepted by the authors or publishers for loss, damage or injury caused by any errors in, or omissions from, the information given.

Contents

Introductory pages

1990 ZX600-A1 (UK ZZ-R600 model shown, US Ninja ZX-6 similar)

1995 ZX600-E3 (UK ZZ-R600R model shown, US Ninja ZX-6 similar)

About this manual

Its purpose

The purpose of this manual is to help you maintain and repair your vehicle. It can do so in several ways. It can help you decide what work must be done, even if you choose to have it done by a dealer service department or a repair shop, it provides information and procedures for routine maintenance and it offers diagnostic and repair procedures to follow when trouble occurs.

It is hoped that you will use the manual to tackle the work yourself. For many simple jobs, doing it yourself may be quicker than arranging an appointment to get the machine into a shop and making the trips to leave it and pick it up. More importantly, a lot of money can be saved by avoiding the expense the shop must pass on to you to cover its labor and overhead costs. An added benefit is the sense of satisfaction and accomplishment that you feel after having done the job yourself.

Using the manual

The manual is divided into Chapters. Each Chapter is divided into numbered Sections which are headed in bold type between horizontal lines. Each Section consists of consecutively numbered paragraphs.

At the beginning of each numbered section you will be referred to any illustrations which apply to the procedures in that section. The reference numbers used in illustration captions pinpoint the pertinent Step within that section. That is, illustration 3.2 means the illustration refers to Section 3 and Step (or paragraph) 2 within that Section.

Procedures, once described in the text, are not normally repeated. When it is necessary to refer to another Chapter, the reference will be given as Chapter and Section number. Cross references given without use of the word "Chapter" apply to Sections and/or paragraphs in the same Chapter. For example, "see Section 8" means in the same Chapter.

Reference to the left or right side of the motorcycle is based on the assumption that one is sitting on the seat, facing forward.

Even though extreme care has been taken during the preparation of this manual, neither the publisher nor the author can accept responsibility for any errors in, or omissions from, the information given.

NOTE

A **Note** provides information necessary to properly complete a procedure or information which will make the procedure easier to understand.

CAUTION

A **Caution** provides a special procedure or special steps which must be taken while completing the procedure where the Caution is found. Not heeding a Caution can result in damage to the assembly being worked on.

WARNING

A **Warning** provides a special procedure or special steps which must be taken while completing the procedure where the Warning is found. Not heeding a Warning can result in personal injury.

Introduction to the Kawasaki ZX600 (Ninja ZX-6 and ZZ-R600)

The Kawasaki Ninja ZX600 (Ninja ZX-6 and ZZ-R600) is one of the most competent high-performance motorcycles in its class. Light weight, high output, outstanding brakes and excellent handling characteristics are what have made this machine one of the more popular mid-size bikes.

The engine is an inline four-cylinder, liquid-cooled, double overhead camshaft unit with four valves per cylinder. Fuel is delivered through four Keihin carburetors.

The front suspension uses telescopic forks.

The rear end uses a shock absorber/spring unit mounted ahead of the swingarm, close to the center of gravity of the machine. The damping characteristics of the rear shock are adjustable, as is the rear spring preload.

The front brake on all models uses a pair of dual-piston calipers. The rear brake uses a single dual-piston caliper.

Identification numbers

The frame serial number is stamped into the right side of the steering head and the engine serial number is stamped into the right engine case. Both of these numbers should be recorded and kept in a safe place so they can be furnished to law enforcement officials in the event of theft.

The frame serial number, engine serial number and carburetor identification number should also be kept in a handy place (such as with your driver's license) so they are always available when purchasing or ordering parts for your machine.

The models covered by this manual are as follows:

ZX600-D1 (1990 Ninja ZX-6/ZZ-R600)
ZX600-D2 (1991 Ninja ZX-6/ZZ-R600)
ZX600-D3 (1992 Ninja ZX-6/ZZ-R600)
ZX600-D4 (1993 Ninja ZX-6/ZZ-R600)
ZX600-E1 (1993 Ninja ZX-6/ZZ-R600)
ZX600-E2 (1994 Ninja ZX-6/ZZ-R600)
ZX600-E3 (1995 Ninja ZX-6/ZZ-R600)

The frame serial number is stamped on the steering head . . .

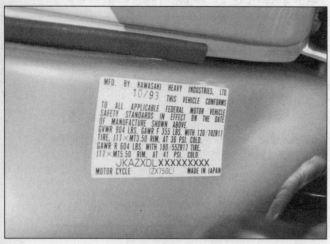

. . . and displayed on a decal

The engine serial number is located on the right side of the crankcase

The following table is a breakdown of the initial frame numbers for each model and year of production:

Year	Model	Initial frame number
1990	ZX600-D1	JKAZX4D1*LA000001, or JKAZX4D1*LB500001, or ZX600D-000001
1991	ZX600-D2	JKAZX4D1*MA014001, or JKAZX4D1*MB502201, or ZX600D-014001, or ZX600D-600001
1992	ZX600-D3	JKAZX4D1*NA028001, or JKAZX4D1*NB505201, or ZX600D-028001, or ZX600D-602501
1993	ZX600-D4	JKAZX4D1*PB508301
1993	ZX600-E1	JKAZX4E1*PA000001, or JKAZX4E1*PB500001, or ZX600E-000001
1994	ZX600-E2	JKAZX4E1*RA020001, or JKAZX4E1*RB503201, or ZX600E-020001
1995	Not available at time of printing	

* This digit in the frame number changes from one machine to another.

Buying parts

Once you have found all the identification numbers, record them for reference when buying parts. Since the manufacturers change specifications, parts and vendors (companies that manufacture various components on the machine), providing the ID numbers is the only way to be reasonably sure that you are buying the correct parts.

Whenever possible, take the worn part to the dealer so direct comparison with the new component can be made. Along the trail from the manufacturer to the parts shelf, there are numerous places that the part can end up with the wrong number or be listed incorrectly.

The two places to purchase new parts for your motorcycle - the accessory store and the franchised dealer - differ in the type of parts they carry. While dealers can obtain virtually every part for your cycle, the accessory dealer is usually limited to normal high wear items such as shock absorbers, tune-up parts, various engine gaskets, cables, chains, brake parts, etc. Rarely will an accessory outlet have major suspension components, cylinders, transmission gears, or cases.

Used parts can be obtained for roughly half the price of new ones, but you can't always be sure of what you're getting. Once again, take your worn part to the wrecking yard (breaker) for direct comparison.

Whether buying new, used or rebuilt parts, the best course is to deal directly with someone who specializes in parts for your particular make.

General specifications

ZX600 (Ninja ZX-6 and ZZ-R600)

Frame and suspension

Wheelbase	
D models	1440 mm (56.74 inches)
E models	1430 mm (56.34 inches)
Overall length	
D models	2075 mm (81.76 inches)
E models	2070 mm (81.56 inches)
Overall width	
D models	700 mm (27.58 inches)
E models	695 mm (27.38 inches)
Overall height	
D models	1170 mm (46.10 inches)
E models	1175 mm (46.30 inches)
Seat height	780 mm (30.73 inches)
Dry weight	
California models	195.5 kg (430.1 pounds)
All other models	195 kg (429 pounds)
Front suspension	Telescopic fork
Rear suspension	Single shock absorber/coil spring
Front brake	Dual hydraulic discs
Rear brake	Single hydraulic disc
Fuel capacity	18 liters (4.7 US gal, 4.0 Imp gal)

Engine

Type	Liquid-cooled, 4-stroke, DOHC inline four-cylinder
Displacement	599 cc
Compression ratio	
D models	11.5 to 1
E models	12.0 to 1
Ignition system	Transistorized
Carburetor type	Four 36 mm Keihin CVKD36 carburetors
Transmission	6-speed, constant mesh

Maintenance techniques, tools and working facilities

Basic maintenance techniques

There are a number of techniques involved in maintenance and repair that will be referred to throughout this manual. Application of these techniques will enable the amateur mechanic to be more efficient, better organized and capable of performing the various tasks properly, which will ensure that the repair job is thorough and complete.

Fastening systems

Fasteners, basically, are nuts, bolts and screws used to hold two or more parts together. There are a few things to keep in mind when working with fasteners. Almost all of them use a locking device of some type (either a lock washer, locknut, locking tab or thread adhesive). All threaded fasteners should be clean, straight, have undamaged threads and undamaged corners on the hex head where the wrench fits. Develop the habit of replacing all damaged nuts and bolts with new ones.

Rusted nuts and bolts should be treated with a penetrating oil to ease removal and prevent breakage. Some mechanics use turpentine in a spout type oil can, which works quite well. After applying the rust penetrant, let it "work" for a few minutes before trying to loosen the nut or bolt. Badly rusted fasteners may have to be chiseled off or removed with a special nut breaker, available at tool stores.

If a bolt or stud breaks off in an assembly, it can be drilled out and removed with a special tool called an E-Z out (or screw extractor). Most dealer service departments and motorcycle repair shops can perform this task, as well as others (such as the repair of threaded holes that have been stripped out).

Flat washers and lock washers, when removed from an assembly, should always be replaced exactly as removed. Replace any damaged washers with new ones. Always use a flat washer between a lock washer and any soft metal surface (such as aluminum), thin sheet metal or plastic. Special locknuts can only be used once or twice before they lose their locking ability and must be replaced.

Tightening sequences and procedures

When threaded fasteners are tightened, they are often tightened to a specific torque value (torque is basically a twisting force). Over-tightening the fastener can weaken it and cause it to break, while under-tightening can cause it to eventually come loose. Each bolt, depending on the material it's made of, the diameter of its shank and the material it is threaded into, has a specific torque value, which is noted in the Specifications. Be sure to follow the torque recommendations closely.

Fasteners laid out in a pattern (i.e. cylinder head bolts, engine case bolts, etc.) must be loosened or tightened in a sequence to avoid warping the component. Initially, the bolts/nuts should go on finger tight only. Next, they should be tightened one full turn each, in a criss-cross or diagonal pattern. After each one has been tightened one full turn, return to the first one tightened and tighten them all one half turn, following the same pattern. Finally, tighten each of them one quarter turn at a time until each fastener has been tightened to the proper torque. To loosen and remove the fasteners the procedure would be reversed.

Disassembly sequence

Component disassembly should be done with care and purpose to help ensure that the parts go back together properly during reassembly. Always keep track of the sequence in which parts are removed. Take note of special characteristics or marks on parts that can be installed more than one way (such as a grooved thrust washer on a shaft). It's a good idea to lay the disassembled parts out on a clean surface in the order that they were removed. It may also be helpful to make sketches or take instant photos of components before removal.

When removing fasteners from a component, keep track of their locations. Sometimes threading a bolt back in a part, or putting the washers and nut back on a stud, can prevent mixups later. If nuts and bolts can't be returned to their original locations, they should be kept in a compartmented box or a series of small boxes. A cupcake or muffin tin is ideal for this purpose, since each cavity can hold the bolts and nuts from a particular area (i.e. engine case bolts, valve cover bolts, engine mount bolts, etc.). A pan of this type is especially helpful when working on assemblies with very small parts (such as the carburetors and the valve train). The cavities can be marked with paint or tape to identify the contents.

Whenever wiring looms, harnesses or connectors are separated, it's a good idea to identify the two halves with numbered pieces of masking tape so they can be easily reconnected.

Gasket sealing surfaces

Throughout any motorcycle, gaskets are used to seal the mating surfaces between components and keep lubricants, fluids, vacuum or pressure contained in an assembly.

Many times these gaskets are coated with a liquid or paste type gasket sealing compound before assembly. Age, heat and pressure can sometimes cause the two parts to stick together so tightly that they are very difficult to separate. In most cases, the part can be loosened by striking it with a soft-faced hammer near the mating surfaces. A regular hammer can be used if a block of wood is placed between the hammer and the part. Do not hammer on cast parts or parts that could be easily damaged. With any particularly stubborn part, always recheck to make sure that every fastener has been removed.

Avoid using a screwdriver or bar to pry apart components, as they can easily mar the gasket sealing surfaces of the parts (which must remain smooth). If prying is absolutely necessary, use a piece of wood, but keep in mind that extra clean-up will be necessary if the wood splinters.

After the parts are separated, the old gasket must be carefully scraped off and the gasket surfaces cleaned. Stubborn gasket material can be soaked with a gasket remover (available in aerosol cans) to soften it so it can be easily scraped off. A scraper can be fashioned from a piece of copper tubing by flattening and sharpening one end. Copper is recommended because it is usually softer than the surfaces to be scraped, which reduces the chance of gouging the part. Some gaskets can be removed with a wire brush, but regardless of the method used, the mating surfaces must be left clean and smooth. If for some reason the gasket surface is gouged, then a gasket sealer thick enough to fill scratches will have to be used during reassembly of the components. For most applications, a non-drying (or semi-drying) gasket sealer is best.

Hose removal tips

Hose removal precautions closely parallel gasket removal precautions. Avoid scratching or gouging the surface that the hose mates against or the connection may leak. Because of various chemical reactions, the rubber in hoses can bond itself to the metal spigot that the hose fits over. To remove a hose, first loosen the hose clamps that secure it to the spigot. Then, with slip joint pliers, grab the hose at the clamp and rotate it around the spigot. Work it back and forth until it is completely free, then pull it off (silicone or other lubricants will ease removal if they can be applied between the hose and the outside of the spigot). Apply the same lubricant to the inside of the hose and the

Spark plug gap adjusting tool

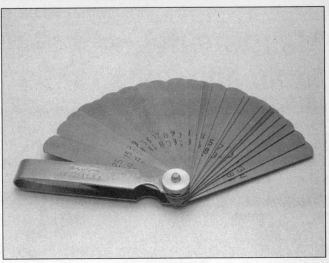

Feeler gauge set

Control cable pressure luber

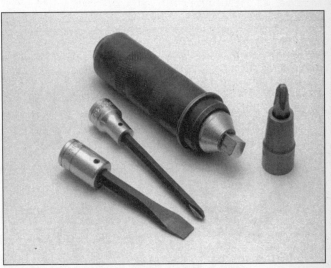

Hand impact screwdriver and bits

the hose and the outside of the spigot to simplify installation.

If a hose clamp is broken or damaged, do not reuse it. Also, do not reuse hoses that are cracked, split or torn.

Tools

A selection of good tools is a basic requirement for anyone who plans to maintain and repair a motorcycle. For the owner who has few tools, if any, the initial investment might seem high, but when compared to the spiraling costs of routine maintenance and repair, it is a wise one.

To help the owner decide which tools are needed to perform the tasks detailed in this manual, the following tool lists are offered: Maintenance and minor repair, Repair and overhaul and Special. The newcomer to practical mechanics should start off with the Maintenance and minor repair tool kit, which is adequate for the simpler jobs. Then, as confidence and experience grow, the owner can tackle more difficult tasks, buying additional tools as they are needed. Eventually the basic kit will be built into the Repair and overhaul tool set. Over a period of time, the experienced do-it-yourselfer will assemble a tool set complete enough for most repair and overhaul procedures and will add tools from the Special category when it is felt that the expense is justified by the frequency of use.

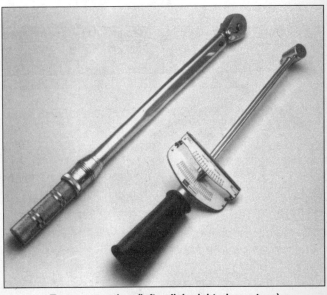

Torque wrenches (left - click; right - beam type)

Snap-ring pliers (top - external; bottom - internal)

Allen wrenches (left), and Allen head sockets (right)

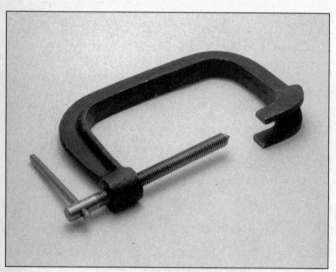

Valve spring compressor

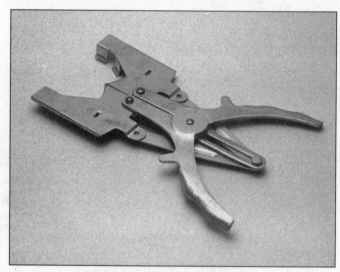

Piston ring removal/installation tool

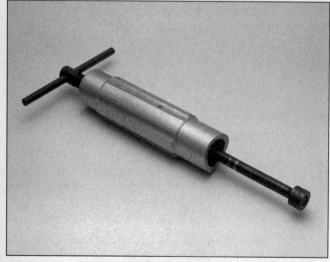

Piston pin puller

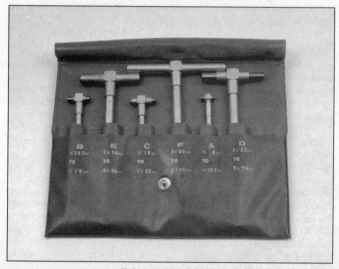

Telescoping gauges

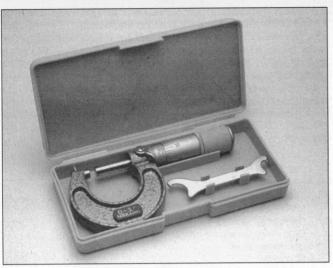

0-to-1 inch micrometer

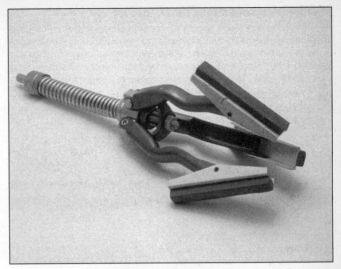

Cylinder surfacing hone

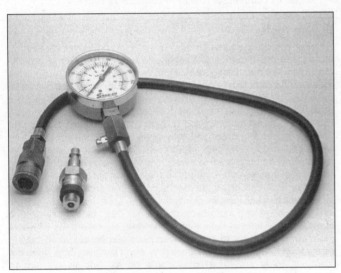

Cylinder compression gauge

Dial indicator set

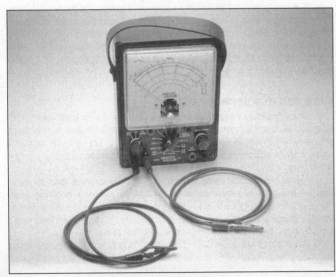

Multimeter (volt/ohm/ammeter)

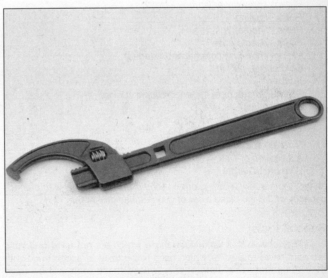

Adjustable spanner

Maintenance and minor repair tool kit

The tools in this list should be considered the minimum required for performance of routine maintenance, servicing and minor repair work. We recommend the purchase of combination wrenches (box end and open end combined in one wrench); while more expensive than open-ended ones, they offer the advantages of both types of wrench.

Combination wrench set (6 mm to 22 mm)
Adjustable wrench - 8 in
Spark plug socket (with rubber insert)
Spark plug gap adjusting tool
Feeler gauge set
Standard screwdriver (5/16 in x 6 in)
Phillips screwdriver (No. 2 x 6 in)
Allen (hex) wrench set (4 mm to 12 mm)
Combination (slip-joint) pliers - 6 in
Hacksaw and assortment of blades
Tire pressure gauge
Control cable pressure luber
Grease gun
Oil can
Fine emery cloth
Wire brush
Hand impact screwdriver and bits
Funnel (medium size)
Safety goggles
Drain pan
Work light with extension cord
Repair and overhaul tool set

These tools are essential for anyone who plans to perform major repairs and are intended to supplement those in the Maintenance and minor repair tool kit. Included is a comprehensive set of sockets which, though expensive, are invaluable because of their versatility (especially when various extensions and drives are available). We recommend the 3/8 inch drive over the 1/2 inch drive for general motorcycle maintenance and repair (ideally, the mechanic would have a 3/8 inch drive set and a 1/2 inch drive set).

Socket set(s)
Reversible ratchet
Extension - 6 in
Universal joint
Torque wrench (same size drive as sockets)
Ball peen hammer - 8 oz
Soft-faced hammer (plastic/rubber)
Standard screwdriver (1/4 in x 6 in)
Standard screwdriver (stubby - 5/16 in)
Phillips screwdriver (No. 3 x 8 in)
Phillips screwdriver (stubby - No. 2)
Pliers - locking
Pliers - lineman's
Pliers - needle nose
Pliers - snap-ring (internal and external)
Cold chisel - 1/2 in
Scriber
Scraper (made from flattened copper tubing)
Center punch
Pin punches (1/16, 1/8, 3/16 in)
Steel rule/straightedge - 12 in
Pin-type spanner wrench
A selection of files
Wire brush (large)

Note: *Another tool which is often useful is an electric drill with a chuck capacity of 3/8 inch (and a set of good quality drill bits).*

Special tools

The tools in this list include those which are not used regularly, are expensive to buy, or which need to be used in accordance with their manufacturer's instructions. Unless these tools will be used frequently, it is not very economical to purchase many of them. A

consideration would be to split the cost and use between yourself and a friend or friends (i.e. members of a motorcycle club).

This list primarily contains tools and instruments widely available to the public, as well as some special tools produced by the vehicle manufacturer for distribution to dealer service departments. As a result, references to the manufacturer's special tools are occasionally included in the text of this manual. Generally, an alternative method of doing the job without the special tool is offered. However, sometimes there is no alternative to their use. Where this is the case, and the tool can't be purchased or borrowed, the work should be turned over to the dealer service department or a motorcycle repair shop.

Valve spring compressor
Piston ring removal and installation tool
Piston pin puller
Telescoping gauges
Micrometer(s) and/or dial/Vernier calipers
Cylinder surfacing hone
Cylinder compression gauge
Dial indicator set
Multimeter
Adjustable spanner
Manometer or vacuum gauge set
Small air compressor with blow gun and tire chuck

Buying tools

For the do-it-yourselfer who is just starting to get involved in motorcycle maintenance and repair, there are a number of options available when purchasing tools. If maintenance and minor repair is the extent of the work to be done, the purchase of individual tools is satisfactory. If, on the other hand, extensive work is planned, it would be a good idea to purchase a modest tool set from one of the large retail chain stores. A set can usually be bought at a substantial savings over the individual tool prices (and they often come with a tool box). As additional tools are needed, add-on sets, individual tools and a larger tool box can be purchased to expand the tool selection. Building a tool set gradually allows the cost of the tools to be spread over a longer period of time and gives the mechanic the freedom to choose only those tools that will actually be used.

Tool stores and motorcycle dealers will often be the only source of some of the special tools that are needed, but regardless of where tools are bought, try to avoid cheap ones (especially when buying screwdrivers and sockets) because they won't last very long. There are plenty of tools around at reasonable prices, but always aim to purchase items which meet the relevant national safety standards. The expense involved in replacing cheap tools will eventually be greater than the initial cost of quality tools.

It is obviously not possible to cover the subject of tools fully here. For those who wish to learn more about tools and their use, there is a book entitled *Motorcycle Workshop Practice Manual* (Book no. 1454) available from the publishers of this manual. It also provides an introduction to basic workshop practice which will be of interest to a home mechanic working on any type of motorcycle.

Care and maintenance of tools

Good tools are expensive, so it makes sense to treat them with respect. Keep them clean and in usable condition and store them properly when not in use. Always wipe off any dirt, grease or metal chips before putting them away. Never leave tools lying around in the work area.

Some tools, such as screwdrivers, pliers, wrenches and sockets, can be hung on a panel mounted on the garage or workshop wall, while others should be kept in a tool box or tray. Measuring instruments, gauges, meters, etc. must be carefully stored where they can't be damaged by weather or impact from other tools.

When tools are used with care and stored properly, they will last a very long time. Even with the best of care, tools will wear out if used frequently. When a tool is damaged or worn out, replace it; subsequent jobs will be safer and more enjoyable if you do.

Working facilities

Not to be overlooked when discussing tools is the workshop. If anything more than routine maintenance is to be carried out, some sort of suitable work area is essential.

It is understood, and appreciated, that many home mechanics do not have a good workshop or garage available and end up removing an engine or doing major repairs outside (it is recommended, however, that the overhaul or repair be completed under the cover of a roof).

A clean, flat workbench or table of comfortable working height is an absolute necessity. The workbench should be equipped with a vise that has a jaw opening of at least four inches.

As mentioned previously, some clean, dry storage space is also required for tools, as well as the lubricants, fluids, cleaning solvents, etc. which soon become necessary.

Sometimes waste oil and fluids, drained from the engine or cooling system during normal maintenance or repairs, present a disposal problem. To avoid pouring them on the ground or into a sewage system, simply pour the used fluids into large containers, seal them with caps and take them to an authorized disposal site or service station. Plastic jugs are ideal for this purpose.

Always keep a supply of old newspapers and clean rags available. Old towels are excellent for mopping up spills. Many mechanics use rolls of paper towels for most work because they are readily available and disposable. To help keep the area under the motorcycle clean, a large cardboard box can be cut open and flattened to protect the garage or shop floor.

Whenever working over a painted surface (such as the fuel tank) cover it with an old blanket or bedspread to protect the finish.

Safety first

Professional mechanics are trained in safe working procedures. However enthusiastic you may be about getting on with the job at hand, take the time to ensure that your safety is not put at risk. A moment's lack of attention can result in an accident, as can failure to observe simple precautions.

There will always be new ways of having accidents, and the following is not a comprehensive list of all dangers; it is intended rather to make you aware of the risks and to encourage a safe approach to all work you carry out on your bike.

Essential DOs and DON'Ts

DON'T start the engine without first ascertaining that the transmission is in neutral.

DON'T suddenly remove the filler cap from a hot cooling system - cover it with a cloth and release the pressure gradually first, or you may get scalded by escaping coolant.

DON'T attempt to drain oil until you are sure it has cooled sufficiently to avoid scalding you.

DON'T grasp any part of the engine or exhaust system without first ascertaining that it is cool enough not to burn you.

DON'T allow brake fluid or antifreeze to contact the machine's paint work or plastic components.

DON'T siphon toxic liquids such as fuel, hydraulic fluid or antifreeze by mouth, or allow them to remain on your skin.

DON'T inhale dust - it may be injurious to health (see *Asbestos* heading).

DON'T allow any spilled oil or grease to remain on the floor - wipe it up right away, before someone slips on it.

DON'T use ill fitting wrenches or other tools which may slip and cause injury.

DON'T attempt to lift a heavy component which may be beyond your capability - get assistance.

DON'T rush to finish a job or take unverified short cuts.

DON'T allow children or animals in or around an unattended vehicle.

DON'T inflate a tire to a pressure above the recommended maximum. Apart from over stressing the carcase and wheel rim, in extreme cases the tire may blow off forcibly.

DO ensure that the machine is supported securely at all times. This is especially important when the machine is blocked up to aid wheel or fork removal.

DO take care when attempting to loosen a stubborn nut or bolt. It is generally better to pull on a wrench, rather than push, so that if you slip, you fall away from the machine rather than onto it.

DO wear eye protection when using power tools such as drill, sander, bench grinder etc.

DO use a barrier cream on your hands prior to undertaking dirty jobs - it will protect your skin from infection as well as making the dirt easier to remove afterwards; but make sure your hands aren't left slippery. Note that long-term contact with used engine oil can be a health hazard.

DO keep loose clothing (cuffs, ties etc. and long hair) well out of the way of moving mechanical parts.

DO remove rings, wristwatch etc., before working on the vehicle-especially the electrical system.

DO keep your work area tidy - it is only too easy to fall over articles left lying around.

DO exercise caution when compressing springs for removal or installation. Ensure that the tension is applied and released in a controlled manner, using suitable tools which preclude the possibility of the spring escaping violently.

DO ensure that any lifting tackle used has a safe working load rating adequate for the job.

DO get someone to check periodically that all is well, when working alone on the vehicle.

DO carry out work in a logical sequence and check that everything is correctly assembled and tightened afterwards.

DO remember that your vehicle's safety affects that of yourself and others. If in doubt on any point, get professional advice.

IF, in spite of following these precautions, you are unfortunate enough to injure yourself, seek medical attention as soon as possible.

Asbestos

Certain friction, insulating, sealing and other products - such as brake pads, clutch linings, gaskets, etc. - contain asbestos. *Extreme care must be taken to avoid inhalation of dust from such products since it is hazardous to health*. If in doubt, assume that they *do* contain asbestos.

Fire

Remember at all times that gasoline (petrol) is highly flammable. Never smoke or have any kind of naked flame around, when working on the vehicle. But the risk does not end there - a spark caused by an electrical short-circuit, by two metal surfaces contacting each other, by careless use of tools, or even by static electricity built up in your body under certain conditions, can ignite gasoline (petrol) vapor, which in a confined space is highly explosive. Never use gasoline (petrol) as a cleaning solvent. Use an approved safety solvent.

Always disconnect the battery ground (earth) terminal before working on any part of the fuel or electrical system, and never risk spilling fuel on to a hot engine or exhaust.

It is recommended that a fire extinguisher of a type suitable for fuel and electrical fires is kept handy in the garage or workplace at all times. Never try to extinguish a fuel or electrical fire with water.

Fumes

Certain fumes are highly toxic and can quickly cause unconsciousness and even death if inhaled to any extent. Gasoline (petrol) vapor comes into this category, as do the vapors from certain solvents such as trichloroethylene. Any draining or pouring of such volatile fluids should be done in a well ventilated area.

When using cleaning fluids and solvents, read the instructions carefully. Never use materials from unmarked containers - they may give off poisonous vapors.

Never run the engine of a motor vehicle in an enclosed space such as a garage. Exhaust fumes contain carbon monoxide which is extremely poisonous; if you need to run the engine, always do so in the open air or at least have the rear of the vehicle outside the workplace.

The battery

Never cause a spark, or allow a naked light near the vehicle's battery. It will normally be giving off a certain amount of hydrogen gas, which is highly explosive.

Always disconnect the battery ground (earth) terminal before working on the fuel or electrical systems (except where noted).

If possible, loosen the filler plugs or cover when charging the battery from an external source. Do not charge at an excessive rate or the battery may burst.

Take care when topping up, cleaning or carrying the battery. The acid electrolyte, even when diluted, is very corrosive and should not be allowed to contact the eyes or skin. Always wear rubber gloves and goggles or a face shield. If you ever need to prepare electrolyte yourself, always add the acid slowly to the water; never add the water to the acid.

Electricity

When using an electric power tool, inspection light etc., always ensure that the appliance is correctly connected to its plug and that, where necessary, it is properly grounded (earthed). Do not use such appliances in damp conditions and, again, beware of creating a spark or applying excessive heat in the vicinity of fuel or fuel vapor. Also ensure that the appliances meet national safety standards.

A severe electric shock can result from touching certain parts of the electrical system, such as the spark plug wires (HT leads), when the engine is running or being cranked, particularly if components are damp or the insulation is defective. Where an electronic ignition system is used, the secondary (HT) voltage is much higher and could prove fatal.

Motorcycle chemicals and lubricants

A number of chemicals and lubricants are available for use in motorcycle maintenance and repair. They include a wide variety of products ranging from cleaning solvents and degreasers to lubricants and protective sprays for rubber, plastic and vinyl.

Contact point/spark plug cleaner is a solvent used to clean oily film and dirt from points, grime from electrical connectors and oil deposits from spark plugs. It is oil free and leaves no residue. It can also be used to remove gum and varnish from carburetor jets and other orifices.

Carburetor cleaner is similar to contact point/spark plug cleaner but it usually has a stronger solvent and may leave a slight oily reside. It is not recommended for cleaning electrical components or connections.

Brake system cleaner is used to remove grease or brake fluid from brake system components (where clean surfaces are absolutely necessary and petroleum-based solvents cannot be used); it also leaves no residue.

Silicone-based lubricants are used to protect rubber parts such as hoses and grommets, and are used as lubricants for hinges and locks.

Multi-purpose grease is an all purpose lubricant used wherever grease is more practical than a liquid lubricant such as oil. Some multi-purpose grease is colored white and specially formulated to be more resistant to water than ordinary grease.

Gear oil (sometimes called gear lube) is a specially designed oil used in transmissions and final drive units, a s well as other areas where high friction, high temperature lubrication is required. It is available in a number of viscosities (weights) for various applications.

Motor oil, of course, is the lubricant specially formulated for use in the engine. It normally contains a wide variety of additives to prevent corrosion and reduce foaming and wear. Motor oil comes in various weights (viscosity ratings) of from 5 to 80. The recommended weight of the oil depends on the seasonal temperature and the demands on the engine. Light oil is used in cold climates and under light load conditions; heavy oil is used in hot climates and where high loads are encountered. Multi-viscosity oils are designed to have characteristics of both light and heavy oils and are available in a number of weights from 5W-20 to 20W-50.

Gas (petrol) additives perform several functions, depending on their chemical makeup. They usually contain solvents that help dissolve gum and varnish that build up on carburetor and intake parts. They also serve to break down carbon deposits that form on the inside surfaces of the combustion chambers. Some additives contain upper cylinder lubricants for valves and piston rings.

Brake fluid is a specially formulated hydraulic fluid that can withstand the heat and pressure encountered in brake systems. Care must be taken that this fluid does not come in contact with painted surfaces or plastics. An opened container should always be resealed to prevent contamination by water or dirt.

Chain lubricants are formulated especially for use on motorcycle final drive chains. A good chain lube should adhere well and have good penetrating qualities to be effective as a lubricant inside the chain and on the side plates, pins and rollers. Most chain lubes are either the foaming type or quick drying type and are usually marketed as sprays.

Degreasers are heavy duty solvents used to remove grease and grime that may accumulate on engine and frame components. They can be sprayed or brushed on and, depending on the type, are rinsed with either water or solvent.

Solvents are used alone or in combination with degreasers to clean parts and assemblies during repair and overhaul. The home mechanic should use only solvents that are non-flammable and that do not produce irritating fumes.

Gasket sealing compounds may be used in conjunction with gaskets, to improve their sealing capabilities, or alone, to seal metal-to-metal joints. Many gasket sealers can withstand extreme heat, some are impervious to gasoline and lubricants, while others are capable of filling and sealing large cavities. Depending on the intended use, gasket sealers either dry hard or stay relatively soft and pliable. They are usually applied by hand, with a brush, or are sprayed on the gasket sealing surfaces.

Thread cement is an adhesive locking compound that prevents threaded fasteners from loosening because of vibration. It is available in a variety of types for different applications.

Moisture dispersants are usually sprays that can be used to dry out electrical components such as the fuse block and wiring connectors. Some types can also be used as treatment for rubber and as a lubricant for hinges, cables and locks.

Waxes and polishes are used to help protect painted and plated surfaces from the weather. Different types of paint may require the use of different types of wax polish. Some polishes utilize a chemical or abrasive cleaner to help remove the top layer of oxidized (dull) paint on older vehicles. In recent years, many non-wax polishes (that contain a wide variety of chemicals such as polymers and silicones) have been introduced. These non-wax polishes are usually easier to apply and last longer than conventional waxes and polishes.

Troubleshooting

Contents

Engine doesn't start or is difficult to start

1   Starter motor does not rotate

1   Engine kill switch Off.
2   Fuse blown. Check fuse block (Chapter 9).
3   Battery voltage low. Check and recharge battery (Chapter 9).
4   Starter motor defective. Make sure the wiring to the starter is secure. Make sure the starter solenoid (relay) clicks when the start button is pushed. If the solenoid clicks, then the fault is in the wiring or motor.
5   Starter solenoid (relay) faulty. Check it according to the procedure in Chapter 9.
6   Starter button not contacting. The contacts could be wet, corroded or dirty. Disassemble and clean the switch (Chapter 9).
7   Wiring open or shorted. Check all wiring connections and harnesses to make sure that they are dry, tight and not corroded. Also check for broken or frayed wires that can cause a short to ground/earth (see wiring diagram, Chapter 9).
8   Ignition switch defective. Check the switch according to the procedure in Chapter 9. Replace the switch with a new one if it is defective.
9   Engine kill switch defective. Check for wet, dirty or corroded contacts. Clean or replace the switch as necessary (Chapter 9).
10   Faulty starter lockout switch. Check the wiring to the switch and the switch itself according to the procedures in Chapter 9.

2   Starter motor rotates but engine does not turn over

1   Starter motor clutch defective. Inspect and repair or replace (Chapter 2).
2   Damaged idler or starter gears. Inspect and replace the damaged parts (Chapter 2).

3   Starter works but engine won't turn over (seized)

Seized engine caused by one or more internally damaged components. Failure due to wear, abuse or lack of lubrication. Damage can include seized valves, camshafts, pistons, crankshaft, connecting rod bearings, or transmission gears or bearings. Refer to Chapter 2 for engine disassembly.

4   No fuel flow

1   No fuel in tank.
2   Fuel tap vacuum hose broken or disconnected.
3   Tank cap air vent obstructed. Usually caused by dirt or water. Remove it and clean the cap vent hole.
4   Fuel filter clogged. Inspect, and if necessary replace the filter (Chapter 4).
5   Fuel line clogged. Pull the fuel line loose and carefully blow through it.
6   Inlet needle valves clogged. For both the valves to be clogged, either a very bad batch of fuel with an unusual additive has been used, or some other foreign object has entered the tank. Many times after a machine has been stored for many months without running, the fuel turns to a varnish-like liquid and forms deposits on the inlet needle valves and jets. The carburetors should be removed and overhauled if draining the float bowls does not alleviate the problem.

5   Engine flooded

1   Float level too high. Check and adjust as described in Chapter 4.

2   Inlet needle valve worn or stuck open. A piece of dirt, rust or other debris can cause the inlet needle to seat improperly, causing excess fuel to be admitted to the float bowl. In this case, the float chamber should be cleaned and the needle and seat inspected. If the needle and seat are worn, then the leaking will persist and the parts should be replaced with new ones (Chapter 4).
3   Starting technique incorrect. Under normal circumstances (i.e., if all the carburetor functions are sound) the machine should start with little or no throttle. When the engine is cold, the choke should be operated and the engine started without opening the throttle. When the engine is at operating temperature, only a very slight amount of throttle should be necessary. If the engine is flooded, turn the fuel tap off and hold the throttle open while cranking the engine. This will allow additional air to reach the cylinders. Remember to turn the fuel back on after the engine starts.

6   No spark or weak spark

1   Ignition switch Off.
2   Engine kill switch turned to the Off position.
3   Battery voltage low. Check and recharge battery as necessary (Chapter 9).
4   Spark plug dirty, defective or worn out. Locate reason for fouled plug(s) using spark plug condition chart and follow the plug maintenance procedures in Chapter 1.
5   Spark plug cap or secondary (HT) wiring faulty. Check condition. Replace either or both components if cracks or deterioration are evident (Chapter 5).
6   Spark plug cap not making good contact. Make sure that the plug cap fits snugly over the plug end.
7   IC igniter defective. Check the unit, referring to Chapter 5 for details.
8   Pickup coil defective. Check the unit, referring to Chapter 5 for details.
9   Ignition coil(s) defective. Check the coils, referring to Chapter 5.
10   Ignition or kill switch shorted. This is usually caused by water, corrosion, damage or excessive wear. The switches can be disassembled and cleaned with electrical contact cleaner. If cleaning does not help, replace the switches (Chapter 9).
11   Wiring shorted or broken between:
   a) *Ignition switch and engine kill switch*
   b) *IC igniter and engine kill switch*
   c) *IC igniter and ignition coil*
   d) *Ignition coil and plug*
   e) *IC igniter and pickup coil*
Make sure that all wiring connections are clean, dry and tight. Look for chafed and broken wires (Chapters 5 and 9).

7   Compression low

1   Spark plug loose. Remove the plug and inspect the threads. Reinstall and tighten to the specified torque (Chapter 1).
2   Cylinder head not sufficiently tightened down. If the cylinder head is suspected of being loose,; then there's a chance that the gasket or head is damaged if the problem has persisted for any length of time. The head bolts should be tightened to the proper torque in the correct sequence (Chapter 2).
3   Improper valve clearance. This means that the valve is not closing completely and compression pressure is leaking past the valve. Check and adjust the valve clearances (Chapter 1).
4   Cylinder and/or piston worn. Excessive wear will cause compression pressure to leak past the rings. This is usually accompanied by worn rings as well. A top end overhaul is necessary (Chapter 2).
5   Piston rings worn, weak, broken, or sticking. Broken or sticking piston rings usually indicate a lubrication or carburetion problem that causes excess carbon deposits to form on the pistons and rings. Top

end overhaul is necessary (Chapter 2).

6   Piston ring-to-groove clearance excessive. This is caused by excessive wear of the piston ring lands. Piston replacement is necessary (Chapter 2).

7   Cylinder head gasket damaged. If the head is allowed to become loose, or if excessive carbon build-up on the piston crown and combustion chamber causes extremely high compression, the head gasket may leak. Retorquing the head is not always sufficient to restore the seal, so gasket replacement is necessary (Chapter 2).

8   Cylinder head warped. This is caused by overheating or improperly tightened head bolts. Machine shop resurfacing or head replacement is necessary (Chapter 2).

9   Valve spring broken or weak. Caused by component failure or wear; the spring(s) must be replaced (Chapter 2).

10   Valve not seating properly. This is caused by a bent valve (from over-revving or improper valve adjustment), burned valve or seat (improper carburetion) or an accumulation of carbon deposits on the seat (from carburetion, lubrication problems). The valves must be cleaned and/or replaced and the seats serviced if possible (Chapter 2).

8   Stalls after starting

1   Improper choke action. Make sure the choke rod is getting a full stroke and staying in the "out" position. Adjustment of the cable slack is covered in Chapter 1.

2   Ignition malfunction. See Chapter 5.

3   Carburetor malfunction. See Chapter 4.

4   Fuel contaminated. The fuel can be contaminated with either dirt or water, or can change chemically if the machine is allowed to sit for several months or more. Drain the tank and float bowls (Chapter 4).

5   Intake air leak. Check for loose carburetor-to-intake manifold connections, loose or missing vacuum gauge access port cap or hose, or loose carburetor top (Chapter 4).

6   Idle speed incorrect. Turn idle speed adjuster screw until the engine idles at the specified rpm (Chapters 1 and 4).

9   Rough idle

1   Ignition malfunction. See Chapter 5.

2   Idle speed incorrect. See Chapter 1.

3   Carburetors not synchronized. Adjust carburetors with vacuum gauge set or manometer as outlined in Chapter 1.

4   Carburetor malfunction. See Chapter 4.

5   Fuel contaminated. The fuel can be contaminated with either dirt or water, or can change chemically if the machine is allowed to sit for several months or more. Drain the tank and float bowls. If the problem is severe, a carburetor overhaul may be necessary (Chapters 1 and 4).

6   Intake air leak.

7   Air cleaner clogged. Service or replace air filter element (Chapter 1).

Poor running at low speed

10   Spark weak

1   Battery voltage low. Check and recharge battery (Chapter 9).

2   Spark plug fouled, defective or worn out. Refer to Chapter 1 for spark plug maintenance.

3   Spark plug cap or high tension wiring defective. Refer to Chapters 1 and 5 for details of the ignition system.

4   Spark plug cap not making contact.

5   Incorrect spark plug. Wrong type, heat range or cap configuration. Check and install correct plugs listed in Chapter 1. A cold plug or one with a recessed firing electrode will not operate at low speeds without fouling.

6   IC igniter defective. See Chapter 5.

7   Pickup coil defective. See Chapter 5.

8   Ignition coil(s) defective. See Chapter 5.

11   Fuel/air mixture incorrect

1   Pilot screw(s) out of adjustment (Chapters 1 and 4).

2   Pilot jet or air passage clogged. Remove and overhaul the carburetors (Chapter 4).

3   Air bleed holes clogged. Remove carburetor and blow out all passages (Chapter 4).

4   Air cleaner clogged, poorly sealed or missing.

5   Air cleaner-to-carburetor boot poorly sealed. Look for cracks, holes or loose clamps and replace or repair defective parts.

6   Fuel level too high or too low. Adjust the floats (Chapter 4).

7   Fuel tank air vent obstructed. Make sure that the air vent passage in the filler cap is open (except California models).

8   Carburetor intake manifolds loose. Check for cracks, breaks, tears or loose clamps or bolts. Repair or replace the rubber boots.

12   Compression low

1   Spark plug loose. Remove the plug and inspect the threads. Reinstall and tighten to the specified torque (Chapter 1).

2   Cylinder head not sufficiently tightened down. If the cylinder head is suspected of being loose, then there's a chance that the gasket and head are damaged if the problem has persisted for any length of time. The head bolts should be tightened to the proper torque in the correct sequence (Chapter 2).

3   Improper valve clearance. This means that the valve is not closing completely and compression pressure is leaking past the valve. Check and adjust the valve clearances (Chapter 1).

4   Cylinder and/or piston worn. Excessive wear will cause compression pressure to leak past the rings. This is usually accompanied by worn rings as well. A top end overhaul is necessary (Chapter 2).

5   Piston rings worn, weak, broken, or sticking. Broken or sticking piston rings usually indicate a lubrication or carburetion problem that causes excess carbon deposits to form on the pistons and rings. Top end overhaul is necessary (Chapter 2).

6   Piston ring-to-groove clearance excessive. This is caused by excessive wear of the piston ring lands. Piston replacement is necessary (Chapter 2).

7   Cylinder head gasket damaged. If the head is allowed to become loose, or if excessive carbon build-up on the piston crown and combustion chamber causes extremely high compression, the head gasket may leak. Retorquing the head is not always sufficient to restore the seal, so gasket replacement is necessary (Chapter 2).

8   Cylinder head warped. This is caused by overheating or improperly tightened head bolts. Machine shop resurfacing or head replacement is necessary (Chapter 2).

9   Valve spring broken or weak. Caused by component failure or wear; the spring(s) must be replaced (Chapter 2).

10   Valve not seating properly. This is caused by a bent valve (from over-revving or improper valve adjustment), burned valve or seat (improper carburetion) or an accumulation of carbon deposits on the seat (from carburetion, lubrication problems). The valves must be cleaned and/or replaced and the seats serviced if possible (Chapter 2).

13   Poor acceleration

1   Carburetors leaking or dirty. Overhaul the carburetors (Chapter 4).

2   Timing not advancing. The pickup coil unit or the IC igniter may be defective. If so, they must be replaced with new ones, as they cannot be repaired.

3   Carburetors not synchronized. Adjust them with a vacuum gauge set or manometer (Chapter 1).

4   Engine oil viscosity too high. Using a heavier oil than that recommended in Chapter 1 can damage the oil pump or lubrication system and cause drag on the engine.

5   Brakes dragging. Usually caused by debris which has entered the brake piston sealing boot, or from a warped disc or bent axle. Repair as necessary (Chapter 7).

Poor running or no power at high speed

14   Firing incorrect

1   Air filter restricted. Clean or replace filter (Chapter 1).

2   Spark plug fouled, defective or worn out. See Chapter 1 for spark plug maintenance.

3   Spark plug cap or secondary (HT) wiring defective. See Chapters 1 and 5 for details of the ignition system.

4   Spark plug cap not in good contact. See Chapter 5.

5   Incorrect spark plug. Wrong type, heat range or cap configuration. Check and install correct plugs listed in Chapter 1. A cold plug or one with a recessed firing electrode will not operate at low speeds without fouling.

6   IC igniter defective. See Chapter 5.

7   Ignition coil(s) defective. See Chapter 5.

15   Fuel/air mixture incorrect

1   Main jet clogged. Dirt, water and other contaminants can clog the main jets. Clean the fuel tap filter, the float bowl area, and the jets and carburetor orifices (Chapter 4).

2   Main jet wrong size. The standard jetting is for sea level atmospheric pressure and oxygen content.

3   Throttle shaft-to-carburetor body clearance excessive. Refer to Chapter 4 for inspection and part replacement procedures.

4   Air bleed holes clogged. Remove and overhaul carburetors (Chapter 4).

5   Air cleaner clogged, poorly sealed or missing.

6   Air cleaner-to-carburetor boot poorly sealed. Look for cracks, holes or loose clamps, and replace or repair defective parts.

7   Fuel level too high or too low. Adjust the float(s) (Chapter 4).

8   Fuel tank air vent obstructed. Make sure the air vent passage in the filler cap is open.

9   Carburetor intake manifolds loose. Check for cracks, breaks, tears or loose clamps or bolts. Repair or replace the rubber boots (Chapter 2).

10   Fuel filter clogged. Clean, and if necessary, replace the filter (Chapter 1).

11   Fuel line clogged. Pull the fuel line loose and carefully blow through it.

16   Compression low

1   Spark plug loose. Remove the plug and inspect the threads. Reinstall and tighten to the specified torque (Chapter 1).

2   Cylinder head not sufficiently tightened down. If the cylinder head is suspected of being loose, then there's a chance that the gasket and head are damaged if the problem has persisted for any length of time. The head bolts should be tightened to the proper torque in the correct sequence (Chapter 2).

3   Improper valve clearance. This means that the valve is not closing completely and compression pressure is leaking past the valve. Check and adjust the valve clearances (Chapter 1).

4   Cylinder and/or piston worn. Excessive wear will cause compression pressure to leak past the rings. This is usually accompanied by worn rings as well. A top end overhaul is necessary (Chapter

2).

5   Piston rings worn, weak, broken, or sticking. Broken or sticking piston rings usually indicate a lubrication or carburetion problem that causes excess carbon deposits or seizures to form on the pistons and rings. Top end overhaul is necessary (Chapter 2).

6   Piston ring-to-groove clearance excessive. This is caused by excessive wear of the piston ring lands. Piston replacement is necessary (Chapter 2).

7   Cylinder head gasket damaged. If the head is allowed to become loose, or if excessive carbon build-up on the piston crown and combustion chamber causes extremely high compression, the head gasket may leak. Retorquing the head is not always sufficient to restore the seal, so gasket replacement is necessary (Chapter 2).

8   Cylinder head warped. This is caused by overheating or improperly tightened head bolts. Machine shop resurfacing or head replacement is necessary (Chapter 2).

9   Valve spring broken or weak. Caused by component failure or wear; the spring(s) must be replaced (Chapter 2).

10   Valve not seating properly. This is caused by a bent valve (from over-revving or improper valve adjustment), burned valve or seat (improper carburetion) or an accumulation of carbon deposits on the seat (from carburetion, lubrication problems). The valves must be cleaned and/or replaced and the seats serviced if possible (Chapter 2).

17   Knocking or pinging

1   Carbon build-up in combustion chamber. Use of a fuel additive that will dissolve the adhesive bonding the carbon particles to the crown and chamber is the easiest way to remove the build-up. Otherwise, the cylinder head will have to be removed and decarbonized (Chapter 2).

2   Incorrect or poor quality fuel. Old or improper grades of gasoline (petrol) can cause detonation. This causes the piston to rattle, thus the knocking or pinging sound. Drain old fuel and always use the recommended fuel grade.

3   Spark plug heat range incorrect. Uncontrolled detonation indicates the plug heat range is too hot. The plug in effect becomes a glow plug, raising cylinder temperatures. Install the proper heat range plug (Chapter 1).

4   Improper air/fuel mixture. This will cause the cylinder to run hot, which leads to detonation. Clogged jets or an air leak can cause this imbalance. See Chapter 4.

18   Miscellaneous causes

1   Throttle valve doesn't open fully. Adjust the cable slack (Chapter 1).

2   Clutch slipping. Caused by damaged, loose or worn clutch components. Refer to Chapter 2 for adjustment and overhaul procedures.

3   Timing not advancing.

4   Engine oil viscosity too high. Using a heavier oil than the one recommended in Chapter 1 can damage the oil pump or lubrication system and cause drag on the engine.

5   Brakes dragging. Usually caused by debris which has entered the brake piston sealing boot, or from a warped disc or bent axle. Repair as necessary.

Overheating

19   Cooling system not operating properly

1   Coolant level low. Check coolant level as described in Chapter 1. If coolant level is low, the engine will overheat.

2   Leak in cooling system. Check cooling system hoses and radiator for leaks and other damage. Repair or replace parts as necessary (Chapter 3).

3   Thermostat sticking open or closed. Check and replace as described in Chapter 3.
4   Faulty radiator cap. Remove the cap and have it pressure checked at a service station.
5   Coolant passages clogged. Have the entire system drained and flushed, then refill with new coolant.
6   Water pump defective. Remove the pump and check the components.
7   Clogged radiator fins. Clean them by blowing compressed air through the fins from the back side.

20   Firing incorrect

1   Spark plug fouled, defective or worn out. See Chapter 1 for spark plug maintenance.
2   Incorrect spark plug.
3   Faulty ignition coil(s) (Chapter 5).

21   Fuel/air mixture incorrect

1   Main jet clogged. Dirt, water and other contaminants can clog the main jets. Clean the fuel tap filter, the float bowl area and the jets and carburetor orifices (Chapter 4).
2   Main jet wrong size. The standard jetting is for sea level atmospheric pressure and oxygen content.
3   Air cleaner poorly sealed or missing.
4   Air cleaner-to-carburetor boot poorly sealed. Look for cracks, holes or loose clamps and replace or repair.
5   Fuel level too low. Adjust the float(s) (Chapter 4).
6   Fuel tank air vent obstructed. Make sure that the air vent passage in the filler cap is open (except California models).
7   Carburetor intake manifolds loose. Check for cracks, breaks, tears or loose clamps or bolts. Repair or replace the rubber boots (Chapter 4).

22   Compression too high

1   Carbon build-up in combustion chamber. Use of a fuel additive that will dissolve the adhesive bonding the carbon particles to the piston crown and chamber is the easiest way to remove the build-up. Otherwise, the cylinder head will have to be removed and decarbonized (Chapter 2).
2   Improperly machined head surface or installation of incorrect gasket during engine assembly. Check Specifications (Chapter 2).

23   Engine load excessive

1   Clutch slipping. Caused by damaged, loose or worn clutch components. Refer to Chapter 2 for overhaul procedures.
2   Engine oil level too high. The addition of too much oil will cause pressurization of the crankcase and inefficient engine operation. Check Specifications and drain to proper level (Chapter 1).
3   Engine oil viscosity too high. Using a heavier oil than the one recommended in Chapter 1 can damage the oil pump or lubrication system as well as cause drag on the engine.
4   Brakes dragging. Usually caused by debris which has entered the brake piston sealing boot, or from a warped disc or bent axle. Repair as necessary.

24   Lubrication inadequate

1   Engine oil level too low. Friction caused by intermittent lack of lubrication or from oil that is "overworked" can cause overheating. The oil provides a definite cooling function in the engine. Check the oil level (Chapter 1).
2   Poor quality engine oil or incorrect viscosity or type. Oil is rated not only according to viscosity but also according to type. Some oils are not rated high enough for use in this engine. Check the Specifications section and change to the correct oil (Chapter 1).

25   Miscellaneous causes

Modification to exhaust system. Most aftermarket exhaust systems cause the engine to run leaner, which makes it run hotter. When installing an accessory exhaust system, always rejet the carburetors.

Clutch problems

26   Clutch slipping

1   Friction plates worn or warped. Overhaul the clutch assembly (Chapter 2).
2   Metal plates worn or warped (Chapter 2).
3   Clutch springs broken or weak. Old or heat-damaged (from slipping clutch) springs should be replaced with new ones (Chapter 2).
4   Clutch release mechanism defective. Check the mechanism and replace any defective parts (Chapter 2).
5   Clutch hub or housing unevenly worn. This causes improper engagement of the discs. Replace the damaged or worn parts (Chapter 2).

27   Clutch not disengaging completely

1   Air in clutch hydraulic system. Bleed the system (Chapter 2).
2   Clutch master or release cylinder worn. Inspect and, if necessary, overhaul the cylinders (Chapter 2).
3   Clutch plates warped or damaged. This will cause clutch drag, which in turn causes the machine to creep. Overhaul the clutch assembly (Chapter 2).
4   Clutch spring tension uneven. Usually caused by a sagged or broken spring. Check and replace the springs (Chapter 2).
5   Engine oil deteriorated. Old, thin, worn out oil will not provide proper lubrication for the discs, causing the clutch to drag. Replace the oil and filter (Chapter 1).
6   Engine oil viscosity too high. Using a heavier oil than recommended in Chapter 1 can cause the plates to stick together, putting a drag on the engine. Change to the correct weight oil (Chap-ter 1).
7   Clutch housing seized on shaft. Lack of lubrication, severe wear or damage can cause the housing to seize on the shaft. Overhaul of the clutch, and perhaps transmission, may be necessary to repair damage (Chapter 2).
8   Clutch release mechanism defective. Worn or damaged release mechanism parts can stick and fail to apply force to the pressure plate. Overhaul the release mechanism (Chapter 2).
9   Loose clutch hub nut. Causes housing and hub misalignment putting a drag on the engine. Engagement adjustment continually varies. Overhaul the clutch assembly (Chapter 2).

Gear shifting problems

28   Doesn't go into gear or lever doesn't return

1   Clutch not disengaging. See Section 27.
2   Shift fork(s) bent or seized. Often caused by dropping the machine or from lack of lubrication. Overhaul the transmission (Chapter 2).
3   Gear(s) stuck on shaft. Most often caused by a lack of lubrication

3   Gear(s) stuck on shaft. Most often caused by a lack of lubrication or excessive wear in transmission bearings and bushings. Overhaul the transmission (Chapter 2).

4   Shift drum binding. Caused by lubrication failure or excessive wear. Replace the drum and bearings (Chapter 2).

5   Shift lever return spring weak or broken (Chapter 2).

6   Shift lever broken. Splines stripped out of lever or shaft, caused by allowing the lever to get loose or from dropping the machine. Replace necessary parts (Chapter 2).

7   Shift mechanism pawl broken or worn. Full engagement and rotary movement of shift drum results. Replace shaft assembly (Chapter 2).

8   Pawl spring broken. Allows pawl to "float", causing sporadic shift operation. Replace spring (Chapter 2).

29   Jumps out of gear

1   Shift fork(s) worn. Overhaul the transmission (Chapter 2).
2   Gear groove(s) worn. Overhaul the transmission (Chapter 2).
3   Gear dogs or dog slots worn or damaged. The gears should be inspected and replaced. No attempt should be made to service the worn parts.

30   Overshifts

1   Pawl spring weak or broken (Chapter 2).
2   Shift drum stopper lever not functioning (Chapter 2).
3   Overshift limiter broken or distorted (Chapter 2).

Abnormal engine noise

31   Knocking or pinging

1   Carbon build-up in combustion chamber. Use of a fuel additive that will dissolve the adhesive bonding the carbon particles to the piston crown and chamber is the easiest way to remove the build-up. Otherwise, the cylinder head will have to be removed and decarbonized (Chapter 2).

2   Incorrect or poor quality fuel. Old or improper fuel can cause detonation. This causes the piston to rattle, thus the knocking or pinging sound. Drain the old fuel and always use the recommended grade (Chapter 4).

3   Spark plug heat range incorrect. Uncontrolled detonation indicates that the plug heat range is too hot. The plug in effect becomes a glow plug, raising cylinder temperatures. Install the proper heat range plug (Chapter 1).

4   Improper air/fuel mixture. This will cause the cylinder to run hot and lead to detonation. Clogged jets or an air leak can cause this imbalance. See Chapter 4.

32   Piston slap or rattling

1   Cylinder-to-piston clearance excessive. Caused by improper assembly. Inspect and overhaul top end parts (Chapter 2).

2   Connecting rod bent. Caused by over-revving, trying to start a badly flooded engine or from ingesting a foreign object into the combustion chamber. Replace the damaged parts (Chapter 2).

3   Piston pin or piston pin bore worn or seized from wear or lack of lubrication. Replace damaged parts (Chapter 2).

4   Piston ring(s) worn, broken or sticking. Overhaul the top end (Chapter 2).

5   Piston seizure damage. Usually from lack of lubrication or overheating. Replace the pistons and bore the cylinders, as necessary

(Chapter 2).

6   Connecting rod bearing and/or piston pin-end clearance excessive. Caused by excessive wear or lack of lubrication. Replace worn parts.

33   Valve noise

1   Incorrect valve clearances. Adjust the clearances by referring to Chapter 1.

2   Valve spring broken or weak. Check and replace weak valve springs (Chapter 2).

3   Camshaft or cylinder head worn or damaged. Lack of lubrication at high rpm is usually the cause of damage. Insufficient oil or failure to change the oil at the recommended intervals are the chief causes. Since there are no replaceable bearings in the head, the head itself will have to be replaced if there is excessive wear or damage (Chapter 2).

34   Other noise

1   Cylinder head gasket leaking. This will cause compression leakage into the cooling system (which may show up as air bubbles in the coolant in the radiator). Also, coolant may get into the oil (which will turn the oil gray and foamy). In either case, have the cooling system checked by a dealer service department.

2   Exhaust pipe leaking at cylinder head connection. Caused by improper fit of pipe(s) or loose exhaust flange. All exhaust fasteners should be tightened evenly and carefully. Failure to do this will lead to a leak.

3   Crankshaft runout excessive. Caused by a bent crankshaft (from over-revving) or damage from an upper cylinder component failure. Can also be attributed to dropping the machine on either of the crankshaft ends.

4   Engine mounting fasteners loose. Tighten all engine mounting fasteners to the specified torque (Chapter 2).

5   Crankshaft bearings worn (Chapter 2).

6   Camshaft chain tensioner defective. Replace according to the procedure in Chapter 2.

7   Camshaft chain, sprockets or guides worn (Chapter 2).

Abnormal driveline noise

35   Clutch noise

1   Clutch housing/friction plate clearance excessive (Chapter 2).
2   Loose or damaged clutch pressure plate and/or bolts (Chapter 2).

36   Transmission noise

1   Bearings worn. Also includes the possibility that the shafts are worn. Overhaul the transmission (Chapter 2).

2   Gears worn or chipped (Chapter 2).

3   Metal chips jammed in gear teeth. Probably pieces from a broken clutch, gear or shift mechanism that were picked up by the gears. This will cause early bearing failure (Chapter 2).

4   Engine oil level too low. Causes a howl from transmission. Also affects engine power and clutch operation (Chapter 1).

37   Chain or final drive noise

1   Chain not adjusted properly (Chapter 1).
2   Sprocket (engine sprocket or rear sprocket) loose. Tighten fasteners (Chapter 6).

3   Sprocket(s) worn. Replace sprocket(s) (Chapter 6).

4   Rear sprocket warped. Replace sprockets and chain as a set (Chapter 6).

5   Wheel coupling worn. Replace coupling (Chapter 6).

Abnormal frame and suspension noise

38   Front end noise

1   Low fluid level or improper viscosity oil in forks. This can sound like "spurting" and is usually accompanied by irregular fork action (Chapter 6).

2   Spring weak or broken. Makes a clicking or scraping sound. Fork oil, when drained, will have a lot of metal particles in it (Chapter 6).

3   Steering head bearings loose or damaged. Clicks when braking. Check and adjust or replace as necessary (Chapters 1 and 6).

4   Fork clamps loose. Make sure all fork clamp pinch bolts are tight (Chapter 6).

5   Fork tube bent. Good possibility if machine has been dropped. Replace tube with a new one (Chapter 6).

6   Front axle or axle clamp bolt loose. Tighten them to the specified torque (Chapter 7).

39   Shock absorber noise

1   Fluid level incorrect. Indicates a leak caused by defective seal. Shock will be covered with oil. Replace shock (Chapter 6).

2   Defective shock absorber with internal damage. This is in the body of the shock and cannot be remedied. The shock must be replaced with a new one (Chapter 6).

3   Bent or damaged shock body. Replace the shock with a new one (Chapter 6).

40   Brake noise

1   Squeal caused by pad shim not installed or positioned correctly (Chapter 7).

2   Squeal caused by dust on brake pads. Usually found in combination with glazed pads. Clean using brake cleaning solvent (Chapter 7).

3   Contamination of brake pads. Oil, brake fluid or dirt causing brake to chatter or squeal. Clean or replace pads (Chapter 7).

4   Pads glazed. Caused by excessive heat from prolonged use or from contamination. Do not use sandpaper, emery cloth, carborundum cloth or any other abrasive to roughen the pad surfaces as abrasives will stay in the pad material and damage the disc. A very fine flat file can be used, but pad replacement is suggested as a cure (Chapter 7).

5   Disc warped. Can cause a chattering, clicking or intermittent squeal. Usually accompanied by a pulsating lever and uneven braking. Replace the disc (Chapter 7).

6   Loose or worn wheel bearings. Check and replace as needed (Chapter 7).

Oil pressure indicator light comes on

41   Engine lubrication system

1   Engine oil pump defective (Chapter 2).

2   Engine oil level low. Inspect for leak or other problem causing low oil level and add recommended lubricant (Chapters 1 and 2).

3   Engine oil viscosity too low. Very old, thin oil or an improper weight of oil used in engine. Change to correct lubricant (Chapter 1).

4   Camshaft or journals worn. Excessive wear causing drop in oil pressure. Replace cam and/or head. Abnormal wear could be caused by oil starvation at high rpm from low oil level or improper oil weight or

type (Chapter 1).

5   Crankshaft and/or bearings worn. Same problems as paragraph 4. Check and replace crankshaft and/or bearings (Chapter 2).

42   Electrical system

1   Oil pressure switch defective. Check the switch according to the procedure in Chapter 9. Replace it if it is defective.

2   Oil pressure indicator light circuit defective. Check for pinched, shorted, disconnected or damaged wiring (Chapter 9).

Excessive exhaust smoke

43   White smoke

1   Piston oil ring worn. The ring may be broken or damaged, causing oil from the crankcase to be pulled past the piston into the combustion chamber. Replace the rings with new ones (Chapter 2).

2   Cylinders worn, cracked, or scored. Caused by overheating or oil starvation. The cylinders will have to be rebored and new pistons installed.

3   Valve oil seal damaged or worn. Replace oil seals with new ones (Chapter 2).

4   Valve guide worn. Perform a complete valve job (Chapter 2).

5   Engine oil level too high, which causes oil to be forced past the rings. Drain oil to the proper level (Chapter 1).

6   Head gasket broken between oil return and cylinder. Causes oil to be pulled into combustion chamber. Replace the head gasket and check the head for warpage (Chapter 2).

7   Abnormal crankcase pressurization, which forces oil past the rings. Clogged breather or hoses usually the cause (Chapter 4).

44   Black smoke

1   Air cleaner clogged. Clean or replace the element (Chapter 1).

2   Main jet too large or loose. Compare the jet size to the Specifications (Chapter 4).

3   Choke stuck, causing fuel to be pulled through choke circuit (Chapter 4).

4   Fuel level too high. Check and adjust the float height as necessary (Chapter 4).

5   Inlet needle held off needle seat. Clean float bowl and fuel line and replace needle and seat if necessary (Chapter 4).

45   Brown smoke

1   Main jet too small or clogged. Lean condition caused by wrong size main jet or by a restricted orifice. Clean float bowl and jets and compare jet size to Specifications (Chapter 4).

2   Fuel flow insufficient. Fuel inlet needle valve stuck closed due to chemical reaction with old fuel. Float height incorrect. Restricted fuel line. Clean line and float bowl and adjust floats if necessary (Chapter 4).

3   Carburetor intake manifolds loose (Chapter 4).

4   Air cleaner poorly sealed or not installed (Chapter 1).

Poor handling or stability

46   Handlebar hard to turn

1   Steering stem locknut too tight (Chapter 6).

2   Bearings damaged. Roughness can be felt as the bars are turned from side-to-side. Replace bearings and races (Chapter 6).

3   Races dented or worn. Denting results from wear in only one position (e. g., straight ahead), from striking an immovable object or hole or from dropping the machine.Replace races and bearings (Chapter 6).

4   Steering stem lubrication inadequate. Causes are grease getting hard from age or being washed out by high pressure car washes. Disassemble steering head and repack bearings (Chapter 6).

5   Steering stem bent. Caused by hitting a curb or hole or from dropping the machine. Replace damaged part. Do not try to straighten stem (Chapter 6).

6   Front tire air pressure too low (Chapter 1).

47   Handlebar shakes or vibrates excessively

1   Tires worn or out of balance (Chapter 7).

2   Swingarm bearings worn. Replace worn bearings by referring to Chapter 6.

3   Rim(s) warped or damaged. Inspect wheels for runout (Chapter 7).

4   Wheel bearings worn. Worn front or rear wheel bearings can cause poor tracking. Worn front bearings will cause wobble (Chapter 7).

5   Handlebar clamp bolts loose (Chapter 6).

6   Steering stem or fork clamps loose. Tighten them to the specified torque (Chapter 6).

7   Engine mount bolts loose. Will cause excessive vibration with increased engine rpm (Chapter 2).

48   Handlebar pulls to one side

1   Frame bent. Definitely suspect this if the machine has been dropped. May or may not be accompanied by cracking near the bend. Replace the frame (Chapter 6).

2   Wheel out of alignment. Caused by improper location of axle spacers or from bent steering stem or frame (Chapter 6).

3   Swingarm bent or twisted. Caused by age (metal fatigue) or impact damage. Replace the arm (Chapter 6).

4   Steering stem bent. Caused by impact damage or from dropping the motorcycle. Replace the steering stem (Chapter 6).

5   Fork leg bent. Disassemble the forks and replace the damaged parts (Chapter 6).

6   Fork oil level uneven.

49   Poor shock absorbing qualities

1   Too hard:

a) *Fork oil level excessive (Chapter 6).*

b) *Fork oil viscosity too high. Use a lighter oil (see the Specifications in Chapter 6).*

c) *Fork tube bent. Causes a harsh, sticking feeling (Chapter 6).*

d) *Shock shaft or body bent or damaged (Chapter 6).*

e) *Fork internal damage (Chapter 6).*

f) *Shock internal damage.*

g) *Tire pressure too high (Chapters 1 and 7).*

2   Too soft:

a) *Fork or shock oil insufficient and/or leaking (Chapter 6).*

b) *Fork oil viscosity too light (Chapter 6).*

c) *Fork springs weak or broken (Chapter 6).*

Braking problems

50   Front brakes are spongy, don't hold

1   Air in brake line. Caused by inattention to master cylinder fluid level or by leakage. Locate problem and bleed brakes (Chapter 7).

2   Pad or disc worn (Chapters 1 and 7).

3   Brake fluid leak. See paragraph 1.

4   Contaminated pads. Caused by contamination with oil, grease, brake fluid, etc. Clean or replace pads. Clean disc thoroughly with brake cleaner (Chapter 7).

5   Brake fluid deteriorated. Fluid is old or contaminated. Drain system, replenish with new fluid and bleed the system (Chapter 7).

6   Master cylinder internal parts worn or damaged causing fluid to bypass (Chapter 7).

7   Master cylinder bore scratched from ingestion of foreign material or broken spring. Repair or replace master cylinder (Chapter 7).

8   Disc warped. Replace disc (Chapter 7).

51   Brake lever or pedal pulsates

1   Disc warped. Replace disc (Chapter 7).

2   Axle bent. Replace axle (Chapter 6).

3   Brake caliper bolts loose (Chapter 7).

4   Brake caliper shafts damaged or sticking, causing caliper to bind. Lube the shafts and/or replace them if they are corroded or bent (Chapter 7).

5   Wheel warped or otherwise damaged (Chapter 7).

6   Wheel bearings damaged or worn (Chapter 7).

52   Brakes drag

1   Master cylinder piston seized. Caused by wear or damage to piston or cylinder bore (Chapter 7).

2   Lever balky or stuck. Check pivot and lubricate (Chapter 7).

3   Brake caliper binds. Caused by inadequate lubrication or damage to caliper shafts (Chapter 7).

4   Brake caliper piston seized in bore. Caused by wear or ingestion of dirt past deteriorated seal (Chapter 7).

5   Brake pad damaged. Pad material separating from backing plate. Usually caused by faulty manufacturing process or from contact with chemicals. Replace pads (Chapter 7).

6   Pads improperly installed (Chapter 7).

Electrical problems

53   Battery dead or weak

1   Battery faulty. Caused by sulfated plates which are shorted through sedimentation or by low electrolyte level. Also, broken battery terminal making only occasional contact (Chapter 9).

2   Battery cables making poor contact (Chapter 9).

3   Load excessive. Caused by addition of high wattage lights or other electrical accessories.

4   Ignition switch defective. Switch either grounds (earths) internally or fails to shut off system. Replace the switch (Chapter 9).

5   Regulator/rectifier defective (Chapter 9).

6   Stator coil open or shorted (Chapter 9).

7   Wiring faulty. Wiring grounded (earthed) or connections loose in ignition, charging or lighting circuits (Chapter 9).

54   Battery overcharged

1   Regulator/rectifier defective. Overcharging is noticed when battery gets excessively warm or "boils" over (Chapter 9).

2   Battery defective. Replace battery with a new one (Chapter 9).

3   Battery amperage too low, wrong type or size. Install manufacturer's specified amp-hour battery to handle charging load (Chapter 9).

Notes

Chapter 1
Tune-up and routine maintenance

Contents

1

Specifications

Engine

Spark plugs
  Type
    D models
      US models .... NGK C9E or ND U27ES-N
      UK and Canadian models .... NGK CR9E or ND U27ESR-N
    E models (US, UK and Canadian) .... NGK CR9E or ND U27ESR-N
  Gap (all models) .... 0.7 to 0.8 mm (0.028 to 0.032 inch)
Engine idle speed
  All except California models .... 1000 to 1100 rpm
  California models .... 1250 to 1350 rpm
Valve clearances (COLD engine)
  Intake .... 0.15 to 0.24 mm (.006 to .009 inch)
  Exhaust .... 0.22 to 0.31 mm (.009 to .012 inch)
Cylinder compression pressure
  Acceptable range .... 960 to 1470 kPa @ 350 rpm (9.8 to 15 kg/cm^2, 139 to 213 psi)
  Maximum difference between cylinders .... 122 kPa (1.2 kg/cm^2, 18 psi)
Carburetor synchronization (vacuum difference
  between cylinders) .... Less than 2.7 kPa (2 cm Hg)
Cylinder numbering (from left side to right side of bike) 1-2-3-4
Firing order 1-2-4-3

Miscellaneous

Brake pad minimum thickness	1 mm (3/64-inch)
Choke cable freeplay	2 to 3 mm (0.08 to 0.12 inch)
Clutch lever freeplay	2 to 3 mm (0.08 to 0.12 inch)
Throttle grip freeplay	2 to 3 mm (0.08 to 0.12 inch)
Drive chain	
Slack	35 to 40 mm (1.38 to 1.57 inch)
20-link length	323 mm (12.73 inch) maximum
Battery electrolyte specific gravity	1.260 minimum
Minimum tire tread depth	
Front	1.0 mm (0.040 inch)
Rear	
Up to 130 km/h (80 mph)	2 mm (0.0788 inch)
Over 130 km/h (80 mph)	3 mm (0.1182 inch)
Tire pressures (cold)	
Front	250 kPa (2.5 kg/cm², 36 psi)
Rear	290 kPa (2.9 kg/cm², 41 psi)

Torque specifications

Oil drain plug	20 N-m (174 in-lbs)
Oil filter	9.8 N-m (87 in-lbs)
Coolant drain bolt	9.8 N-m (87 in-lbs)
Spark plugs	14 N-m (120 in-lbs)
Valve cover bolts	9.8 N-m (87 in-lbs)

Recommended lubricants and fluids

Engine/transmission oil	
Type	API grade SE, SF or SG multi-viscosity
Viscosity	
In cold climates	SAE 10W40 or 10W50
In warm climates	SAE 20W40 or 20W50
Capacity	3.2L (3.4 qts)
Coolant	
Type	50/50 mixture of ethylene glycol-based antifreeze and soft water
Capacity	2.5 liters (2.64 quarts)
Brake fluid grade	
D models	DOT 3
E models	DOT 4
Fork oil	
Type	SAE 10W20 fork oil
Capacity	
D models	
At oil change	384 cc
Completely dry	452 cc
E models	
At oil change	429 cc
Completely dry	505 cc
Oil level (distance from oil to top of fork tube, fork fully compressed, without spring)	
D models	140 mm (5.52 inches)
E models	98 mm (3.86 inches)

Miscellaneous

Wheel bearings	Medium weight, lithium-based multi-purpose grease
Swingarm pivot bearings	Medium weight, lithium-based multi-purpose grease
Cables and lever pivots	Chain and cable lubricant or 10W30 motor oil
Sidestand/centerstand pivots	Chain and cable lubricant or 10W30 motor oil
Brake pedal/shift lever pivots	Chain and cable lubricant or 10W30 motor oil
Throttle grip	Multi-purpose grease or dry film lubricant

1 Kawasaki ZX600
Routine maintenance intervals

Note: *The pre-ride inspection outlined in the owner's manual covers checks and maintenance that should be carried out on a daily basis. It's condensed and included here to remind you of its importance. Always perform the pre-ride inspection at every maintenance interval (in addition to the procedures listed). The intervals listed below are the shortest intervals recommended by the manufacturer for each particular operation during the model years covered in this manual. Your owner's manual may have different intervals for your model.*

Daily or before riding

Check the engine oil level
Check the fuel level and inspect for leaks
Check the engine coolant level and look for leaks
Check the operation of both brakes - also check the fluid level and look for leakage
Check the tires for damage, the presence of foreign objects and correct air pressure
Check the throttle for smooth operation and correct freeplay
Check the operation of the clutch - make sure the freeplay is correct
Make sure the steering operates smoothly
Check for proper operation of the headlight, tail light, brake light, turn signals, indicator lights and horn
Make sure the sidestand and centerstand return to their fully up positions and stay there under spring pressure
Make sure the engine STOP switch works properly

Every 200 miles

Lubricate the drive chain

After the initial 500 miles

Perform all of the daily checks plus:
Check and adjust the valve clearances
Clean the air filter element
Check/adjust the idle speed
Check/adjust the carburetor synchronization
Check/adjust the drive chain slack
Change the engine oil and oil filter
Check the evaporative emission control system (California models)
Check the cooling system hoses
Check the battery electrolyte level
Check the tightness of all fasteners

Every 500 miles

Check/adjust the drive chain slack

Every 3000 miles

Clean and gap the spark plugs
Check the operation of the air suction valve (if equipped)
Check/adjust the idle speed
Check/adjust the carburetor synchronization
Check the evaporative emission control system (California models)
Adjust the clutch freeplay
Check the drive chain and sprockets for wear
Check the brake fluid level
Check the brake discs and pads
Check/adjust the brake pedal position
Check the operation of the brake light
Lubricate all cables
Lubricate the clutch and brake lever pivots
Lubricate the shift/brake lever pivots and the sidestand/centerstand pivots
Change the engine oil and oil filter
Clean the air filter element
Check the steering
Check the tires and wheels
Check the battery electrolyte level (if possible)
Check the exhaust system for leaks and check the tightness of the fasteners

Every 6000 miles

All of the items above plus:
Check the cleanliness of the fuel system and the condition of the fuel and vacuum hoses
Lubricate the swingarm needle bearings and suspension linkage
Replace the spark plugs

Every 18,000 miles

Check the cooling system and replace the coolant
Change the fork oil

Once a year

Clean the coolant filter (UK models only)

Every two years

Change the brake fluid (Chapter 7)
Rebuild the brake calipers and master cylinders (Chapter 7)
Lubricate the steering head bearings (Chapter 6)
Check and lubricate the wheel bearings (Chapter 7)
Lubricate the speedometer gear

Every four years

Replace the fuel hoses (Chapter 4)
Replace the brake hoses (Chapter 7)

3.3 The engine oil level must be between the Minimum and Maximum marks (arrows) on the window

3.4 If the oil level is below the Minimum mark, remove the oil filler cap (arrow) from the right crankcase cover and add enough oil of the recommended grade and type to bring the level up to the Maximum mark; don't overfill the engine!

3.7 The brake fluid level in the front master cylinder must be above the lower mark (arrow) at the inspection window

2   Introduction to tune-up and routine maintenance

This Chapter covers in detail the checks and procedures necessary for the tune-up and routine maintenance of your motorcycle. Section 1 includes the routine maintenance schedule, which is designed to keep the machine in proper running condition and prevent possible problems. The remaining Sections contain detailed procedures for carrying out the items listed on the maintenance schedule, as well as additional maintenance information designed to increase reliability.

Since routine maintenance plays such an important role in the safe and efficient operation of your motorcycle, it is presented here as a comprehensive check list. For the rider who does all his own maintenance, these lists outline the procedures and checks that should be done on a routine basis.

Deciding where to start or plug into the routine maintenance schedule depends on several factors. If you have a motorcycle whose warranty has recently expired, and if it has been maintained according to the warranty standards, you may want to pick-up routine maintenance as it coincides with the next mileage or calendar interval. If you have owned the machine for some time but have never performed any maintenance on it, then you may want to start at the nearest interval and include some additional procedures to ensure that nothing important is overlooked. If you have just had a major engine overhaul, then you may want to start the maintenance routine from the beginning. If you have a used machine and have no knowledge of its history or maintenance record, you may desire to combine all the checks into one large service initially and then settle into the maintenance schedule prescribed.

The Sections which actually outline the inspection and maintenance procedures are written as step-by-step comprehensive guides to the actual performance of the work. They explain in detail each of the routine inspections and maintenance procedures on the check list. References to additional information in applicable Chapters is also included and should not be overlooked.

Before beginning any actual maintenance or repair, the machine should be cleaned thoroughly, especially around the oil filter housing, spark plugs, cylinder head covers, side covers, carburetors, etc. Cleaning will help ensure that dirt does not contaminate the engine and will allow you to detect wear and damage that could otherwise easily go unnoticed.

3   Fluid levels - check

Engine oil

Refer to illustrations 3.3 and 3.4

1   Place the motorcycle on the centerstand, then start the engine and allow it to reach normal operating temperature. **Caution:** *Do not run the engine in an enclosed space such as a garage or shop.*

2   Stop the engine and allow the machine to sit undisturbed on the centerstand for about five minutes.

3   With the engine off, check the oil level in the window located at the lower part of the right crankcase cover. The oil level should be between the Maximum and Minimum level marks on the window **(see illustration)**.

4   If the level is below the Minimum mark, remove the oil filler cap from the right crankcase cover **(see illustration)** and add enough oil of the recommended grade and type to bring the level up to the Maximum mark. Do not overfill.

Brake fluid

Refer to illustrations 3.7, 3.13a and 3.13b

5   In order to ensure proper operation of the hydraulic disc brakes, the fluid level in the master cylinder reservoirs must be properly maintained.

6   With the motorcycle on the centerstand, turn the handlebars until the top of the master cylinder is as level as possible. If necessary, loosen the brake lever clamp bolts and rotate the master cylinder assembly slightly to make it level.

7   Look closely at the inspection window in the master cylinder reservoir. Make sure that the fluid level is above the Lower mark on the reservoir **(see illustration)**.

8   If the level is low, the fluid must be replenished. Before removing the master cylinder cap, cover the gas tank to protect it from brake fluid spills (which will damage the paint) and remove all dust and dirt from the area around the cap.

9   Remove the screws and lift off the cap and rubber diaphragm. **Note:** *Do not operate the brake lever with the cap removed.*

10   Add new, clean brake fluid of the recommended type until the level is above the inspection window. Do not mix different brands of brake fluid in the reservoir, as they may not be compatible.

11   Replace the rubber diaphragm and the cover. Tighten the screws evenly, but do not overtighten them.

12   Wipe any spilled fluid off the reservoir body and reposition and tighten the brake lever and master cylinder assembly if it was moved.

13   A sight window **(see illustration)** is provided for checking the fluid level in the rear master cylinder reservoir. However, unless the reservoir is clean, it is difficult to read the fluid level through the slot. You may have to remove the right side cover (see Chapter 8) and wipe off the side of the reservoir. The fluid level should be between the Upper and Lower marks **(see illustration)**. If it isn't, wipe off and unscrew the cap, and add the type of brake fluid recommended in this Chapter's Specifications until the level is at the Upper mark.

14   If the brake fluid level was low in either check, inspect the front or rear brake system for leaks.

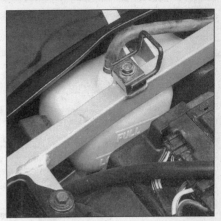

3.13a You can read the fluid level in the rear brake reservoir through this sight window in the right side cover - but only with a small flashlight

3.13b The brake fluid level in the rear master cylinder reservoir must be between the Upper and Lower marks (arrows)

3.15 After removing the seat, you'll find the coolant reservoir under the right frame rail; the Full and Low marks (arrows) are visible on the side of the reservoir facing in

Coolant

Refer to illustration 3.15

Note: *The engine must be cold for the results to be accurate, so always perform this check before starting the engine for the first time each day.*

15 Remove the seat. The coolant reservoir **(see illustration)** is located under the right frame rail of the seat subframe.

16 The coolant level is satisfactory if it is between the Low and Full marks on the reservoir**(see illustration 3.15)** If the level is at or below the Low mark, remove the right side cover (see Chapter 8), unscrew the reservoir filler cap and add the recommended coolant mixture (see this Chapter's Specifications) until the Full level is reached. If the coolant level seems to be consistently low, check the entire cooling system for leaks.

---

4   **Battery condition - check**

Battery electrolyte level/specific gravity (D models)

Refer to illustration 4.5

Warning: *Be extremely careful when handling or working around the battery. The electrolyte is very caustic and an explosive gas (hydrogen) is given off when the battery is charging.*

1   Remove the seat, then remove the air cleaner intake duct (see Chapter 4).

2   Remove the bolts securing the battery cables to the battery terminals (remove the negative cable first, positive cable last) **(see illustration 4.12)**. Pull the battery straight up to remove it. The electrolyte level will now be visible through the opaque battery case - it should be between the Upper and Lower level marks.

3   If it is low, remove the cell caps and fill each cell to the upper level mark with distilled water. Do not use tap water (except in an emergency), and do not overfill. The cell holes are quite small, so it may help to use a plastic squeeze bottle with a small spout to add the water. If the level is within the marks on the case, additional water is not necessary.

4   Next, check the specific gravity of the electrolyte in each cell with a small hydrometer made especially for motorcycle batteries (if the electrolyte level is known to be sufficient it won't be necessary to remove the battery. These are available from most dealer parts departments or motorcycle accessory stores.

5   Remove the caps, draw some electrolyte from the first cell into the hydrometer **(see illustration)** and note the specific gravity. Compare the reading to the Specifications listed in this Chapter.

4.5 On D models, check the battery's specific gravity with a hydrometer

Note: *Add 0.004 points to the reading for every 10-degrees F above 68-degrees F - subtract 0.004 points from the reading for every 10-degrees below 68-degrees F.* Return the electrolyte to the appropriate cell and repeat the check for the remaining cells. When the check is complete, rinse the hydrometer thoroughly with clean water.

6   If the specific gravity of the electrolyte in each cell is as specified, the battery is in good condition and is apparently being charged by the machine's charging system.

7   If the specific gravity is low, the battery is not fully charged. This may be due to corroded battery terminals, a dirty battery case, a malfunctioning charging system, or loose or corroded wiring connections. On the other hand, it may be that the battery is worn out, especially if the machine is old, or that infrequent use of the motorcycle prevents normal charging from taking place.

8   Be sure to correct any problems and charge the battery if necessary. Refer to Chapter 9 for additional battery maintenance and charging procedures.

9   Install the battery cell caps, tightening them securely. Reconnect the cables to the battery, attaching the positive cable first and the negative cable last. Make sure to install the insulating boot over the positive terminal. Install the fuel tank mount and the seat. Be very careful not to pinch or otherwise restrict the battery vent tube (if equipped), as the battery may build up enough internal pressure during normal charging system operation to explode.

1

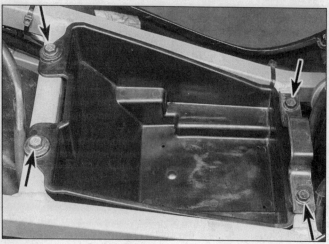

4.10 To remove the package tray on E models, remove these four bolts (arrows); don't lose the metal piece that's attached by the two front bolts - it secures the front end of the seat

Battery charging condition (E models)

Refer to illustrations 4.10, 4.11 and 4.12

Note: *E models use a maintenance-free battery. Do not attempt to remove the caps to check the specific gravity or to add electrolyte or water.*

10   Remove the seat and remove the small black plastic package tray **(see illustration)**.

11   Using a digital voltmeter, measure the battery voltage as shown **(see illustration)**. It should be at least 12.6 volts. If it isn't, try charging the battery (see Chapter 9). If the battery can't be charged to the specified voltage, replace it.

12   To replace the battery, remove the bolts securing the battery cables to the battery terminals (remove the negative cable first, positive cable last) **(see illustration)**. Pull the battery straight up to remove it. Don't worry about disconnecting the vent hose - there isn't one. Maintenance-free batteries don't use a vent hose.

13   Installation is the reverse of removal.

5   Brake pad thickness - check

Refer to illustrations 5.2a, 5.2b and 5.3

1   The brake pads should be checked at the recommended intervals and replaced with new ones when worn beyond the limit listed in this Chapter's Specifications.

2   To check the front brake pads, turn the front wheel to each side and remove the pad spring **(see illustration)**. The brake pads are visible from this angle and should have at least the specified minimum amount of lining material remaining on the metal backing plate **(see illustration)**. Be sure to check the pads in both calipers.

3   Check the rear brake pads by looking into the caliper from the rear of the machine **(see illustration)**.

4   If the pads are worn excessively, they must be replaced with new ones (see Chapter 7).

6   Brake system - general check

Refer to illustration 6.6

1   A routine general check of the brakes will ensure that any problems are discovered and remedied before the rider's safety is jeopardized.

2   Check the brake lever and pedal for loose connections, excessive play, bends, and other damage. Replace any damaged parts with new ones (see Chapter 7).

3   Make sure all brake fasteners are tight. Check the brake pads for wear (see Section 5) and make sure the fluid level in the reservoir is

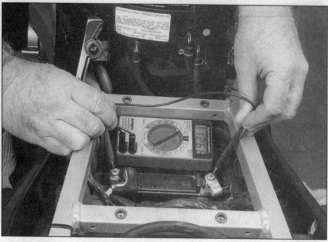

4.11 On E models, use a digital voltmeter to measure the battery voltage; it should be at least 12.6 volts. If it isn't, try charging the battery (see Chapter 9). If the battery can't be charged to the specified voltage, replace it.

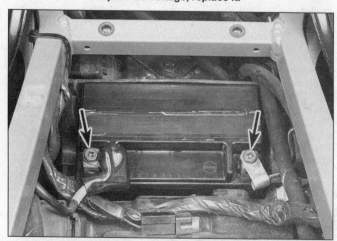

4.12 To replace the battery, remove the bolts securing the battery cables to the battery terminals (remove the negative cable first, positive cable last). Pull the battery straight up to remove it.

correct (see Section 3). Look for leaks at the hose connections and check for cracks in the hoses. If the lever is spongy, bleed the brakes as described in Chapter 7.

4   Make sure the brake light operates when the brake lever is depressed.

5   Make sure the brake light is activated when the rear brake pedal is depressed approximately 11 mm (7/16 inch).

6   If adjustment is necessary, hold the switch and turn the adjusting nut on the switch body **(see illustration)** until the brake light is activated when required. The factory recommends 10mm (0.39 inch) of pedal freeplay. Moving the switch up activates the brake lights sooner; lowering the switch activates the lights later. If the brake lights don't come on when the brake pedal is depressed, check the switch (see Chapter 9).

7   The front brake light switch is not adjustable. If it fails to operate properly, replace it with a new one (see Chapter 9).

Brake pedal position - check and adjustment

Refer to illustration 6.9

8   Rear brake pedal position is largely a matter of personal preference. Locate the pedal so that the rear brake can be engaged quickly and easily without excessive foot movement. The recommended factory setting is approximately 55 mm (2-1/64 inches) below the top of the footpeg.

5.2a To gain access to the front brake pads, turn the front wheel to each side, remove these two screws (arrows) and remove the pad spring from each caliper

5.2b The front brake pads should have at least the specified minimum amount of lining material remaining on the metal backing plate (be sure to check the pads in both calipers)

5.3 Check the rear brake pads by looking into the caliper from the rear of the machine

6.6 Hold the switch and turn the adjusting nut on the switch body until the brake light is activated - turning the switch out will cause the brake light to come on sooner, while turning it in will cause it to come on later

6.9 To adjust the position of the pedal, loosen the locknut on the clevis, then screw the pushrod with the hex head in or out of the clevis to adjust the position of the brake pedal

7.4 Check the tire pressures when the tires are cold and keep them properly inflated

1

9   To adjust the position of the pedal, loosen the locknut on the clevis, then screw the pushrod with the hex head in or out of the clevis to adjust the position of the brake pedal **(see illustration)**.
10   If necessary, adjust the brake light switch (see Steps 5 and 6).

7   Tires/wheels - general check

Refer to illustration 7.4

1   Routine tire and wheel checks should be made with the realization that your safety depends to a great extent on their condition.
2   Check the tires carefully for cuts, tears, embedded nails or other sharp objects and excessive wear. Operation of the motorcycle with excessively worn tires is extremely hazardous, as traction and handling are directly affected. Measure the tread depth at the center of the tire and replace worn tires with new ones when the tread depth is less than specified.
3   Repair or replace punctured tires as soon as damage is noted. Do not try to patch a torn tire, as wheel balance and tire reliability may be impaired.
4   Check the tire pressures when the tires are cold and keep them properly inflated **(see illustration)**. Proper air pressure will increase tire life and provide maximum stability and ride comfort. Keep in mind that

low tire pressures may cause the tire to slip on the rim or come off, while high tire pressures will cause abnormal tread wear and unsafe handling.
5   The cast wheels used on this machine are virtually maintenance free, but they should be kept clean and checked periodically for cracks and other damage. Never attempt to repair damaged cast wheels; they must be replaced with new ones.
6   Check the valve stem locknuts to make sure they are tight. Also, make sure the valve stem cap is in place and tight. If it is missing, install a new one made of metal or hard plastic.

8   Throttle operation/grip freeplay - check and adjustment

Check

1   Make sure the throttle grip rotates easily from fully closed to fully open with the front wheel turned at various angles. The grip should return automatically from fully open to fully closed when released. If the throttle sticks, check the throttle cables for cracks or kinks in the housings. Also, make sure the inner cables are clean and well-lubricated.
2   Check for a small amount of freeplay at the grip and compare the freeplay to the value listed in this Chapter's Specifications.

Adjustment

Refer to illustrations 8.3, 8.5, 8.7a and 8.7b

Note: *These motorcycles use two throttle cables - an accelerator cable and a decelerator cable.*

3   Freeplay adjustments can be made at the throttle end of the cable. Loosen the lockwheel on the cable **(see illustration)** and turn the adjuster until the desired freeplay is obtained, then retighten the lockwheel.

4   If the cables can't be adjusted at the grip end, you'll have to adjust them at the other (carburetor) end. To do so, remove the fuel tank (see Chapter 4).

5   Loosen the locknuts on both throttle cables **(see illustration)**, then turn both adjusting nuts in completely.

6   Turn out the adjusting nut of the decelerator cable until the inner cable becomes tight, then tighten the locknut.

7   Turn the accelerator adjusting nut until the desired freeplay is obtained, then tighten the locknut. Make sure the throttle linkage lever contacts the idle adjusting screw when the throttle grip is released **(see illustration)** and stops against the carburetor stopper with the throttle grip open **(see illustration)**.

---

9   Choke cable - check and adjustment

Check

Refer to illustration 9.2

1   Remove the fuel tank (see Chapter 4).

2   To calculate the amount of choke cable freeplay at the choke lever, pull the choke lever until the starter plunger lever at the carburetor contacts the starter plunger **(see illustration)**. The amount of choke lever travel is equal to the amount of choke cable freeplay. Compare your measurement to the choke cable freeplay listed in this Chapter's Specifications. If the freeplay is incorrect, adjust the choke cable.

Adjustment

Refer to illustration 9.3

3   Loosen the locknut and turn the adjuster at the middle of the cable **(see illustration)** until the proper amount of freeplay is obtained.

4   Tighten the locknut against the adjuster when you're done.

---

10   Clutch - check and adjustment

Refer to illustrations 10.2, 10.4 and 10.6

1   Correct clutch freeplay is necessary to ensure proper clutch operation and reasonable clutch service life. Freeplay normally

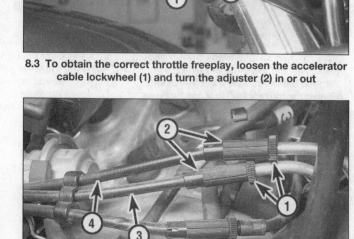

8.3   To obtain the correct throttle freeplay, loosen the accelerator cable lockwheel (1) and turn the adjuster (2) in or out

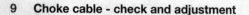

8.5   Throttle cable details

1	Locknuts	3	Decelerator cable
2	Adjusting nuts	4	Accelerator cable

changes because of cable stretch and clutch wear, so it should be checked and adjusted periodically.

2   Check clutch cable freeplay at the clutch lever on the handlebar. Slowly pull in the lever until resistance is felt, then note how far the lever has moved away from its bracket at the pivot end **(see illustration)**.

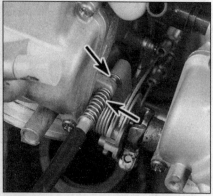

8.7a   Make sure the throttle linkage lever (upper arrow) contacts the idle adjusting screw (lower arrow) when the throttle grip is released (carburetors removed from head for clarity) . . .

8.7b   . . . and stops against the carburetor stopper (arrow) with the throttle grip open

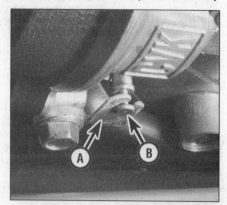

9.2   To calculate the amount of choke cable freeplay at the choke lever, pull the choke lever at the handlebar until the starter plunger lever at the carburetor (A) contacts the starter plunger (B); choke lever travel equals choke cable freeplay

9.3 To adjust the choke cable, loosen the locknut and turn the adjuster at the middle of the cable (arrow) until the correct freeplay is obtained

10.2 To check clutch cable freeplay at the clutch lever on the handlebar, slowly pull in the lever until resistance is felt, then note how far the lever has moved away from its bracket at the pivot end; if the cable is adjusted correctly, there should be about 2 to 3 mm of clearance between the lever and the bracket (arrow)

10.4 If the lever adjuster on the handlebar reaches the end of its travel, adjust the cable at its bracket (arrow) on the lower right side of the engine; first, loosen the two adjusting nuts (arrows) at the bracket completely

Compare this distance with the freeplay listed in this Chapter's Specifications. Too little freeplay can prevent the clutch from fully engaging. Too much freeplay can prevent the clutch from fully releasing.

3   To adjust freeplay at the clutch lever, loosen (turn counterclockwise) the knurled lock wheel, then turn the threaded adjuster in or out until the desired freeplay is obtained. Always retighten (turn clockwise) the lock wheel once the adjustment is complete.

4   If the lever adjuster on the handlebar reaches the end of its travel, pull back the dust boot and adjust the cable at its bracket just ahead of the clutch lever on the lower right side of the engine **(see illustration)**.

5   Loosen the two adjusting nuts at the bracket completely.

6   Loosen the knurled lock wheel at the clutch lever and turn the adjuster in or out until the gap between the adjuster and lock wheel is about 5 to 6 mm **(see illustration)**.

7   Pull the clutch cable tight to remove all slack, then tighten the adjusting nuts against the bracket at the lower end of the cable.

8   Turn the adjuster at the clutch lever until the correct freeplay is obtained. When the cable is properly adjusted, the angle between the cable and the release lever should be approximately 80 to 90-degrees.

9   If the proper amount of freeplay still can't be obtained, the cable must be replaced (see Chapter 2).

11 Drive chain and sprockets - check, adjustment and lubrication

Check

Refer to illustrations 11.3 and 11.5

1   A neglected drive chain won't last long and can quickly damage the sprockets. Routine chain adjustment and lubrication isn't difficult and will ensure maximum chain and sprocket life.

2   To check the chain, place the bike on its centerstand and shift the transmission into Neutral. Make sure the ignition switch is off.

3   Push up on the bottom run of the chain and measure the slack midway between the two sprockets **(see illustration)**, then compare your measurements to the value listed in this Chapter's Specifications. As wear occurs, the chain will actually stretch, which means adjustment usually involves removing some slack from the chain. In some cases where lubrication has been neglected, corrosion and galling may cause the links to bind and kink, which effectively shortens the chain's length. If the chain is tight between the sprockets, rusty or kinked, it's time to replace it with a new one.

1

10.6 Loosen the knurled lock wheel at the clutch lever and turn the adjuster in or out until the gap between the adjuster and lock wheel is about 5 to 6 mm, then tighten the lock wheel

11.3 Push up on the bottom run of the chain and measure the slack (how far the chain deflects) midway between the two sprockets; if it's not within the specified limits, adjust the slack in the chain

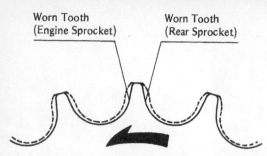

Worn Tooth (Engine Sprocket)   Worn Tooth (Rear Sprocket)

Direction of rotation

11.5 Check the teeth on both sprockets in the indicated areas to determine whether they are excessively worn

4   Remove the chain guard (it's held on by two bolts). Check the entire length of the chain for damaged rollers, loose links and pins. Hang a 20-lb weight on the bottom run of the chain and measure the length of 20 links along the top run. Rotate the wheel and repeat this check at several places on the chain, since it may wear unevenly. Compare your measurements with the maximum 20-link length listed in this Chapter's Specifications. If any of your measurements exceed the maximum, replace the chain. **Note:** *Never install a new chain on old sprockets, and never use the old chain if you install new sprockets - replace the chain and sprockets as a set.*
5   Remove the engine sprocket cover (see Chapter 7, Section 15). Check the teeth on the engine sprocket and the rear sprocket for wear **(see illustration)**.

Adjustment

Refer to illustrations 11.7, 11.8, 11.9 and 11.11
6   Place the bike on its centerstand and shift the transmission into Neutral. Make sure the ignition switch is off. Rotate the rear wheel until the chain is positioned with the least amount of slack present.
7   Loosen both torque link nuts **(see illustration)**.
8   Remove the cotter pin and loosen the axle nut **(see illustration)**.
9   Loosen and back-off the locknuts on the chain adjuster bolts **(see illustration)**.
10   Turn the axle adjusting bolts on both sides of the swingarm until the proper chain tension is obtained. Be sure to turn the adjusting bolts evenly to keep the rear wheel in alignment. If the adjusting bolts reach the end of their travel, the chain is excessively worn and should be replaced with a new one (see Chapter 6).
11   When the chain has the correct amount of slack, make sure the marks on the adjusters correspond to the same relative marks on each side of the swingarm **(see illustration)**. Tighten the axle nut to the torque listed in the Chapter 7 Specifications, then install a new cotter pin. If necessary, turn the nut an additional amount to line up the cotter pin

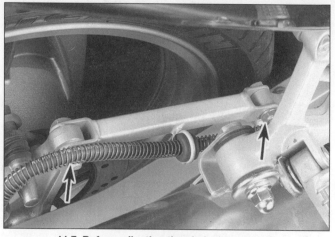

11.7 Before adjusting the chain, loosen both torque link nuts (arrows)

hole with the castellations in the nut - don't loosen the nut to do this.
12   Tighten the locknuts and the torque link nut securely.

Lubrication

Refer to illustration 11.13
Note: *If the chain is extremely dirty, it should be removed and cleaned before it is lubricated (see Chapter 6).*
13   The best time to lubricate the chain is after the motorcycle has been ridden. When the chain is warm, the lubricant will penetrate the joints between the side plates, pins, bushings and rollers to provide lubrication of the internal load bearing areas. Use a good quality chain lubricant and apply it to the area where the side plates overlap - not the middle of the rollers **(see illustration)**. After applying the lubricant, let it soak in a few minutes before wiping off any excess.

12   Engine oil/filter - change

Refer to illustrations 12.6, 12.7a and 12.7b
1   Consistent routine oil and filter changes are the single most important maintenance procedure you can perform on a motorcycle. The oil not only lubricates the internal parts of the engine, transmission and clutch, but it also acts as a coolant, a cleaner, a sealant, and a protectant. Because of these demands, the oil takes a terrific amount of abuse and should be replaced often with new oil of the recommended grade and type. Saving a little money on the difference in cost between a good oil and a cheap oil won't pay off if the engine is damaged.

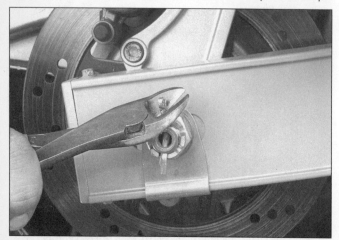

11.8 Remove the cotter pin and loosen the axle nut

11.9 Loosen and back-off the locknuts on the chain adjuster bolts

11.11 When the chain has the correct amount of slack, make sure the marks on the adjusters correspond to the same relative marks on each side of the swingarm

11.13 Apply chain lubricant to the joints between the side plates, pins, bushings and rollers to provide lubrication of the internal load bearing areas - not the middle of the rollers. With the bike on its centerstand, hold the plastic nozzle near the edge of the chain and turn the wheel by hand as the lubricant sprays out; repeat this procedure on the inside edge of the chain

2   Before changing the oil and filter, warm up the engine so the oil will drain easily. Be careful when draining the oil, as the exhaust pipes, the engine, and the oil itself can cause severe burns.
3   Put the motorcycle on the centerstand over a clean drain pan.
4   Remove the lower fairing (see Chapter 8).
5   Remove the oil filler cap to vent the crankcase (and serve as a reminder that there's no oil in the engine!).
6   Remove the drain plug **(see illustration)** from the engine and allow the oil to drain into the pan. Discard the drain plug sealing washer.
7   While the oil is draining, remove the oil filter with an oil filter wrench **(see illustrations)**.
8   Wipe any residual oil off the filter sealing surface on the crankcase. And be sure to wipe off any oil spilled on the exhaust headers. If the headers are oily when the engine is started, this oil will smoke and may even burst into flame.
9   Coat the gasket on the new filter with clean engine oil. Install the filter and hand tighten it. The filter should be snug, but do not overtighten it or you'll have difficulty removing it next time.
10   Check the condition of the drain plug threads. Using a new sealing washer, install the drain plug and tighten it to the torque listed in this Chapter's Specifications. Do not overtighten the drain plug! Overtightening the plug can strip out the threads in the pan. If this happens, you will at least have to rethread the hole and you may even have to replace the pan.

11   Before refilling the engine, check the old oil carefully. If the oil was drained into a clean pan, small pieces of metal or other material can be easily detected. If the oil is very metallic colored, then the engine is experiencing wear from break-in (new engine) or from insufficient lubrication. If there are flakes or chips of metal in the oil, then something is drastically wrong internally and the engine will have to be disassembled for inspection and repair.
12   If there are pieces of fiber-like material in the oil, the clutch is experiencing excessive wear and should be checked.
13   If the inspection of the oil turns up nothing unusual, refill the crankcase to the proper level with the recommended oil and install the filler cap. Start the engine and let it run for two or three minutes. Shut it off, wait a few minutes, then check the oil level. If necessary, add more oil to bring the level up to the Maximum mark. Check around the drain plug and filter housing for leaks.
14   The old oil drained from the engine cannot be reused in its present state and should be disposed of. Oil reclamation centers, auto repair shops and gas stations will normally accept the oil, which can be refined and used again (be sure to check with the repair shop or gas station first). After the oil has cooled, it can be drained into a suitable container (capped plastic jugs, topped bottles, milk cartons, etc.) for transport to one of these disposal sites.

12.6 Remove the drain plug (arrow) from the engine and allow the oil to drain into the pan; always discard the old drain plug sealing washer and replace it with a new one

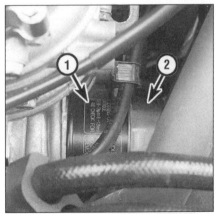

12.7a While the oil is draining, remove the oil filter (1) with an oil filter wrench (2)

12.7b Properly engaged, the filter and filter wrench look like this (filter removed from bike for clarity)

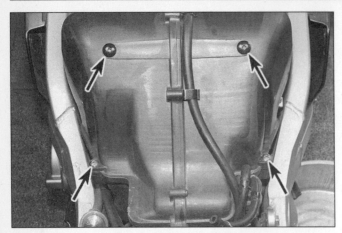

13.2a To remove the upper half of the air cleaner housing on D models, remove these screws (arrows)

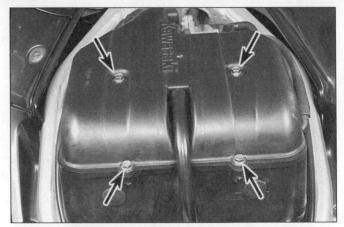

13.2b To remove the upper half of the air cleaner housing on E models, remove these bolts (arrows) . . .

13 Air filter element - servicing

Refer to illustrations 13.2a, 13.2b, 13.2c, 13.3a and 13.3b
Note: *Replace the air filter element every five cleanings (or more frequently, if the bike is operated in dusty conditions).*
1   Remove the seat (see Chapter 8) and the fuel tank (see Chapter 4).
2   Remove the upper half of the air cleaner housing **(see illustrations).**
3   Remove the air filter element **(see illustrations).** Wipe out the housing with a clean rag.
4   If the filter element is extremely dirty or torn, replace it. If it's still in reasonable condition, wash it in clean solvent, then dry it out with compressed air. After cleaning the element, saturate it with SE or SF class SAE30 oil, squeeze out the excess oil, then wrap it in a clean rag and squeeze it as dry as possible. Make sure you don't tear the filter.
5   Installation is the reverse of removal. Make sure the element is seated properly in the filter housing before installing the cover. Reinstall the fuel tank bracket, fuel tank and seat.

13.2c . . . and remove these bolts (arrows); to ensure proper reassembly, clearly label all emission hoses

14 Cylinder compression - check

Refer to illustration 14.5
1   Among other things, poor engine performance may be caused by leaking valves, incorrect valve clearances, a leaking head gasket, or worn pistons, rings and/or cylinder walls. A cylinder compression check will help pinpoint these conditions and can also indicate the presence of excessive carbon deposits in the cylinder heads.
2   The only tools required are a compression gauge and a spark plug wrench. Depending on the outcome of the initial test, a squirt-type oil can may also be needed.
3   Start the engine and allow it to reach normal operating temperature. Place the motorcycle on the centerstand, remove the fuel tank, then remove the spark plugs (see Section 15, if necessary). Work carefully - don't strip the spark plug hole threads and don't burn your hands.
4   Disable the ignition by unplugging the primary wires from the coils (see Chapter 5). Be sure to mark the locations of the wires before detaching them.

13.3a Removing the air filter on a D model

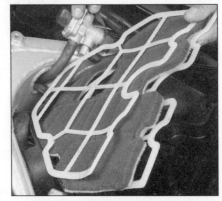

13.3b Removing the air filter on an E model

14.5 A compression gauge with a threaded fitting for the spark plug hole is preferable to the type that requires hand pressure to maintain the seal

15.2 This is the special spark plug removal tool contained in the bike's tool kit; if the tool kit is missing, or this tool isn't there, you can obtain one from the dealer or use an extension and a 16mm deep socket (preferably one designed for removing spark plugs, i.e. with a rubber insert inside to grip the plug)

5   Install the compression gauge in one of the spark plug holes **(see illustration)**. Hold or block the throttle wide open.
6   Crank the engine over a minimum of four or five revolutions (or until the gauge reading stops increasing) and observe the initial movement of the compression gauge needle as well as the final total gauge reading. Repeat the procedure for the other cylinders and compare the results to the value listed in this Chapter's Specifications.
7   If the compression in all cylinders built up quickly and evenly to the specified amount, you can assume the engine upper end is in reasonably good mechanical condition. Worn or sticking piston rings and worn cylinders will produce very little initial movement of the gauge needle, but compression will tend to build up gradually as the engine spins over. Valve and valve seat leakage, or head gasket leakage, is indicated by low initial compression which does not tend to build up.
8   To further confirm your findings, add a small amount of engine oil to each cylinder by inserting the nozzle of a squirt-type oil can through the spark plug holes. The oil will tend to seal the piston rings if they are leaking. Repeat the test for all cylinders.
9   If the compression increases significantly after the addition of the oil, the piston rings and/or cylinders are definitely worn. If the compression does not increase, the pressure is leaking past the valves or the head gasket. Leakage past the valves may be due to insufficient valve clearances, burned, warped or cracked valves or valve seats or valves that are hanging up in the guides.
10   If compression readings are considerably higher than specified,

the combustion chambers are probably coated with excessive carbon deposits. It is possible (but not very likely) for carbon deposits to raise the compression enough to compensate for the effects of leakage past rings or valves. Refer to Chapter 2, remove the cylinder head and carefully decarbonize the combustion chambers.

15 Spark plugs - replacement

Refer to illustrations 15.2, 15.6a, 15.6b and 15.7
1   Make sure your spark plug socket is the correct size before attempting to remove the plugs. This motorcycle is equipped with very small spark plugs. The diameter of the threaded portion of the plugs is 12 mm; the hex for tightening a plug is 16 mm. The factory-equipped tool kit includes a 16mm hex wrench. If you don't have this tool, use a 16mm deep socket. We recommend a quarter-inch-drive socket; most 3/8-inch-drive sockets won't fit down into the spark plug holes.
2   Remove the fuel tank (see Chapter 4), then disconnect the spark plug caps from the spark plugs. If available, use compressed air to blow out any accumulated debris from the spark plug holes. You'll need the special tool in the bike's tool kit **(see illustration)** to remove the plugs, or use an extension and a 16mm deep socket (preferably one with a rubber insert to prevent damage to the plug and to grip the plug when lifting it out of its hole).
3   Inspect the electrodes for wear. Both the center and side electrodes should have square edges and the side electrode should be of uniform thickness. Look for excessive deposits and evidence of a cracked or chipped insulator around the center electrode. Compare your spark plugs to the color spark plug reading chart. Check the threads, the washer and the porcelain insulator body for cracks and other damage.
4   If the electrodes are not excessively worn, and if the deposits can be easily removed with a wire brush, the plugs can be regapped and reused (if no cracks or chips are visible in the insulator). If in doubt concerning the condition of the plugs, replace them with new ones, as the expense is minimal.
5   Cleaning spark plugs by sandblasting is permitted, provided you clean the plugs with a high flash-point solvent afterwards.
6   Before installing new plugs, make sure they are the correct type and heat range. Check the gap between the electrodes, as they are not preset. For best results, use a wire-type gauge rather than a flat gauge to check the gap **(see illustration)**. If the gap must be adjusted, bend the side electrode only and be very careful not to chip or crack the insulator nose **(see illustration)**. Make sure the washer is in place before installing each plug.
7   Since the cylinder heads are made of aluminum, which is soft and easily damaged, thread the plugs into the heads by hand. Since the plugs are quite recessed, slip a short length of hose over the end of the plug to use as a tool to thread it into place **(see illustration)**. The hose

15.6a Spark plug manufacturers recommend using a wire-type gauge for checking the spark plug gap; you should feel a slight drag as the wire slides between the electrode - if you don't feel this drag, adjust the gap

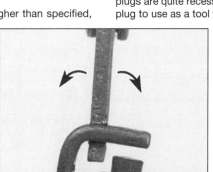

15.6b To change the gap, bend the side electrode only, as indicated by the arrows, and be very careful not to crack or chip the ceramic insulator surrounding the center electrode

15.7 A length of rubber hose will save time and prevent damaged threads when installing the spark plugs

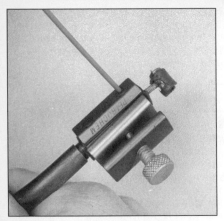

16.3a A pressure lube adapter makes lubing a cable easier and neater (available at most bike shops)

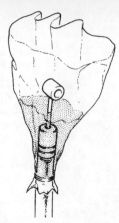

16.3b If you don't have a pressure lube adapter, make a funnel at one end of the cable with a small piece of plastic, tape it to the cable and carefully pour a small amount of oil into the funnel

17.6a To position the number 1 piston at Top Dead Center (TDC) on the compression stroke, turn the crankshaft until the TDC mark on the rotor ("T,1 4") is aligned with the timing mark on the crankcase (don't try to turn the engine with the timing rotor Allen bolt or the bolt may snap off).

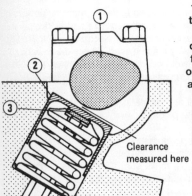

17.6b Note the position of the no. 1 cylinder camshaft lobes; they should not be depressing the valve lifters for either the intake valves or the exhaust valves (if they are, turn the crankshaft one complete revolution and realign the timing rotor mark; piston number 1 is now at TDC compression)

Clearance measured here

1   Cam lobe
2   Valve lifter
3   Valve adjusting shim

will grip the plug well enough to turn it, but will start to slip if the plug begins to cross-thread in the hole - this will prevent damaged threads and the accompanying repair costs.

8   Once the plugs are finger tight, the job can be finished with a socket. If a torque wrench is available, tighten the spark plugs to the torque listed in this Chapter's Specifications. If you do not have a torque wrench, tighten the plugs finger tight (until the washers bottom on the cylinder head) then use a wrench to tighten them an additional 1/4 turn. Regardless of the method used, do not over-tighten them.

9   Reconnect the spark plug caps.

16 Lubrication - general

Refer to illustrations 16.3a and 16.3b

1   Since the controls, cables and various other components of a motorcycle are exposed to the elements, they should be lubricated periodically to ensure safe and trouble-free operation.

2   The footpegs, clutch and brake lever, brake pedal, shift lever and side and centerstand pivots should be lubricated frequently. In order for the lubricant to be applied where it will do the most good, the component should be disassembled. However, if chain and cable lubricant is being used, it can be applied to the pivot joint gaps and will usually work its way into the areas where friction occurs. If motor oil or light grease is being used, apply it sparingly as it may attract dirt (which could cause the controls to bind or wear at an accelerated rate).
Note: *One of the best lubricants for the control lever pivots is a dry-film*

lubricant (available from many sources by different names).

3   The throttle, choke and clutch cables should be separated from the handlebar lever and bracket before they're lubricated. They should be treated with motor oil or a commercially available cable lubricant which is specially formulated for use on motorcycle control cables. Small adapters for pressure lubricating the cables with spray can lubricants are available and ensure that the cable is lubricated along its entire length **(see illustration)**. If motor oil is being used, tape a funnel-shaped piece of heavy paper or plastic to the end of the cable, then pour oil into the funnel and suspend the end of the cable upright **(see illustration)**. Leave it until the oil runs down into the cable and out the other end. When attaching the cable to the lever, be sure to lubricate the barrel-shaped fitting at the end with multi-purpose grease.

4   Speedometer and tachometer cables should be removed from their housings and lubricated with motor oil or cable lubricant in a similar fashion.

5   The procedures for lubricating the swingarm bearings and rear shock absorber linkage are in Chapter 6.

17 Valve clearances - check and adjustment

Refer to illustrations 17.6a, 17.6b, 17.7, 17.8, 17.12, 17.16a and 17.16b

1   The engine must be completely cool for this maintenance procedure, so let the machine sit overnight before beginning.

2   Disconnect the cable from the negative terminal of the battery.

3   Refer to Chapter 4 and remove the fuel tank.

4   Remove the valve cover (see Chapter 2).

5   Remove the pick-up coil cover (see Chapter 5).

6   Position the number 1 piston (on the left side of the engine) at Top Dead Center (TDC) on the compression stroke. Do this by turning the crankshaft, with a wrench placed on the timing rotor hex, until the TDC mark on the rotor ("T,1 4") is aligned with the timing mark on the crankcase **(see illustration)**. **Caution:** *Don't try to turn the engine with the timing rotor Allen bolt or the bolt may snap off.* Now, check the position of the no. 1 cylinder camshaft lobes; they should not be depressing the valve lifters for either the intake valves or the exhaust valves **(see illustration)**. If they are, turn the crankshaft one complete revolution and realign the timing rotor mark. Piston number 1 is now at TDC compression.

7   With the engine in this position, all of the valves for cylinder no. 1 can be checked, as well as the exhaust valves for cylinder no. 2 and the intake valves for cylinder no. 3 **(see illustration)**.

Spark plug maintenance: Checking plug gap with feeler gauges

Altering the plug gap. Note use of correct tool

Spark plug conditions: A brown, tan or grey firing end is indicative of correct engine running conditions and the selection of the appropriate heat rating plug

White deposits have accumulated from excessive amounts of oil in the combustion chamber or through the use of low quality oil. Remove deposits or a hot spot may form

Black sooty deposits indicate an over-rich fuel/air mixture, or a malfunctioning ignition system. If no improvement is obtained, try one grade hotter plug

Wet, oily carbon deposits form an electrical leakage path along the insulator nose, resulting in a misfire. The cause may be a badly worn engine or a malfunctioning ignition system

A blistered white insulator or melted electrode indicates over-advanced ignition timing or a malfunctioning cooling system. If correction does not prove effective, try a colder grade plug

A worn spark plug not only wastes fuel but also overloads the whole ignition system because the increased gap requires higher voltage to initiate the spark. This condition can also affect air pollution

Measuring Valves ■

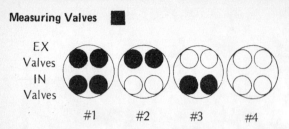

17.7 With cylinder no. 1 at TDC compression, the shaded valves can be adjusted

Measuring Valves ■

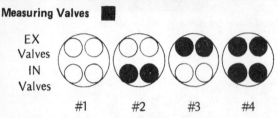

17.12 With cylinder no. 4 at TDC compression, the shaded valves can be adjusted

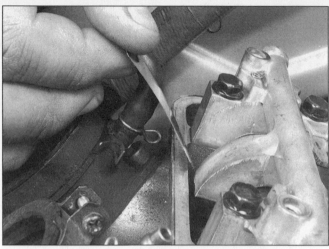

17.8 Insert a feeler gauge of the thickness listed in this Chapter's Specifications between the valve lifter and cam lobe, then slowly pull out the feeler gauge. You should feel a slight drag. If there's no drag, the clearance is too loose; if there's a heavy drag, the clearance is too tight.

8   Start with the no. 1 intake valve clearance. Insert a feeler gauge of the thickness listed in this Chapter's Specifications between the valve lifter and cam lobe **(see illustration)**. Pull the feeler gauge out slowly - you should feel a slight drag. If there's no drag, the clearance is too loose. If there's a heavy drag, the clearance is too tight.
9   If the clearance is incorrect, write down the actual measured clearance. You'll need this information later to select a new valve adjusting shim.
10   Now measure the no. 1 exhaust valves, following the same procedure you used for the intake valves. Make sure to use a feeler gauge of the specified thickness and write down the actual clearances of any valves that aren't within the Specifications.

VALVE CLEARANCE ADJUSTMENT CHART – INLET VALVE

PRESENT SHIM — Example

PART No. (92180 -)	1014	1016	1018	1020	1022	1024	1026	1028	1030	1032	1034	1036	1038	1040	1042	1044	1046	1048	1050	1052	1054
MARK	50	55	60	65	70	75	80	85	90	95	00	05	10	15	20	25	30	35	40	45	50
THICKNESS (mm)	2.50	2.55	2.60	2.65	2.70	2.75	2.80	2.85	2.90	2.95	3.00	3.05	3.10	3.15	3.20	3.25	3.30	3.35	3.40	3.45	3.50

VALVE CLEARANCE MEASUREMENT:

Measurement																					
0.00 ~ 0.03					2.50	2.55	2.60	2.65	2.70	2.75	2.80	2.85	2.90	2.95	3.00	3.05	3.10	3.15	3.20	3.25	3.30
0.04 ~ 0.08				2.50	2.55	2.60	2.65	2.70	2.75	2.80	2.85	2.90	2.95	3.00	3.05	3.10	3.15	3.20	3.25	3.30	3.35
0.09 ~ 0.13			2.50	2.55	2.60	2.65	2.70	2.75	2.80	2.85	2.90	2.95	3.00	3.05	3.10	3.15	3.20	3.25	3.30	3.35	3.40
0.14 ~ 0.17		2.50	2.55	2.60	2.65	2.70	2.75	2.80	2.85	2.90	2.95	3.00	3.05	3.10	3.15	3.20	3.25	3.30	3.35	3.40	3.45
0.18 ~ 0.23	SPECIFIED CLEARANCE/NO CHANGE REQUIRED																				
0.24 ~ 0.28	2.55	2.60	2.65	2.70	2.75	2.80	2.85	2.90	2.95	3.00	3.05	3.10	3.15	3.20	3.25	3.30	3.35	3.40	3.45	3.50	
0.29 ~ 0.33	2.60	2.65	2.70	2.75	2.80	2.85	2.90	2.95	3.00	3.05	3.10	3.15	3.20	3.25	3.30	3.35	3.40	3.45	3.50		
0.34 ~ 0.38	2.65	2.70	2.75	2.80	2.85	2.90	2.95	3.00	3.05	3.10	3.15	3.20	3.25	3.30	3.35	3.40	3.45	3.50			
0.39 ~ 0.43	2.70	2.75	2.80	2.85	2.90	2.95	3.00	3.05	3.10	3.15	3.20	3.25	3.30	3.35	3.40	3.45	3.50				
0.44 ~ 0.48	2.75	2.80	2.85	2.90	2.95	3.00	3.05	3.10	3.15	3.20	3.25	3.30	3.35	3.40	3.45	3.50					
0.49 ~ 0.53	2.80	2.85	2.90	2.95	3.00	3.05	3.10	3.15	3.20	3.25	3.30	3.35	3.40	3.45	3.50						
0.54 ~ 0.58	2.85	2.90	2.95	3.00	3.05	3.10	3.15	3.20	3.25	3.30	3.35	3.40	3.45	3.50							
0.59 ~ 0.63	2.90	2.95	3.00	3.05	3.10	3.15	3.20	3.25	3.30	3.35	3.40	3.45	3.50								
0.64 ~ 0.68	2.95	3.00	3.05	3.10	3.15	3.20	3.25	3.30	3.35	3.40	3.45	3.50									
0.69 ~ 0.73	3.00	3.05	3.10	3.15	3.20	3.25	3.30	3.35	3.40	3.45	3.50										
0.74 ~ 0.78	3.05	3.10	3.15	3.20	3.25	3.30	3.35	3.40	3.45	3.50											
0.79 ~ 0.83	3.10	3.15	3.20	3.25	3.30	3.35	3.40	3.45	3.50												
0.84 ~ 0.88	3.15	3.20	3.25	3.30	3.35	3.40	3.45	3.50													
0.89 ~ 0.93	3.20	3.25	3.30	3.35	3.40	3.45	3.50														
0.94 ~ 0.98	3.25	3.30	3.35	3.40	3.45	3.50															
0.99 ~ 1.03	3.30	3.35	3.40	3.45	3.50																
1.04 ~ 1.08	3.35	3.40	3.45	3.50																	
1.09 ~ 1.13	3.40	3.45	3.50																		
1.14 ~ 1.18	3.45	3.50																			
1.19 ~ 1.23	3.50																				

(Example arrow points to the 0.39 ~ 0.43 measurement row.)

INSTALL THE SHIM OF THIS THICKNESS (mm)

17.16a Intake valve shim selection chart

11   Proceed to measure the clearances of the no. 2 exhaust valves and the no. 3 intake valves. Again, write down the measured clearances of any valves that aren't within the Specifications.

12   Rotate the crankshaft one complete revolution and align the TDC mark on the rotor (T 1,4) with the timing mark on the crankcase, which will position piston no. 4 at TDC compression. Measure all four valves on cylinder no. 4, followed by the no. 3 exhaust valves and the no. 2 intake valves **(see illustration)**. Again, write down the measured clearances of any valves that aren't within the Specifications.

13   If any of the clearances need to be adjusted, go to Step 14. If all of the clearances are within the Specifications, go to Step 20.

14   Remove the camshafts (see Chapter 2). Remove the valve lifters and adjusting shims from any valves that needed adjustment. Be sure to keep the lifters and shims in order so they can be returned to the locations from which they were removed.

15   Determine the thickness of the shim(s) you removed. It should be marked on the bottom of the shim, but the ideal way is to measure it with a micrometer.

16   If the clearance was too large, you need a thicker shim. If the clearance was too small, you need a thinner shim. Calculate the thickness of the replacement shim by referring to the accompanying charts **(see illustrations)**.

17   To use the charts, find the actual measured clearance of the valve in the left-hand column, and the thickness of the existing shim in the top row. Follow across and down to where the row and column meet; the shim listed at that point is the one you need. For example:

a) If the actual measured clearance was 0.28 mm, find the 0.25 to 0.29 mm entry on the left-hand side of the chart.

b) If the existing shim thickness is 2.60 mm, find the 2.60 entry in the top row of the chart.

c) Follow the lines across and down from these two entries until they meet. The number listed in that space (2.65 mm) is the needed shim thickness. **Note:** In addition to the shims listed in the charts, shims are available in the following thicknesses: 2.43 mm, 2.48 mm, 2.53 mm and 2.58 mm.

18   Perform Steps 15 through 17 to select a new shim for each of the valves that needed adjustment.

19   Install the shims, lifters and camshafts and recheck the clearances (see Chapter 2 and Steps 6 through 12 above).

20   With all of the clearances within the Specifications, install the valve cover and all of the components that had to be removed to get it off.

21   Install the fuel tank and reconnect the cable to the negative terminal of the battery.

18   Idle speed - check and adjustment

Refer to illustration 18.3a and 18.3b

1   The idle speed should be checked and adjusted when it is obviously too high or too low, but only after the carburetors are synchronized. Before adjusting the idle speed, make sure the valve clearances and spark plug gaps are correct. Also, turn the handlebars back-and-forth and see if moving the bars changes the idle speed. If it does, the throttle cable may not be adjusted correctly, or it may be worn out. Be sure to correct this problem before proceeding.

VALVE CLEARANCE ADJUSTMENT CHART – EXHAUST VALVE

PART No. (92180 -)	1014	1016	1018	1020	1022	1024	1026	1028	1030	1032	1034	1036	1038	1040	1042	1044	1046	1048	1050	1052	1054
MARK	50	55	60	65	70	75	80	85	90	95	00	05	10	15	20	25	30	35	40	45	50
THICKNESS (mm)	2.50	2.55	2.60	2.65	2.70	2.75	2.80	2.85	2.90	2.95	3.00	3.05	3.10	3.15	3.20	3.25	3.30	3.35	3.40	3.45	3.50
VALVE CLEARANCE MEASUREMENT																					
0.00 ~ 0.05						2.50	2.55	2.60	2.65	2.70	2.75	2.80	2.85	2.90	2.95	3.00	3.05	3.10	3.15	3.20	3.25
0.06 ~ 0.10					2.50	2.55	2.60	2.65	2.70	2.75	2.80	2.85	2.90	2.95	3.00	3.05	3.10	3.15	3.20	3.25	3.30
0.11 ~ 0.15				2.50	2.55	2.60	2.65	2.70	2.75	2.80	2.85	2.90	2.95	3.00	3.05	3.10	3.15	3.20	3.25	3.30	3.35
0.16 ~ 0.20			2.50	2.55	2.60	2.65	2.70	2.75	2.80	2.85	2.90	2.95	3.00	3.05	3.10	3.15	3.20	3.25	3.30	3.35	3.40
0.21 ~ 0.24		2.50	2.55	2.60	2.65	2.70	2.75	2.80	2.85	2.90	2.95	3.00	3.05	3.10	3.15	3.20	3.25	3.30	3.35	3.40	3.45
0.25 ~ 0.30	SPECIFIED CLEARANCE/NO CHANGE REQUIRED																				
0.31 ~ 0.35	2.55	2.60	2.65	2.70	2.75	2.80	2.85	2.90	2.95	3.00	3.05	3.10	3.15	3.20	3.25	3.30	3.35	3.40	3.45	3.50	
0.36 ~ 0.40	2.60	2.65	2.70	2.75	2.80	2.85	2.90	2.95	3.00	3.05	3.10	3.15	3.20	3.25	3.30	3.35	3.40	3.45	3.50		
0.41 ~ 0.45	2.65	2.70	2.75	2.80	2.85	2.90	2.95	3.00	3.05	3.10	3.15	3.20	3.25	3.30	3.35	3.40	3.45	3.50			
0.46 ~ 0.50	2.70	2.75	2.80	2.85	2.90	2.95	3.00	3.05	3.10	3.15	3.20	3.25	3.30	3.35	3.40	3.45	3.50				
0.51 ~ 0.55	2.75	2.80	2.85	2.90	2.95	3.00	3.05	3.10	3.15	3.20	3.25	3.30	3.35	3.40	3.45	3.50					
0.56 ~ 0.60	2.80	2.85	2.90	2.95	3.00	3.05	3.10	3.15	3.20	3.25	3.30	3.35	3.40	3.45	3.50						
0.61 ~ 0.65	2.85	2.90	2.95	3.00	3.05	3.10	3.15	3.20	3.25	3.30	3.35	3.40	3.45	3.50							
0.66 ~ 0.70	2.90	2.95	3.00	3.05	3.10	3.15	3.20	3.25	3.30	3.35	3.40	3.45	3.50								
0.71 ~ 0.75	2.95	3.00	3.05	3.10	3.15	3.20	3.25	3.30	3.35	3.40	3.45	3.50									
0.76 ~ 0.80	3.00	3.05	3.10	3.15	3.20	3.25	3.30	3.35	3.40	3.45	3.50										
0.81 ~ 0.85	3.05	3.10	3.15	3.20	3.25	3.30	3.35	3.40	3.45	3.50											
0.86 ~ 0.90	3.10	3.15	3.20	3.25	3.30	3.35	3.40	3.45	3.50												
0.91 ~ 0.95	3.15	3.20	3.25	3.30	3.35	3.40	3.45	3.50													
0.96 ~ 1.00	3.20	3.25	3.30	3.35	3.40	3.45	3.50														
1.01 ~ 1.05	3.25	3.30	3.35	3.40	3.45	3.50															
1.06 ~ 1.10	3.30	3.35	3.40	3.45	3.50																
1.11 ~ 1.15	3.35	3.40	3.45	3.50																	
1.16 ~ 1.20	3.40	3.45	3.50																		
1.21 ~ 1.25	3.45	3.50																			
1.26 ~ 1.30	3.50																				

INSTALL THE SHIM OF THIS THICKNESS (mm)

17.16b Exhaust valve shim selection chart

18.3a On D models, the idle speed adjustment screw (arrow) is located underneath the carburetors; using the bike's tachometer, turn the knob until the idle speed is correct

18.3b On E models, the idle speed adjustment screw (arrow) is located on the left side of the engine, right above and ahead of the countershaft sprocket cover; using the bike's tachometer, turn the knob until the idle speed is correct

2   The engine should be at normal operating temperature, which is usually reached after 10 to 15 minutes of stop-and-go riding. Place the motorcycle on the centerstand and make sure the transmission is in Neutral.

3   Locate the idle adjusting screw on the left side of the bike, just above the engine and just behind and below the left carburetor **(see illustrations)**. Turn the screw until the idle speed listed in this Chapter's Specifications is obtained.

4   Snap the throttle open and shut a few times, then recheck the idle speed. If necessary, repeat the adjustment procedure.

5   If a smooth, steady idle can't be achieved, the fuel/air mixture may be incorrect. Refer to Chapter 4 for additional carburetor information.

19   Carburetor synchronization - check and adjustment

Refer to illustrations 19.9a, 19.9b and 19.13

Warning: *Gasoline (petrol) is extremely flammable, so take extra precautions when you work on any part of the fuel system. Don't smoke or allow open flames or bare light bulbs near the work area, and don't work in a garage where a natural gas-type appliance (such as a water heater or clothes dryer) with a pilot light is present. Since gasoline is carcinogenic, wear latex gloves when there's a possibility of being exposed to fuel, and, if you spill any fuel on your skin, rinse it off immediately with soap and water. Mop up any spills immediately and do not store fuel-soaked rags where they could ignite. When you perform any kind of work on the fuel system, wear safety glasses and have a fire extinguisher suitable for a class B type fire (flammable liquids) on hand.*

1   Out-of-sync carburetors will reduce fuel mileage, increase engine temperature, respond unevenly to throttle inputs and increase engine vibration levels. Carburetor synchronization is the process of adjusting the carburetors so they deliver the same amount of air/fuel mixture to each cylinder. The carbs are synched by measuring the vacuum produced in each cylinder, then adjusting all four carbs to the same vacuum reading. Four identical carburetors producing the same intake vacuum will theoretically deliver the same amount of fuel at a given throttle setting.

2   To properly synchronize the carburetors, you will need some sort of vacuum gauge setup, preferably with a gauge for each cylinder, or a mercury manometer, which is a calibrated tube arrangement that utilizes columns of mercury to indicate engine vacuum.

3   A manometer can be purchased from a motorcycle dealer or accessory shop and should have the necessary rubber hoses supplied with it for hooking into the vacuum hose fittings on the carburetors.

4   A vacuum gauge setup can also be purchased from a dealer or fabricated from commonly available hardware and automotive vacuum gauges.

5   The manometer is the more reliable and accurate instrument, and

19.9a Clearly label, then disconnect the vacuum hoses from these vacuum pipes (arrows) (carburetors removed for clarity) . . .

for that reason is preferred over the vacuum gauge setup; however, since the mercury used in the manometer is a liquid, and extremely toxic, extra precautions must be taken during use and storage of the instrument.

6   Because of the need for a carb synchronization setup like one of the two described above, most owners leave this task to a dealer service department or a reputable motorcycle repair shop. But if you want to tackle this job, here's how it's done:

7   Start the engine and let it run until it reaches normal operating temperature, then check and, if necessary, adjust the idle speed (see Section 18). Shut off the engine.

8   Remove the fuel tank (see Chapter 4) and place it on a nearby bench or tool cart right next to the bike. The tank must be higher than the carburetor float bowls. Or, have an assistant hold the fuel tank out of the way, but in such a position that fuel can still be delivered and access to the carburetors is unobstructed. Place the fuel tap lever in the Prime position.

9   Clearly label, then detach the vacuum hoses from the vacuum pipes on the top of the intake boots **(see illustration)**, then hook up the vacuum gauge set or the manometer according to the manufacturer's instructions. Make sure there are no leaks in the setup, as false readings will result **(see illustration)**.

10   Reconnect the fuel line to the fuel tank (it's not necessary to hook-up the vacuum line to the fuel tap).

11   Start the engine and make sure the idle speed is correct.

19.9b . . . then attach your carburetor synchronization gauges as shown

19.13 First, turn the synchronizing screw between the carburetors for no. 1 and no. 2 cylinders (A); then, turn the screws for nos. 3 and 4 carburetors (B); then synchronize the two pairs of carburetors with the center screw (C) (carburetors pulled out of intake boots and emissions hoses removed for clarity)

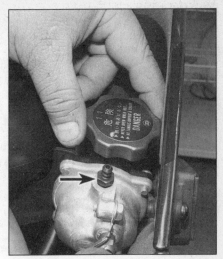

20.6 Push down on the radiator cap, slowly turn it counterclockwise to the first stop and allow all pressure to escape before removing it (the arrow points to the thermostat housing bleeder bolt)

11   Start the engine and make sure the idle speed is correct.

12   The vacuum readings for all of the cylinders should be the same, or at least within the tolerance listed in this Chapter's Specifications. If the vacuum readings vary, adjust as necessary.

13   To perform the adjustment, synchronize the carburetors for cylinders 1 and 2 by turning the butterfly valve adjusting screw between those two carburetors, as needed, until the vacuum is identical or nearly identical for those two cylinders (see illustration).

14   Next, synchronize the carburetors for cylinders 3 and 4, using the butterfly valve adjusting screw situated between those two carburetors (see illustration 19.13).

15   Finally, synchronize the carburetors for cylinders 1 and 2 to the carburetors for cylinders 3 and 4 by turning the center adjusting screw (see illustration 19.13).

16   When the adjustment is complete, recheck the vacuum readings and idle speed, then stop the engine. Remove the vacuum gauge or manometer and attach the hoses to the fittings on the carburetors. Reinstall the fuel tank and seat.

20   Cooling system - check

Refer to illustrations 20.6 and 20.7

Warning: The engine must be cool before beginning this procedure.

Note: Refer to Section 3 and check the coolant level before performing this check.

1   The entire cooling system should be checked carefully at the recommended intervals. Look for evidence of leaks, check the condition of the coolant, check the radiator for clogged fins and damage and make sure the fan operates when required.

2   Examine each of the rubber coolant hoses along its entire length. Look for cracks, abrasions and other damage. Squeeze each hose at various points. They should feel firm, yet pliable, and return to their original shape when released. If they are dried out or hard, replace them with new ones.

3   Check for evidence of leaks at each cooling system joint. Tighten the hose clamps carefully to prevent future leaks.

4   Check the radiator for evidence of leaks and other damage. Remove the fairings if necessary (see Chapter 8). Leaks in the radiator leave tell-tale scale deposits or coolant stains on the outside of the core below the leak. If leaks are noted, remove the radiator (refer to Chapter 3) and have it repaired at a radiator shop or replace it with a new one. **Caution:** Do not use a liquid leak stopping compound to try to repair leaks.

5   Check the radiator fins for mud, dirt and insects, which may impede the flow of air through the radiator. If the fins are dirty, force water or low pressure compressed air through the fins from the backside. If the fins are bent or distorted, straighten them carefully with a screwdriver.

6   Remove the trim panel between the tank and the right fairing (see Chapter 8), then remove the radiator cap by turning it counterclockwise until it reaches a stop. If you hear a hissing sound (indicating there is still pressure in the system), wait until it stops. Now, press down on the cap and continue turning the cap counterclockwise until it can be removed (see illustration). Check the condition of the coolant in the radiator. If it is rust colored or if accumulations of scale are visible in the radiator, drain, flush and refill the system with new coolant. Check the cap gaskets for cracks and other damage. Have the cap tested by a dealer service department or replace it with a new one. Install the cap by turning it clockwise until it reaches the first stop, then push down on the cap and continue turning until it can turn no further.

7   Check the antifreeze content of the coolant with an antifreeze hydrometer (see illustration). Sometimes coolant may look like it's in good condition, but might be too weak to offer adequate protection. If the hydrometer indicates a weak mixture, drain, flush and refill the cooling system (see Section 21).

8   Start the engine and let it reach normal operating temperature,

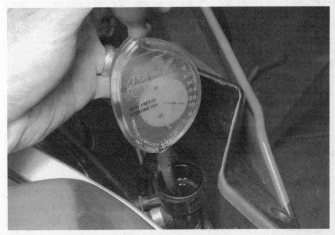

20.7 An antifreeze hydrometer is helpful for determining the condition of the coolant

21.3 Remove the bolt from the water pump outlet pipe and allow the coolant to drain (hose disconnected from inlet pipe for clarity)

8   Start the engine and let it reach normal operating temperature, then check for leaks again. As the coolant temperature increases, the fan should come on automatically and the temperature should begin to drop. If it does not, refer to Chapter 3 and check the fan and fan circuit carefully.

9   If the coolant level is consistently low, and no evidence of leaks can be found, have the entire system pressure checked by a Kawasaki dealer service department, motorcycle repair shop or service station.

21 Cooling system - draining, flushing and refilling

Warning: *Allow the engine to cool completely before performing this maintenance operation. Also, don't allow antifreeze to come into contact with your skin or painted surfaces of the vehicle. Rinse off spills immediately with plenty of water. Antifreeze is highly toxic if ingested. Never leave antifreeze lying around in an open container or in puddles on the floor; children and pets are attracted by its sweet smell and may drink it. Check with local authorities about disposing of used antifreeze. Many communities have collection centers which will see that antifreeze is disposed of safely. Antifreeze is also combustible, so don't store or use it near open flames.*

Draining

Refer to illustration 21.3

1   Remove the plastic trim panel between the right side of the fairing and the fuel tank (see Chapter 8). Loosen the radiator cap **(see illustration 20.6)**. Place a large, clean drain pan under the left side of the engine.

2   Remove the lower fairing (see Chapter 8).

3   Remove the drain bolt from the water pump outlet pipe (the one closer to the engine) and allow the coolant to drain into the pan **(see illustration)**. **Note:** *The coolant will rush out with considerable force, so position the drain pan accordingly. Remove the radiator cap completely to ensure that all of the coolant can drain.*

4   Remove the reservoir (see Chapter 3) and drain it. Wash out the reservoir with water.

Flushing

5   Flush the system with clean tap water by inserting a garden hose in the radiator filler neck. Allow the water to run through the system until it is clear when it exits the drain bolt hole. If the radiator is extremely corroded, remove it by referring to Chapter 3 and have it cleaned at a radiator shop.

6   Check the drain bolt gasket. Replace it with a new one if necessary.

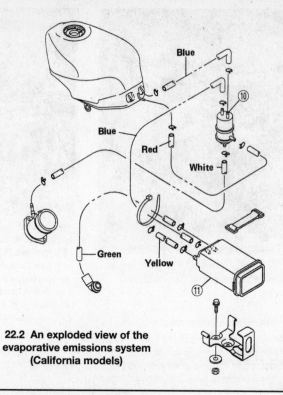

22.2 An exploded view of the evaporative emissions system (California models)

7   Clean the hole, then install the drain bolt and tighten it to the torque listed in this Chapter's Specifications.

8   Fill the cooling system with clean water mixed with a flushing compound. Make sure the flushing compound is compatible with aluminum components, and follow the manufacturer's instructions carefully.

9   Start the engine and allow it to reach normal operating temperature. Let it run for about ten minutes.

10   Stop the engine. Let the machine cool for awhile, then cover the radiator cap with a heavy rag and turn it counterclockwise to the first stop, releasing any pressure that may be present in the system. Once the hissing stops, push down on the cap and remove it completely.

11   Drain the system once again.

12   Fill the system with clean water, then repeat Steps 9, 10 and 11.

Refilling

13   Fill the system with the proper coolant mixture (see this Chapter's Specifications). When the system is full (all the way up to the top of the radiator cap filler neck), loosen the bleeder bolts on the water pump **(see illustration 9.5 in Chapter 3)** and the thermostat housing **(see illustration 20.6)**. When coolant free of air bubbles flows from the bleeders, tighten them securely. Start the engine (radiator cap removed) and allow it to run until no air bubbles remain in the coolant.

14   Add coolant until it reaches the top of the filler neck. Reinstall the cap.

15   Check the coolant level in the reservoir (see Section 3). If the coolant level is low, add the specified mixture until it reaches the FULL mark in the reservoir.

16   Check the system for leaks.

17   Do not dispose of the old coolant by pouring it down a drain. Instead, pour it into a heavy plastic container, cap it tightly and take it to an authorized disposal site or a service station.

22 Evaporative emission control system (California models only) - check

1   This system, installed on California models to conform to Califor-

22.3 The liquid/vapor separator (arrow) is located on the right side of the bike, just below and in front of the IC igniter

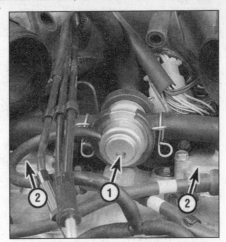

23.1 Details of the air suction valves and hoses

1   *Vacuum switching valve*
2   *Air suction valve*

23.4 To disconnect the hoses from the air switching valve covers, simply pull them straight up

California emission control standards, routes fuel vapors from the fuel system into the engine to be burned, instead of letting them evaporate into the atmosphere. When the engine isn't running, vapors are stored in a carbon canister.

Hoses

Refer to illustration 22.2
2   To begin the inspection of the system, remove the seat and side covers (see Chapter 8 if necessary). Inspect the hoses connecting the fuel tank, carburetors and liquid/vapor separator to the canister for cracking, kinks or other signs of deterioration **(see illustration)**.

Liquid/vapor separator

Refer to illustration 22.3
Warning: *Gasoline (petrol) is extremely flammable, so take extra precautions when you work on any part of the fuel system. Don't smoke or allow open flames or bare light bulbs near the work area, and don't work in a garage where a natural gas-type appliance (such as a water heater or clothes dryer) with a pilot light is present. Since gasoline is carcinogenic, wear latex gloves when there's a possibility of being exposed to fuel, and, if you spill any fuel on your skin, rinse it off immediately with soap and water. Mop up any spills immediately and do not store fuel-soaked rags where they could ignite. When you perform any kind of work on the fuel system, wear safety glasses and have a fire extinguisher suitable for a class B type fire (flammable liquids) on hand.*
3   To check the liquid/vapor separator, label and disconnect the hoses from it **(see illustration)**, then remove it from the machine. Check it closely for cracks or other signs of damage. Reinstall the separator and connect the hoses, except for the breather hose. Using a syringe, inject approximately 20 mL of gasoline into the separator.
4   Disconnect the fuel return hose from the fuel tank and direct the end of the hose into an approved gasoline container. Hold the container level with the top of the fuel tank.
5   Start the engine and allow it to idle. If the fuel that was squirted into the separator comes out of the hose, it's working properly. If fuel doesn't come out of the hose, replace the separator.

Canister

6   Remove the canister from under the passenger's seat and inspect it for cracks or other signs of damage. Tip the canister so the nozzles point down. If fuel runs out of the canister, the liquid/vapor separator is probably bad - check it as described above. The fuel inside the canister has probably caused damage, so it would be a good idea to replace it also.

23.5a To remove a reed plate, remove the two retaining bolts and the cover, then carefully pry the plate out of the valve cover with a small screwdriver; make sure you don't gouge or scratch the plate, the reeds or the valve cover

23 Clean Air System - check

Refer to illustrations 23.1, 23.4, 23.5a and 23.5b
1   The Clean Air System **(see illustration)**, installed on US models only, consists of a pair of one-way check valves that allow fresh air to flow into the exhaust ports. The suction developed by the exhaust pulses pulls the air from the air cleaner, through a hose to the vacuum switch valve, through a pair of hoses and two pairs of reed valves, and finally into the exhaust ports. The introduction of fresh air helps ignite any fuel that may not have been burned by the normal combustion process.
2   Remove the fuel tank (see Chapter 4).
3   Remove the ignition coils (see Chapter 5).
4   Disconnect the hoses from the air suction valves **(see illustration)**. Remove the bolts and lift off the suction valve covers.
5   Pry the reed valve plates out of the valve cover **(see illustration)**. Check the valves for cracks, warping, burning or other damage **(see illustration)**. Check the area where the reeds contact the valve holder for scratches, separation and grooves. If any of these conditions are

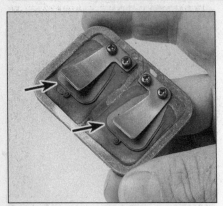

23.5b Check the reeds (arrows) on the air suction valve for damage and carbon build-up

24.2 The exhaust pipe flange nuts (arrow) should be checked frequently and tightened if necessary

25.4 Try to move the forks back-and-forth as shown - they shouldn't move; if you feel any play, adjust the steering head bearings

noted on either valve, replace it.
6   Wash the valves with solvent if carbon has accumulated between the reed and the valve holder.
7   Installation of the valves is the reverse of removal. Be sure to use a new gasket.

24 Exhaust system - check

Refer to illustration 24.2
1   Periodically check all of the exhaust system joints for leaks and loose fasteners. The lower fairing will have to be removed to do this properly (see Chapter 8). If tightening the clamp bolts fails to stop any leaks, replace the gaskets with new ones (a procedure which requires disassembly of the system).
2   The exhaust pipe flange nuts at the cylinder heads **(see illustration)** are especially prone to loosening, which could cause damage to the head. Check them frequently and keep them tight.

25 Steering head bearings - check and adjustment

1   This vehicle is equipped with ball-and-cone type steering head bearings which can become dented, rough or loose during normal use of the machine. In extreme cases, worn or loose steering head bearings can cause steering wobble that is potentially dangerous.

Check

Refer to illustration 25.4
2   To check the bearings, place the motorcycle on the centerstand and block the machine so the front wheel is in the air.
3   Point the wheel straight ahead and slowly move the handlebars from side-to-side. Dents or roughness in the bearing races will be felt and the bars will not move smoothly.
4   Next, grasp the fork legs and try to move the wheel forward and backward **(see illustration)**. Any looseness in the steering head bearings will be felt. If play is felt in the bearings, adjust the steering head as follows:

Adjustment

Refer to illustrations 25.7a, 25.7b and 25.8
5   Remove the fuel tank (see Chapter 4).
6   Remove the lower inner fairing (the small access panel on the underside of the upper fairing, above the front wheel, used for accessing the brake junction pipe and the horn) in order to reach the fork lower pinch bolts (see Chapter 8).
7   Loosen the steering head nut and the fork lower pinch bolts **(see illustrations)**. **Note:** *While it isn't absolutely necessary to remove the upper triple clamp, doing so will make it easier to turn the special spanner wrench since clearance is limited by the instrument cluster and the frame.*

25.7a Loosen the steering head nut . . .

8   Carefully tighten the steering stem locknut until the steering head is tight but does not bind when the forks are turned from side-to-side **(see illustration)**.
9   Retighten the steering head nut and the fork pinch bolts, in that order, to the torque values listed in the Chapter 6 Specifications.
10   Recheck the steering head bearings for play as described above. If necessary, repeat the adjustment procedure. Reinstall all parts previously removed.
11   Refer to Chapter 6 for steering head bearing lubrication and replacement procedures.

26 Fasteners - check

1   Since vibration of the machine tends to loosen fasteners, all nuts, bolts, screws, etc. should be periodically checked for proper tightness.
2   Pay particular attention to the following:

Spark plugs
Engine oil drain plug
Oil filter cover bolt
Gearshift lever
Footpegs and sidestand
Engine mount bolts
Shock absorber mount bolts
Rear suspension linkage bolts
Front axle and clamp bolt
Rear axle nut

3   If a torque wrench is available, use it along with the Torque specifications at the beginning of this, or other, Chapters.

25.7b . . . and loosen the fork lower pinch bolts (fairing removed for clarity)

25.8 Tighten the steering stem locknut with an adjustable spanner wrench such as the special Kawasaki tool shown (no. 57001-1100) or a suitable equivalent tool (upper triple clamp removed for clarity)

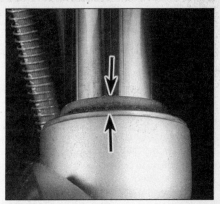

28.3 Inspect each fork seal for oil leaks at the indicated areas (arrows); if oil is leaking past either seal, replace the seal

29.2 Remove this drain screw (arrow) to drain each fork leg (D models)

27 Fuel system - check and filter cleaning

Warning: *Gasoline (petrol) is extremely flammable, so take extra precautions when you work on any part of the fuel system. Don't smoke or allow open flames or bare light bulbs near the work area, and don't work in a garage where a natural gas-type appliance (such as a water heater or clothes dryer) with a pilot light is present. Since gasoline is carcinogenic, wear latex gloves when there's a possibility of being exposed to fuel, and, if you spill any fuel on your skin, rinse it off immediately with soap and water. Mop up any spills immediately and do not store fuel-soaked rags where they could ignite. When you perform any kind of work on the fuel system, wear safety glasses and have a fire extinguisher suitable for a class B type fire (flammable liquids) on hand.*

1   Check the fuel tank, the fuel tap, the lines and the carburetors for leaks and evidence of damage.
2   If carburetor gaskets are leaking, the carburetors should be disassembled and rebuilt by referring to Chapter 4.
3   If the fuel tap is leaking, tightening the screws may help. If leakage persists, the tap should be disassembled and repaired or replaced with a new one.
4   If the fuel lines are cracked or otherwise deteriorated, replace them with new ones.
5   Check the vacuum hose connected to the fuel tap. If it is cracked or otherwise damaged, replace it with a new one.
6   The fuel filter, which is attached to the fuel tap, may become clogged and should be removed and cleaned periodically. In order to clean the filter, the fuel tank must be drained and the fuel tap removed.
7   Remove the fuel tank (see Chapter 4). Drain the fuel into an

approved fuel container.
8   Once the tank is emptied, loosen and remove the screws that attach the fuel tap to the tank. Remove the tap and filter.
9   Clean the filter with solvent and blow it dry with compressed air. If the filter is torn or otherwise damaged, replace the entire fuel tap with a new one. Check the mounting flange O-ring and the gaskets on the screws. If they are damaged, replace them with new ones.
10   Install the O-ring, filter and fuel tap on the tank, then install the tank. Refill the tank and check carefully for leaks around the mounting flange and screws.

28 Suspension - check

Refer to illustration 28.3
1   The suspension components must be maintained in top operating condition to ensure rider safety. Loose, worn or damaged suspension parts decrease the vehicle's stability and control.
2   While standing alongside the motorcycle, lock the front brake and push on the handlebars to compress the forks several times. See if they move up-and-down smoothly without binding. If binding is felt, the forks should be disassembled and inspected as described in Chapter 6.
3   Carefully inspect the area around the fork seals for any signs of fork oil leakage **(see illustration)**. If leakage is evident, the seals must be replaced as described in Chapter 6.
4   Check the tightness of all suspension nuts and bolts to be sure none have worked loose.
5   Inspect the shock for fluid leakage and tightness of the mounting nuts. If leakage is found, the shock should be replaced.
6   Set the bike on its centerstand. Grab the swingarm on each side, just ahead of the axle. Rock the swingarm from side to side - there should be no discernible movement at the rear. If there's a little movement or a slight clicking can be heard, make sure the pivot shaft nuts are tight. If the pivot nuts are tight but movement is still noticeable, the swingarm will have to be removed and the bearings replaced as described in Chapter 6.
7   Inspect the tightness of the rear suspension nuts and bolts.

29 Fork oil - replacement

Draining and adding oil

D models

Refer to illustration 29.2
1   Place the motorcycle on the centerstand.
2   Place a drain pan under one fork leg and remove the drain screw **(see illustration). Warning:** *Do not allow the fork oil to contact the brake discs or pads. If it does, clean the discs with brake system*

1

brake discs or pads. If it does, clean the discs with brake system cleaner and replace the pads with new ones before riding the motorcycle.

3   After most of the oil has drained, slowly compress and release the forks to pump out the remaining oil. An assistant will most likely be required to do this procedure.

4   Check the drain screw gasket for damage. Replace it if necessary. Apply sealant to the threads of the drain screw, install the screw and gasket and tighten it securely.

5   Repeat Steps 2, 3 and 4 for the other fork leg.

6   Remove the lower fairing (see Chapter 8) and place a floor jack underneath the engine. Put a block of wood between the jack head and the engine to protect the engine cases. (The purpose of this step is to take the weight of the bike off the front wheel so that the forks are fully extended when adding new oil.)

7   Remove the handlebar *from one side* (see Chapter 6).

8   Depress the top plug with a large punch or Phillips screwdriver and remove the wire retaining ring **(see illustration 29.24a)**. Inspect the top plug O-ring - if it's damaged, replace it. Pull out the spacer, spring seat (large washer) and fork spring **(see illustrations 29.24b through 29.24e)**.

9   Pour the type and amount of fork oil listed in this Chapter's Specifications into the fork tube through the opening at the top.

10   Install the fork spring with the smaller (tapered) end facing down into the fork tube. Install the spring seat and spacer.

11   Install the top plug (don't forget the O-ring!), depress it with a large punch or Phillips screwdriver, and install the wire retaining ring. Make sure the ring is properly seated in its groove in the tube before releasing the plug.

12   Install the handlebar (see Chapter 6).

13   Repeat this procedure for the other fork leg.

E models

Refer to illustrations 29.16a, 29.16b, 29.16c, 29.16d and 29.16e

14   Remove the fork legs (see Chapter 6).

15   Place one fork leg in a bench vise. Push down on the top plug and remove the wire retaining ring.

16   Depress the top plug with a large punch or Phillips screwdriver and remove the wire retaining ring **(see illustration)**. Remove the top plug and inspect the plug O-ring - if it's damaged, replace it **(see illustration)**. Pull out the spacer, spring seat (large washer) and fork spring **(see illustrations)**.

17   Pour out the old fork oil into a suitable container, then firmly grasp the fork tube and pump the fork slider up and down several times to make sure *all* the old oil is expelled.

18   Pour the type and amount of fork oil listed in this Chapter's Specifications into the fork tube through the opening at the top.

19   Install the fork spring with the smaller (tapered) end facing down into the fork tube. Install the spring seat and spacer.

20   Install the top plug (don't forget the O-ring!), depress it with a

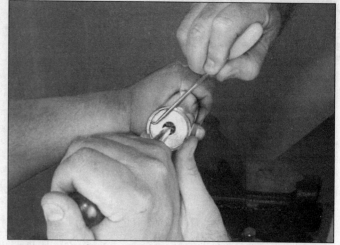

29.16a Push the top plug down into the fork tube with a large punch or screwdriver and remove the wire retaining ring, then remove the plug

large punch or Phillips screwdriver, and install the wire retaining ring. Make sure the ring is properly seated in its groove in the tube before releasing the plug.

21   Repeat this procedure for the other fork leg.

22   Install the fork legs (see Chapter 6).

Calculating the amount of fork oil without draining the forks

Refer to illustrations 29.24a, 29.24b, 29.24c, 29.24d, 29.24e and 29.26

Note: *If one fork seal has been leaking, or if the oil in one fork leg is simply lower or higher than the other leg for some reason, you can use the following method to calculate the correct amount of oil in each leg without draining the old oil.*

23   Remove the handlebar *from one side* (see Chapter 6).

24   Remove the top plug from the exposed fork tube **(see illustration)**. Inspect the top plug O-ring - if it's damaged, discard it and get a new one **(see illustration 29.16b)**. Pull out the spacer, spring seat (large washer) and fork spring **(see illustrations)**.

25   Place a small jack under the front wheel, then slowly pump it up until the front fork sliders (the lower part of the forks) are fully compressed.

26   Insert a tape measure into the fork tube and measure the distance from the top of the tube to the oil **(see illustration)**. Compare your measurement to the distance listed in this Chapter's Specifications, then add or subtract oil as necessary. If you're removing oil, use a small syringe.

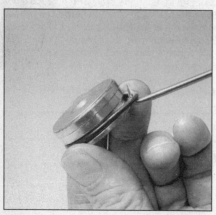

29.16b Inspect the top plug O-ring - if it's damaged, discard it and get a new one

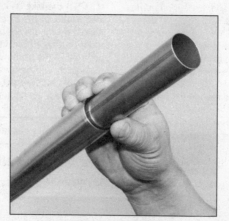

29.16c Pull out the spacer . . .

29.16d . . . and remove the spring seat (a magnet may be required to do this)

29.16e Pull out the spring; note the slight taper at the lower end of the spring (not shown here) - the tapered end must face down when you install the spring

29.24a To remove the top plug from the exposed fork tube, depress the plug with a large punch or Phillips screwdriver, depress the plug and remove the wire retaining ring . . .

29.24b . . . and remove the plug

29.24c Pull out the spacer . . .

29.24d . . . and remove the spring seat (the large washer) (you'll need a magnet to extract it from the tube)

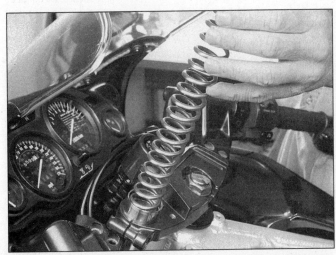

29.24e Remove the fork spring and remember which end faces down (the slightly tapered end)

29.26 After raising the front wheel as high as it will go, insert a tape measure into the fork tube and measure the distance from the top of the tube to the oil, compare your measurement to the distance listed in this Chapter's Specifications, then add or subtract oil as necessary

1

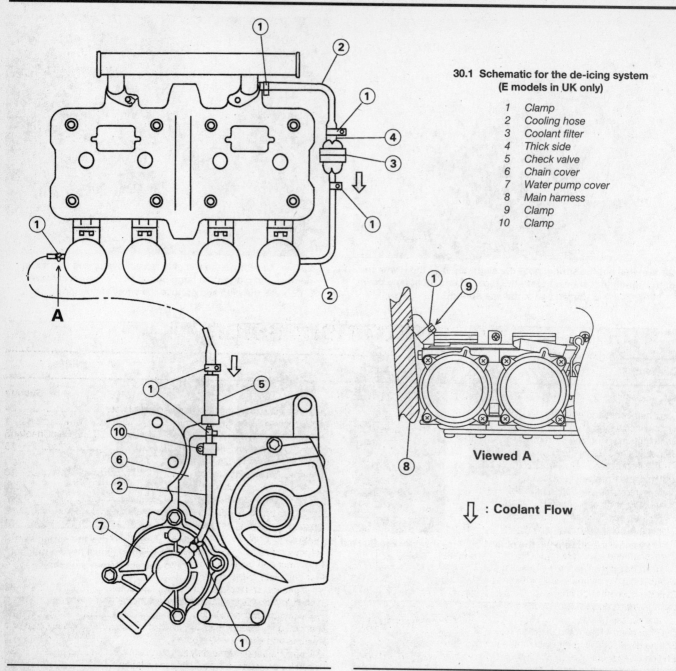

30.1 Schematic for the de-icing system (E models in UK only)

1   Clamp
2   Cooling hose
3   Coolant filter
4   Thick side
5   Check valve
6   Chain cover
7   Water pump cover
8   Main harness
9   Clamp
10   Clamp

Viewed A

⬇ : Coolant Flow

---

30 Coolant filter (U.K. E models only) - description and maintenance

Description

Refer to illustration 30.1

1   E models sold in the United Kingdom are equipped with a carburetor de-icing system **(see illustration)** that uses engine coolant to prevent icing around the mouths of the carburetors.

Maintenance

2   Every year, prior to the winter riding season, clean the coolant filter.
3   Drain the coolant (see Section 21).
4   Remove the fuel tank (see Chapter 4).
5   Remove the filter **(see illustration 30.1).**
6   Blow off any dirt and sediment on the filter with compressed air.
7   Installation is the reverse of removal.

Chapter 2
Engine, clutch and transmission

Contents

Specifications

General

Bore	64.0 mm (2.522 inches)
Stroke	46.6 mm (1.836 inches)
Displacement	599 cc
Compression ratio	
D models	11.5 : 1
E models	12.0 : 1
Cylinder numbering	1-2-3-4 (from left end of engine)
Firing order	1-2-4-3

Camshafts

Lobe height (D models)
   Intake
      Standard .... 34.93 to 35.07 mm (1.376 to 1.382 inches)
      Minimum .... 34.83 mm (1.372 inches)
   Exhaust
      Standard .... 34.43 to 34.57 mm (1.357 to 1.362 inches)
      Minimum .... 34.33 mm (1.353 inches)
Lobe height (E models)
   Intake
      Standard .... 34.946 to 35.054 mm (1.377 to 1.381 inches)
      Minimum .... 34.846 mm (1.349 inches)
   Exhaust
      Standard .... 34.346 to 34.454 mm (1.353 to 1.357 inches)
      Minimum .... 34.246 mm (1.349 inches)
Bearing oil clearance
   Standard .... 0.028 to 0.071 mm (0.0011 to 0.0028 inch)
   Maximum .... 0.16 mm (0.0063 inch)
Journal diameter
   Standard .... 23.950 to 23.972 mm (0.9436 to 0.9445 inch)
   Minimum .... 23.92 mm (0.9425 inch)
Bearing journal inside diameter
   Standard .... 24.000 to 24.021 mm (0.9449 to 0.9457 inch)
   Maximum .... 24.08 mm (0.9480 inch)
Camshaft runout
   Standard .... 0.02 mm (0.0008 inch) or less
   Maximum .... 0.1 mm (0.0039 inch)
Cam chain 20-link length
   Standard .... 127.0 to 127.4 mm (5.0 to 5.0157 inches)
   Maximum .... 128.9 mm (5.0748 inches)

Cylinder head, valves and valve springs

Cylinder head warpage limit .... 0.05 mm (0.0020 inch)
Valve clearances .... See Chapter 1
Valve stem runout
   Standard .... 0.01 mm (0.0004 inch) or less
   Maximum .... 0.05 mm (0.0020 inch
Valve stem diameter
   D models
      Intake valve
         Standard .... 4.475 to 4.490 mm (0.1763 to 0.1769 inch)
         Minimum .... 4.46 mm (0.1757 inch)
      Exhaust valve
         Standard .... 4.455 to 4.470 mm (0.1755 to 0.1761 inch)
         Minimum .... 4.44 mm (0.1749 inch)
   E models
      Intake valve
         Standard .... 3.975 to 3.990 mm (0.1566 to 0.1572 inch)
         Minimum .... 3.945 mm (0.1554 inch)
      Exhaust valve
         Standard .... 3.955 to 3.970 mm (0.1558 to 0.1564 inch)
         Minimum .... 3.925 mm (0.1547 inch)
Valve guide inside diameter (intake and exhaust)
   D models
      Standard .... 4.500 to 4.512 mm (0.1773 to 0.1778 inch)
      Maximum .... 4.58 mm (0.1805 inch)
   E models
      Standard .... 4.000 to 4.012 mm (0.1576 to 0.1581 inch)
      Maximum .... 4.07 mm (0.1604 inch)
Valve stem-to-guide clearance
   Intake valve
      Standard .... 0.034 to 0.116 mm (0.0013 to 0.0045 inch)
      Maximum .... 0.33 mm (0.0130 inch)
   Exhaust valve
      Standard .... 0.088 to 0.167 mm (0.0347 to 0.0066 inch)
      Maximum .... 0.37 mm (0.0146 inch)
Valve seat width (intake and exhaust) .... 0.5 to 1.0 mm (0.0197 to 0.0394 inch)

Valve spring free length
    D models
        Intake (up to DE021419)
            Standard.. 42.9 mm (1.6903 inch)
            Maximum.. 41.2 mm (1.6233 inch)
        Intake (DE021420 on)
            Inner spring
                Standard.. 44.5 mm (1.7533 inch)
                Maximum.. 43.1 mm (1.6981 inch(
            Outer spring
                Standard.. 44.1 mm (1.7375 inch)
                Maximum.. 42.7 mm (1.6824 inch)
        Exhaust
            Standard.. 46.8 mm (1.8439 inch)
            Maximum.. 45.1 mm (1.7770 inch)
    E models
        Intake
            Inner spring
                Standard.. 40.00 mm (1.576 inch)
                Maximum.. 38.6 mm (1.5208 inch)
            Outer spring
                Standard.. 42.69 mm (1.6820 inch)
                Maximum.. 41.29 mm (1.6268 inch)
        Exhaust
            Standard.. 43.95 mm (1.7316 inch)
            Maximum.. 42.25 mm (1.6647 inch)

Cylinder block

Bore diameter
    Standard.. 64.000 to 64.012 mm (2.5216 to 2.5221 inch)
    Maximum.. 64.10 mm (2.5255 inch)

Pistons

Piston diameter
    Standard.. 63.940 to 63.960 mm (2.5192 to 2.5200 inch)
    Minimum.. 63.79 mm (2.5133 inch)
Piston-to-cylinder clearance.. 0.040 to 0.072 mm (0.0016 to 0.0028 inch)
Piston ring-to-groove clearance
    Standard.. 0.03 to 0.07 mm (0.0012 to 0.0028 inch)
    Maximum.. 0.17 mm (0.0067 inch)
Piston ring groove width
    Standard.. 0.82 to 0.84 mm (0.0323 to 0.0331 inch)
    Maximum.. 1.12 mm (0.0441 inch)
Piston ring thickness
    Standard.. 0.77 to 0.79 mm (0.0303 to 0.0311 inch)
    Minimum.. 0.70 mm (0.0276 inch)
Piston ring end gap
    Standard.. 0.15 to 0.30 mm (0.0059 to 0.0118 inch)
    Maximum.. 0.60 mm (0.0236 inch)

Crankshaft and bearings

Crankshaft endplay
    Standard.. 0.05 to 0.21 mm (0.0020 to 0.0083 inch)
    Maximum.. 0.40 mm (0.0158 inch)
Crankshaft runout
    Standard.. 0.02 mm (0.0008 inch)
    Maximum.. 0.05 mm (00020 inch)
Main bearing oil clearance
    Standard.. 0.014 to 0.038 mm (0.0006 to 0.0015 inch)
    Maximum.. 0.070 mm (0.0028 inch)
Crankcase main bearing bore diameter
    '0' mark on crankcase.. 36.000 to 36.008 mm (1.4184 to 1.4187 inch)
    No mark on crankcase.. 36.009 to 36.016 mm (1.4188 to 1.4190 inch)
Main bearing journal diameter
    No mark on crank throw.. 31.984 to 31.992 mm (1.2601 to 1.2605 inch)
    '1' mark on crank throw.. 31.993 to 32.000 mm (1.2605 to 1.2608 inch)

2

Crankshaft and bearings (continued)

Connecting rod big end side clearance
  D models
    Standard .... 0.05 to 0.21 mm (0.0020 to 0.0083 inch)
    Maximum .... 0.40 mm (0.0158 inch)
  E models
    Standard .... 0.13 mm to 0.33 mm (0.0051 to 0.0130 inch)
    Maximum .... 0.50 mm (0.0217 inch)
Connecting rod bearing oil clearance
  D models
    Standard .... 0.035 to 0.059 mm (0.0014 to 0.002 inch)
    Maximum .... 0.10 mm (0.0043 inch)
  E models
    Standard .... 0.036 to 0.066 mm (0.0014 to 0.0026 inch)
    Maximum .... 0.10 mm (0.0043 inch)
Connecting rod big end inside diameter
  D models
    No mark on side of rod .... 36.000 to 36.008 mm (1.4184 to 1.4187 inch)
    '0' mark on side of rod .... 36.009 to 36.016 mm (1.4188 to 1.4190 inch)
  E models
    No mark on side of rod .... 33.000 to 33.008 mm (1.3002 to 1.3005 inch)
    '0' mark on side of rod .... 33.009 to 33.016 mm (1.3006 to 1.3008 inch)
Connecting rod journal (crankpin) diameter
  D models
    No mark on crank throw .... 32.984 to 32.992 mm (1.2996 to 1.2999 inch)
    '0' mark on crank throw .... 32.993 to 33.000 mm (1.2999 to 1.3002 inch)
  E models
    No mark on crank throw .... 29.984 to 29.994 mm (1.1814 to 1.1818 inch)
    '0' mark on crank throw .... 29.995 to 30.000 mm (1.1818 to 1.182 inch)

Oil pump and relief valve

Oil pressure @ 4000 rpm .... 410 to 470 kPa (4.2 to 4.8 kg/cm², 60 to 68 psi)
Relief valve opening pressure .... 375 to 530 kPa (3.8 to 5.4 kg/cm², 54 to 77 psi)

Clutch

Spring free length
  Standard .... 33.6 mm (1.3238 inches)
  Minimum .... 32.6 mm (1.2844 inches)
Friction and steel plate warpage
  Standard .... 0.2 mm (0.0079 inch) or less
  Maximum .... 0.3 mm (0.0118 inch)
Friction plate thickness
  Standard .... 2.9 to 3.1 mm (0.1143 to 0.1221 inch)
  Maximum .... 2.8 mm (0.1103 inch)

Transmission

Shift fork ear thickness
  Standard .... 4.9 to 5.0 mm (0.1929 to 0.1969 inch)
  Minimum .... 4.8 mm (0.189 inch)
Shift fork groove width in gears
  Standard .... 5.05 to 5.15 mm (0.1988 to 0.2028 inch)
  Maximum .... 5.2 mm (0.2049 inch)
Shift fork guide pin diameter
  Standard .... 7.9 to 8.0 mm (0.3110 to 0.315 inch)
  Minimum .... 7.8 mm (0.3071 inch)
Shift drum groove width
  Standard .... 8.05 to 8.20 mm (0.3169 to 0.3228 inch)
  Maximum .... 8.3 mm (0.3268 inch)

Torque specifications

Engine top end

Valve cover bolts .... 9.8 Nm (87 in-lbs)
Camshaft bearing cap bolts .... 12 Nm (104 in-lbs)
Camshaft sprocket bolts .... 15 Nm (11 ft-lbs)
Cam chain tensioner mounting bolts .... 12 Nm (104 in-lbs)
Cylinder head bolts
  New bolts, washers, cylinder head .... 47 Nm (35 ft-lbs)
  Used bolts, washers, cylinder head .... 43 Nm (32 ft-lbs)

Clutch

Clutch cover bolts	8.8 Nm (78 in-lbs)
Clutch cover noise damper bolts	5.9 Nm (52 in-lbs)
Clutch spring bolts	8.8 Nm (78 in-lbs)
Clutch hub nut	130 Nm (98 ft-lbs)

Engine lubrication system

External oil line banjo bolts	25 Nm (18 ft-lbs)
Oil pan bolts	8.8 Nm (78 in-lbs)
Oil pressure relief valve	15 Nm (11 ft-lbs)
Oil pressure switch	15 Nm (11 in-lbs)
Oil separator cover bolts (upper crankcase)	9.8 Nm (87 in-lbs)

Engine bottom end

Crankcase bolts (see illustration 22.8)

T1	9.8 Nm (87 in-lbs)
T2	8.8 Nm (78 in-lbs)
T3	15 Nm (132 in-lbs)
T4	20 Nm (174 in-lbs)
T5	12 Nm (104 in-lbs)
T6	36 Nm (27 ft-lbs)
T7	27 Nm (20 ft-lbs)
T8	25 Nm (216 in-lbs)
T9	98 Nm (72 ft-lbs)
Connecting rod cap nuts	36 Nm (27 ft-lbs)
Alternator stator bolts	12 Nm (104 in-lbs)
Engine mounting bolts/nuts	
D models	44 Nm (33 ft-lbs)
E models	49 Nm (36 ft-lbs)
Engine mounting bracket Allen bolts	
D models	20 Nm (174 in-lbs)
E models	23 Nm (198 in-lbs)

1 General information

The engine/transmission unit is of the water-cooled, in-line, four-cylinder design, installed transversely across the frame. The sixteen valves are operated by double overhead camshafts which are chain driven off the crankshaft. the engine/transmission assembly is constructed from aluminum alloy. The crankcase is divided horizontally.

The crankcase incorporates a wet sump, pressure-fed lubrication system which uses a gear-driven, dual-rotor oil pump, an oil filter and by-pass valve assembly, a relief valve and an oil pressure switch. Also contained in the crankcase is the secondary shaft and the starter motor clutch.

Power from the crankshaft is routed to the transmission via the clutch, which is of the wet, multi-plate type and is chain-driven off the crankshaft. The transmission is a six-speed, constant-mesh unit.

2 Operations possible with the engine in the frame

The components and assemblies listed below can be removed without having to remove the engine from the frame. If, however, a number of areas require attention at the same time, removal of the engine is recommended.

Gear selector mechanism external components
Water pump
Starter motor
Alternator
Clutch assembly
Oil pan, oil pump and relief valve
Valve cover, camshafts, shims and buckets
Cam chain tensioner
Cylinder head (D models only)
Cylinder block and pistons (D models only)

3 Operations requiring engine removal

It is necessary to remove the engine/transmission assembly from the frame and separate the crankcase halves to gain access to the following components:

Crankshaft, connecting rods and bearings
Transmission shafts
Shift drum and forks
Camshaft chain

4 Major engine repair - general note

1   It is not always easy to determine when or if an engine should be completely overhauled, as a number of factors must be considered.
2   High mileage is not necessarily an indication that an overhaul is needed, while low mileage, on the other hand, does not preclude the need for an overhaul. Frequency of servicing is probably the single most important consideration. An engine that has regular and frequent oil and filter changes, as well as other required maintenance, will most likely give many miles of reliable service. Conversely, a neglected engine, or one which has not been broken in properly, may require an overhaul very early in its life.
3   Exhaust smoke and excessive oil consumption are both indications that piston rings and/or valve guides are in need of attention. Make sure oil leaks are not responsible before deciding that the rings and guides are bad. Refer to Chapter 1 and perform a cylinder compression check to determine for certain the nature and extent of the work required.
4   Low oil pressure is usually an indicator of excessive crankshaft bearing wear or a worn out oil pump. To check the oil pressure, refer to Section 17. If the oil pressure is lower than specified, inspect the oil passages for clogging, and inspect the oil pump, oil pressure relief valves and the crankshaft bearing inserts for excessive wear.

5.9a To remove the external oil line, remove these two banjo bolts (arrows) from the cylinder head . . .

5.9b . . . and this banjo bolt (arrow) from the crankcase; discard the copper sealing washers - you'll have to use new ones during reassembly

5.14 Remove this bolt (arrow) from the top of the case and detach the ground strap

5.15a To detach the center heat guard, remove these two bolts (arrows)

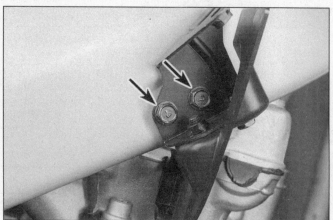

5.15b To detach the side heat guards from the frame, remove these two bolts (arrows) (right heat guard shown, left guard similar)

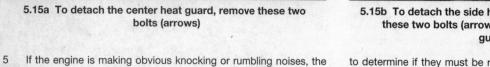

5 If the engine is making obvious knocking or rumbling noises, the connecting rod and/or main bearings are probably at fault.

6 Loss of power, rough running, excessive valve train noise and high fuel consumption rates may also point to the need for an overhaul, especially if they are all present at the same time. If a complete tune-up does not remedy the situation, major mechanical work is the only solution.

7 An engine overhaul generally involves restoring the internal parts to the specifications of a new engine. During an overhaul the piston rings are replaced and the cylinder walls are bored and/or honed. If a rebore is done, then new pistons are also required. The main and connecting rod bearings are generally replaced with new ones and, if necessary, the crankshaft is also replaced. Generally the valves are serviced as well, since they are usually in less than perfect condition at this point. While the engine is being overhauled, other components such as the carburetors and the starter motor can be rebuilt also. The end result should be a like-new engine that will give as many trouble free miles as the original.

8 Before beginning the engine overhaul, read through all of the related procedures to familiarize yourself with the scope and requirements of the job. Overhauling an engine is not all that difficult, but it is time consuming. Plan on the motorcycle being tied up for a minimum of two (2) weeks. Check on the availability of parts and make sure that any necessary special tools, equipment and supplies are obtained in advance.

9 Most work can be done with typical shop hand tools, although a number of precision measuring tools are required for inspecting parts

to determine if they must be replaced. Often a dealer service department or motorcycle repair shop will handle the inspection of parts and offer advice concerning reconditioning and replacement. As a general rule, time is the primary cost of an overhaul so it doesn't pay to install worn or substandard parts.

10 As a final note, to ensure maximum life and minimum trouble from a rebuilt engine, everything must be assembled with care in a spotlessly clean environment.

5 Engine - removal and installation

Warning: *Engine removal and installation should be done with the aid of at least one assistant - and preferably two - to avoid back injuries, or injuries that could occur if the engine is dropped. A hydraulic floor jack should be used to support and lower the engine if possible (available at any equipment rental yard).*

Removal

Refer to illustrations 5.9a, 5.9b, 5.14, 5.15a, 5.15b, 5.16, 5.17a, 5.17b, 5.18a, 5.18b and 5.19

1 Set the bike on its centerstand.

2 Remove the seat, the side covers and the upper and lower fairings (see Chapter 8).

3 Remove the fuel tank (see Chapter 4).

4 Drain the coolant and the engine oil (see Chapter 1).

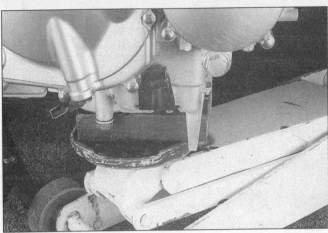

5.16 Support the engine with a floor jack; place a block of wood between the jack head and the engine as shown, to protect the oil pan (put the block of wood *between* the two projections on the pan - allowing the weight of the engine to rest on these projections could damage them)

5.17a Remove the front left engine bolt

5.17b Remove the right front engine bolt, the two Allen bolts above it and the right engine mounting bracket

5.18a Hold the bolt on the left side of the frame and unscrew the lower rear engine mounting nut

5.18b Use the same technique to remove the upper rear engine mounting bolt

5   Remove the ignition coils (see Chapter 5).
6   Remove the air suction valve and the vacuum switching valve (see Chapter 1).
7   Remove the carburetors (see Chapter 4) and plug the intake openings with rags.
8   Remove the radiator, radiator hoses and oil cooler (see Chapter 3).
9   Remove the external oil line from the front of the engine **(see illustrations)**.
10   Remove the exhaust system (see Chapter 4).
11   Disconnect the lower end of the clutch cable from the lever and bracket (see Chapter 1).
12   Remove the engine sprocket cover, unbolt the engine sprocket and detach the sprocket and chain from the engine (see Chapter 7).
13   Mark and disconnect the wires from the oil pressure switch, the neutral switch and the starter motor. Unplug the alternator, sidestand and pickup coil electrical connectors (see Chapters 5 and 9).
14   Remove the bolt securing the ground wire to the engine case **(see illustration)**.
15   Remove the heat guards **(see illustrations)**.
16   Support the engine with a floor jack and a wood block **(see illustration)**.
17   Remove the front engine mounting nuts and bolts **(see illustrations)**.
18   Pry the plugs from the holes in the frame and remove the rear

engine mounting nuts and bolts **(see illustrations)**.
19   Slowly and carefully lower the engine assembly until the jack is fully collapsed **(see illustration)**.
20   Have a couple of assistants lift the engine by hand just high

5.19 Carefully lower the engine from the frame until the floor jack is fully collapsed, then have a couple of assistants lift the engine slightly and pull out the jack and the block of wood

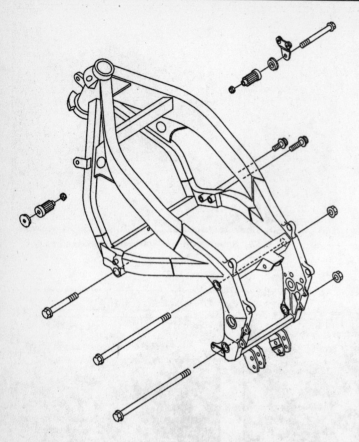

5.22 Engine mounting bolts, nuts and bushings (D model shown, E model similar)

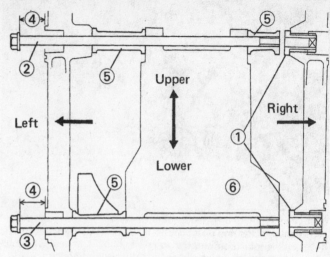

5.24 Engine adjustment details (D models)

1   Mounting adjusters
2   Rear upper mounting bolt
3   Rear lower mounting bolt
4   About 25 mm
5   Collars
6   Engine

enough so you can slip the jack and wood block out from under the engine assembly.

21   Place a block of wood under the front wheel and have one assistant tilt the bike to one side while you and the other helper drag the engine assembly out from under the right side of the bike.

Installation

Refer to illustrations 5.22, 5.24 and 5.25

22   Be sure to inspect all engine mounting bushings **(see illustration)** for cracks and tears. Replace any damaged or worn bushings.

23   Once the engine is in position, install the front and rear mounting bolts, but don't tighten them until the engine has been correctly aligned with the frame. This may seem like an unnecessary step, but it's not. On these models, the engine is a "stressed-member," i.e. part of the frame. Because of manufacturing tolerances, the engine must be correctly aligned, or it could affect handling and/or wear on the drive chain and the countershaft and rear sprockets. A pair of "adjusters" (actually bushings with internal hexes) take up the clearance between the engine and the frame in both rear mounting bolt holes on D models; a single adjuster - in the lower rear hole only - does the same thing on E models. You'll find the adjuster(s) inside the rear engine mounting bolt hole(s) on the right side of the frame.

24   To align the engine on D models, insert the collars and the rear upper and lower engine mounting bolts from the left side of the engine, but don't shove the bolts all the way through yet; leave about 25 mm (.985 inch) protruding as shown **(see illustration)**. Screw the lower engine mounting adjuster in a clockwise direction until it contacts the engine, then tighten it to the torque listed in this Chapter's Specifications. Now do the same thing with the upper adjuster: Turn it in until it contacts the engine, then tighten to the torque listed in this Chapter's Specifications. Push both mounting bolts the rest of the way through

the holes in the adjusters, install the nuts and tighten them to the torque listed in this Chapter's Specifications.

25   The alignment procedure for E models **(see illustration)** is exactly the same except that there's only one adjuster - for the lower rear engine mounting bolt.

26   The remainder of installation is essentially the reverse of removal, with the following additions:

a) Use new gaskets at all exhaust pipe connections.
b) Make sure all wires and hoses are routed properly (refer to the cable, wire and hose routing diagrams at the end this book).
c) Adjust the drive chain, throttle cables, choke cable and clutch cable following the procedures in Chapter 1.
d) Fill the engine with the specified oil (see Chapter 1).
e) Add the specified 50/50 mixture of antifreeze and water (see Chapter 1) and bleed the air from the cooling system.
f) Synchronize the carburetors and adjust the idle (see Chapter 1).

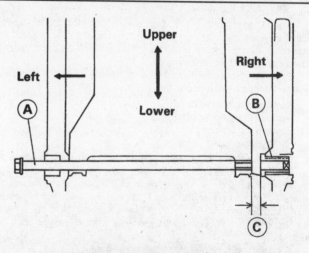

5.25 Engine adjustment details (E models)

A   Lower rear engine mounting bolt
B   Engine mounting bolt adjuster
C   10mm (0.394 inch)

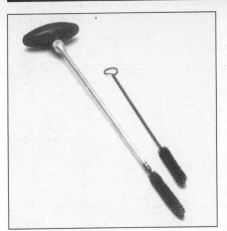

6.2a A selection of brushes is required for cleaning holes and passages in the engine components

6.2b Type HPG-1 Plastigage is needed to check the crankshaft, connecting rod and camshaft oil clearance

6.3 Construct an engine stand with short lengths of 2X4s and lag bolts or nails

6   Engine disassembly and reassembly - general information

Refer to illustrations 6.2a, 6.2b and 6.3

1   Before disassembling the engine, clean the exterior with a degreaser and rinse it with water. A clean engine will make the job easier and prevent the possibility of getting dirt into the internal areas of the engine.

2   In addition to the precision measuring tools mentioned earlier, you will need a torque wrench, a valve spring compressor, oil galley brushes, a piston ring removal and installation tool, a piston ring compressor, a pin-type spanner wrench and a clutch holder tool (which is described in Section 20). Some new, clean engine oil of the correct grade and type, some engine assembly lube (or moly-based grease), a tube of Kawasaki Bond liquid gasket (part no. 92104-1003) or equivalent, and a tube of Kawasaki Bond silicone sealant (part no. 56019-120) or equivalent, will also be required. Although it may not be considered a tool, some Plastigage (type HPG-1) should also be obtained to use for checking bearing oil clearances **(see illustrations)**.

3   An engine support stand made from short lengths of 2x4s bolted together will facilitate the disassembly and reassembly procedures **(see illustration)**. The perimeter of the mount should be just big enough to accommodate the engine oil pan.

4   When disassembling the engine, keep "mated" parts together (including gears, cylinders, pistons, etc. that have been in contact with each other during engine operation). These "mated" parts must be reused or replaced as an assembly.

5   Engine/transmission disassembly should be done in the following general order with reference to the appropriate Sections.

Remove the cylinder head
Remove the cylinder block
Remove the pistons
Remove the clutch
Remove the oil pan
Remove the external shift mechanism
Remove the alternator rotor/starter clutch from the left end of the crank (see Chapter 9)
Remove the starter gear from the left end of the crankshaft
Remove the timing rotor from the right end of the crankshaft (see Chapter 5)
Separate the crankcase halves
Remove the crankshaft and connecting rods
Remove the transmission shafts/gears
Remove the shift drum/forks

6   Reassembly is accomplished by reversing the general disassembly sequence.

7   Valve cover - removal and installation

Refer to illustrations 7.8 and 7.10

Note: *The valve cover can be removed with the engine in the frame. If the engine has been removed, ignore the steps which don't apply.*

Removal

1   Set the bike on its centerstand.

2   Remove the seat and the front screws from both side covers (see Chapter 8).

3   Remove the fuel tank (see Chapter 4).

4   Remove the upper and lower fairings (see Chapter 8).

5   Remove the Air Suction Valve and the Vacuum Switching Valve (see Chapter 1).

6   Remove the ignition coils and their brackets, along with the spark plug wires (see Chapter 5).

7   Remove the heat guards **(see illustration 5.15a and 5.15b)**.

8   Remove the valve cover bolts **(see illustration)**.

9   Lift the cover off the cylinder head. If it's stuck, don't attempt to pry it off - tap around the sides of it with a plastic hammer to dislodge it.

7.8 To remove the valve cover, remove these eight bolts (arrows)

2

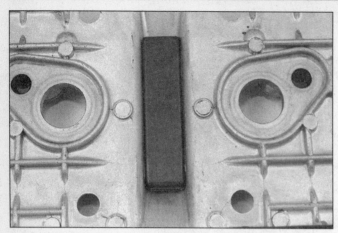

7.10 Flip the valve cover upside-down and inspect the chain rubbing block - if it's worn, replace it

10   Check the rubbing block in the center of the cover - if it's excessively worn, pry it out and install a new one **(see illustration)**.

Installation

Refer to illustration 7.12

11   Peel the rubber gasket from the cover. If it is cracked, hardened, has soft spots or shows signs of general deterioration, replace it.

12   Clean the mating surfaces of the cylinder head and the valve cover with lacquer thinner, acetone or brake system cleaner. Apply a thin film of RTV sealant to the half-circle cutouts on each side of the head **(see illustration)**.

13   Install the gasket to the cover. Position the cover on the cylinder head, making sure the gasket doesn't slip out of place.

14   Check the rubber seals on the valve cover bolts; if they're cracked, dried out or worn, replace them. Install the bolts, tightening them evenly to the torque listed in this Chapter's Specifications.

15   The remainder of installation is the reverse of removal.

---

8   Camshaft chain tensioner - removal and installation

Removal

Refer to illustrations 8.3 and 8.5

Note: *The camshaft chain tensioner can be removed with the engine in*

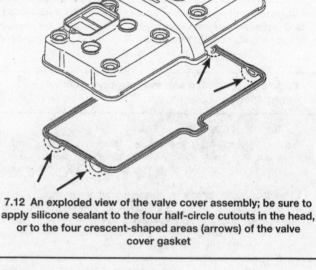

7.12 An exploded view of the valve cover assembly; be sure to apply silicone sealant to the four half-circle cutouts in the head, or to the four crescent-shaped areas (arrows) of the valve cover gasket

the frame. If the engine has been removed, ignore the steps which don't apply.

1   Set the bike on its centerstand.

2   Remove the fuel tank and carburetors (see Chapter 4).

3   Remove the tensioner cap bolt, sealing washer and spring **(see illustration)**.

4   Remove the tensioner mounting bolts and detach the tensioner from the cylinder block. **Caution:** *This is a "non-return" type cam chain*

8.3 To detach the tensioner from the cylinder block, remove the cap bolt (center arrow), washer and spring, then remove the tensioner mounting bolts (outer arrows)

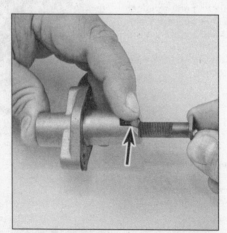

8.5 To fish the guide pin out of the tensioner, depress the stopper (arrow) with your finger and push in the plunger, then turn the tensioner upside down and tap it in your hand - the guide pin will fall out

8.9 Install the cam chain tensioner with the arrow on top

8.10 Install the spring and guide pin into the tensioner, then collapse the spring with the cap bolt - don't forget to put the copper sealing washer on the cap bolt

9.3 Before loosening or removing anything in the valve train, remove the timing rotor cover from the right end of the crankshaft and turn the crankshaft until the "T" (Top Dead Center) mark for "1,4" (cylinders 1 and 4) is aligned with the stationary pointer on the case

tensioner; the tensioner plunger doesn't return to its original position once it has moved out to take up slack in the cam chain. When removing the tensioner, NEVER take out the bolts only halfway; if you retighten them from this position, you could damage the tensioner and the cam chain. Once the bolts are removed, the tensioner must be removed and reset as described below. And once the tensioner is removed, NEVER turn over the crankshaft. Doing so could upset cam chain timing and damage the valves.

5   Push the stopper to release the ratchet mechanism **(see illustration)**, depress the tensioner plunger and fish out the guide pin from the spring side of the tensioner. Wash the tensioner components with solvent.

Installation

Refer to illustrations 8.9 and 8.10

6   Lubricate the friction surfaces of the components with moly-based grease.
7   Inspect the tensioner gasket for cracks or hardening. If it's damaged, replace it.
8   Depress the stopper to release the ratchet mechanism **(see illustration 8.5)** and push in the tensioner plunger.
9   Position the tensioner body on the cylinder block with the arrow on the tensioner at the top **(see illustration)**, install the tensioner mounting bolts and tighten them to the torque listed in this Chapter's Specifications.
10   Insert the guide pin into the spring and install the spring and guide pin into the tensioner, then push them in with the cap bolt **(see illustration)**.
11   Using a wrench on the crankshaft bolt at the right end of the engine (see *Timing rotor - removal and installation* in Chapter 5), slowly turn the crankshaft over a couple of turns in the normal direction of rotation.

9   Camshafts and lifters - removal, inspection and installation

Camshafts

Removal

Refer to illustrations 9.3, 9.5, 9.6a, 9.6b, 9.6c, 9.6d, 9.6e, 9.6f and 9.7
Note: *This procedure can be performed with the engine in the frame.*
1   Remove the front retaining screws from both side covers (see Chapter 8), and remove the fuel tank and the carburetors (see Chapter 4).

9.5 To remove the camshaft bearing caps, remove these bolts (arrows) in the reverse order in which they're numbered; the numbers are embossed into the caps next to each bolt (see illustration 9.21)

2   Remove the valve cover (see Section 7).
3   Remove the pickup coil cover from the right side of the engine (see Chapter 5). Using a wrench on the large engine turning hex on the end of the crankshaft, rotate the engine clockwise until the T 1,4 mark on the timing rotor aligns with the static index mark on the casing **(see illustration)**.
4   Remove the cam chain tensioner (see Section 8).
5   Note the small numbers embossed on the bearing caps next to each pair of cap bolts; these numbers indicate the order in which the bearing cap bolts are to be tightened **(see illustration 9.21)**. When loosening the cap bolts, reverse this order. Unscrew the bearing cap bolts **(see illustration)** evenly, a little at a time, until they are all loose, then lift off the bearing caps. **Caution:** *If the bearing cap bolts aren't loosened evenly, the camshaft may bind.* Also note the "L" (bearing cap for the left side of the head) and "R" (bearing cap for right side) embossed on each bearing cap; when you reinstall the caps, be sure to install them in the same positions.
6   Look for marks on the camshafts. The intake camshaft should have an IN mark and the exhaust camshaft should have an EX mark. If you can't find these marks, label the camshafts to ensure they are

2

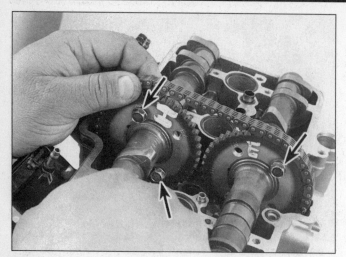

9.6a Clearly label the intake and exhaust camshaft sprockets and remove the three bolts (arrows) you can see; the other bolt, on the exhaust cam sprocket, is difficult to remove until you can rotate the exhaust cam slightly (which you can't do until you have removed the intake cam and sprocket and have some slack in the chain)

installed in their original locations **(see illustration)**. Now loosen both intake camshaft sprocket bolts and the bolt that's visible on the exhaust cam sprocket. Pull up on the camshaft chain and carefully guide the intake camshaft out of the intake sprocket and remove the sprocket **(see illustrations)**. Now that you have some chain slack, pull up on the chain so it isn't engaged with the exhaust sprocket teeth, rotate the exhaust cam just enough to reach that fourth sprocket bolt and remove the bolt **(see illustration)**. **Caution:** *DON'T rotate the crankshaft or the cam chain!* Now remove the exhaust cam and sprocket **(see illustration)**. Finally, remove all four spark plug hole O-rings and all four dowels **(see illustration)**. You can use these dowels again, but discard the O-rings and install new ones when you reassemble the camshaft assembly.

7   While the camshafts are out, don't allow the chain to go slack - if you do, it will become detached from the gear on the crankshaft and may bind between the crankshaft and case, which could cause damage to these components. Wire the chain to another component, or hang it from a wooden dowel **(see illustration)**, to prevent it from dropping down into the cam chain tunnel. Also, cover the top of the cylinder head with a rag to prevent foreign objects from falling into the engine.

Inspection

Refer to illustrations 9.9a, 9.9b, 9.11, 9.13a, 9.13b and 9.16
Note: *Before replacing camshafts or the cylinder head and bearing*

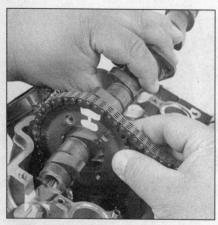

9.6b Slide the intake cam through the intake sprocket and remove it . . .

9.6c . . . then remove the intake cam sprocket

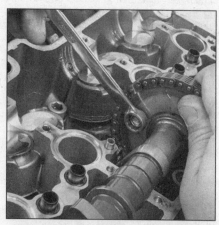

9.6d Lift the cam chain off the exhaust cam sprocket and rotate the cam slightly to get at the other sprocket bolt and remove it

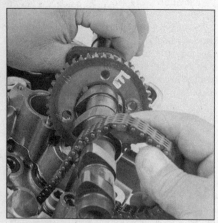

9.6e Remove the exhaust cam and sprocket

9.6f Remove all four spark plug hole O-rings and discard them; and don't lose the four dowels (arrows) (it's a good idea to pull them out and put them in a small plastic bag)

9.7 An old wooden broom handle makes a good hanger for the cam chain so the chain won't fall down into the cam tunnel

9.9a Check the lobes of the camshaft for wear - here's a good example of damage which will require replacement - or repair - of the camshaft

9.9b Measure the height of the camshaft lobes with a micrometer

9.11 Lay a strip of Plastigage (type HPG-1) across each camshaft bearing journal, parallel with the camshaft centerline, as shown

caps because of damage, check with local machine shops specializing in motorcycle engine work. In the case of the camshafts, it may be possible for cam lobes to be welded, reground and hardened, at a cost far lower than that of a new camshaft. If the bearing surfaces in the cylinder head are damaged, it may be possible for them to be bored out to accept bearing inserts. Because of the high cost of a new cylinder head, we recommend that all options be explored before condemning it as trash!

8 Inspect the cam bearing surfaces of the head and the bearing caps. Look for score marks, deep scratches and evidence of spalling (a pitted appearance).

9 Check the camshaft lobes for heat discoloration (blue appearance), score marks, chipped areas, flat spots and spalling **(see illustration)**. Measure the height of each lobe with a micrometer **(see illustration)** and compare the results to the minimum lobe height listed in this Chapter's Specifications. If damage is noted or wear is excessive, the camshaft must be replaced. Also, be sure to check the condition of the followers as described later in this Section.

10 Next, check the camshaft bearing oil clearances. Clean the camshafts, the bearing surfaces in the cylinder head and bearing caps with a clean lint-free cloth, then lay the cams in place in the cylinder head. Engage the cam chain with the sprockets, so the camshafts don't turn as the bearing caps are tightened.

11 Cut eight strips of Plastigage (type HPG-1) and lay one piece on each bearing journal, parallel with the camshaft centerline **(see illustration)**. Install the bearing caps in their proper positions **(see illustra-**

tion 9.21) and install the bolts. Tighten the bolts evenly in a criss-cross pattern until the specified torque is reached. While doing this, don't let the camshafts rotate.

12 Now unscrew the bolts a little at a time, and carefully lift off the bearing caps.

13 To determine the oil clearance, compare the crushed Plastigage (at its widest point) on each journal to the scale printed on the Plastigage container **(see illustration)**. Compare the results to this Chapter's Specifications, noting that the figures differ depending on the cylinder number. If the oil clearance is greater than specified, measure the diameter of the cam bearing journal with a micrometer **(see illustration)**. If the journal diameter is less than the specified limit, replace the camshaft with a new one and recheck the clearance. If the clearance is still too great, replace the cylinder head and bearing caps with new parts.

14 Except in cases of oil starvation, the cam chain wears very little. If the chain has stretched excessively, which makes it difficult to maintain proper tension, replace it with a new one (see Section 27 for chain stretch measurement and replacement).

15 Check the sprockets for wear, cracks and other damage, replacing them if necessary. If the sprockets are worn, the cam chain is also worn, and so is the sprocket on the crankshaft. If severe wear is apparent, the entire engine should be disassembled for inspection.

16 Replace the camshaft sprockets if necessary. Install the new sprocket so that its marked side faces away from the flange to which it's attached, toward the right of the engine **(see illustration)**. Apply

2

9.13a Compare the width of the crushed Plastigage to the scale printed on the Plastigage container to obtain the clearance

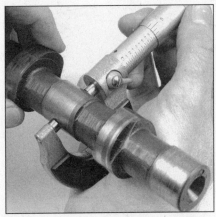

9.13b Measure the cam bearing journal with a micrometer

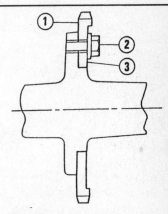

9.16 Correct installation of the camshaft sprockets

1 Sprocket   3 Marked face
2 Bolt

thread locking compound to the sprocket bolts and tighten them to the specified torque when installing the camshafts.

17   Inspect the front (exhaust side) and rear (intake side) cam chain guides (the long black rubbing blocks that protect the cam chain tunnel from the chain) (see Section 27). If the front cam chain guide must be replaced, you'll have to remove the cylinder head (see Section 10). If the rear guide must be replaced, the cylinder block must be removed (see Section 13). If the cam chain itself must be replaced, you'll have to split the cases (see Section 22).

Installation

Refer to illustrations 9.19a, 9.19b and 9.21

18   Make sure the bearing surfaces in the cylinder head and the bearing caps are clean, then apply engine oil to each of them. Install four new spark plug hole O-rings.

19   Apply engine oil (or a coat of engine assembly lube if new camshafts are being fitted) to the lobes. Make sure the camshaft bearing journals are clean, then lay the exhaust camshaft, followed by the intake camshaft, in the cylinder head - do not mix them up **(see illustration)**. Verify that the T 1.4 mark on the timing rotor is still aligned (see Step 3) and align the marks on the cam sprockets exactly with the cylinder head surface **(see illustration)**.

20   Make sure that the timing marks are aligned as described in Step 19, then mesh the chain with the camshaft sprockets. Count the number of chain link pins between the EX mark and the IN mark **(see illustration 9.19b)**. There should be no slack in the chain between the two sprockets.

21   Install the dowels in their locations. Carefully set the bearing caps in place in their proper positions **(see illustration)** and install the bolts. Snug all of the bolts evenly, in the order of the number next to each bolt, then tighten them in this same order to the torque listed in this Chapter's Specifications.

22   Insert your finger or a wood dowel into the cam chain tensioner hole and apply pressure to the cam chain. Check the timing marks to make sure they are aligned (see Step 19) and there are still the correct number of link pins between the EX and IN marks on the cam sprockets. If necessary, change the position of the sprocket(s) on the chain to bring all of the marks into alignment. **Caution:** *If the marks are not aligned exactly as described, the valve timing will be incorrect and the valves may contact the pistons, causing extensive damage to the engine.*

23   Install the cam chain tensioner (see Section 8).

24   Check the valve clearances (see Chapter 1) and install the pickup

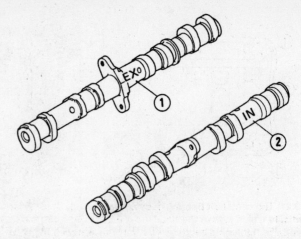

9.19a Don't mix up the camshafts during installation! The exhaust cam has the letters EX embossed on it; the intake cam has IN on it

coil cover (see Chapter 5).

25   Install the valve cover (see Section 7).

26   Install the carburetors and the fuel tank (see Chapter 4). Install and tighten the front retaining screws for the side covers (see Chapter 8). Install the seat.

Lifters

Removal

27   Remove the camshafts.

28   Obtain a container with at least 16 compartments and label each compartment with the number of its corresponding valve in the cylinder head. Or write the cylinder number and position of the lifter on top with a laundry marking pen (for example: cylinder no. 1, intake, left; cyl no. 2, intake, right; etc.) and stick the lifter and shim into a plastic bag. Whatever method you use, DON'T MIX UP THE LIFTERS! Not only will you have to measure the valve clearances all over again - and probably have to remove the camshafts again as well, but you may also damage valve train parts.

29   Using a magnet if necessary, lift each follower out of the cylinder head and store it in its corresponding compartment in the container.

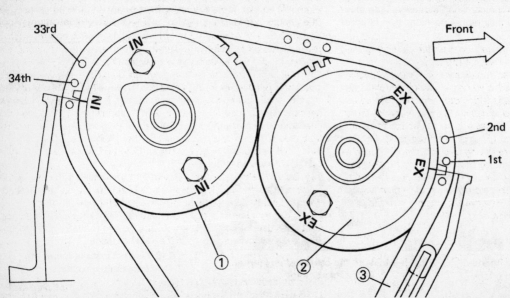

9.19b Make sure the camshaft sprockets are properly aligned with the cylinder head before installing and tighten the sprocket bolts

1   *Intake sprocket*
2   *Exhaust sprocket*
3   *Pull the exhaust side taut*

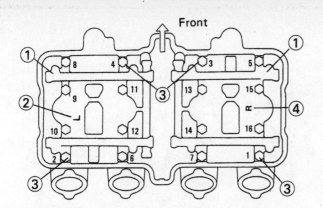

9.21 The camshaft bearing caps are marked "L" and "R" to indicate which side of the head they're attached - don't switch them! The tightening sequence for the camshaft bearing caps is indicated by the number embossed into the cap next to each bolt

1	Camshaft caps	3	Longer bolts
2	"L" mark	4	"R" mark

The shim is likely to stick to the inside of the follower so take great care not to lose it when removing the follower. Remove the shims and store each one with its respective follower.

Inspection

30   No figures are available to determine wear of the lifters or bore. Inspect the lifters for signs of excessive wear or scoring, and if necessary replace them. Wear of their bores will necessitate cylinder head replacement.

Installation

31   Fit each shim to the top of its correct valve making sure it is correctly seated in the valve spring retainer. **Note:** *It is essential that the shims are returned to their original valves, otherwise the valve clearances will be inaccurate.*
32   Lubricate the surface of the followers with engine oil, then install them in their respective positions in the cylinder head, making sure each one squarely enters its bore.
33   Install the camshafts and check the valve clearances.

---

10 Cylinder head - removal and installation

Removal

Caution: *The engine must be completely cool before beginning this procedure, or the cylinder head may become warped.*
Note: *On D models, the cylinder head can be removed with the engine in the frame (although it's difficult); so, if you have already removed the engine on a D model, ignore the steps which don't apply. It should be noted, however, that removing and installing the four outer cylinder head bolts on D models is tricky with the engine still attached to the frame. So we recommend removing the engine before removing the head even on D models. Although removing and installing the engine certainly adds more time to head removal and installation, it makes the job itself easier. At any rate, if you're removing the head on a D model, read through the following procedure before you decide which way to go. Finally, on E models, you MUST remove the engine from the bike before the cylinder head can be removed.*

D models

1   Remove the fuel tank and the carburetors (see Chapter 4).
2   Remove the upper and lower fairings (see Chapter 8).
3   Remove the radiator (see Chapter 3).
4   Remove the exhaust system (see Chapter 4).

10.14 Remove the old cylinder head gasket and remove the dowels (arrow points to right dowel, other dowel not visible in this photo)

5   Remove the upper coolant pipe from the cylinder head (see Chapter 3).
6   Remove the external oil line banjo bolts and washers from the cylinder head and the crankcase **(see illustrations 5.9a and 5.9b** and remove the external oil line.

E models

7   Remove the engine (see Section 5).

All models

Refer to illustration 10.14
8   Remove the valve cover (see Section 7),
9   Remove the camshaft chain tensioner (see Section 8).
10   Remove the camshafts (see Section 9).
11   Remove the cylinder block-to-cylinder head bolts in the reverse order of the tightening sequence **(see illustration 10.19a)**. Besides the eight bolts within the perimeter of the head, don't forget the two bolts on each end of the head. To remove these outer bolts on D models with the engine still installed in the frame, you'll need Kawasaki's hex wrench (tool no. 57001-1234) or a suitable equivalent.
12   On D models with the engine in the frame, raise the head slightly and remove the two left and two right bolts. On D models with the engine removed, and on all E models, simply pull the cylinder head off the cylinder block. If the head is stuck, tap around the side of the head with a rubber mallet to jar it loose, or use two wooden dowels inserted into the intake or exhaust ports to lever the head off. Don't attempt to pry the head off by inserting a screwdriver between the head and the cylinder block - you'll damage the sealing surfaces.
13   Pull out the front cam chain guide and inspect it (see Section 27). You can't remove the rear cam chain guide without pulling off the cylinder block, but now is the time to inspect it anyway, just in case it needs to be replaced (see Section 27). Stuff a clean rag into the cam chain tunnel to prevent the entry of debris. Remove all of the washers from their seats, using a pair of needle-nose pliers.
14   Remove the old head gasket and the two dowel pins from the cylinder block **(see illustration)**.
15   Check the cylinder head gasket and the mating surfaces on the cylinder head and block for leakage, which could indicate warpage. Refer to Section 12 and check the flatness of the cylinder head.
16   Clean all traces of old gasket material from the cylinder head and block. Be careful not to let any of the gasket material fall into the crankcase, the cylinder bores or the water passages.

Installation

Refer to illustrations 10.17, 10.19a and 10.19b
17   Install the two dowel pins, then lay the new gasket in place on the

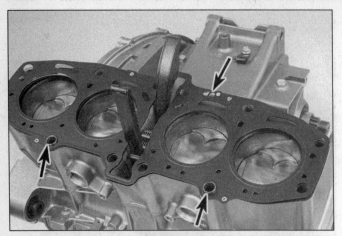

10.17 Install the new head gasket with the "UP" mark (upper arrow) to the left of the cam chain tunnel and make sure both dowels (lower arrows) are in place

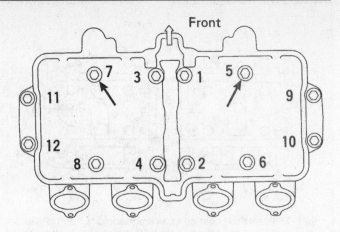

10.19a Cylinder head bolt tightening sequence; note that bolts 5 and 7 are longer than the rest and must be installed in the correct holes

cylinder block. Make sure the UP mark on the gasket is positioned on the left-hand side of the engine **(see illustration)**. Never reuse the old gasket and don't use any type of gasket sealant.

18   Carefully lower the cylinder head over the studs. It is helpful to have an assistant support the camshaft chain with a piece of wire so it doesn't fall and become kinked or detached from the crankshaft. When the head is resting against the cylinder block, wire the cam chain to another component to keep tension on it.

19   Install the cylinder head-to-block bolts and gradually and evenly tighten them in the specified sequence **(see illustration)** to the torque listed in this Chapter's Specifications. Note that the head bolts which are longer than the others must be installed in the correct holes. If you're installing the head on a D model with the engine in the frame, the two bolts on each end of the head can be tightened to the speci- fied torque with a hex wrench. At a point 150 mm (5-29/32 inches) from the working end of the hex wrench, apply 32 kg of force to each outer bolt (29.4 kg for a used bolt) **(see illustration)**.

20   Install the front camshaft chain guide with its "UP" mark at the top. Push the guide all the way down (see Section 27).

21   Install the camshafts (see Section 9), the camshaft chain ten- sioner (see Section 8) and the valve cover (see Section 7).

22   On E models, install the engine (see Section 5).

23   On D models, install the upper coolant pipe (see Chapter 3) and the external oil line **(see illustrations 5.9a and 5.9b)**. Be sure to use new sealing washers and tighten the banjo bolts to the torque listed in this Chapter's Specifications. Then install the exhaust system (see Chapter 4), the radiator (see Chapter 3), the upper and lower fairings (see Chapter 8) and the carburetors and fuel tank (see Chapter 4).

24   On all models, change the engine oil (see Chapter 1).

11   Valves/valve seats/valve guides - servicing

1   Because of the complex nature of this job and the special tools and equipment required, servicing of the valves, the valve seats and the valve guides (commonly known as a valve job) is best left to a pro- fessional.

2   The home mechanic can, however, remove and disassemble the head, do the initial cleaning and inspection, then reassemble and deliver the head to a dealer service department or properly equipped motorcycle repair shop for the actual valve servicing. Refer to Section 12 for those procedures.

3   The dealer service department will remove the valves and springs, recondition or replace the valves and valve seats, replace the valve guides, check and replace the valve springs, spring retainers and keepers (as necessary), replace the valve seals with new ones and reassemble the valve components.

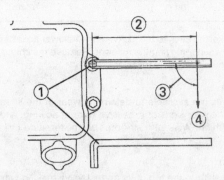

10.19b If you're installing the head on a D model, and the engine is in the frame:

1   *Insert a Kawasaki hex wrench (tool no. 57001-1234) or similar Allen wrench into each outer head bolt*

2   *Measure off 150 mm from the working end of the hex wrench out, toward the end of the handle*

3   *Maintaining the force at an angle of 90-degrees to the wrench . . .*

4   *. . . apply 32 kg (70.5 lbs) of force to the head bolt (29.4 kg [65 lbs] for used bolts)*

4   After the valve job has been performed, the head will be in like- new condition. When the head is returned, be sure to clean it again very thoroughly before installation on the engine to remove any metal particles or abrasive grit that may still be present from the valve service operations. Use compressed air, if available, to blow out all the holes and passages.

12   Cylinder head and valves - disassembly, inspection and reassembly

1   As mentioned in the previous Section, valve servicing and valve guide replacement should be left to a dealer service department or motorcycle repair shop. However, disassembly, cleaning and inspec- tion of the valves and related components can be done (if the neces- sary special tools are available) by the home mechanic. This way no expense is incurred if the inspection reveals that service work is not required at this time.

2   To properly disassemble the valve components without the risk of damaging them, a valve spring compressor is absolutely necessary. If the special tool is not available, have a dealer service department or

12.7a Compress the valve spring with a valve spring compressor . . .

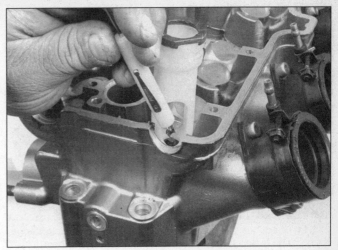

12.7b . . . and remove the collets (keepers)

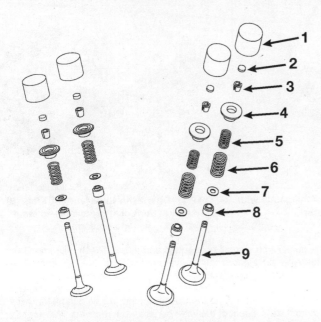

**12.7c An exploded view of the exhaust (left) and intake (right)
valve assemblies**

1	Lifter (bucket)	6	Outer valve spring
2	Shim	7	Valve spring seat
3	Collets (keepers)	8	Valve guide seal
4	Valve spring retainer	9	Valve
5	Inner valve spring		

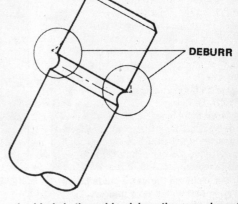

**12.7d If the valve binds in the guide, deburr the area above the
collet (keeper) groove**

motorcycle repair shop handle the entire process of disassembly, inspection, service or repair (if required) and reassembly of the valves.

Disassembly

Refer to illustrations 12.7a, 12.7b, 12.7c and 12.7d

3   Remove the lifters and their shims if you haven't already done so (see Section 9). Store the components in such a way that they can be returned to their original locations without getting mixed up (labeled plastic bags work well).

4   Before the valves are removed, scrape away any traces of gasket material from the head gasket sealing surface. Work slowly and do not nick or gouge the soft aluminum of the head. Gasket removing solvents, which work very well, are available at most motorcycle shops and auto parts stores.

5   Carefully scrape all carbon deposits out of the combustion chamber area. A hand-held wire brush or a piece of fine emery cloth can be used once the majority of deposits have been scraped away. Do not use a wire brush mounted in a drill motor, or one with extremely stiff bristles, as the head material is soft and may be eroded away or scratched by the wire brush.

6   Before proceeding, arrange to label and store the valves along with their related components so they can be kept separate and reinstalled in the same valve guides they are removed from (again, plastic bags work well for this).

7   Compress the valve spring on the first valve with a spring compressor, then remove the keepers **(see illustrations)** and the retainer from the valve assembly. Do not compress the springs any more than is absolutely necessary. Carefully release the valve spring compressor and remove the springs and the valve from the head **(see illustration)**. If the valve binds in the guide (won't pull through), push it back into the head and deburr the area around the keeper groove with a very fine file or whetstone **(see illustration)**.

8   Repeat the procedure for the remaining valves. Remember to keep the parts for each valve together so they can be reinstalled in the same location.

9   Once the valves have been removed and labeled, pull off the valve stem seals with pliers and discard them (the old seals should never be reused), then remove the spring seats.

10   Next, clean the cylinder head with solvent and dry it thoroughly. Compressed air will speed the drying process and ensure that all holes and recessed areas are clean.

2

12.14 Check the gasket surface for flatness with a straightedge and feeler gauge; measure in the directions shown

12.15 Measuring valve seat width

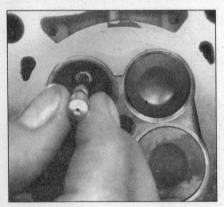

12.16a Measure the valve guide inside diameter with a hole gauge . . .

12.16b . . . then measure the gauge with a micrometer

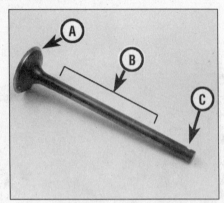

12.17 Check the valve face (A), stem (B) and keeper/collet groove (C) for wear and damage

11   Clean all of the valve springs, keepers, retainers and spring seats with solvent and dry them thoroughly. Do the parts from one valve at a time so that no mixing of parts between valves occurs.

12   Scrape off any deposits that may have formed on the valve, then use a motorized wire brush to remove deposits from the valve heads and stems. Again, make sure the valves do not get mixed up.

Inspection

Refer to illustrations 12.14, 12.15, 12.16a, 12.16b, 12.17, 12.18a, 12.18b, 12.18c, 12.19a and 12.19b

13   Inspect the head very carefully for cracks and other damage. If cracks are found, a new head will be required. Check the cam bearing surfaces for wear and evidence of seizure. Check the camshafts and rocker arms for wear as well (see Section 9).

14   Using a precision straightedge and a feeler gauge, check the head gasket mating surface for warpage. Lay the straightedge length-wise, across the head and diagonally (corner-to-corner), intersecting the head bolt holes, and try to slip a 0.002 in (0.05 mm) feeler gauge under it, on either side of each combustion chamber **(see illustration)**. If the feeler gauge can be inserted between the head and the straight-edge, the head is warped and must either be machined or, if warpage is excessive, replaced with a new one.

15   Examine the valve seats in each of the combustion chambers. If they are pitted, cracked or burned, the head will require valve service that is beyond the scope of the home mechanic. Measure the valve seat width **(see illustration)** and compare it to this Chapter's Specifi-cations. If it is not within the specified range, or if it varies around its circumference, valve service work is required.

16   Clean the valve guides to remove any carbon buildup, then mea-sure the inside diameters of the guides (at both ends and the center of

the guide) with a small hole gauge and a 0-to-1-inch micrometer **(see illustrations)**. Record the measurements for future reference. These measurements, along with the valve stem diameter measurements, will enable you to compute the valve stem-to-guide clearance. This clear-ance, when compared to the Specifications, will be one factor that will determine the extent of the valve service work required. The guides are measured at the ends and at the center to determine if they are worn in a bell-mouth pattern (more wear at the ends). If they are, guide replacement is an absolute must.

17   Carefully inspect each valve face for cracks, pits and burned spots. Check the valve stem and the keeper groove area for cracks **(see illustration)**. Rotate the valve and check for any obvious indica-tion that it is bent. Check the end of the stem for pitting and excessive wear and make sure the bevel is the specified width. The presence of any of the above conditions indicates the need for valve servicing.

18   Measure the valve stem diameter **(see illustration)**. By subtract-ing the stem diameter from the valve guide diameter, the valve stem-to-guide clearance is obtained. If the stem-to-guide clearance is greater than listed in this Chapter's Specifications, the guides and valves will have to be replaced with new ones. Also check the valve stem for bending. Set the valve in a V-block with a dial indicator touch-ing the middle of the stem **(see illustration)**. Rotate the valve and note the reading on the gauge. If the stem runout exceeds the value listed in this Chapter's Specifications, replace the valve **(see illustration)**.

19   Check the end of each valve spring for wear and pitting. Measure the free length **(see illustration)** and compare it to this Chapter's Specifications. Any springs that are shorter than specified have sagged and should not be reused. Stand the spring on a flat surface and check it for squareness **(see illustration)**.

20   Check the spring retainers and keepers for obvious wear and

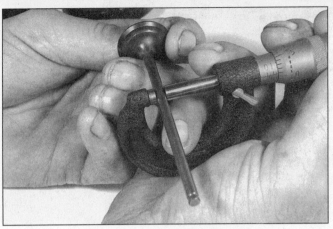

12.18a Measuring valve stem diameter

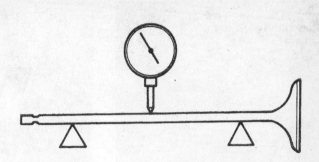

12.18b Check the valve stem for bends with a V-block (or V-blocks, as shown here) and a dial indicator

12.18c Measuring valve head margin thickness

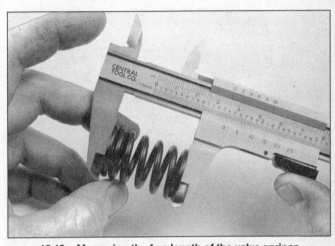

12.19a Measuring the free length of the valve springs

2

cracks. Any questionable parts should not be reused, as extensive damage will occur in the event of failure during engine operation.
21   If the inspection indicates that no service work is required, the valve components can be reinstalled in the head.

Reassembly

Refer to illustrations 12.23, 12.24a, 12.24b, 12.26 and 12.27
22   Before installing the valves in the head, they should be lapped to ensure a positive seal between the valves and seats. This procedure requires fine valve lapping compound (available at auto parts stores)

and a valve lapping tool. If a lapping tool is not available, a piece of rubber or plastic hose can be slipped over the valve stem (after the valve has been installed in the guide) and used to turn the valve.
23   Apply a small amount of fine lapping compound to the valve face **(see illustration)**, then slip the valve into the guide. **Note:** *Make sure the valve is installed in the correct guide and be careful not to get any lapping compound on the valve stem.*
24   Attach the lapping tool (or hose) to the valve and rotate the tool between the palms of your hands. Use a back-and-forth motion rather than a circular motion **(see illustration)**. Lift the valve off the seat and

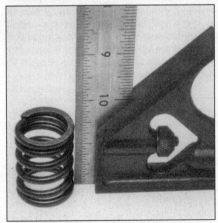

12.19b Checking the valve springs for squareness

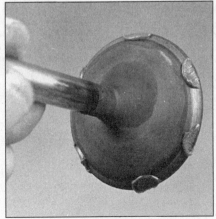

12.23 Apply the lapping compound very sparingly, in small dabs, to the valve face only

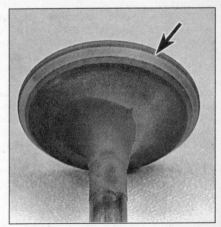

12.24a After lapping, the valve face should exhibit a uniform, unbroken contact pattern (arrow) . . .

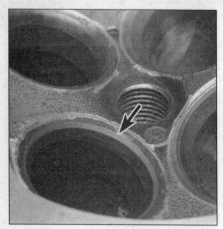

12.24b . . . and the seat should be the specified width (arrow) with a smooth, unbroken appearance

12.26 Using the wooden handle of a hammer, an extension and a small socket of the correct diameter, gently tap the new valve guide seals onto the guides

12.27 A small dab of grease will help hold the keepers/collets in place on the valve while the spring compressor is released

13.3a To pry the cylinder block loose from the crankcase, insert the prybar between an engine mounting bolt boss on the crankcase and a boss for the lower water pipe mounting bolt as shown; do NOT attempt to insert any prying tool into the gap between the gasket mating surfaces of the block and the crankcase

13.3b If the cylinder block is stuck, use a rubber mallet to knock it loose

turn it at regular intervals to distribute the lapping compound properly. Continue the lapping procedure until the valve face and seat contact area is of uniform width and unbroken around the entire circumference of the valve face and seat **(see illustrations)**.

25   Carefully remove the valve from the guide and wipe off all traces of lapping compound. Use solvent to clean the valve and wipe the seat area thoroughly with a solvent soaked cloth. Repeat the procedure for the remaining valves.

26   Lay the spring seats in place in the cylinder head, then install new valve stem seals on each of the guides **(see illustration)**. Use an appropriate size deep socket to push the seals into place until they are properly seated. Don't twist or cock them, or they will not seal properly against the valve stems. Also, don't remove them again or they will be damaged.

27   Coat the valve stems with assembly lube or moly-based grease, then install one of them into its guide. Next, install the springs and retainers, compress the springs and install the keepers. **Note:** *Install the springs with the tightly wound coils at the bottom (next to the spring seat). When compressing the springs with the valve spring compressor, depress them only as far as is absolutely necessary to slip the keepers into place. Apply a small amount of grease to the keepers* **(see illustration)** *to help hold them in place as the pressure is released from*

the springs. Make certain that the keepers are securely locked in their retaining grooves.

28   Support the cylinder head on blocks so the valves can't contact the workbench top, then very gently tap each of the valve stems with a soft-faced hammer. This will help seat the keepers in their grooves.

29   Once all of the valves have been installed in the head, check for proper valve sealing by pouring a small amount of solvent into each of the valve ports. If the solvent leaks past the valve(s) into the combustion chamber area, disassemble the valve(s) and repeat the lapping procedure, then reinstall the valve(s) and repeat the check. Repeat the procedure until a satisfactory seal is obtained.

13 Cylinder block - removal, inspection and installation

Removal

Refer to illustrations 13.3a, 13.3b, 13.3c, 13.4 and 13.5

1   On E models, remove the engine. On all models, remove the valve cover (see Section 7), the camshaft chain tensioner (see Section 8), the camshafts (see Section 9) and the cylinder head (see Section 10). Make sure the crankshaft is positioned at Top Dead Center (TDC) for cylinders 1 and 4.

2   Remove the lower water pipe from the cylinder block (see Chapter 3).

13.3c To remove the cylinder block, lift it straight up off the pistons

13.4 To remove the front chain guide, pull it straight up

3   Pry the cylinder block loose as shown **(see illustration)**. Do NOT try to insert the prybar between the gasket mating surfaces of the block and the crankcase. If it's stuck, tap around its perimeter with a soft-faced hammer **(see illustration)**. Lift the cylinder block straight up to remove it **(see illustration)**.

4   Lift out the camshaft chain front guide **(see illustration)**.

5   Remove the dowel pins from the mating surface of the crankcase **(see illustration)**. Be careful not to let these drop into the engine. Stuff rags around the pistons and remove the gasket and all traces of old gasket material from the surfaces of the cylinder block and the cylinder head.

Inspection

Refer to illustration 13.7

Caution: *Don't attempt to separate the liners from the cylinder block.*

6   Check the cylinder walls carefully for scratches and score marks.

7   Using the appropriate precision measuring tools, check each cylinder's diameter at the specified distances from the top of the cylinder, parallel to the crankshaft axis **(see illustration)**. Next, measure each cylinder's diameter at the same two locations across the crankshaft axis. Compare the results to this Chapter's Specifications. If the cylinder walls are tapered, out-of-round, worn beyond the specified limits, or badly scuffed or scored, have them rebored and honed by a dealer service department or a motorcycle repair shop. If a rebore is

done, oversize pistons and rings will be required as well. **Note:** *Kawasaki supplies pistons in only one oversize - +0.5 mm (+0.020 inch).*

8   As an alternative, if the precision measuring tools are not available, a dealer service department or motorcycle repair shop will make the measurements and offer advice concerning servicing of the cylinders. If they are in reasonably good condition and not worn to the outside of the limits, and if the piston-to-cylinder clearances can be maintained properly (see Section 14), then the cylinders do not have to be rebored; honing is all that is necessary.

9   To perform the honing operation you will need the proper size flexible hone with fine stones, or a "bottle brush" type hone, plenty of light oil or honing oil, some shop towels and an electric drill motor. Hold the cylinder block in a vise (cushioned with soft jaws or wood blocks) when performing the honing operation. Mount the hone in the drill motor, compress the stones and slip the hone into the cylinder. Lubricate the cylinder thoroughly, turn on the drill and move the hone up and down in the cylinder at a pace which will produce a fine crosshatch pattern on the cylinder wall with the crosshatch lines intersecting at approximately a 60-degree angle. Be sure to use plenty of lubricant and do not take off any more material than is absolutely necessary to produce the desired effect. Do not withdraw the hone from the cylinder while it is running. Instead, shut off the drill and continue moving the hone up and down in the cylinder until it comes to a complete stop, then compress the stones and withdraw the hone. Wipe the oil out of

13.5 Remove the positioning dowels from the crankcase (if you leave them installed while the cylinder block is removed, they could fall into the crankcase

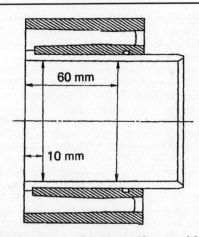

13.7 Measure the cylinder diameter at 10 mm and 60 mm from the top of the cylinder, in front-to-rear and side-to-side directions

13.12 Use pieces of wire to hold the pistons in position

13.13 Install the new base gasket with the "UP" to the left of the cam chain tunnel

Wipe the oil out of the cylinder and repeat the procedure on the remaining cylinder. Remember, do not remove too much material from the cylinder wall. If you do not have the tools, or do not desire to perform the honing operation, a dealer service department or motorcycle repair shop will generally do it for a reasonable fee.

10   Next, the cylinders must be thoroughly washed with warm soapy water to remove all traces of the abrasive grit produced during the honing operation. Be sure to run a brush through the bolt holes and flush them with running water. After rinsing, dry the cylinders thoroughly and apply a coat of light, rust-preventative oil to all machined surfaces.

Installation

Refer to illustrations 13.12, 13.13 and 13.14

11   Lubricate the cylinder bores with plenty of clean engine oil. Apply a thin film of moly-based grease to the piston skirts.

12   Slowly rotate the crankshaft until all of the pistons are at the same level. Slide lengths of welding rod or pieces of a straightened-out coat hanger under the pistons, on both sides of the connecting rods **(see illustration)**. This will help keep the pistons level as the cylinder block is lowered onto them.

13   Install the dowel pins, then lower a new cylinder base gasket over the studs, with the UP mark on the left-hand side of the engine **(see illustration)**.

14   Attach four piston ring compressors to the pistons and compress the piston rings **(see illustration)**. Large hose clamps can be used instead - just make sure they don't scratch the pistons, and don't tighten them too much.

15   Install the cylinder block over the studs and carefully lower it down until the piston crowns fit into the cylinder liners. While doing this, pull the camshaft chain up, using a hooked tool or a piece of coat hanger. Push down on the cylinder block, making sure the pistons don't get cocked sideways, until the bottom of the cylinder liners slide down past the piston rings. A wood or plastic hammer handle can be used to gently tap the block down, but don't use too much force or the pistons will be damaged.

16   Remove the piston ring compressors or hose clamps, being careful not to scratch the pistons. Remove the rods from under the pistons.

17   Install the cam chain front guide (see Section 27).

18   Install the cylinder head (see Section 10), the camshafts (see Section 9), the camshaft chain tensioner (see Section 8) and the valve cover (see Section 7).

19   On E models, install the engine (see Section 5).

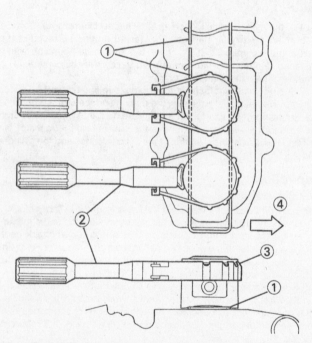

13.14 To install the cylinder block, squeeze the piston rings with four piston ring compressors

1   Piston base (Kawasaki tool no. 57001-1336)
2   Piston ring compressor assembly (Kawasaki tool no. 57001-1094)
3   Chamfer on piston base tool faces up
4   Front of engine (tools must be installed from rear)

14 Pistons - removal, inspection and installation

1   The pistons are attached to the connecting rods with piston pins that are a slip fit in the pistons and rods.

2   Before removing the pistons from the rods, stuff a clean shop towel into each crankcase hole, around the connecting rods. This will prevent the circlips from falling into the crankcase if they are inadvertently dropped.

Removal

Refer to illustrations 14.3a, 14.3b, 14.3c, 14.4a and 14.4b

3   Using a sharp scribe, scratch the number of each piston into its

14.3a Scribe or mark the number of each piston into the piston crown

14.3b Pry the piston pin circlip loose with a small screwdriver

14.3c Pull out the piston pin circlip with a pair of needle-nose pliers

14.4a Working from the opposite side of the piston, push the piston pin through far enough to grasp it and pull it out of the piston

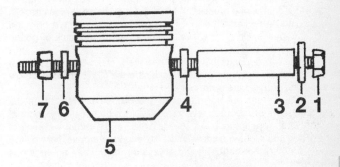

14.4b The piston pins should come out with hand pressure - if they don't, this removal tool can be fabricated from readily available parts

1 Bolt	7 Nut (B)
2 Washer	8 Large enough for piston
3 Pipe (A)	pin to fit inside
4 Padding (A)	9 Small enough to fit
5 Piston	through piston pin bore
6 Washer (B)	

2

crown **(see illustration)**. Each piston should also have an arrow pointing toward the front of the engine. If not, scribe an arrow into the piston crown before removal. Support the first piston and pry out the circlip with a small screwdriver **(see illustration)**. Grasp the circlip with needle-nose pliers and remove it from the groove **(see illustration)**.

4   Push out the piston pin far enough to get a hold of it and pull it out of the piston **(see illustration)**. If the pin won't come out, use a special piston pin removal tool (Kawasaki tool no. 57001-910) **(see illustration)**. You may have to deburr the area around the groove to enable the pin to slide out (use a triangular file for this procedure). Repeat the procedure for the remaining pistons.

Inspection

Refer to illustrations 14.6, 14.11, 14.13, 14.14 and 14.15

5   Before the inspection process can be carried out, the pistons must be cleaned and the old piston rings removed.

6   Using a piston ring installation tool, carefully remove the rings from the pistons **(see illustration)**. Do not nick or gouge the pistons in the process.

7   Scrape all traces of carbon from the tops of the pistons. A hand-held wire brush or a piece of fine emery cloth can be used once the majority of the deposits have been scraped away. Do not, under any circumstances, use a wire brush mounted in a drill motor to remove deposits from the pistons; the piston material is soft and will be eroded away by the wire brush.

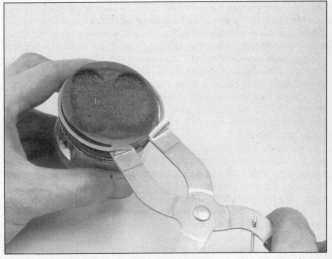

14.6 Remove the piston rings with a ring removal and installation tool

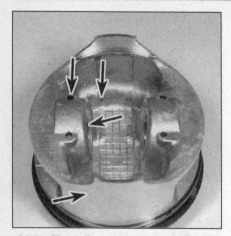

14.11 Check the piston pin bore and the skirt for wear, and make sure the oil holes are clear (arrows)

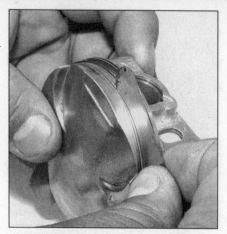

14.13 Measure the piston ring-to-groove clearance with a feeler gauge

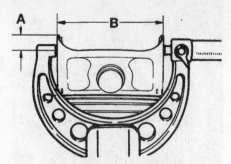

14.14 Measure the piston diameter with a micrometer

1   *5 mm (13/64-inch) from bottom of piston*
2   *Piston diameter*

8   Use a piston ring groove cleaning tool to remove any carbon deposits from the ring grooves. If a tool is not available, a piece broken off the old ring will do the job. Be very careful to remove only the carbon deposits. Do not remove any metal and do not nick or gouge the sides of the ring grooves.

9   Once the deposits have been removed, clean the pistons with solvent and dry them thoroughly. Make sure the oil return holes below the oil ring grooves are clear.

10   If the pistons are not damaged or worn excessively and if the cylinders are not rebored, new pistons will not be necessary. Normal piston wear appears as even, vertical wear on the thrust surfaces of the piston and slight looseness of the top ring in its groove. New piston rings, on the other hand, should always be used when an engine is rebuilt.

11   Carefully inspect each piston for cracks around the skirt, at the pin bosses and at the ring lands **(see illustration)**.

12   Look for scoring and scuffing on the thrust faces of the skirt, holes in the piston crown and burned areas at the edge of the crown. If the skirt is scored or scuffed, the engine may have been suffering from overheating and/or abnormal combustion, which caused excessively high operating temperatures. The oil pump and cooling system should be checked thoroughly. A hole in the piston crown, an extreme to be sure, is an indication that abnormal combustion (pre-ignition) was occurring. Burned areas at the edge of the piston crown are usually evidence of spark knock (detonation). If any of the above problems exist, the causes must be corrected or the damage will occur again.

13   Measure the piston ring-to-groove clearance by laying a new piston ring in the ring groove and slipping a feeler gauge in beside it **(see illustration)**. Check the clearance at three or four locations around the groove. Be sure to use the correct ring for each groove; they are different. If the clearance is greater then specified, new pistons will have to be used when the engine is reassembled.

14   Check the piston-to-bore clearance by measuring the bore (see Section 13) and the piston diameter. Make sure that the pistons and cylinders are correctly matched. Measure the piston across the skirt on the thrust faces at a 90-degree angle to the piston pin, about 1/2-inch (13 mm) up from the bottom of the skirt **(see illustration)**. Subtract the piston diameter from the bore diameter to obtain the clearance. If it is greater than specified, the cylinders will have to be rebored and new oversized pistons and rings installed. If the appropriate precision measuring tools are not available, the piston-to-cylinder clearances can be obtained, though not quite as accurately, using feeler gauge stock. Feeler gauge stock comes in 12-inch lengths and various thicknesses and is generally available at auto parts stores. To check the clearance, select a 0.07 mm (0.002 inch) feeler gauge and slip it into the cylinder along with the appropriate piston. The cylinder should be upside down and the piston must be positioned exactly as it normally would be. Place the feeler gauge between the piston and

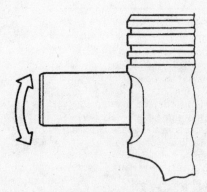

14.15 Slip the pin into the piston and try to wiggle it back-and-forth; if it's loose, replace the piston and the pin

cylinder on one of the thrust faces (90-degrees to the piston pin bore). The piston should slip through the cylinder (with the feeler gauge in place) with moderate pressure. If it falls through, or slides through easily, the clearance is excessive and a new piston will be required. If the piston binds at the lower end of the cylinder and is loose toward the top, the cylinder is tapered, and if tight spots are encountered as the piston/feeler gauge is rotated in the cylinder, the cylinder is out-of-round. Repeat the procedure for the remaining pistons and cylinders. Be sure to have the cylinders and pistons checked by a dealer service department or a motorcycle repair shop to confirm your findings before purchasing new parts.

15   Apply clean engine oil to the pin, insert it into the piston and check for freeplay by rocking the pin back-and-forth **(see illustration)**. If the pin is loose, new pistons and possibly new pins must be installed.

16   Refer to Section 15 and install the rings on the pistons.

Installation

Note: *Install the pistons for cylinders 2 and 3 first.*

17   Install the pistons in their original locations with the arrows pointing to the front of the engine. Lubricate the pins and the rod bores with clean engine oil. Install new circlips in the grooves in the inner sides of the pistons (don't reuse the old circlips). Push the pins into position from the opposite side and install new circlips. Compress the circlips only enough for them to fit in the piston. Make sure the clips are properly seated in the grooves.

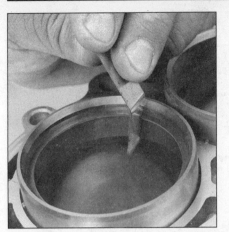

15.3 Measure the piston ring end gap with a feeler gauge

15.5 If the end of the gap is too small, clamp a file in a vise and file the ring ends (from the outside in only) to enlarge the gap slightly

15.9a When installing the oil ring expander, make sure the ends don't overlap

15 Piston rings - installation

Refer to illustrations 15.3, 15.5, 15.9a, 15.9b, 15.11a, 15.11b and 15.14

1   Before installing the new piston rings, the ring end gaps must be checked.

2   Lay out the pistons and the new ring sets so the rings will be matched with the same piston and cylinder during the end gap measurement procedure and engine assembly.

3   Insert the top (No. 1) ring into the bottom of the first cylinder and square it up with the cylinder walls by pushing it in with the top of the piston. The ring should be about one inch above the bottom edge of the cylinder. To measure the end gap, slip a feeler gauge between the ends of the ring **(see illustration)** and compare the measurement to the Specifications.

4   If the gap is larger or smaller than specified, double check to make sure that you have the correct rings before proceeding.

5   If the gap is too small, it must be enlarged or the ring ends may come in contact with each other during engine operation, which can cause serious damage. The end gap can be increased by filing the ring ends very carefully with a fine file **(see illustration)**. When performing this operation, file only from the outside in.

6   Excess end gap is not critical unless it is greater than 0.040 in (1 mm). Again, double check to make sure you have the correct rings for your engine.

7   Repeat the procedure for each ring that will be installed in the first cylinder and for each ring in the remaining cylinder. Remember to keep the rings, pistons and cylinders matched up.

8   Once the ring end gaps have been checked/corrected, the rings can be installed on the pistons.

9   The oil control ring (lowest on the piston) is installed first. It is composed of three separate components. Slip the expander into the groove, then install the upper side rail **(see illustrations)**. Do not use a piston ring installation tool on the oil ring side rails as they may be damaged. Instead, place one end of the side rail into the groove between the spacer expander and the ring land. Hold it firmly in place and slide a finger around the piston while pushing the rail into the groove. Next, install the lower side rail in the same manner.

10   After the three oil ring components have been installed, check to make sure that both the upper and lower side rails can be turned smoothly in the ring groove.

11   Install the no. 2 (middle) ring in the middle groove on the piston **(see illustration)**. Make sure that the "R" identification mark is facing up **(see illustration)**. And don't mix up the top and middle rings. They can be readily distinguished by their different cross-section shapes. Finally, don't expand the ring any more than is necessary to slide it into place.

12   Install the no. 1 (top) ring in the same manner. Again, make sure the identifying mark is facing up.

15.9b Do NOT use a ring installation tool to install the oil ring side rails

15.11a Install the second (middle) ring into the middle groove in the piston

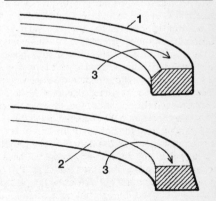

15.11b Don't confuse the top ring with the second (middle) ring

1   Top ring
2   Middle (second) ring
3   "R" identification mark

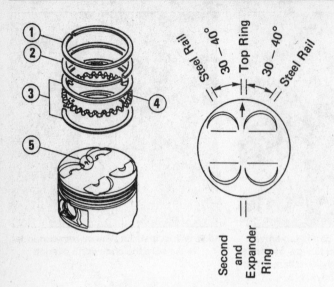

15.14 Ring gap positioning details

1   *Top ring*
2   *Second (middle ring)*
3   *Oil ring side rails*
4   *Oil ring expander*
5   *Arrowhead mark (must point toward front of engine)*

13   Repeat the procedure for the remaining piston and rings. Be very careful not to confuse the no. 1 and no. 2 rings.
14   Once the rings have been properly installed, stagger the end gaps, including those of the oil ring side rails **(see illustration)**.

16   Oil pan - removal and installation

Removal

Refer to illustration 16.5
Note: *The oil pan can be removed with the engine in the frame.*

16.7a Inspect the screen on the oil pick-up tube for signs of engine damage (these pieces of "casting flash" and gasket material look worse than they are; they're fairly typical on a relatively new engine such as the one shown here); if you find little chunks of gear teeth or bearing material on the pick-up tube screen on an older engine, it's overhaul time

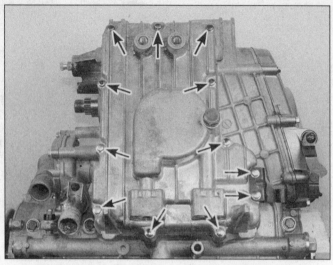

16.5 To remove the oil pan, remove these bolts (arrows)

1   Set the bike on its centerstand.
2   Drain the engine oil (see Chapter 1).
3   Remove the exhaust system (see Chapter 4).
4   Remove the banjo bolts that attach the oil cooler lines to the oil pan (see Chapter 3).
5   Remove the oil pan bolts **(see illustration)** and detach the pan from the crankcase.
6   Remove all traces of old gasket material from the mating surfaces of the oil pan and crankcase.

Installation

Refer to illustrations 16.7a, 16.7b and 16.7c
7   Inspect the screen on the oil pick-up tube **(see illustration)**. The presence of chunks of metal could indicate serious wear or damage in the bottom end or gearbox. Inspect the O-rings on the pick-up tube and the oil pipe **(see illustrations)**. If they're cracked, torn or deteriorated, replace them. Be sure to wash the screen before installing the pick-up.
8   Position a new gasket on the oil pan. A thin film of RTV sealant can be used to hold the gasket in place. Install the oil pan and bolts, tightening the bolts to the torque listed in this Chapter's Specifications, using a criss-cross pattern.

16.7b To remove the oil pick-up tube, simply pull it straight off. Inspect the O-ring (arrow) for cracks, tears or deterioration; if it's damaged, replace it

16.7c To remove the oil pipe, simply pull it straight off. Inspect the O-rings (arrows) for cracks, tears or deterioration; if they're damaged, replace them

17.2 To check the oil pressure, remove the bolt from the right end of the main oil passage, attach an oil pressure gauge and start the engine - note the oil pressure as the engine rpm goes up and down

17.9 Remove the oil pump gear snap-ring

17.10 Remove the oil pump gear

17.11 Remove the oil pump gear drive pin

17.12 To remove the oil pump cover, remove these three screws (arrows)

9   The remainder of installation is the reverse of removal. Install a new filter and fill the crankcase with oil (see Chapter 1), then run the engine and check for leaks.

17 Oil pump - pressure check, removal, inspection and installation

Check

Refer to illustration 17.2

Warning: *If the oil passage plug is removed when the engine is hot, hot oil will drain out - wait until the engine is cold before beginning this check (it must be cold to perform the relief valve opening pressure check, anyway).*

Note: *The oil pump can be removed with the engine in the frame.*

1   Remove the lower fairing (see Chapter 8).
2   Remove the plug at the bottom of the crankcase on the right-hand side and hook up Kawasaki's oil pressure gauge and adapter (tool nos. 57001-164 and 57001-1278, respectively) or a suitable equivalent gauge and adapter **(see illustration)**.
3   Start the engine and watch the gauge while varying the engine rpm. The pressure should stay within the relief valve opening pressure

listed in this Chapter's Specifications. If the pressure is too high, a relief valve is stuck closed. To check it, see Section 18.
4   If the pressure is lower than the standard, either a relief valve is stuck open, the oil pump is faulty, or there is other engine damage. Begin diagnosis by checking the relief valves (see Section 18), then the oil pump (see below). If those items check out okay, chances are the bearing oil clearances are excessive and the engine needs to be overhauled.
5   If the pressure reading is in the desired range, allow the engine to warm up to normal operating temperature and check the pressure again, at the specified engine rpm. Compare your findings with this Chapter's Specifications.
6   If the pressure is significantly lower than specified, check the relief valve and the oil pump.

Removal

Refer to illustrations 17.9, 17.10, 17.11, 17.12, 17.13, 17.14a and 17.14b

7   Place the bike on its centerstand.
8   Remove the clutch cover and clutch assembly (see Section 20).
9   Remove the oil pump gear snap-ring **(see illustration)**.
10   Remove the oil pump gear **(see illustration)**.
11   Remove the oil pump gear roll pin **(see illustration)**.
12   Remove the oil pump cover **(see illustration)**.

2

17.13 Remove the oil pump outer rotors (A) and the oil pump housing (B)

17.14a Remove the oil pump shaft (A) and inner rotors (B); don't lose the dowel pins (C)

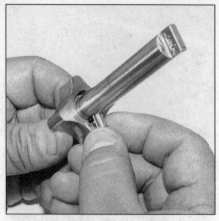

17.14b Don't lose this pin that locks the inner rotors to the shaft; when installing the shaft, make sure this pin is horizontal so that it doesn't fall out

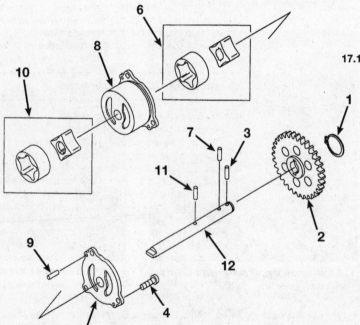

17.16 An exploded view of the oil pump assembly

1   Snap-ring
2   Gear (hub must face in during reassembly)
3   Roll pin for gear
4   Oil pump cover retaining screw (2)
5   Oil pump cover
6   Outer rotors
7   Roll pin for outer rotors
8   Oil pump housing
9   Dowel pin (2) for oil pump housing and cover
10 Inner rotors
11 Roll pin for inner rotors
12 Shaft

13   Remove the oil pump outer rotors and the oil pump housing **(see illustration)**.
14   Remove the oil pump shaft, inner rotors and the roll pin **(see illustrations)**.

Inspection

15   Wash all the components in solvent, then dry them off. Check the pump cover, housing, rotors and shaft for scoring and wear. Kawasaki doesn't publish clearance specifications, so if any damage or uneven or excessive wear is evident, replace the pump. If you're rebuilding the engine, it's a good idea to install a new oil pump anyway. Finally, if you see any sign of wear, be sure to remove the oil pan (see Section 16) and make sure the pick-up screen isn't clogged **(see illustration 16.7a)**.

Installation

Refer to illustration 17.16
16   Installation is basically the reverse of removal **(see illustration)**. However, there are a few things that must be done a certain way:

a) *Don't forget to install the roll pin before installing the inner rotors. When installing the shaft and inner rotors, the roll pin must be horizontal, or it will fall out (if the inner rotor roll pin is horizontal, the outer roll pin will also be horizontal - they're in the same plane).*
b) *When installing the inner rotors and shaft, the projection on the end of the shaft must engage the notch in the water pump shaft (see Chapter 3).*
c) *Don't forget to install the roll pin for the outer rotors before installing the pump cover.*
d) *Before installing the pump cover, pack the cavities between the rotors with petroleum jelly to ensure that the pump develops suction quickly and begins oil circulation as soon as the engine is started.*
e) *Tighten the pump cover screws securely.*
f) *When installing the pump gear, the gear hub must face in (toward the engine). And don't forget the gear drive pin!*
g) *If the pump gear circlip has lost its tensile "memory" (its ability to spring back to its original shape), replace it. Using a weak circlip could cause serious damage to the engine if the gear comes off.*

18.2a The oil pressure relief valve (arrow) for the oil cooler and transmission is screwed into the oil pan

18.2b The oil pressure relief valve (arrow) for the main oil passage is screwed into the crank web

18 Oil pressure relief valves - removal, inspection and installation

Removal

Refer to illustrations 18.2a and 18.2b

1 Remove the oil pan (see Section 16).

2 There are two oil pressure relief valves: The valve screwed into the pan **(see illustration)** is for the oil cooler and transmission; the valve screwed into the crank web **(see illustration)** is for the main oil passage. Both of these valves are normally trouble-free; their only function is to prevent excessive oil pressure (which can cause seals to leak) in the event an oil passage becomes clogged. However, if you're installing a new oil pan, or planning to soak the engine bottom end or pan in some sort of cleaning solution, the relief valve(s) must be removed. When installing either relief valve, be sure to coat the threads with a non-locking thread agent and tighten it to the torque listed in this Chapter's Specifications.

Inspection

3 Clean the valve with solvent and dry it, using compressed air if available.

4 Using a wood or plastic tool, depress the steel ball inside the valve and see if it moves smoothly. Make sure it returns to its seat completely. If it doesn't, replace it with a new one (don't attempt to disassemble and repair it).

Installation

5 Apply a non-hardening thread locking compound to the threads of the valve, install it into the crank web or oil pan, and tighten it to the torque listed in this Chapter's Specifications.

6 The remainder of installation is the reverse of removal.

19 Clutch cable - replacement

Refer to illustrations 19.5, 19.6 and 19.7

1 Place the bike on its centerstand.

2 Remove the lower fairing (see Chapter 8).

3 To put some slack in the cable, pull back the dust boot and fully loosen the adjuster nuts at the bracket just in front of the clutch lever on the right side of the engine **(see illustration 10.4 in Chapter 1)**.

4 To put some more slack in the cable, loosen the knurled lock wheel at the clutch lever on the handlebar **(see illustration 10.6 in Chapter 1)** and turn the threaded adjuster all the way in until it stops.

5 Align the slots in both the lock wheel and the adjuster so that they're both facing forward and pull out the cable **(see illustration)**.

6 To disconnect the clutch cable from the clutch lever, align the cable with the slot in the bottom of the lever and disengage the cable end from the lever **(see illustration)**.

7 Release the other end of the cable from the release lever **(see illustration)**.

19.5 To put some slack in the clutch cable, back off the knurled lock wheel and turn the adjuster in as far as it will go; then align the slots in the lock wheel and adjuster as shown, so that they're both facing forward and pull out the cable

19.6 To disconnect the clutch cable from the clutch lever, pull it out of the slot in the front of the lever, then slide the cable end out of the lever

19.7 To disconnect the clutch cable from the release lever, push the lever forward and disengage the cable end from the slot in the lever

20.4 To remove the clutch cover, remove these bolts (arrows)

20.5 Remove the bolts and springs (arrows) from the clutch spring plate, then remove the spring plate and pushrod (center arrow)

20.6 Remove the clutch friction and steel plates

20.7a Hold the clutch hub with a clutch holder tool (Kawasaki tool no. 57001-1243, or an equivalent tool such as the one being used here) and break the clutch hub nut loose

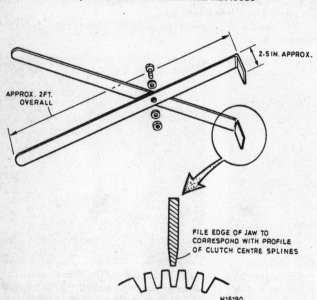

20.7b Homemade version of the Kawasaki clutch holding tool

8   Before removing the cable from the bike, tape the lower end of the new cable to the upper end of the old cable. Slowly pull the lower end of the old cable out, guiding the new cable down into position. Using this method will ensure the cable is routed correctly.
9   Lubricate the cable (see Chapter 1).
10   Installation is the reverse of removal.
11   Adjust the cable (see Chapter 1).

20 Clutch - removal, inspection and installation

Note: The clutch can be removed with the engine in the frame. Refer to illustrations 20.4, 20.5, 20.6, 20.7a, 20.7b, 20.7c, 20.7d, 20.8a through 20.8g

Removal

1   Set the bike on its centerstand. Remove the lower fairing (see Chapter 8).
2   Drain the engine oil (see Chapter 1).
3   Completely loosen the rear adjustment nuts on the clutch cable at its bracket on the clutch cover. Pull the cable out of the bracket, then detach the cable end from the lever (see Section 19).
4   Remove the clutch cover bolts **(see illustration)** and take off the cover. If the cover is stuck, tap around its perimeter with a soft-face hammer.
5   Remove the clutch springs and bolts **(see illustration)**. To

20.7c An even easier-to-make clutch holding tool can be fabricated by drilling and bolting together an old steel plate and a friction plate

20.7d Make sure the bolts of your holding tool are long enough to serve as removal handles

20.8a Remove the thrust washer

20.8b Remove the clutch hub

20.8c Remove the large washer

20.8d To separate the sleeve from the housing, install a couple of bolts as shown, screw them in and pull it out

20.8e Remove the clutch housing

prevent the assembly from turning, thread one of the cover mounting bolts into the case and wedge a screwdriver between the bolt and the clutch housing. Remove the clutch spring plate, bearing and pushrod.

6   Remove the friction and steel plates from the clutch housing **(see illustration)**.

7   Remove the clutch hub nut, using a special holding tool (Kawasaki tool no. 57001-1243, or a suitable equivalent) to prevent the clutch housing from turning **(see illustration)**. An alternative to this tool can be fabricated from some steel strap, bent at the ends and bolted

together in the middle **(see illustration)**. Or, if you're planning to replace the clutch plates, drill holes in a friction plate and a steel plate and bolt them together as they would be installed **(see illustrations)**. Slip the bolted plates into their installed positions; the clutch hub will be locked to the clutch housing. Shift the transmission into a low gear and have an assistant apply and hold the rear brake. Unscrew the nut and remove it.

8   Remove the thrust washer, clutch hub, large washer, clutch housing, sleeve, large washer and small washer **(see illustrations)**.

20.8f Remove the large washer

20.8g Remove the small washer

20.9 Inspect the clutch hub splines (arrows) for wear and distortion

20.10 Measure the clutch spring free length

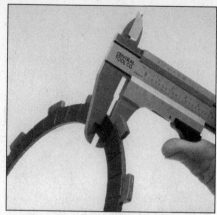

20.11 Measure the thickness of the friction plates

Inspection

Refer to illustrations 20.9, 20.10, 20.11, 20.12, 20.14 and 20.16

9   Examine the splines on both the inside and the outside of the clutch hub **(see illustration)**. If any wear is evident, replace the hub with a new one.

10   Measure the free length of the clutch springs **(see illustration)** and compare the results to this Chapter's Specifications. If the springs have sagged, or if cracks are noted, replace them with new ones as a set.

11   If the lining material of the friction plates smells burnt or if it is glazed, new parts are required. If the metal clutch plates are scored or discolored, they must be replaced with new ones. Measure the thickness of each friction plate **(see illustration)** and compare the results to this Chapter's Specifications. Replace with new parts any friction plates that are near the wear limit.

12   Lay the metal plates, one at a time, on a perfectly flat surface (such as a piece of plate glass) and check for warpage by trying to slip a 0.019-inch feeler gauge between the flat surface and the plate **(see illustration)**. Do this at several places around the plate's circumference. If the feeler gauge can be slipped under the plate, it is warped and should be replaced with a new one.

13   Check the tabs on the friction plates for excessive wear and mushroomed edges. They can be cleaned up with a file if the deformation is not severe.

14   Check the edges of the slots in the clutch housing for indentations made by the friction plate tabs **(see illustration)**. If the indentations are deep they can prevent clutch release, so the housing should be replaced with a new one. If the indentations can be removed easily with a file, the life of the housing can be prolonged to an extent. Also, check the primary gear teeth for cracks, chips and excessive wear. If the gear is worn or damaged, the clutch housing must be replaced with a new one. Check the bearing for score marks, scratches and excessive wear.

15   Check the bearing journal on the transmission mainshaft for score marks, heat discoloration and evidence of excessive wear. Check the clutch spring plate for wear and damage.

16   Clean all traces of old gasket material from the clutch cover. If the seal for the oil level window **(see illustration)** has been leaking, pry out the old seal and install a new one. If the release shaft seal has been leaking, pull out the release shaft, pry out the seal and drive in a new seal with a hammer and a small socket with an outside diameter slightly smaller than that of the seal. While the release shaft is removed, inspect the two small needle bearings that support the shaft at each end. It's unlikely that either of these bearings will ever need replacement; if either one is worn or damaged, take the cover to an automotive or motorcycle machine shop and have them pressed out and new ones installed. Finally, if you're planning to install a new cover, remove the noise damper from the old cover and install it on the new cover.

20.12 Check all plates for warpage by trying to slide a 0.3 mm (0.011-inch) feeler gauge between each plate and a flat surface - it shouldn't fit; if it does, replace the plate (0.2 mm, or 0.008-inch is acceptable)

20.14 Inspect the edges (arrows) of the slots in the clutch housing for signs of heavy wear; minor damage can be removed with a file. Also inspect the bushing surface (arrow) for wear

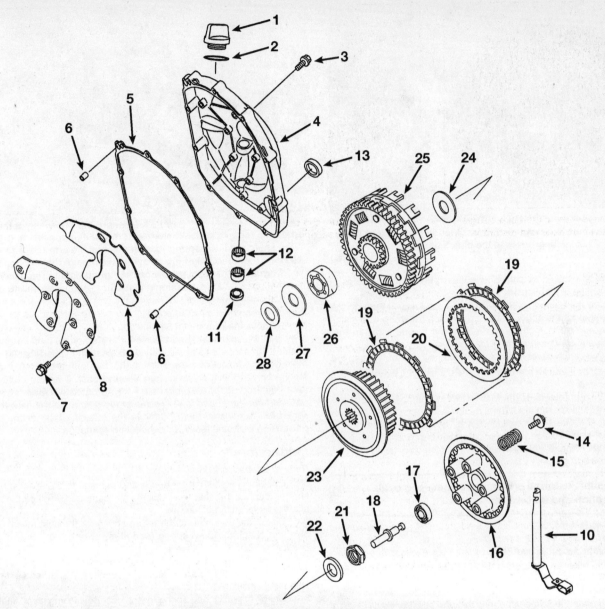

20.16 An exploded view of the clutch assembly

1	Oil filler cap	11	Clutch release shaft oil seal
2	O-ring	12	Clutch release shaft needle
3	Clutch cover bolt (10)		bearings (2)
4	Clutch cover	13	Oil level window seal
5	Clutch cover gasket	14	Spring bolt (5)
6	Clutch cover positioning dowels (2)	15	Spring (5)
7	Clutch noise damper bolt (9)	16	Spring plate
8	Clutch noise damper plate	17	Spring plate bearing
9	Clutch noise damper plate	18	Pushrod
10	Clutch release shaft	19	Friction plate

20	Steel plate
21	Clutch hub nut
22	Hub nut washer
23	Clutch hub
24	Large washer
25	Clutch housing
26	Sleeve
27	Large washer
28	Small washer

Installation

Refer to illustration 20.20

17 Installation is basically the reverse of removal **(see illustration 20.16)**, with the following points:

18 Be sure to lubricate all bearing and friction surfaces with engine oil to protect them when the engine is started for the first time after reassembly.

19 Use one of the holding techniques described in Step 7 to prevent the hub from turning while tightening the hub nut to the torque listed in this Chapter's Specifications.

20 Coat the clutch friction plates with engine oil and install the plates, starting with a friction plate and alternating them with steel plates. There are seven friction plates and six steel plates (Therefore, the last plate installed should also be a friction plate - if it isn't, you've got them out of sequence - check your work). Make sure the last

20.20 Make sure the tangs on the last friction plate fit into these special grooves in the clutch housing

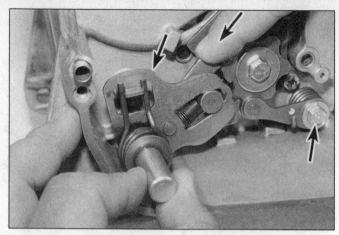

21.4a To remove the shift shaft/external shift mechanism, grasp the shaft, push the spring-loaded mechanism arm toward the shaft (in the direction of the arrow) to disengage the mechanism from the shift drum (arrow on the right points to the gear positioning lever) . . .

friction plate is installed as shown **(see illustration)**, with its tangs in the groove on the clutch housing.

21   Lubricate the pushrod with moly grease and install it through the spring plate. Mount the spring plate to the clutch assembly and install the springs and bolts, tightening them to the torque listed in this Chapter's Specifications in a criss-cross pattern.

22   Install the clutch cover and bolts, using a new gasket. Tighten the bolts, in a criss-cross pattern, to the torque listed in this Chapter's Specifications.

23   Connect the clutch cable to the release lever and adjust the freeplay (see Chapter 1).

24   Fill the crankcase with the recommended type and amount of engine oil (see Chapter 1).

25   Install the lower fairing (see Chapter 8).

21 Shift shaft/external shift mechanism - removal, inspection and installation

Removal

Refer to illustrations 21.4a and 21.4b

1   Set the bike on its centerstand. Drain the engine oil (see Chapter 1).

2   Turn the shift lever to the first-gear position and leave it there. **Note:** *Don't rotate the shift shaft during this procedure or you'll have to find first gear again before you can remove the shift shaft and external shift mechanism.* Remove the shift lever, engine sprocket cover and

the engine sprocket (see Chapter 7).

3   Remove the clutch (see Section 20).

4   With the shift shaft (and therefore the shift drum) in the first gear position, grasp the end of the shift shaft, push the spring-loaded shift mechanism arm toward the shift shaft, then pull the external shift mechanism and shift shaft out **(see illustrations)**. **Caution:** *Don't pull either shift rod out of the crankcase - the shift forks will fall into the oil pan, and the upper and lower halves of the crankcase will have to be separated to reinstall them.* Remove the retaining bolt for the gear positioning lever and remove the lever and spring.

Inspection

Refer to illustration 21.6

5   Check the shift shaft for bends and damage to the splines. If the shaft is bent or the shift lever splines are damaged, replace the shift shaft/external shift mechanism.

6   Check the condition of the return spring for the shift mechanism arm and check the pawl spring **(see illustration)**. If either spring is cracked or distorted, replace it.

7   Check the shift mechanism arm for cracks, distortion and wear. If any of these conditions are found, replace the shift shaft and external shift mechanism.

8   Check the collar and spring for the gear positioning lever. If either part is cracked or distorted, replace it.

9   Check the condition of the shift shaft seals and the oil level window seal in the clutch cover (see Section 20). If they have been

21.4b . . . and pull out the shift shaft and external shift mechanism

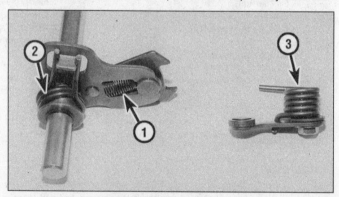

21.6 Check the condition of:

1   *The return spring for the shift mechanism arm*
2   *Pawl spring*
3   *Return spring for gear positioning lever*

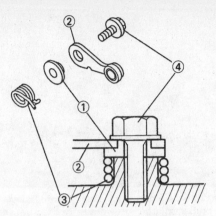

21.11 Installation details of the gear positioning lever assembly

1   *Flanged collar (installed flat against raised boss on case, with hub side projecting through lever)*
2   *Gear positioning lever*
3   *Return spring (installed over boss, between case and collar; both ends of spring face to the rear, inner end flat against case projection, outer end hooked around outer face of lever)*
4   *Retaining bolt*

leaking, drive them out with a hammer and punch. New seals can be installed by driving them in with a socket.

Installation

Refer to illustration 21.11

10   Slide the external shift mechanism into place, push in the shift mechanism arm to clear the shift drum and push the shift shaft all the way through the case until the splined end comes out the other side. Make sure the shift mechanism arm and pawl springs are positioned correctly.

11   Install the gear positioning lever return spring, collar, lever and bolt **(see illustration)**. Make sure the spring is positioned correctly.

12   Install the clutch and clutch cover (see Section 20).

13   Install the engine sprocket and chain, engine sprocket cover and the shift lever (see Chapter 7).

14   Add engine oil (see Chapter 1).

22 Crankcase - disassembly and reassembly

1   To examine and repair or replace the crankshaft, connecting rods, bearings, and/or transmission components, the engine must be removed (see Section 5) and the crankcase must be split into two parts.

2   If the crankcase is being separated to remove the crankshaft, remove the cylinder head, cylinder block and pistons (see Sections 10, 13 and 14).

3   Before splitting the cases, remove the following components:

   a) *Coolant hoses, pipes and water pump (see Chapter 3).*
   b) *Alternator cover and alternator rotor (see Chapter 9).* **Note:** *The cover has to come off for everything, but the alternator rotor can remain installed on the crankshaft if you're only servicing the transmission.*
   c) *Starter motor, starter idler gear and starter clutch (see Chapter 9).* **Note:** *The starter clutch must come off if you're servicing the crankshaft, but can remain on the crank if you're only servicing the transmission.*
   d) *Timing rotor and pick-up coil (see Chapter 5).* **Note:** *The timing rotor must come off if you're servicing the crank, but can remain on the crank if you're only servicing the transmission.*
   e) *Clutch cover and clutch (see Section 20).* **Note:** *The cover has to come off for everything, but the clutch can remain on the transmission input shaft if you're only servicing the crankshaft.*

22.4a Lower crankcase bolts (arrows); remove the 6 mm bolts (the ones along the front) first

22.4b Don't forget these three bolts (arrows) inside the engine

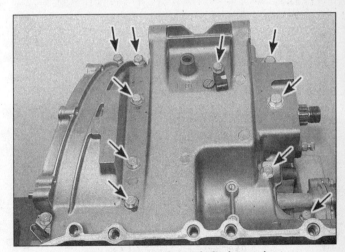

22.4c Upper crankcase bolts (arrows)

   f) *Shift shaft/external shift mechanism (see Section 21).*
   g) *Oil filter (see Chapter 1), oil pan and oil pump (see Sections 16 and 17).*
   h) *Cam chain guides (see Section 27).*

Disassembly

Refer to illustrations 22.4a, 22.4b, 22.4c, 22.5a and 22.5b

4   Remove the lower crankcase bolts (6 mm bolts first), then remove the upper crankcase bolts **(see illustrations)**.

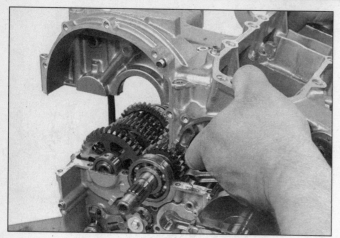

22.5a Separate the crankcase halves

22.5b If the crankcase halves are stuck together, lever them apart with a prybar or large screwdriver inserted between any convenient bosses or projections, but DO NOT pry between the gasket mating surfaces of the crankcase halves or you might damage their sealing ability

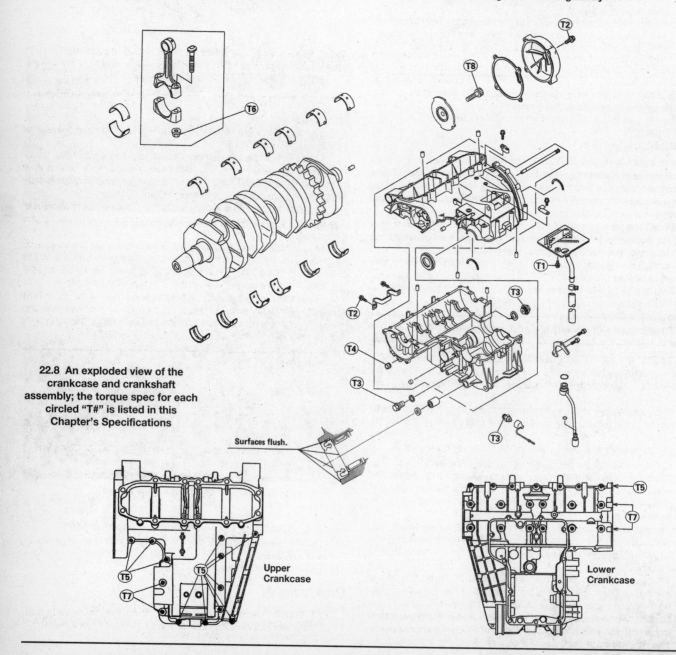

22.8 An exploded view of the crankcase and crankshaft assembly; the torque spec for each circled "T#" is listed in this Chapter's Specifications

Surfaces flush.

Upper Crankcase

Lower Crankcase

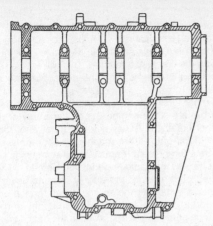

22.10 Apply Kawasaki Bond liquid gasket (part no. 92104-1003) or a similar substance to the shaded areas of the gasket mating surfaces

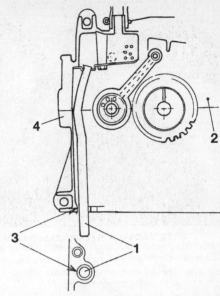

22.12 Make sure the oil return hose (1) is routed properly through the upper crankcase half (2) and through its hole (3) in the lower crankcase half (4)

5   Separate the crankcase halves (**see illustration**). If they're stuck, carefully pry the case halves apart by inserting a prybar between suitable bosses or projections (**see illustration**). **Caution:** *Do NOT try to stick a prybar between the gasket mating surfaces of the case halves or you will damage their sealing ability.*

6   Remove the crankshaft (see Section 25), shift drum and forks (see Section 29) and transmission shafts (see Section 28).

Reassembly

Refer to illustrations 22.8, 22.10, 22.12, 22.13, 22.15 and 22.17

7   Remove all traces of sealant from the crankcase mating surfaces. Be careful not to let any old sealant fall into the case.

8   Make sure the four dowel pins are in place in their holes in the mating surfaces of the crankcase halves - two in the upper half, two in the lower half (**see illustration**).

9   Pour some engine oil over the transmission gears, the crankshaft main bearings and the shift drum. Don't get any oil on the crankcase mating surface.

10   Apply a thin, even bead of Kawasaki Bond liquid gasket (part no. 92104-1003) to the indicated areas of the crankcase mating surfaces (**see illustration**). Also apply RTV sealant to the areas near the ends of the crankshaft seal areas (lay it over the Kawasaki Bond). **Caution:** *Don't apply an excessive amount of either type of sealant, as it will ooze out when the case halves are assembled and may obstruct oil passages.*

11   Check the position of the shift drum - make sure it's in the neutral position (see Section 29).

12   Carefully place the upper crankcase half onto the lower crankcase half. While doing this, make sure the shift forks fit into their gear grooves, and the oil return hose is properly routed through its hole in the lower crankcase half (**see illustration**).

13   Install the bolts in the lower crankcase half (**see illustration**) and tighten them so they are just snug. The two longer 8 mm bolts go into the number 1 and number 3 holes.

14   In two steps, tighten the larger (8 mm) bolts, in the sequence embossed on the case (also indicated in **illustration 22.13**) to the torque listed in this Chapter's Specifications. Then tighten the smaller (6 mm) bolts to the torque listed in this Chapter's Specifications.

15   Turn the case over and install the upper crankcase half bolts (**see illustration**) until they're all snug. Then tighten them evenly and gradually, in a criss-cross pattern, to the torque listed in this Chapter's Specifications.

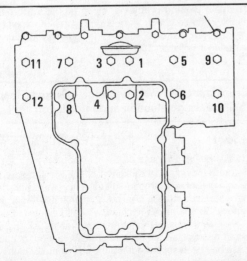

22.13 Bolt tightening sequence for bolts in lower crankcase half (do the larger 8 mm bolts first, then the smaller 6 mm bolts)

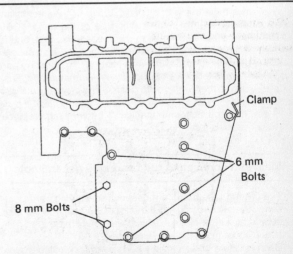

22.15 Tighten the bolts for the upper crankcase half evenly and gradually in a criss-cross pattern to the specified torque

22.17 Install the new output shaft seal with a large socket with an outer diameter slightly smaller than the outside diameter of the seal - drive it in so its face is flush with the surface of the case halves

16 Turn the main drive shaft and the output shaft to make sure they turn freely. Install the shift lever on the shift shaft and, while turning the output shaft, shift the transmission through the gears, first through sixth, then back to first. If the transmission doesn't shift properly, the case will have to be separated again to correct the problem. Also make sure the crankshaft turns freely.

17 Apply high temperature grease to the lips of the output shaft oil seal, press the seal into its bore in the crankcase until the face of the seal is flush with the case halves **(see illustration)**.

18 The remainder of installation is the reverse of removal.

23 Crankcase components - inspection and servicing

1 After the crankcases have been separated and the crankshaft, shift drum and forks and transmission components removed, the crankcases should be cleaned thoroughly with new solvent and dried with compressed air. All oil passages should be blown out with compressed air and all traces of old gasket sealant should be removed from the mating surfaces. **Caution:** *Be very careful not to nick or gouge the crankcase mating surfaces or leaks will result. Check both crankcase sections very carefully for cracks and other damage.*

2 Check the ball and needle bearings in the case. If they don't turn smoothly, drive them out with a bearing driver or a socket having an outside diameter slightly smaller than that of the bearing. Before installing them, allow them to sit in the freezer overnight, and about fifteen-minutes before installation, place the case half in an oven, set to about 200-degrees F, and allow it to heat up. The bearings are an interference fit, and this will ease installation. **Warning:** *Before heating the case, wash it thoroughly with soap and water so no explosive fumes are present. Also, don't use a flame to heat the case.*

3 If any damage is found that can't be repaired, replace the crankcase halves as a set.

24 Main and connecting rod bearings - general note

1 Even though main and connecting rod bearings are generally replaced with new ones during the engine overhaul, the old bearings should be retained for close examination as they may reveal valuable information about the condition of the engine.

2 Bearing failure occurs mainly because of lack of lubrication, the presence of dirt or other foreign particles, overloading the engine and/or corrosion. Regardless of the cause of bearing failure, it must be corrected before the engine is reassembled to prevent it from

happening again.

3 When examining the bearings, remove the main bearings from the case halves and the rod bearings from the connecting rods and caps and lay them out on a clean surface in the same general position as their location on the crankshaft journals. This will enable you to match any noted bearing problems with the corresponding side of the crankshaft journal.

4 Dirt and other foreign particles get into the engine in a variety of ways. It may be left in the engine during assembly or it may pass through filters or breathers. It may get into the oil and from there into the bearings. Metal chips from machining operations and normal engine wear are often present. Abrasives are sometimes left in engine components after reconditioning operations such as cylinder honing, especially when parts are not thoroughly cleaned using the proper cleaning methods. Whatever the source, these foreign objects often end up imbedded in the soft bearing material and are easily recognized. Large particles will not imbed in the bearing and will score or gouge the bearing and journal. The best prevention for this cause of bearing failure is to clean all parts thoroughly and keep everything spotlessly clean during engine reassembly. Frequent and regular oil and filter changes are also recommended.

5 Lack of lubrication or lubrication breakdown has a number of interrelated causes. Excessive heat (which thins the oil), overloading (which squeezes the oil from the bearing face) and oil leakage or throw off (from excessive bearing clearances, worn oil pump or high engine speeds) all contribute to lubrication breakdown. Blocked oil passages will also starve a bearing and destroy it. When lack of lubrication is the cause of bearing failure, the bearing material is wiped or extruded from the steel backing of the bearing. Temperatures may increase to the point where the steel backing and the journal turn blue from overheating.

6 Riding habits can have a definite effect on bearing life. Full throttle low speed operation, or lugging the engine, puts very high loads on bearings, which tend to squeeze out the oil film. These loads cause the bearings to flex, which produces fine cracks in the bearing face (fatigue failure). Eventually the bearing material will loosen in pieces and tear away from the steel backing. Short trip driving leads to corrosion of bearings, as insufficient engine heat is produced to drive off the condensed water and corrosive gases produced. These products collect in the engine oil, forming acid and sludge. As the oil is carried to the engine bearings, the acid attacks and corrodes the bearing material.

7 Incorrect bearing installation during engine assembly will lead to bearing failure as well. Tight fitting bearings which leave insufficient bearing oil clearances result in oil starvation. Dirt or foreign particles trapped behind a bearing insert result in high spots on the bearing which lead to failure.

8 To avoid bearing problems, clean all parts thoroughly before reassembly, double check all bearing clearance measurements and lubricate the new bearings with engine assembly lube or moly-based grease during installation.

25 Crankshaft and main bearings - removal, inspection, main bearing selection and installation

Removal

Refer to illustrations 25.1 and 25.2

1 Before removing the crankshaft check the endplay. This can be done with a dial indicator mounted in-line with the crankshaft, or feeler gauges inserted between the no. 2 crankcase main journal **(see illustration)**. Compare your findings with this Chapter's Specifications. If the endplay is excessive, the case halves must be replaced. Crankshaft removal is a simple matter of lifting it out of place once the crankcase has been separated and the starter motor clutch/secondary sprocket assembly has been removed.

2 The main bearing inserts can be removed from their saddles by pushing their centers to the side, then lifting them out **(see**

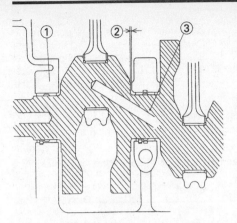

25.1 Crankshaft endplay measurement

1   *Crankcase*
2   *Measure here*
3   *No. 2 journal*

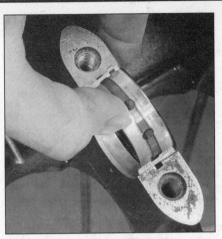

25.2 To remove a main bearing insert, push it sideways and lift it out

25.8 Lay the Plastigage strips (arrow) on the journals, parallel to the crankshaft centerline

illustration). Keep the bearing inserts in order. The main bearing oil clearance should be checked, however, before removing the inserts (see Step 8).

Inspection

3   Mark and remove the connecting rods from the crankshaft (see Section 26).
4   Clean the crankshaft with solvent, using a rifle-cleaning brush to scrub out the oil passages. If available, blow the crank dry with compressed air. Check the main and connecting rod journals for uneven wear, scoring and pits. Rub a penny across the journal several times - if a journal picks up copper from the penny, it's too rough. Replace the crankshaft.
5   Check the camshaft chain gear and the primary chain gear on the crankshaft for chipped teeth and other wear. If any undesirable conditions are found, replace the crankshaft. Check the chains as described in Section 27.
6   Check the rest of the crankshaft for cracks and other damage. It should be magnafluxed to reveal hidden cracks - a dealer service department or motorcycle machine shop will handle the procedure.
7   Set the crankshaft on V-blocks and check the runout with a dial indicator touching the center main journal, comparing your findings with this Chapter's Specifications. If the runout exceeds the limit, replace the crank.

Main bearing selection

Refer to illustrations 25.8, 25.10, 25.11, 25.13, 25.15, 25.16 and 25.17
8   To check the main bearing oil clearance, clean off the bearing

inserts (and reinstall them, if they've been removed from the case) and lower the crankshaft into the upper half of the case. Cut five pieces of Plastigage (type HPG-1) and lay them on the crankshaft main journals, parallel with journal axis (see illustration).
9   Very carefully, guide the lower case half down onto the upper case half. Install the large (8 mm) bolts and tighten them, using the recommended sequence, to the torque listed in this Chapter's Specifications (see Section 22). Don't rotate the crankshaft!
10   Now, remove the bolts and carefully lift the lower case half off. Compare the width of the crushed Plastigage on each journal to the scale printed on the Plastigage envelope to obtain the main bearing oil clearance (see illustration). Write down your findings, then remove all traces of Plastigage from the journals, using your fingernail or the edge of a credit card.
11   If the oil clearance falls into the specified range, no bearing replacement is required (provided they are in good shape). If the clearance is between 0.038 mm (0.0015 inch) and the 0.070 mm (0.0028 inch) service limit, and the bearings are excessively worn, replace the old bearing inserts with new inserts that have *blue* paint marks (see illustration), then check the oil clearance once again. Always replace all of the inserts at the same time.
12   If the bearings are not excessively worn, the clearance can slightly exceed the standard clearance, as long as it isn't greater than the maximum clearance or less than the minimum clearance.
13   If the clearance *is* greater than the service limit listed in this Chapter's Specifications, measure the diameter of the crankshaft journals with a micrometer (see illustration) and compare your findings with this Chapter's Specifications. Also, by measuring the

2

25.10 Measure the width of the crushed Plastigage (be sure to use the correct scale - standard and metric are included)

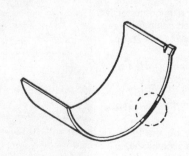

25.11 Location of the bearing insert color code

25.13 Measure the diameter of each crankshaft journal at several points to detect taper and out-of-round conditions

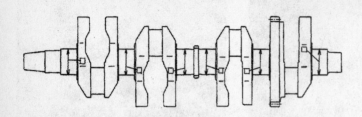

25.15 Crankshaft main journal size marking locations (#1 mark or no mark); use in conjunction with . . .

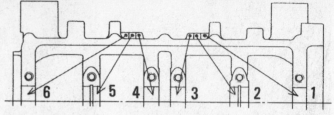

25.16 . . . crankcase markings to determine insert size

Main Bearing Insert Selection

Crankcase Main Bearing Bore Diameter Mark	Crankshaft Main Journal Diameter Mark	Crankshaft Bearing Insert*		
		Size Color	Part Number	Journal Nos.
O	1	Brown	13034-1016	1, 2, 5
			13034-1066	3, 4, 6
None	1	Black	13034-1017	1, 2, 5
O	None		13034-1065	3, 4, 6
None	None	Blue	13034-1018	1, 2, 5
			13034-1064	3, 4, 6

25.17 Main bearing insert size selection table

*The bearing inserts for Nos. 1, 2, and 5 journals have an oil groove, respectively.

diameter at a number of points around each journal's circumference, you'll be able to determine whether or not the journal is out-of-round. Take the measurement at each end of the journal, near the crank throws, to determine if the journal is tapered.

14   If any crank journal has worn down past the service limit, replace the crankshaft.

15   If the diameters of the journals aren't less than the service limit but differ from the original markings on the crankshaft **(see illustration)**, apply new marks with a hammer and punch.

a) *If the journal measures between 31.984 to 31.992 mm (1.2602 to 1.2605 inches) don't make any marks on the crank (there shouldn't be any marks there, anyway).*

b) *If the journal measures between 31.993 to 32.000 mm (1.2605 to 1.2608 inches), make a "1" mark on the crank in the area indicated (if it's not already there).*

16   Remove the main bearing inserts and assemble the case halves (see Section 22). Using a telescoping gauge and a micrometer, measure the diameters of the main bearing bores, then compare the measurements with the marks on the upper case half **(see illustration)**.

a) *If the bores measure between 36.000 to 36.008 mm (1.4184 to 1.4187-inches), there should be a "0" mark in the indicated areas.*

b) *If the bores measure between 36.009 to 36.016 mm (1.4187 to 1.4190-inches), there shouldn't be any marks in the indicated areas.*

17   Using the marks on the crank and the marks on the case, determine the bearing sizes required by referring to the accompanying bearing selection chart **(see illustration)**.

Installation

Refer to illustration 25.18

18   Separate the case halves once again. Clean the bearing saddles

in the case halves, then install the bearing inserts in their webs in the case **(see illustration)**. The bearing inserts for all except the two middle journals have oil grooves. When installing the bearings, use your hands only - don't tap them into place with a hammer.

19   Lubricate the bearing inserts with engine assembly lube or moly-based grease.

20   Install the connecting rods, if they were removed (see Section 26).

21   Loop the camshaft chain over the crankshaft sprocket.

22   Carefully lower the crankshaft into place.

23   Assemble the case halves (see Section 22) and make sure the crankshaft and the transmission shafts turn freely.

25.18 Make sure the tabs on the bearing inserts fit into the notches in the crank web

26.1 Check the connecting rod side clearance with a feeler gauge

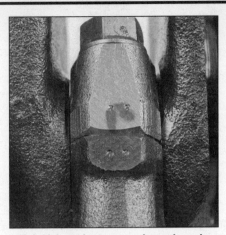

26.2 Using a hammer and punch, make matching cylinder number marks in the connecting rod and its cap

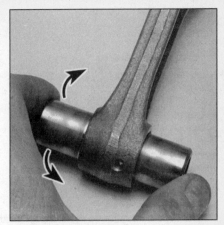

26.5 Check the piston pin and connecting rod bore for excessive wear by rocking the pin back-and-forth as shown

26 Connecting rods and bearings - removal, inspection, bearing selection and installation

Removal

Refer to illustrations 26.1 and 26.2

1   Before removing the connecting rods from the crankshaft, measure the side clearance of each rod with a feeler gauge **(see illustration)**. If the clearance on any rod is greater than that listed in this Chapter's Specifications, that rod will have to be replaced with a new one.

2   Using a center punch, mark the position of each rod and cap, relative to its position on the crankshaft **(see illustration)**.

3   Unscrew the bearing cap nuts, separate the cap from the rod, then detach the rod from the crankshaft. If the cap is stuck, tap on the ends of the rod bolts with a soft face hammer to free them.

4   Separate the bearing inserts from the rods and caps, keeping them in order so they can be reinstalled in their original locations. Wash the parts in solvent and dry them with compressed air, if available.

Inspection

Refer to illustration 26.5

5   Check the connecting rods for cracks and other obvious damage. Lubricate the piston pin for each rod, install it in the proper rod and check for play **(see illustration)**. If it is loose, replace the connecting rod and/or the pin.

6   Refer to Section 24 and examine the connecting rod bearing inserts. If they are scored, badly scuffed or appear to have been seized, new bearings must be installed. Always replace the bearings in the connecting rods as a set. If they are badly damaged, check the corresponding crankshaft journal. Evidence of extreme heat, such as discoloration, indicates that lubrication failure has occurred. Be sure to thoroughly check the oil pump and pressure relief valve as well as all oil holes and passages before reassembling the engine.

7   Have the rods checked for twist and bending at a dealer service department or other motorcycle repair shop.

Bearing selection

Refer to illustrations 26.18, 26.20a, 26.20b and 26.21

8   If the bearings and journals appear to be in good condition, check the oil clearances as follows:

9   Start with the rod for the number one cylinder. Wipe the bearing inserts and the connecting rod and cap clean, using a lint-free cloth.

10   Install the bearing inserts in the connecting rod and cap. Make sure the tab on the bearing engages with the notch in the rod or cap.

11   Wipe off the connecting rod journal with a lint-free cloth. Lay a strip of Plastigage (type HPG-1) across the top of the journal, parallel with the journal axis **(see illustration 25.8)**.

12   Position the connecting rod on the bottom of the journal, then install the rod cap and nuts. Tighten the nuts to the torque listed in this Chapter's Specifications, but don't allow the connecting rod to rotate at all.

13   Unscrew the nuts and remove the connecting rod and cap from the journal, being very careful not to disturb the Plastigage. Compare the width of the crushed Plastigage to the scale printed in the Plastigage envelope **(see illustration 25.10)** to determine the bearing oil clearance.

14   If the clearance is within the range listed in this Chapter's Specifications and the bearings are in perfect condition, they can be reused. If the clearance is between 0.059 mm (0.0023-inch) and the service limit 0.10 mm (0.0039-inch), replace the bearing inserts with inserts that have blue paint marks, then check the oil clearance once again. Always replace all of the inserts at the same time.

15   The clearance might be slightly greater than the standard clearance, but that doesn't matter, as long as it isn't greater than the maximum clearance or less than the minimum clearance.

16   If the clearance is greater than the service limit listed in this Chapter's Specifications, measure the diameter of the connecting rod journal with a micrometer and compare your findings with this Chapter's Specifications. Also, by measuring the diameter at a number of points around the journal's circumference, you'll be able to determine whether or not the journal is out-of-round. Take the measurement at each end of the journal to determine if the journal is tapered.

17   If any journal has worn down past the service limit, replace the crankshaft.

18   If the diameter of the journal isn't less than the service limit but differs from the original markings on the crankshaft **(see illustration)**, apply new marks with a hammer and punch.

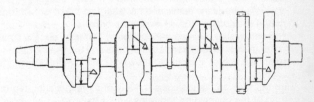

△ : Crankpin Diameter Marks, "O" mark or no mark

26.18 The marking locations (D) for the connecting rod journal sizes (either a "0" mark, or no mark); used in conjunction with . . .

2

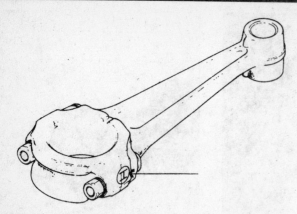

26.20a . . . the mark (or no mark) on the connecting rod (arrow) to determine insert size - the letter is a weight grade mark

a) *If the journal measures between 32.984 to 33.992 mm (1.2996 to 1.2999-inches), don't make any marks on the crank (there shouldn't be one there anyway).*

b) *If the journal measures between 32.993 to 33.000 mm (1.2999 to 1.3002-inches), make a "0" mark on the crank in the area indicated (if not already there).*

19 Remove the bearing inserts from the connecting rod and cap, then assemble the cap to the rod. Tighten the nuts to the torque listed in this Chapter's Specifications.

20 Using a telescoping gauge and a micrometer, measure the inside diameter of the connecting rod **(see illustration)**. The mark on the connecting rod (if any) should coincide with the measurement, but if it doesn't, make a new mark **(see illustration)**.

a) *If the inside diameter measures between 36.000 to 36.008 mm (1.4184 to 1.4187-inches), don't make any mark on the rod (there shouldn't be any there anyway).*

b) *If the inside diameter measures between 36.009 to 36.016 mm (1.4187 to 1.4190-inches), make a 0 mark on the rod (it should already be there).*

21 By referring to the accompanying chart **(see illustration)**, select the correct connecting rod bearing inserts.

22 Repeat the bearing selection procedure for the remaining connecting rods.

Installation

23 Wipe off the bearing inserts and connecting rods and caps. Install the inserts into the rods and caps, using your hands only, making sure the tabs on the inserts engage with the notches in the rods and caps. When all the inserts are installed, lubricate them with engine assembly lube or moly-based grease. Don't get any lubricant on the mating surfaces of the rod or cap.

24 Assemble each connecting rod to its proper journal, making sure the previously applied matchmarks correspond to each other. **Note:** *The letter present at the rod/cap seam on one side of the connecting rod is a weight mark. If new rods are being installed and they don't all have the same letter on them, two rods with the same letter should be installed on one side of the crank, and the letters on the other two rods should match each other. This will minimize vibration.*

25 When you're sure the rods are positioned correctly, apply a small amount of engine oil to the threads of the bolts and the seating surface of the nuts, then tighten the nuts to the torque listed in this Chapter's Specifications.

26 Turn the rods on the crankshaft. If any of them feel tight, tap on the bottom of the connecting rod caps with a hammer - this should relieve stress and free them up. If it doesn't, recheck the bearing clearance.

27 As a final step, recheck the connecting rod side clearances (see Step 1). If the clearances aren't correct, find out why before proceeding with engine assembly.

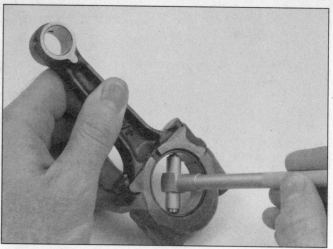

26.20b Measure the internal diameter of the connecting rod with a telescoping gauge, then measure the gauge with a micrometer

Big End Bearing Insert Selection

Con-Rod Big End Bore Diameter Marking	Crankpin Diameter Marking	Bearing Insert	
		Size Color	Part Number
None	O	Brown	13034-1069
None	None	Black	13034-1068
O	O		
O	None	Blue	13034-1067

26.21 Connecting rod bearing insert selection table

27 Camshaft chain and guides - removal, inspection and installation

Removal

Camshaft chain

1 Remove the engine (see Section 5).
2 Separate the crankcase halves (see Section 22).
3 Remove the crankshaft (see Section 25).
4 Remove the chains from the crankshaft.

Chain guides

Refer to illustration 27.6

5 The cam chain front guide can be lifted from the cylinder block after the head has been removed, or from the crankcase after the head and block have been removed **(see illustration 13.4)**.

6 The cam chain rear guide is fastened to the crankcase with a bracket and two bolts **(see illustration)**. Remove the bolts and detach the guide and bracket from the case.

Inspection

Camshaft chain

Refer to illustration 27.7

7 Pull the chain tight to eliminate all slack and measure the length of twenty links, pin-to-pin **(see illustration)**. Compare your findings to the length listed in this Chapter's Specifications.

8 Also check the chain for binding and obvious damage.

9 If the twenty-link length is not as specified, or there is visible damage, replace the chain.

27.6 To remove the rear cam chain guide, remove these two Allen bolts from the crank web

Chain guides

10 Check the guides for deep grooves, cracking and other obvious damage, replacing them if necessary.

Installation

Refer to illustration 27.11

11 Installation of the chain and guides is the reverse of removal. Make sure the "UP" mark on the front camshaft chain guide is at the top and facing forward **(see illustration)**. When installing the bracket for the cam chain rear guide, apply a non-hardening thread locking compound to the threads of the bolts. Tighten the bolts to the torque listed in this Chapter's Specifications. Apply engine oil to the faces of the guides and to the chains.

28 Transmission shafts - removal and installation

Removal

Refer to illustration 28.2

1 Remove the engine and clutch, then separate the case halves (see Sections 5, 20 and 22).

2 The shafts can simply be lifted out of the upper half of the case **(see illustration)**. If they are stuck, use a soft-face hammer and gently

28.2 Once the crankcase has been separated, the transmission shafts can be lifted out

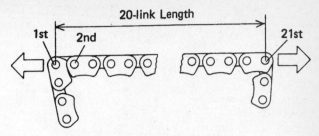

27.7 Cam chain stretch measurement

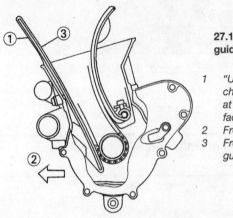

27.11 Cam chain guide installation details

1 "UP" mark on front chain guide at the top and facing forward
2 Front of the bike
3 Front cam chain guide

tap on the bearings on the ends of the shafts to free them. The shaft nearest the rear of the case is the output shaft - the other shaft is the main drive shaft.

3 Refer to Section 29 for information pertaining to the shift drum and forks and to Section 30 for information pertaining to transmission shaft service.

Installation

Refer to illustration 28.4

4 Check to make sure the set pins and rings are present in the upper case half, where the shaft bearings seat **(see illustration)**.

5 Carefully lower each shaft into place. The holes in the needle bearing outer races must engage with the set pins, and the grooves in the ball bearing outer races must engage with the set rings.

6 The remainder of installation is the reverse of removal.

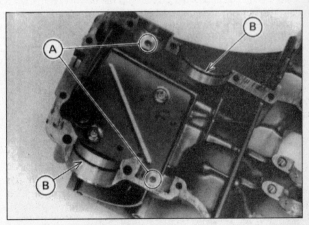

28.4 When installing the transmission shafts, make sure the shaft bearings are properly engaged with the set pins (A) and set rings (B), or the case halves will not bolt together; if you have trouble fitting the cases together, this is the most likely cause of the problem

29.2 To remove the shift drum assembly, remove the:

1	Shift drum retainer plate screws	3	Shift rod for output shaft
2	Shift drum retainer plate	4	Shift rod for input shaft
		5	Shift drum assembly

29 Shift drum and forks - removal, inspection and installation

Removal

Refer to illustrations 29.2, 29.3a, 29.3b and 29.4

1   Remove the engine, separate the crankcase halves and remove the external shift mechanism (see Sections 5, 21 and 22).

2   Remove the retaining plate for the shift drum and shift rods **(see illustration)**.

3   Support the shift forks and pull the shift rods out **(see illustration)**. The driveshaft shift forks and the shift rods are interchangeable, but it's a good idea to reassemble them as soon as they're removed from the engine so they can be returned to their original positions **(see illustration)**.

4   Slide the shift drum out of the crankcase **(see illustration)**.

Inspection

Refer to illustrations 29.5, 29.6 and 29.7

5   Check the edges of the grooves in the drum for signs of excessive wear **(see illustration)**. Measure the widths of the grooves and compare your findings to this Chapter's Specifications.

6   Put the shift drum in a bench vise and remove the drum cam bolt and disassemble the drum **(see illustration)**. Check the pin plate and pins for wear or damage and replace them as necessary. Spin the

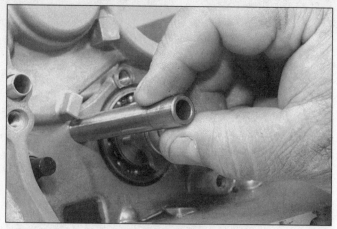

29.3a Remove the shift rods for the output shaft (shown) and the input shaft (not shown), . . .

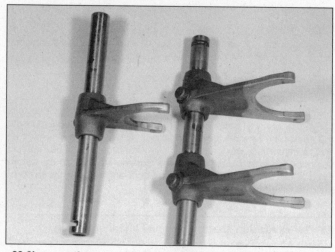

29.3b . . . and reassemble them so they can be returned to their original positions

bearing and check for roughness, noise or looseness. Replace the bearing if defects are found. To reassemble the shift drum, fit the spacer and the drum cam onto the shift drum so that the Woodruff key fits into the groove in the spacer and the cam.

7   Check the shift forks for distortion and wear, especially at the fork ears. Measure the thickness of the fork ears and compare your findings

29.4 Remove the shift drum assembly

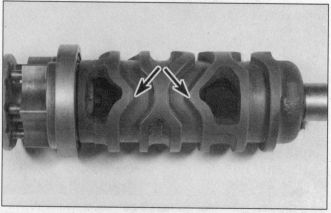

29.5 Inspect the edges of the fork grooves for wear, especially at their points (arrows)

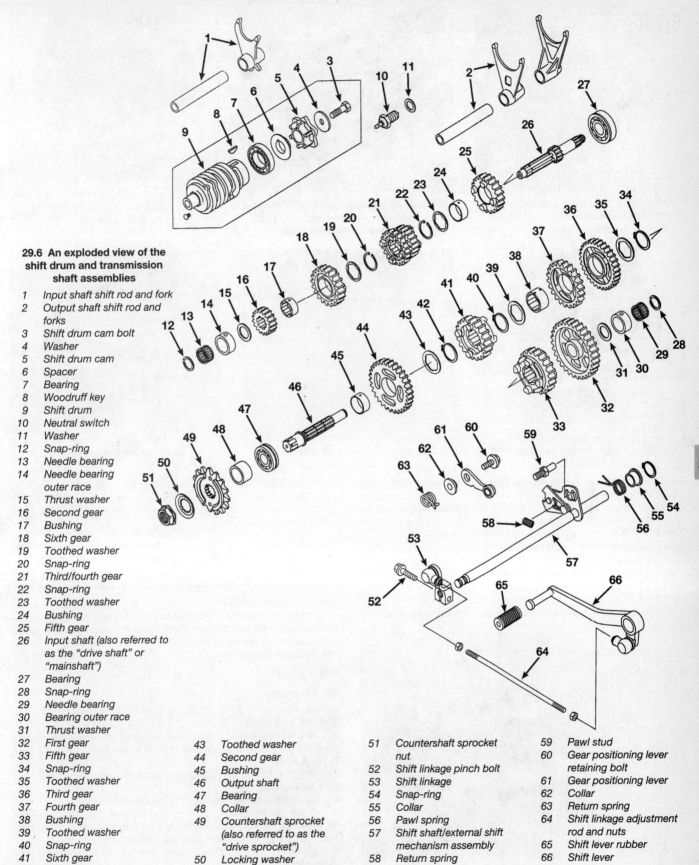

29.6 An exploded view of the shift drum and transmission shaft assemblies

1 Input shaft shift rod and fork
2 Output shaft shift rod and forks
3 Shift drum cam bolt
4 Washer
5 Shift drum cam
6 Spacer
7 Bearing
8 Woodruff key
9 Shift drum
10 Neutral switch
11 Washer
12 Snap-ring
13 Needle bearing
14 Needle bearing outer race
15 Thrust washer
16 Second gear
17 Bushing
18 Sixth gear
19 Toothed washer
20 Snap-ring
21 Third/fourth gear
22 Snap-ring
23 Toothed washer
24 Bushing
25 Fifth gear
26 Input shaft (also referred to as the "drive shaft" or "mainshaft")
27 Bearing
28 Snap-ring
29 Needle bearing
30 Bearing outer race
31 Thrust washer
32 First gear
33 Fifth gear
34 Snap-ring
35 Toothed washer
36 Third gear
37 Fourth gear
38 Bushing
39 Toothed washer
40 Snap-ring
41 Sixth gear
42 Snap-ring

43 Toothed washer
44 Second gear
45 Bushing
46 Output shaft
47 Bearing
48 Collar
49 Countershaft sprocket (also referred to as the "drive sprocket")
50 Locking washer

51 Countershaft sprocket nut
52 Shift linkage pinch bolt
53 Shift linkage
54 Snap-ring
55 Collar
56 Pawl spring
57 Shift shaft/external shift mechanism assembly
58 Return spring

59 Pawl stud
60 Gear positioning lever retaining bolt
61 Gear positioning lever
62 Collar
63 Return spring
64 Shift linkage adjustment rod and nuts
65 Shift lever rubber
66 Shift lever

2

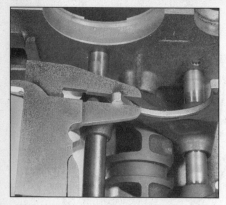

29.7 Measure the thickness of the shift fork ears and replace the shift forks if they're worn

30.1 Place the transmission parts in order on a rod; a large rubber band will keep them from being disturbed

30.2a Slide off the needle bearing outer race . . .

30.2b . . . then remove the snap-ring and bearing

30.3 Remove the thrust washer and second gear

30.4a Slide off sixth gear . . .

with this Chapter's Specifications **(see illustration)**. If they are discolored or severely worn they are probably bent. If damage or wear is evident, check the shift fork groove in the corresponding gear as well. Inspect the guide pins and the shaft bore for excessive wear and distortion and replace any defective parts with new ones.

8   Check the shift fork shafts for evidence of wear, galling and other damage. Make sure the shift forks move smoothly on the shafts. If the shafts are worn or bent, replace them with new ones.

Installation

9   Installation is the reverse of removal; note the following points:

30.4b . . . and its bushing

a) Lubricate all parts with engine oil before installing them.
b) Use non-permanent thread locking agent on the threads of the shift drum and shift rod retaining plate bolts. Tighten the bolts securely.

30 Transmission shafts - disassembly, inspection and reassembly

Refer to illustration 30.1

1   Remove the shafts from the case (see Section 28). **Note:** When disassembling the transmission shafts, place the parts on a long rod or thread a wire through them to keep them in order and facing the proper direction **(see illustration)**.

Mainshaft

Disassembly

Refer to illustrations 30.2a, 30.2b, 30.3, 30.4a, 30.4b, 30.5a, 30.5b, 30.6, 30.7a, 30.7b and 30.7c

2   Remove the needle bearing outer race, then remove the snap-ring from the end of the shaft and slide the needle bearing off **(see illustrations)**.
3   Remove the thrust washer and slide second gear off the shaft **(see illustration)**.
4   Remove sixth gear and bushing **(see illustrations)**.
5   Slide the toothed washer off and remove the snap-ring **(see illustration)**. To keep the snap-ring from bending as it's expanded, hold the back of it with pliers **(see illustration)**.
6   Remove the third/fourth gear cluster from the shaft **(see illustration)**.
7   Remove the next snap-ring, then slide the washer, fifth gear and its bushing off the shaft **(see illustrations)**.

30.5a Remove the toothed washer and snap-ring . . .

30.5b . . . holding the back of the snap-ring with pliers to prevent it from twisting

30.6 Slide the third/fourth gear off the shaft

30.7a Remove the snap-ring . . .

30.7b . . . the toothed washer and fifth gear . . .

30.7c . . . and its bushing

Inspection

Refer to illustrations 30.9 and 30.11

8   Wash all of the components in clean solvent and dry them off. Rotate the ball bearing on the shaft, feeling for tightness, rough spots, excessive looseness and listening for noises. If any of these conditions are found, replace the bearing. This will require the use of a hydraulic press or a bearing puller setup. If you don't have access to these tools, take the shaft and bearing to a Kawasaki dealer or other motorcycle repair shop and have them press the old bearing off the shaft and install the new one.

9   Measure the shift fork groove between third and fourth gears **(see illustration)**. If the groove width exceeds the figure listed in this Chapter's Specifications, replace the third/fourth gear assembly, and also check the third/fourth gear shift fork (see Section 29).

10   Check the gear teeth for cracking and other obvious damage. Check the bushing and surface in the inner diameter of the fifth and sixth gears for scoring or heat discoloration. If either one is damaged, replace it.

11   Inspect the dogs and the dog holes in the gears for excessive wear **(see illustration 30.9 and the accompanying illustration)**. Replace the paired gears as a set if necessary.

12   Check the needle bearing and race for wear or heat discoloration and replace them if necessary.

30.9 Measure the gear grooves; if they're too wide, replace the gear - also replace the gear if the dogs (arrows) are worn

30.11 Inspect the bushing (left arrow) in gears so equipped; replace the gear if it's worn - if the edges of the slots (right arrow) are rounded, replace the gear

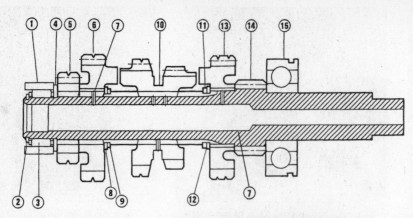

30.13a Mainshaft gear details

1	Needle bearing outer race
2	Snap-ring
3	Needle bearing
4	Thrust washer
5	2nd gear
6	6th gear
7	Bushing
8	Toothed washer
9	Snap-ring
10	3rd/4th gear
11	Snap-ring
12	Toothed washer
13	5th gear
14	1st gear
15	Ball bearing

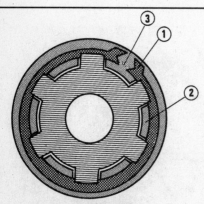

30.13b When installing snap-rings (1), align the opening (3) with a spline groove (2)

30.13c Be sure to align the bushing oil hole with the shaft oil hole (arrows)

30.14a Slide off the bearing outer race . . .

Reassembly

Refer to illustrations 30.13a, 30.13b and 30.13c

13 Reassembly is the basically the reverse of the disassembly procedure, but take note of the following points **(see illustration)**:

a) *Always use new snap-rings and align the opening of the ring with a spline groove* **(see illustration)**. *Face the sharp side of the snap-ring toward the gear being secured; the rounded side faces away from the gear.*

b) *When installing the gear bushings on the shaft, align the oil hole in the shaft with the oil hole in the bushing* **(see illustration)**.

c) *Lubricate the components with engine oil before assembling them.*

Driveshaft

Disassembly

Refer to illustrations 30.14a, 30.14b, 30.15, 30.16a, 30.16b, 30.17a through 30.17d, 30.18a, 30.18b, 30.18c, 30.19a, 30.19b, 30.19c and 30.20

14 Remove the needle bearing outer race and slide the needle bearing off **(see illustrations)**.

15 Remove the thrust washer and first gear from the shaft **(see illustration)**.

16 Remove fifth gear from the shaft. Fifth gear has three steel balls in it for the positive neutral finder mechanism. These lock fifth gear to the

30.14b . . . and the bearing

30.15 Remove the thrust washer (arrow) and first gear

30.16a Hold third gear (A) with one hand and spin the transmission shaft while lifting up on fifth gear (B); it may take several tries to disengage fifth gear from the shaft, but it will slide off easily once it is disengaged

30.16b These three balls ride in slots in the transmission shaft; they must be flung outward by centrifugal force before fifth gear can be removed

30.17a Remove the snap-ring . . .

30.17b . . . the toothed washer . . .

30.17c . . . third gear . . .

30.17d . . . its bushing and fourth gear

30.18a Remove the toothed washer . . .

30.18b . . . the snap-ring . . .

30.18c . . . and sixth gear

30.19a Remove the snap-ring . . .

30.19b . . . the toothed washer and second gear . . .

shaft unless it is spun rapidly enough to fling the balls outward. To remove fifth gear, grasp third gear and hold the shaft in a vertical position with one hand, and with the other hand, spin the shaft back and forth, holding onto fifth gear and pulling up (see illustration). **Caution:** *Don't pull the gear up too hard or fast - the balls will fly out of the gear. After fifth gear is removed, collect the three steel balls* (see illustration).

17   Remove the snap-ring, toothed washer, third gear, bushing and fourth gear from the shaft (see illustrations).

18   Remove the toothed washer, snap-ring and sixth gear (see illustrations).

19   Remove the next snap-ring, toothed washer, second gear and its bushing (see illustrations).

30.19c . . . and its bushing

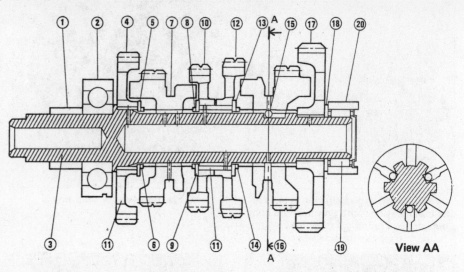

View AA

30.22 Driveshaft gear details

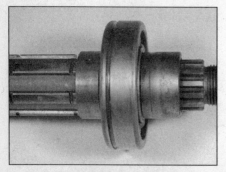

30.20 The bearing and collar can be left on the shaft unless they're worn or damaged

1	Collar	8	Snap-ring	15	Steel ball
2	Ball bearing	9	Toothed washer	16	5th gear
3	Driveshaft	10	4th gear	17	1st gear
4	2nd gear	11	Bushing	18	Thrust washer
5	Toothed washer	12	3rd gear	19	Needle bearing
6	Snap-ring	13	Toothed washer	20	Needle bearing outer
7	6th gear	14	Snap-ring		race

20   The ball bearing and collar can remain on the shaft unless they need to be replaced **(see illustration)**.

Inspection

21   Refer to Steps 8 through 12 for the inspection procedures. They are the same, except when checking the shift fork groove width you'll be checking it on fifth and sixth gears.

Reassembly

Refer to illustration 30.22

22   Reassembly is the basically the reverse of the disassembly procedure, but take note of the following points **(see illustration)**:
a) *Always use new snap-rings and align the opening of the ring with a spline groove* **(see illustration 30.13b)**. *Face the sharp side of each snap-ring toward the gear being secured; face the rounded side of snap-ring away from the gear.*
b) *When installing the bushing for third and fourth gear and second gear, align the oil hole in the bushing with the hole in the shaft.*
c) *When installing fifth gear, don't use grease to hold the balls in place - to do so would impair the positive neutral finder mechanism. Just set the balls in their holes (the holes that they can't pass through), keep the gear in a vertical position and carefully set it on the shaft (engine oil will help keep them in place). The spline grooves that contain the holes with the balls must be aligned with the slots in the shaft spline grooves. Lubricate the components with engine oil before assembling them.*

31   Initial start-up after overhaul

Note: *Make sure the cooling system is checked carefully (especially the coolant level) before starting and running the engine.*
1   Make sure the engine oil level is correct, then remove the spark plugs from the engine. Place the engine STOP switch in the Off position and unplug the primary (low tension) wires from the coil.
2   Turn on the key switch and crank the engine over with the starter

until the oil pressure indicator light goes off (which indicates that oil pressure exists). Reinstall the spark plugs, connect the wires and turn the switch to On.
3   Make sure there is fuel in the tank, then turn the fuel tap to the Prime position and operate the choke.
4   Start the engine and allow it to run at a moderately fast idle until it reaches operating temperature. **Warning:** *If the oil pressure indicator light doesn't go off, or it comes on while the engine is running, stop the engine immediately.*
5   Check carefully for oil leaks and make sure the transmission and controls, especially the brakes, function properly before road testing the machine. Refer to Section 32 for the recommended break-in procedure.
6   Upon completion of the road test, and after the engine has cooled down completely, recheck the valve clearances (see Chapter 1).

32   Recommended break-in procedure

1   Any rebuilt engine needs time to break-in, even if parts have been installed in their original locations. For this reason, treat the machine gently for the first few miles to make sure oil has circulated throughout the engine and any new parts installed have started to seat.
2   Even greater care is necessary if the engine has been rebored or a new crankshaft has been installed. In the case of a rebore, the engine will have to be broken in as if the machine were new. This means greater use of the transmission and a restraining hand on the throttle until at least 500 miles have been covered. There's no point in keeping to any set speed limit - the main idea is to keep from lugging the engine and to gradually increase performance until the 500 mile mark is reached. These recommendations can be lessened to an extent when only a new crankshaft is installed. Experience is the best guide, since it's easy to tell when an engine is running freely.
3   If a lubrication failure is suspected, stop the engine immediately and try to find the cause. If an engine is run without oil, even for a short period of time, irreparable damage will occur.

Chapter 3
Cooling system

Contents

3

Specifications

General

Coolant type	See Chapter 1
Mixture ratio	See Chapter 1
Radiator cap pressure rating	93 to 123 kPa (0.95 to 1.25 kg/cm², 14 to 18 psi)
Thermostatic fan switch rating	
Rising temperature	From Off to On at 96 to 100-degrees C (205 to 212-degrees F)
Falling temperature	From On to Off at 91 to 95-degrees C (196 to 203-degrees F)
Resistance	
On	Less than 0.5 ohms
Off	More than 1 M-ohm
Coolant temperature sensor resistance	
At 80-degrees C (176-degrees F)	47 to 57 ohms
At 100-degrees C (212-degrees F)	26 to 30 ohms

Thermostat rating

Valve opening temperature	80 to 84-degrees C (176 to 183-degrees F)
Valve fully open at	95-degrees C (203-degrees F)
Valve travel (when fully open)	Not less then 8 mm (5/16-inch)

Torque specifications

Thermostatic fan switch	18 Nm (156 in-lbs)
Coolant temperature sensor	7.8 Nm (69 in-lbs)
Oil cooler	
Hose-to-cooler banjo bolts	25 Nm (216 in-lbs)
Hose-to-engine flange bolts	12 Nm (104 in-lbs)

1   General information

Refer to illustration 1.1

The models covered by this manual are equipped with a liquid cooling system **(see illustration)** which utilizes a water/antifreeze mixture to carry away excess heat produced during the combustion process. The cylinders are surrounded by water jackets, through which the coolant is circulated by the water pump. The pump is mounted to the left side of the crankcase and is driven by a gear mounted on the secondary shaft. The coolant passes up through a flexible hose and a coolant pipe, which distributes the water around the four cylinders. It flows through the water passages in the cylinder head, through another pipe (or hoses) and into the thermostat housing. The hot coolant then flows down into the radiator (which is mounted on the frame downtubes to take advantage of maximum air flow), where it is cooled by the passing air, through another hose and back to the water

pump, where the cycle is repeated.

An electric fan, mounted behind the radiator and automatically controlled by a thermostatic switch, provides a flow of cooling air through the radiator when the motorcycle is not moving. Under certain conditions, the fan may come on even after the engine is stopped, and the ignition switch is off, and may run for several minutes.

The coolant temperature sending unit, threaded into the thermostat housing, senses the temperature of the coolant and controls the coolant temperature gauge on the instrument cluster.

The entire system is sealed and pressurized. The pressure is controlled by a valve which is part of the radiator cap. By pressurizing the coolant, the boiling point is raised, which prevents premature boiling of the coolant. An overflow hose, connected between the radiator and reservoir tank, directs coolant to the tank when the radiator cap valve is opened by excessive pressure. The coolant is automatically siphoned back to the radiator as the engine cools.

Many cooling system inspection and service procedures are

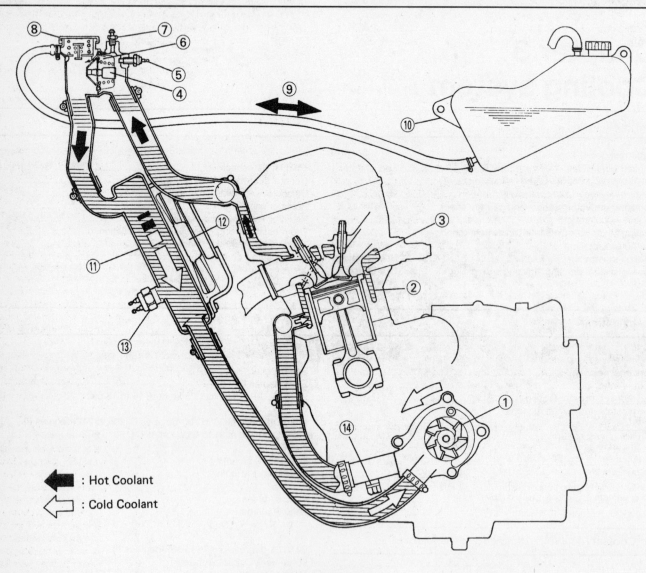

1.1 The cooling system

1	Water pump	6	Air bleeder hole	11	Radiator
2	Cylinder cooling jacket	7	Air bleeder bolt	12	Radiator fan
3	Cylinder head cooling passage	8	Radiator cap	13	Thermostatic fan switch
4	Thermostat	9	Reservoir-to-radiator cap hose	14	Drain bolt
5	Coolant temperature sensor	10	Reservoir tank		

➡ : Hot Coolant

⇨ : Cold Coolant

3.2 To detach the coolant reservoir from the frame, disconnect the two hoses (arrows), then remove the two retaining bolts (arrows)

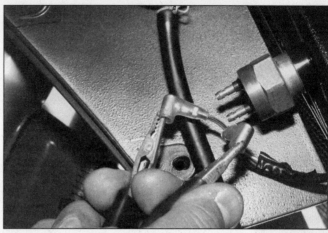

4.1 To check the fan motor, unplug the fan switch electrical leads and bridge them with a jumper wire; if the fan doesn't come on, check the motor, wiring and connectors

considered part of routine maintenance and are included in Chapter 1.

On later UK models, the coolant is also used to warm the carburetor bodies via an arrangement of small hoses. The coolant travels from the rear of the cylinder block, through a filter, through the carburetor castings and then rejoins the main cooling system at the water pump. A check valve is fitted above the water pump to ensure the correct flow of coolant.

Warning 1: *Do not allow antifreeze to come in contact with your skin or painted surfaces of the vehicle. Rinse off spills immediately with plenty of water. Antifreeze is highly toxic if ingested. Never leave antifreeze lying around in an open container or in puddles on the floor; children and pets are attracted by it's sweet smell and may drink it. Check with local authorities about disposing of used antifreeze. Many communities have collection centers which will see that antifreeze is disposed of safely.*

Warning 2: *Do not remove the radiator cap when the engine and radiator are hot. Scalding hot coolant and steam may be blown out under pressure, which could cause serious injury. To open the radiator cap, remove the rear screw from the right side panel on the inside of the fairing (if equipped). When the engine has cooled, lift up the panel and place a thick rag, like a towel, over the radiator cap; slowly rotate the cap counterclockwise to the first stop. This procedure allows any residual pressure to escape. When the steam has stopped escaping, press down on the cap while turning counterclockwise and remove it.*

2   Radiator cap - check

If problems such as overheating and loss of coolant occur, check the entire system as described in Chapter 1. The radiator cap opening pressure should be checked by a dealer service department or service station equipped with the special tester required to do the job. If the cap is defective, replace it with a new one.

3   Coolant reservoir - removal and installation

Refer to illustration 3.2

1   Remove the right side cover (see Chapter 8).
2   Disconnect the hoses from the reservoir **(see illustration)**. It's a good idea to mark the positions of the hoses so they aren't attached to the wrong fitting when the reservoir is installed.
3   Remove the reservoir retaining bolts and detach the reservoir from the frame.
4   Installation is the reverse of removal.

4   Cooling fan and thermostatic fan switch - check and replacement

Check

Refer to illustrations 4.1 and 4.3

1   If the engine is overheating and the cooling fan isn't coming on, remove the seat and check the (10A) fan fuse (see Chapter 9). If the fuse is blown, check the fan circuit for a short to ground (see the *Wiring diagrams* at the end of this book). If the fuse is good, remove the lower fairing (see Chapter 8) and unplug the electrical leads from the thermostatic fan switch. Using a jumper wire, connect these two leads **(see illustration)**. If the fan still doesn't come on, check the wiring, connectors and fan motor.
2   To check the motor, remove the fuel tank and trace the wiring harness from the fan motor to its electrical connector, located between the steering head and the cross brace and accessible from above (it's a two-wire black connector). Unplug the connector and, using two jumper wires connected to the battery terminals, apply battery voltage to the fan-side of the electrical connector. If the fan doesn't rotate, replace the fan motor. If it does rotate, the problem is either in the wiring, connectors or the thermostatic fan switch
3   To check the fan switch, remove the switch (see Step 10) and test it as shown **(see illustration)**. Note the temperature at which the

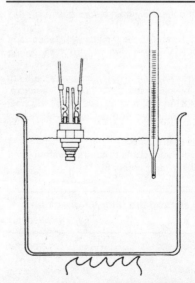

4.3 To check the fan switch, suspend it in water, connect an ohmmeter to the switch terminals, heat up the water and note the temperature at which the switch closes the circuit; compare your results to the switching temperature in this Chapter's Specifications

3

4.6 To detach the fan motor and mounting bracket assembly from the radiator, remove the three bolts (arrows); to separate the motor from its mounting bracket, remove the three screws (arrows)

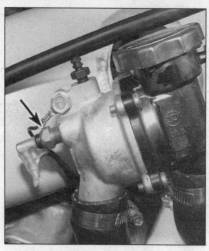

5.2 The coolant temperature sensor (arrow) is threaded into the thermostat housing on the right side of the frame

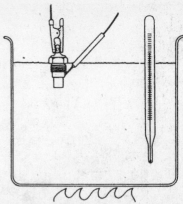

5.4 To determine if the coolant temperature sensor is operating properly, suspend the temperature sensing projection and the threaded portion of the sensor in a pot of water, measure the resistance of the sensor as the water heats up and compare your observations to the specified resistance listed in this Chapter's Specifications

switch closes the circuit and compare this to the temperature listed in this Chapter's Specifications. If the switch doesn't perform as described, replace it.

Replacement

Fan motor

Refer to illustration 4.6

Warning: *The engine must be completely cool before beginning this procedure.*

4   Disconnect the cable from the negative terminal of the battery.

5   Remove the radiator (see Section 8).

6   Remove the three bolts securing the fan bracket to the radiator **(see illustration)**. Separate the fan and bracket from the radiator.

7   Remove the screws that retain the fan blades to the fan motor shaft and remove the fan blade assembly from the motor.

8   Remove the screws that secure the fan motor to the bracket and detach the motor from the bracket.

9   Installation is the reverse of the removal procedure.

Thermostatic fan switch

Warning: *The engine must be completely cool before beginning this procedure.*

10   Prepare the new switch by wrapping the threads with Teflon tape or by coating the threads with RTV sealant. Remove the lower fairing (see Chapter 8).

11   Place a drain pan under the radiator and have some rags handy to soak up the coolant that will inevitably spill out. Unscrew the switch from the radiator **(see illustration 4.1)** and quickly install the new switch, tightening it to the torque listed in this Chapter's Specifications.

12   Plug in the electrical leads to the switch.

13   Check and, if necessary, add coolant to the system (see Chapter 1). Install the lower fairing (see Chapter 8).

---

5   Coolant temperature sensor and gauge - check and replacement

Check

Refer to illustrations 5.2 and 5.4

1   If the engine has been overheating but the coolant temperature

gauge hasn't been indicating a hotter than normal condition, begin with a check of the coolant level (see Chapter 1). If it's low, add the recommended type of coolant and be sure to locate the source of the leak.

2   Remove the seat and the fuel tank (see Chapter 4). Locate the coolant temperature sensor **(see illustration)**, which is screwed into the thermostat housing. Unplug the electrical connector from the sensor, turn the ignition key to the Run position (don't crank the engine over) and note the temperature gauge - it should read Cold.

3   With the ignition key still in the run position, connect one end of a jumper wire to the sending unit wire and ground the other end. The needle on the temperature gauge should swing over past the Hot mark. **Caution:** *Don't ground the wire any longer than necessary or the gauge may be damaged.*

4   If the gauge passes both of these tests, but doesn't operate correctly under normal riding conditions, the temperature sending unit is probably defective. To test the sensor, remove it, suspend the temperature sensing projection and threaded portion of the sensor in a pot of water **(see illustration)** and, using an ohmmeter, see if the sensor's resistance goes down as the temperature increases. Compare your results to the resistance values listed in this Chapter's Specifications. If the sensor doesn't perform as specified, replace it.

5   If the gauge doesn't respond to these two tests as described, either the wire to the gauge is bad or the gauge itself is defective.

Replacement

Coolant temperature sensor

Warning: *The engine must be completely cool before beginning this procedure.*

6   Prepare the new sending unit by wrapping the threads with Teflon tape or by coating the threads with RTV sealant.

7   Unscrew the sending unit from the thermostat housing and quickly install the new unit, tightening it to the torque listed in this Chapter's Specifications.

8   Reconnect the electrical connector to the sending unit. Check and, if necessary, add coolant to the system (see Chapter 1).

Coolant temperature gauge

9   Refer to Chapter 9 for the coolant temperature gauge replacement procedure.

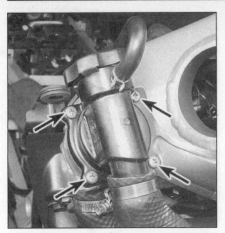

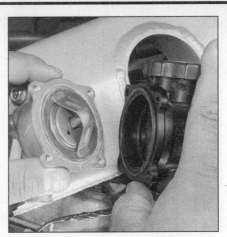

6.4 Remove the four screws (arrows) that attach the cover to the thermostat housing

6.5 Remove the thermostat cover

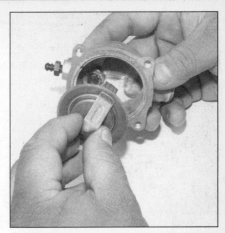

6.6a Remove the thermostat from the housing, noting how it's installed . . .

6   Thermostat - removal, check and installation

Removal

Refer to illustrations 6.4, 6.5, 6.6a and 6.6b

Warning: *The engine must be completely cool before beginning this procedure.*

1   If the thermostat is functioning properly, the coolant temperature gauge should rise to the normal operating temperature quickly and then stay there, only rising above the normal position occasionally when the engine gets unusually hot. If the engine does not reach normal operating temperature quickly, or if it overheats, the thermostat should be removed and checked, or replaced with a new one.

2   Drain the cooling system (see Chapter 1).

3   Remove the trim panel between the upper fairing and the right side of the fuel tank (see Chapter 8).

4   Remove the four screws that attach the cover to the thermostat housing **(see illustration)**.

5   Remove the thermostat cover **(see illustration)**. It isn't necessary to disconnect the hoses from the cover.

6   Withdraw the thermostat from the housing and remove the O-ring from the cover **(see illustrations)**.

Check

Refer to illustration 6.8

7   Remove any coolant deposits, then visually check the thermostat for corrosion, cracks and other damage. If it was open when it was removed, it is defective. Check the O-ring for cracks and other damage.

8   To check the thermostat's operation, submerge it in a container of water along with a thermometer **(see illustration)**. **Warning:** *Antifreeze is poisonous. Don't use a cooking pan.* The thermostat should be suspended so it does not touch the container.

9   Gradually heat the water in the container with a hot plate or stove and check the temperature when the thermostat first starts to open. Continue heating the water and check the temperature when the thermostat is fully open.

10   Compare your results to the specified thermostat opening temperature range listed in this Chapter's Specifications.

11   If the thermostat does not open as described, replace it.

Installation

12   Install the thermostat into the housing, spring end first **(see illustration 6.6a)**.

13   Install a new O-ring in the groove in the thermostat cover.

14   Place the cover on the housing and install the cover screws, tightening them securely.

15   The remainder of installation is the reverse of the removal procedure. Fill the cooling system with the recommended coolant (see Chapter 1).

3

6.6b . . . and remove the O-ring from the cover

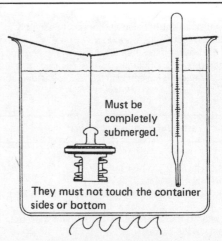

Must be completely submerged.

They must not touch the container sides or bottom

6.8 To check the thermostat, submerge it in a container of water along with a thermometer (thermostat should not touch the container), gradually heat the water in the container and note the temperature at which the thermostat begins to open and the temperature at which the thermostat is fully open

7.4 To remove the thermostat housing assembly, loosen the hose clamps and disconnect all three hoses, then remove the two bolts (arrows) that secure the thermostat housing bracket to the frame

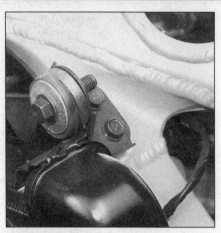

8.6 Remove the two bolts that attach the upper corners of the radiator to their frame brackets (upper left bracket and bolt shown, upper right the same)

8.7 After the upper bolts have been removed, lift the radiator slightly to disengage the positioning pin on its lower edge from the rubber grommet (arrow) and bracket on top of the oil cooler

7   Thermostat housing - removal and installation

Removal

Refer to illustration 7.4

Warning: *The engine must be completely cool before beginning this procedure.*

1   Drain the cooling system (see Chapter 1).
2   Remove the trim panel between the upper fairing and the right side of the fuel tank (see Chapter 8).
3   Unplug the electrical lead from the coolant temperature sensor and disconnect the ground wire from the bolt right above the sensor **(see illustration 5.2)**.
4   Detach the hoses from the thermostat cover and housing **(see illustration)**.
5   Remove the two bolts which attach the thermostat housing bracket to the frame **(see illustration 7.4)**.
6   Remove the thermostat housing and mounting bracket assembly. To separate the housing from the bracket, remove the two cover screws on the bracket side of the cover.

Installation

7   Place the thermostat housing and bracket assembly in position, install the bolts and tighten them securely.
8   Connect the hoses to the thermostat cover and housing.
9   The remainder of installation is the reverse of the removal procedure. Fill the cooling system with the recommended coolant (see Chapter 1).

8   Radiator - removal and installation

Removal

Refer to illustrations 8.6 and 8.7

Warning: *The engine must be completely cool before beginning this procedure.*

1   Set the bike on its centerstand. Disconnect the cable from the negative terminal of the battery.
2   Remove the upper and lower fairings (see Chapter 8).
3   Drain the coolant (see Chapter 1).
4   Remove the fuel tank (see Chapter 4). Follow the wiring harness from the fan motor to the electrical connector, then unplug the connector. Detach any other wiring that may interfere with radiator removal.

5   Loosen the hose clamps on both radiator hoses (one at the lower left corner and one at the upper right corner of the radiator) and detach the hoses (on some models it may be easier to detach the left side hose at the water pump, instead of the radiator).
6   Remove the radiator mounting bolts **(see illustration)**.
7   Lift the radiator up slightly to detach the positioning pin on the bottom of the radiator from the rubber grommet located in the bracket on top of the oil cooler **(see illustration)**. Remove the radiator.
8   If the radiator is to be repaired or replaced, remove the cooling fan (see Section 4).
9   Carefully examine the radiator for evidence of leaks and damage. It is recommended that any necessary repairs be performed by a reputable radiator repair shop.
10   If the radiator is clogged, or if large amounts of rust or scale have formed, the repair shop will also do a thorough cleaning job.
11   Make sure the spaces between the cooling tubes and fins are clear. If necessary, use compressed air or running water to remove anything that may be clogging them. If the fins are bent or flattened, straighten them very carefully with a small screwdriver.

Installation

12   Installation is the reverse of the removal procedure. Be sure to replace the hoses if they are deteriorated, and refill the cooling system with the recommended coolant (see Chapter 1).

9   Water pump - check, removal and installation

Check

Refer to illustrations 9.5, 9.7 and 9.9

Warning: *The engine must be completely cool before beginning this procedure.*

Note: *The water pump on these models can't be overhauled - it must be replaced as a unit.*

1   Visually check around the area of the water pump for coolant leaks. Try to determine if the leak is simply the result of a loose hose clamp or deteriorated hose.
2   Set the bike on its centerstand.
3   Remove the lower fairing (see Chapter 8).
4   Drain the engine coolant (see Chapter 1).
5   Loosen the hose clamp and detach the inlet hose from the water pump cover **(see illustration)**.
6   Remove the cover bolts **(see illustration 9.5)** and separate the cover from the water pump body.

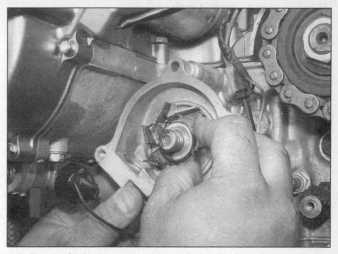

9.5 To remove the water pump cover, loosen the hose clamp (arrow) and detach the hose from the cover, then remove the four cover bolts (arrows) (the upper and lower bolts are also the water pump-to-engine retaining bolts)

9.7 Try to wiggle the water pump impeller back-and-forth and in-and-out; if you feel any play, replace the pump

7   Try to wiggle the water pump impeller back-and-forth and in-and-out **(see illustration)**. If you can feel movement, the water pump must be replaced.

8   Check the impeller blades for corrosion. If they are heavily corroded, replace the water pump and flush the system thoroughly (it would also be a good idea to check the internal condition of the radiator).

9   If the cause of the leak was just a defective cover O-ring, remove the old O-ring **(see illustration)** and install a new one.

Removal

Refer to illustrations 9.12, 9.13 and 9.14

10   Drain the coolant (see Chapter 1).

11   Disconnect the inlet hose from the pump cover **(see illustration 9.5)**.

12   Disconnect the outlet hose and drain bolt housing from the water pump **(see illustration)**.

13   Pull the pump straight out to remove it **(see illustration)**.

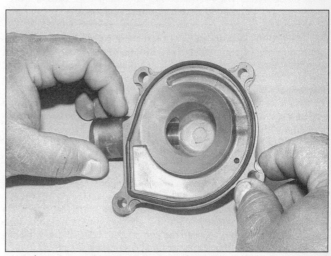

9.9 Inspect the water pump cover O-ring for cracks; if it's damaged or deteriorated, replace it

9.12 Before removing the water pump, remove the drain plug housing retaining bolt and detach the housing and outlet hose from the water pump (it's not necessary to loosen the hose clamp and detach the hose itself from the drain plug housing unless you're planning to replace the hose or the housing)

9.13 To remove the water pump assembly, pull it straight out of the engine

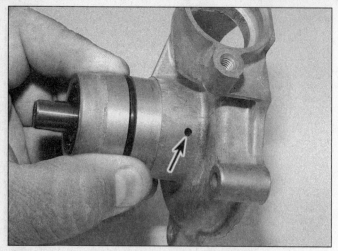

9.14 Inspect the "weep hole" carefully; if it's leaking coolant, the mechanical seal inside the pump has failed and the pump must be replaced. Also inspect the O-ring for cracks and tears; if it's damaged or deteriorated, replace it

14   Check the "weep hole" (coolant drainage passage) in the underside of the pump body **(see illustration)**. If there is coolant residue around it, the water pump is defective (when coolant gets past the mechanical seal inside the pump, it leaks out the weep hole). Replace the pump.

15   If the original water pump is to be installed, check the O-ring on the pump sleeve **(see illustration 9.14)**. If it's cracked or otherwise deteriorated, replace it with a new one.

Installation

Refer to illustration 9.16

16   Installation is basically the reverse of removal. Before installing the pump, smear a little engine oil on the sleeve O-ring. The water pump is driven off the left end of the oil pump shaft. Make sure the pump is engaged properly with the D-shaped end of this shaft **(see illustration)**. Be sure to tighten the pump cover bolts securely. Fill the cooling system with the recommended coolant (see Chapter 1).

10   Coolant pipe(s) - removal and installation

Warning: *The engine must be completely cool before beginning this procedure.*

1   Place the bike on its centerstand.

2   Remove the lower fairing (see Chapter 8).

3   Drain the engine coolant (see Chapter 1).

Upper coolant pipe

Refer to illustration 10.5

4   Loosen the hose clamp and detach the coolant hose from the right end of the upper coolant pipe.

5   Remove the coolant pipe-to-cylinder head bolts **(see illustration)** and separate the pipe from the cylinder head.

6   Remove the O-rings from the ends of the pipe and install new ones. If one of the ends doesn't have an O-ring, be sure to retrieve it from one of the holes in the cylinder head.

7   Check the holes in the head for corrosion, and remove all traces of corrosion if any exists.

8   Lubricate the new O-rings with clean engine oil, then install them on the pipe ends.

9   Install the ends of the coolant pipe into the holes in the cylinder head. Make sure the O-rings don't bunch up or tear. Install the mounting bolts and tighten them securely.

10   Inspect the upper coolant hose. If it's cracked, torn or otherwise

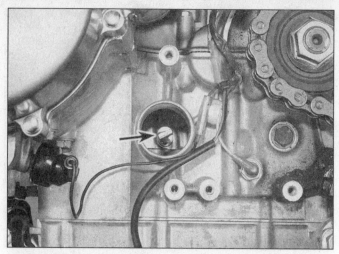

9.16 When you install the water pump, make sure that it's properly engaged with the D-shaped nose (arrow) on the oil pump shaft

10.5 To remove the upper coolant pipe, loosen the hose clamp and detach the coolant hose from the right end of the pipe, then remove these two bolts (arrows) and pull the pipe ends out of the cylinder head; discard the old O-rings

deteriorated, this is a good time to replace it. Reattach the coolant hose and tighten the hose clamp securely.

Lower coolant pipe

Refer to illustration 10.12

11   Loosen the hose clamp and detach the coolant hose from the left end of the lower coolant pipe.

12   Remove the two coolant pipe-to-engine block bolts **(see illustration)**.

13   Separate the pipe from the cylinder block. Make sure all the O-rings come out with the pipe - if not, be sure to retrieve them.

14   Check the pipe ends and the holes in the cylinder block for corrosion, and remove all traces of corrosion if any exists.

15   Lubricate the new O-rings with clean engine oil and install them on the pipe ends.

16   Install the ends of the coolant pipe into the holes in the cylinder block. Install the mounting bolts and tighten them securely.

Upper and lower coolant pipes

17   Fill the cooling system with the recommended coolant (see Chapter 1) and check for leaks.

10.12 To remove the lower coolant pipe, loosen the hose clamp and detach the coolant hose from the lower left end of the pipe, then remove these two bolts (arrows) and pull the pipe ends out of the cylinder block; discard the old O-rings

11.3 To disconnect the hoses from the oil cooler, remove the banjo bolts (arrow); discard the old sealing washers (left hose shown, right hose similar)

11.4 To detach the oil cooler from the frame, remove these two bolts (arrows)

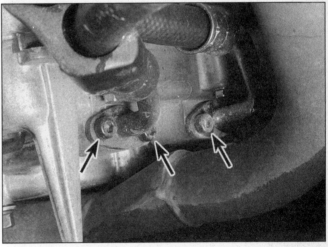

11.5 To detach the oil cooler hoses from the engine, remove these flange bolts (arrows); discard the old flange O-rings

18   The remainder of installation is the reverse of the removal procedure.

11   Oil cooler - removal and installation

Refer to illustrations 11.3, 11.4 and 11.5
Note: *Wait until the engine is cool before beginning this procedure.*
1   Set the bike on its centerstand and drain the engine oil (see Chapter 1).
2   Remove the lower fairing (see Chapter 8).
3   Place a drain pan under the oil cooler and remove the hose-to-oil cooler banjo bolts **(see illustration)**. Discard the sealing washers.
4   Remove the oil cooler retaining bolts **(see illustration)**.
5   Inspect both oil cooler hoses for cracks and tears. If either hose is damaged or otherwise deteriorated, replace it. To detach the hoses from the engine, remove the bolts **(see illustration)** that attach the hose flanges to the pan. Discard the old O-rings. Lubricate the new O-rings with clean engine oil and tighten the flange bolts to the torque listed in this Chapter's Specifications.
6   Installation of the oil cooler is the reverse of removal. Be sure to use new sealing washers when installing the hose-to-cooler banjo bolts. Tighten the banjo bolts to the torque listed in this Chapter's Specifications. Fill the crankcase with the recommended type and amount of oil (see Chapter 1).

3

Notes

Chapter 4
Fuel and exhaust systems

Contents

Specifications

General

Carburetor type	Keihin Seiki CVK-D36 (four)
Fuel pressure (E models)	11 to kPa (0.11 to 0.16 kg/cm^2, 1.6 to 2.3 psi)

Jet sizes - D models

Main jet (except high-altitude)	
California models	145
All others	142
Main jet (high-altitude)	
California models	142
All others	140
Main air jet	70
Needle jet	6
Needle jet mark	N14G
Pilot jet (slow jet)	
Except high-altitude	35
High-altitude	32
Pilot air jet (slow air jet)	110
Starter jet	
California models	48
All others	52

Jet sizes - E models

Main jet (except high-altitude)	
California models	140
All others	135
Main jet (high-altitude)	
California models	138
All others	132

4

Jet sizes - E models (continued)

Main air jet	50
Needle jet	6
Needle jet mark	N1VC
Pilot jet (slow jet)	
Except high-altitude	35
High-altitude	32
Pilot air jet (slow air jet)	110
Starter jet	52

Carburetor adjustments

Choke cable freeplay	2 to 3 mm (0.08 to 0.12 inch)
Float height	9 to 13 mm (0.3546 to 0.5122 inch)
Fuel level	2 to 4 mm below the mark

Torque specifications

Carburetor holder bolts	12 Nm (104 in-lbs)

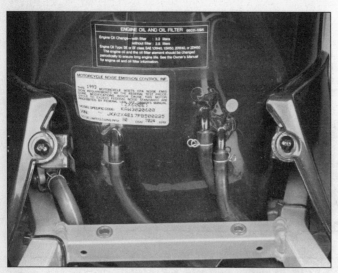

2.4 If your bike is equipped with evaporative emissions hoses, they should already be labeled with colored dots on the tank and matching color bands on the hoses; if not, be sure to mark or label them to prevent confusion during reassembly (D model shown, E models similar)

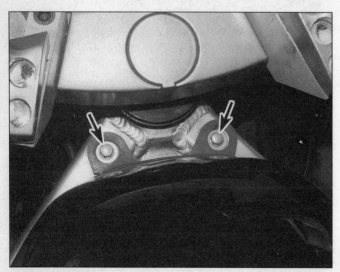

2.5 To detach the front of the fuel tank from the frame, remove these two bolts (arrows) (E model shown, D models similar)

1   General information

The fuel system consists of the fuel tank, the fuel tap and filter, the carburetors and the connecting lines, hoses and control cables. The carburetors used on these motorcycles are four constant vacuum Keihins with butterfly-type throttle valves. For cold starting, an enrichment circuit is actuated by a cable and the choke lever mounted on the left handlebar.

The exhaust system is a four-into-two design with a crossover pipe.

Many of the fuel system service procedures are considered routine maintenance items and for that reason are included in Chapter 1.

2   Fuel tank - removal, cleaning, repair and installation

Removal

Refer to illustrations 2.4, 2.5, 2.6a, 2.6b and 2.7

Warning: *Gasoline (petrol) is extremely flammable, so take extra precautions when you work on any part of the fuel system. Don't smoke or allow open flames or bare light bulbs near the work area, and don't work in a garage where a natural gas-type appliance (such as a water heater or clothes dryer) with a pilot light is present. Since gasoline is carcinogenic, wear latex gloves when there's a possibility of being exposed to fuel, and, if you spill any fuel on your skin, rinse it off immediately with soap and water. Mop up any spills immediately and do not store fuel-soaked rags where they could ignite. When you perform any kind of work on the fuel system, wear safety glasses and*

2.6a To detach the rear of the fuel tank on D models, remove these two bolts (upper arrows); to remove the inlet duct, remove these two screws (lower arrows)

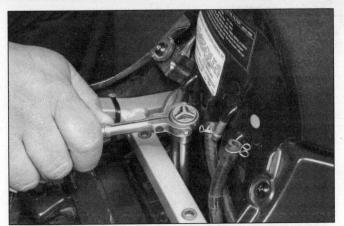

2.6b To detach the rear of the fuel tank from the frame on E models, remove the bolt that's located just underneath and ahead of this frame crossmember

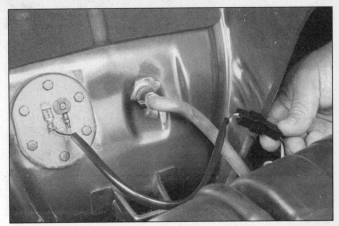

2.7 On E models, lift up the tank and unplug the electrical connector for the fuel level sensor

have a fire extinguisher suitable for a class B type fire (flammable liquids) on hand.

1   Remove the seat (see Chapter 8).

2   Disconnect the cable from the negative terminal of the battery.

3   Remove the front screws from the left and right side covers (see Chapter 8).

4   Mark and disconnect the breather hose from the rear of the fuel tank. On California models, mark and disconnect the evaporative emission hoses **(see illustration)**.

5   Remove the two bolts that attach the front of the tank to the frame **(see illustration)**.

6   On D models, remove the two rear mounting bolts **(see illustration)**. On E models, there's only one rear mounting bolt **(see illustration)**.

7   On E models, lift up the rear of the tank and unplug the electrical connector for the fuel level sensor **(see illustration)**.

8   Disconnect the fuel line from the fuel tap.

9   Carefully lift the tank away from the machine.

Cleaning and repair

10   All repairs to the fuel tank should be carried out by a professional who has experience in this critical and potentially dangerous work. Even after cleaning and flushing of the fuel system, explosive fumes can remain and ignite during repair of the tank.

11   If the fuel tank is removed from the vehicle, it should not be placed in an area where sparks or open flames could ignite the fumes coming out of the tank. Be especially careful inside garages where a natural gas-type appliance is located, because the pilot light could cause an explosion.

Installation

Refer to illustrations 2.12a and 2.12b

12   Before installing the tank, check the condition of the rubber bushings in the front and rear mounting brackets **(see illustrations)**. If they're hardened, cracked, or show any other signs of deterioration, replace them.

13   Installation is the reverse of removal. Make sure the tank seats

4

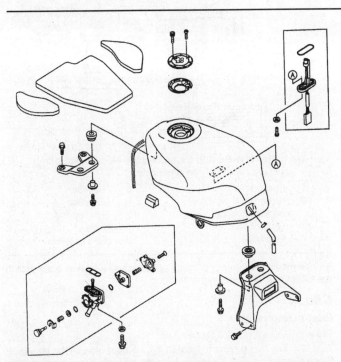

2.12a An exploded view of the fuel tank assembly (D models)

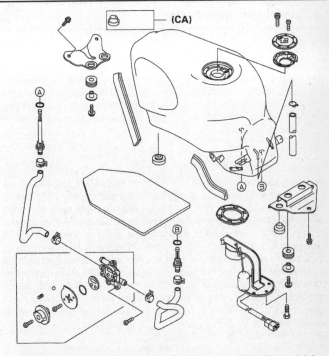

2.12b An exploded view of the fuel tank assembly (E models)

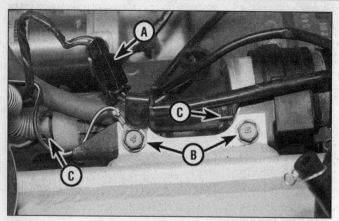

3.5 To remove the electric fuel pump from an E model, unplug the connector (A), remove the mounting bolts (B), loosen the hose clamps (C), and label and detach the hoses

3.7 The fuel pump relay (arrow) is located on the right side of the bike in front of the coolant reservoir and behind the rear brake master cylinder; to remove it, simply pull it out of its rubber holder and unplug the electrical connector

Fuel Pump Relay Internal Resistance

Range	Tester (+) Lead Connection			
x 1 kΩ	1	2	3	4
* 1	–	∞	∞	∞
2	∞	–	∞	∞
3	∞	10-100	–	∞
4	∞	20-200	1 - 5	–

*: Tester (–) Lead Connection

3.9a Resistance table for testing the electric fuel pump on E models

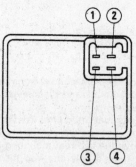

3.9b Terminal guide for testing the electric fuel pump on E models

properly and does not pinch any control cables or wires. If it's difficult to align the holes in the tank brackets with the holes in the frame, stop and check to see if a hose or cable is in the way.

3   Fuel pump (E models) - description, check and component replacement

Description

1   The fuel pump operates when the starter button is depressed and, under certain conditions, when the engine is running. When the fuel level in the float chambers is low, the fuel pump supplies fuel to the carburetors; when the fuel reaches the predetermined level, the fuel pressure rises and the fuel pump goes off. The fuel pressure sensor is integral with the pump.

Removal

Refer to illustration 3.5

Warning: *Gasoline (petrol) is extremely flammable, so take extra precautions when you work on any part of the fuel system. Don't smoke or allow open flames or bare light bulbs near the work area, and don't work in a garage where a natural gas-type appliance (such as a water heater or clothes dryer) with a pilot light is present. Since gasoline is carcinogenic, wear latex gloves when there's a possibility of being exposed to fuel, and, if you spill any fuel on your skin, rinse it off immediately with soap and water. Mop up any spills immediately and do not store fuel-soaked rags where they could ignite. When you perform any kind of work on the fuel system, wear safety glasses and have a fire extinguisher suitable for a class B type fire (flammable liquids) on hand.*

2   Remove the seat (see Chapter 8).
3   Disconnect the cable from the negative terminal of the battery.
4   Remove the fuel tank (see Section 2).
5   Unplug the electrical connector for the pump **(see illustration)**.

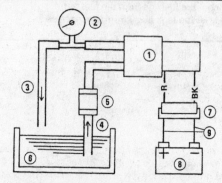

3.11 This is the setup for testing the electric fuel pump on E models

1	Fuel pump	5	Fuel filter
3	Automotive-type fuel	6	Kerosene
	pressure gauge	7	2-pin connector
3	Outlet hose	8	Battery
4	Inlet hose	9	Jumper leads

6   Remove the pump mounting bolts **(see illustration 3.5)**, detach the fuel hoses and remove the pump.

Check

Fuel pump relay

Refer to illustration 3.7, 3.9a and 3.9b

7   The fuel pump relay is located on the right side of the bike **(see illustration)**. To get at it, remove the right side cover (see Chapter 8).
8   Pull the relay out of its rubber holder and unplug the electrical connector.

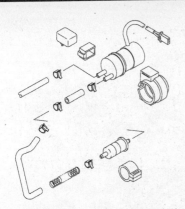

3.13 An exploded view of the electric fuel pump assembly used on E models

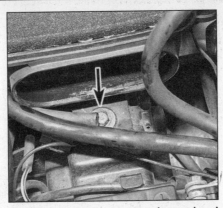

4.4 Remove the front screws (arrows) and rear bolt (arrow) from the air filter housing (D models)

4.5a Remove the screen . . .

4.5b . . . remove the rear mounting bolts (arrows) . . .

4.5c . . . and remove the air filter housing (E models). Note the access plugs (arrows) on the back of the housing; these plugs allow access to the rear bolts without removing the upper half of the housing, but it's tricky trying to install the bolts through the holes

9   Using a digital high-impedance (10 meg-ohm) multimeter, set the ohmmeter scale to the 1 X k-ohms range and measure the resistance at the indicated terminals **(see illustrations)**. **Caution:** *Using an analog meter without 10 meg-ohm internal circuitry will produce inaccurate results and damage the fuel pump relay. If your readings are not as specified, replace the fuel pump relay. If your readings are okay, check the fuel pump itself.*

Fuel pump

Refer to illustration 3.11

Warning: *To protect your eyes from spilled or splashed kerosene, wear safety goggles during the following test procedure.*

Note: *If you don't have a suitable automotive-type fuel pressure gauge for this procedure, take the pump to a Kawasaki dealer and it tested there.*

10   Remove the fuel pump (see Steps 2 through 6 above) and the fuel filter.

11   Fill a container with kerosene and hook up the fuel pump, hoses and filter as shown **(see illustration)**. Connect a fuel pressure gauge to the high pressure side with a T-fitting as shown. **Warning:** *Do NOT use gasoline for this test! It's unnecessary and dangerous.*

12   Hook up the pump leads to a 12-volt battery as shown **(see illustration 3.11)** and note whether the pump is energized:

a) *If the pump operates, check the pump relay.*

b) *If the pump does not operate, it's defective - replace it.*

c) *If the pump operates AND the fuel pump relay is also okay, close the outlet hose momentarily while the pump is running - when the pump stops, note the indicated pressure on the fuel pressure gauge and compare this reading to the fuel pressure listed in this Chapter's Specifications. If the gauge reading is outside that spec, the pump is defective - replace it.*

Installation

Refer to illustration 3.13

13   Installation is the reverse of removal **(see illustration)**. Make sure the hose clamps are all snug; if they're not, replace them.

---

4   Air filter housing - removal and installation

Refer to illustrations 4.4, 4.5a, 4.5b, 4.5c, 4.6a and 4.6b

1   Remove the seat and loosen the front screws on the side covers (see Chapter 8).

2   Remove the fuel tank (see Section 2).

3   On D models, remove the inlet duct **(see illustration 2.6a)**.

4   On D models, remove the front screws **(see illustration 13.2a in Chapter 1)** and the rear bolt from the air filter housing **(see illustration)**, label and detach the drain hose and crankcase breather hose, move the lower half of the housing forward to clear the hook and remove the housing.

5   On E models, detach the crankcase breather hose, remove the upper half of the housing (see Chapter 1), remove the screen, remove the rear mounting bolts and remove the lower half of the housing assembly **(see illustrations)**. (Kawasaki also provides a pair of removable plugs on the rear of the housing to allow you to get at the rear mounting bolts without having to remove the upper half of the housing; this is the faster removal method, but you'll still have to remove the upper half of the housing when *installing* the bolts.)

4

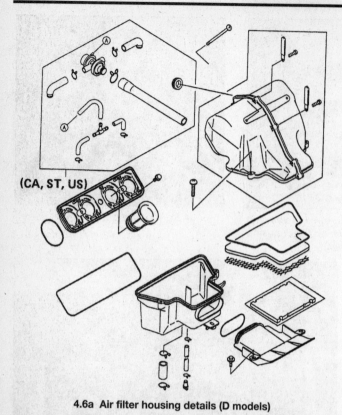

4.6a Air filter housing details (D models)

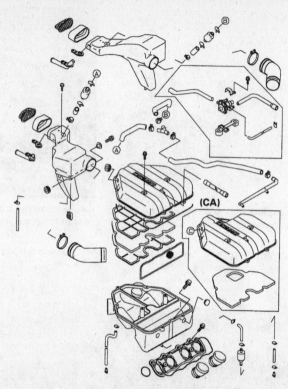

(CA)

4.6b Air filter housing details (E models)

6   Installation is the reverse of removal **(see illustrations)**. If you chose the faster method to remove the air filter housing on an E model, remove the upper half of the housing (see Chapter 1); it's very difficult to install the rear bolts through the access holes in the housing. Make sure all hoses are reattached correctly.

5   Carburetors - removal and installation

Removal

Refer to illustrations 5.6, 5.7a, 5.7b and 5.7c

Warning: *Gasoline (petrol) is extremely flammable, so take extra precautions when you work on any part of the fuel system. Don't smoke or allow open flames or bare light bulbs near the work area, and don't work in a garage where a natural gas-type appliance (such as a water heater or clothes dryer) with a pilot light is present. Since gasoline is carcinogenic, wear latex gloves when there's a possibility of being exposed to fuel, and, if you spill any fuel on your skin, rinse it off immediately with soap and water. Mop up any spills immediately and do not store fuel-soaked rags where they could ignite. When you perform any kind of work on the fuel system, wear safety glasses and have a fire extinguisher suitable for a class B type fire (flammable liquids) on hand.*

1   Remove the seat (see Chapter 8). Remove the fuel tank (see Section 2).
2   Remove the air filter housing (see Section 4).
3   Disconnect the choke cable from the carburetor assembly (see Section 11).
4   Loosen the lockwheel on the throttle cable adjuster at the handlebar and turn the adjuster in all the way **(see illustration 8.3 in Chapter 1)**. If this doesn't give you sufficient slack in the cable to disconnect it from the carburetors, disassemble the switch housing and disconnect the cable from the twist grip (see Section 10).
5   Mark and disconnect all vacuum hoses from the carburetors. On U.K. E models, disconnect and plug the coolant hoses (see Chapter 1).
6   Loosen the clamp screws on the intake manifolds (the rubber

tubes that connect the carburetors to the engine) and pull the carburetor assembly to the rear, clear of the intake manifold tubes **(see illustration)**.
7   Raise the carburetor assembly up far enough to disconnect the throttle cables from the throttle pulley **(see illustrations)**, then remove the carburetors.
8   After the carburetors have been removed, stuff clean rags into the intake manifold tubes to prevent the entry of dirt or other objects.

Installation

9   Position the assembly over the intake manifold tubes. Lightly lubricate the ends of the throttle cables with multi-purpose grease and attach them to the throttle pulley. Make sure the accelerator and decelerator cables are in their proper positions.
10   Tilt the front of the assembly down and insert the fronts of the carburetors into the intake manifold tubes. Push the assembly forward and tighten the clamps.
11   Adjust the throttle grip freeplay at the handlebar (see Chapter 1).
12   Connect and adjust the choke cable (see Section 11).
13   Install the air filter housing (see Section 4).
14   On U.K. E models, connect the coolant lines to the carburetors (see Chapter 1). Connect all vacuum hoses that were disconnected.
15   Install the air filter housing (see Section 4).
16   Install the fuel tank, turn the fuel tap to PRI and check for leaks.
17   Check and, if necessary, adjust the idle speed and carburetor synchronization (see Chapter 1).
18   Install the seat (see Chapter 8).

6   Carburetor overhaul - general information

1   Poor engine performance, hesitation, hard starting, stalling, flooding and backfiring are all signs that major carburetor maintenance may be required.
2   Keep in mind that many so-called carburetor problems are really not carburetor problems at all, but mechanical problems within the

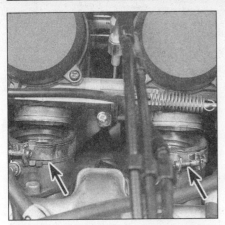

5.6 Pull the carburetors out of the rubber intake boots (arrows point to two middle intake boots, outer boots not visible in this photo)

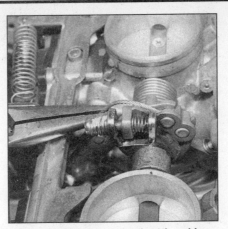

5.7a To disconnect the throttle cables from the carburetors, lift the carburetor assembly up, flip it over, pull the cable toward the pulley to create some slack . . .

5.7b . . . disengage the throttle cables from the throttle pulley . . .

5.7c . . . then remove the elbow-shaped cable housings from their brackets on the carburetor

7.2a Remove the choke shaft spring (arrow) . . .

engine or ignition system malfunctions. Try to establish for certain that the carburetors are in need of maintenance before beginning a major overhaul.

3   Check the fuel tap filter, the fuel lines, the gas tank cap vent, the intake manifold hose clamps, the vacuum hoses, the air filter element, the cylinder compression, the spark plugs, and the carburetor synchronization before assuming that a carburetor overhaul is required.

4   Most carburetor problems are caused by dirt particles, varnish and other deposits which build up in and block the fuel and air passages. Also, in time, gaskets and O-rings shrink or deteriorate and cause fuel and air leaks which lead to poor performance.

5   When the carburetor is overhauled, it is generally disassembled completely and the parts are cleaned thoroughly with a carburetor cleaning solvent and dried with filtered, unlubricated compressed air. The fuel and air passages are also blown through with compressed air to force out any dirt that may have been loosened but not removed by the solvent. Once the cleaning process is complete, the carburetor is reassembled using new gaskets, O-rings and, generally, a new inlet needle valve and seat.

6   Before disassembling the carburetors, make sure you have a carburetor rebuild kit (which will include all necessary O-rings and other parts), some carburetor cleaner, a supply or rags, some means of blowing out the carburetor passages and a clean place to work. It is recommended that only one carburetor be overhauled at a time to avoid mixing up parts.

7   Carburetors - disassembly, cleaning and inspection

Warning: *Gasoline (petrol) is extremely flammable, so take extra precautions when you work on any part of the fuel system. Don't smoke or allow open flames or bare light bulbs near the work area, and don't work in a garage where a natural gas-type appliance (such as a water heater or clothes dryer) with a pilot light is present. Since gasoline is carcinogenic, wear latex gloves when there's a possibility of being exposed to fuel, and, if you spill any fuel on your skin, rinse it off immediately with soap and water. Mop up any spills immediately and do not store fuel-soaked rags where they could ignite. When you perform any kind of work on the fuel system, wear safety glasses and have a fire extinguisher suitable for a class B type fire (flammable liquids) on hand.*

Disassembly

Refer to illustrations 7.2a through 7.2h, 7.3a through 7.3e, 7.4a, 7.4b, 7.5a, 7.5b, 7.6a through 7.6d, 7.7, 7.8, 7.9a, 7.9b, 7.10a, 7.10b, 7.11a and 7.11b

1   Remove the carburetors from the machine as described in Section 5. Set the assembly on a clean working surface. **Note:** *Unless the O-rings on the fuel and vent fittings between the carburetors are leaking, don't detach the carburetors from their mounting brackets. Also, work on one carburetor at a time to avoid getting parts mixed up.*

2   If the carburetors must be separated from each other, remove the

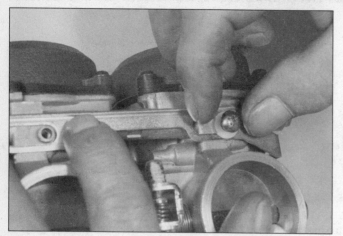
7.2b ... and the three choke shaft screws ...

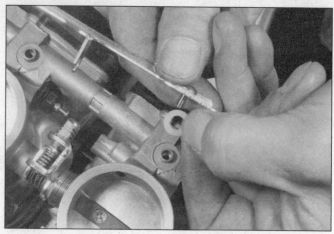
7.2c ... there are two plastic washers for each screw, one on each side of the choke shaft ...

7.2d ... separate the choke shaft from the carburetors

7.2e Intake boot mounting screws (arrows) (D models)

choke lever spring and choke lever by removing the three screws and six plastic washers (two washers per screw, one on each side of the lever) **(see illustrations)**, then remove the screws securing the mounting plate to the carburetors **(see illustrations)**. Mark the position of each carburetor and gently separate them, noting how the throttle linkage is connected **(see illustration)** and being careful not to lose

any springs or fuel and vent fittings that are present between the carburetors **(see illustration)**.

3   Remove the four screws securing the vacuum chamber cover to the carburetor body. Lift the cover off and remove the piston spring **(see illustrations)**. Peel the diaphragm away from its groove in the carburetor body, being careful not to tear it **(see illustration)**. Lift out

7.2f Intake boot mounting screws (arrows) (E models)

7.2g The synchronizing screws and springs (arrows) should look like this

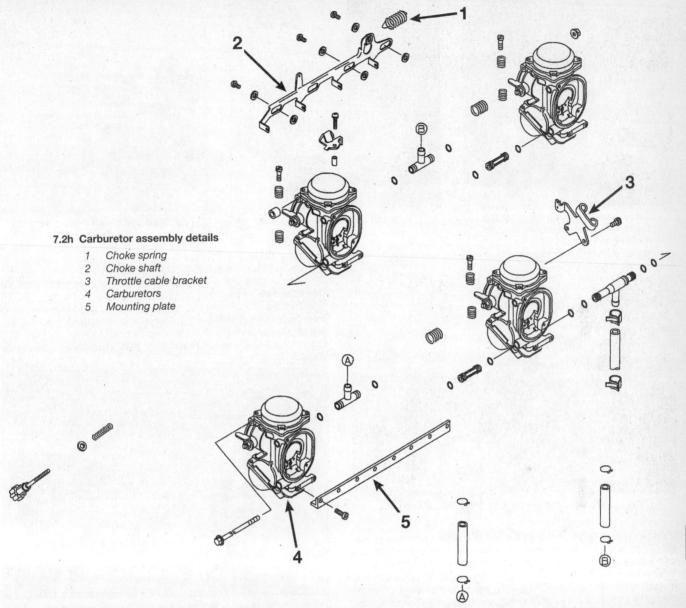

7.2h Carburetor assembly details

1   Choke spring
2   Choke shaft
3   Throttle cable bracket
4   Carburetors
5   Mounting plate

7.3a Remove the vacuum chamber cover screws (arrows) . . .

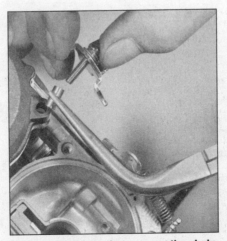

7.3b . . . the screw that secures the choke cable bracket has a dowel pin . . .

7.3c . . . lift off the cover and spring . . .

4

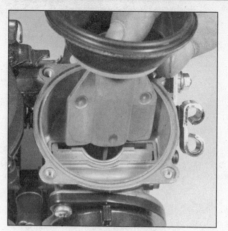

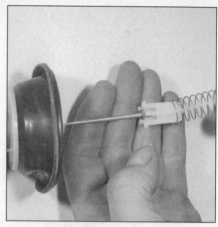

7.3d . . . and carefully separate the diaphragm from its groove and the locating tab (arrow) from its notch

7.3e Lift the throttle piston out

7.4a Separate the jet needle from the throttle piston

the diaphragm/piston assembly **(see illustration)**.

4   Remove the piston spring seat and separate the needle from the piston **(see illustrations)**.

5   Remove the four screws retaining the float chamber to the carburetor body, then detach the chamber **(see illustrations)**.

6   Push the float pivot pin out and detach the float (and fuel inlet valve needle) from the carburetor body **(see illustrations)**. Detach the

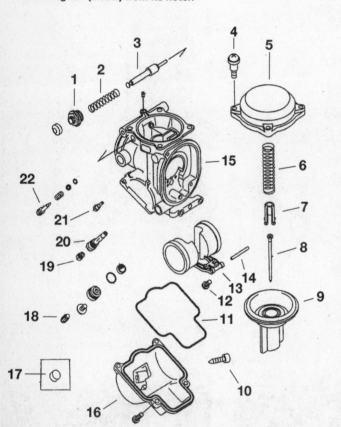

7.4b Carburetor - exploded view

1 Choke plunger cap	12 Retaining screw
2 Spring	13 Floats
3 Choke plunger	14 Float pivot pin
4 Screw	15 Carburetor body
5 Vacuum chamber cover	16 Float chamber
6 Vacuum piston spring	17 Pilot screw plug (US
7 Spring seat	models)
8 Jet needle	18 Needle valve and seat
9 Throttle piston	19 Main jet
10 Float chamber drain	20 Needle jet holder
screw	21 Pilot jet
11 Float chamber gasket	22 Pilot screw

7.5a Remove the float chamber cover screws . . .

7.5b . . . and lift off the cover

7.6a Loosen the screw shown . . .

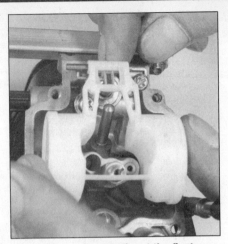

7.6b . . . then push out the float pivot pin . . .

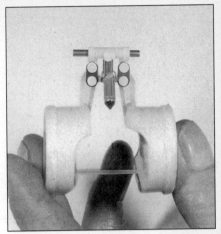

7.6c . . . and lift out the float, together with the needle valve

valve needle from the float. Remove the retaining screw and remove the needle valve seat **(see illustration)**.

7   Unscrew the main jet from the needle jet holder **(see illustration)**.

8   Unscrew the needle jet holder/air bleed pipe **(see illustration)**.

9   Using a small, flat-bladed screwdriver, remove the pilot jet **(see illustrations)**.

10   The pilot (idle mixture) screw is located in the bottom of the carburetor body **(see illustrations)**. On US models, this screw is hidden behind a plug which will have to be removed if the screw is to be taken out. To do this, punch a hole in the plug with an awl or a scribe, then pry it out. On all models, turn the pilot screw in, counting the number of turns until it bottoms lightly. Record that number for use

7.6d Remove the retaining screw and lift out the needle valve seat

7.7 Prevent the needle jet holder from turning with a wrench and unscrew the main jet with a screwdriver; be sure the screwdriver fits the slot exactly so it isn't stripped out

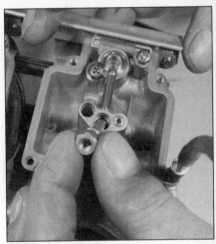

7.8 Unscrew the needle jet holder

7.9a Unscrew the pilot jet . . .

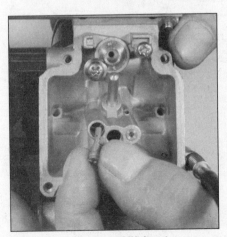

7.9b . . . and lift it out

7.10a The pilot screw on US models is beneath a plug (arrow)

4

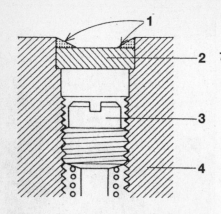

7.10b On installation, apply bonding agent around the plug

1 *Bonding agent*
2 *Plug*
3 *Pilot screw*
4 *Carburetor body*

approximately thirty minutes (or longer, if the directions recommend it).

13   After the carburetor has soaked long enough for the cleaner to loosen and dissolve most of the varnish and other deposits, use a brush to remove the stubborn deposits. Rinse it again, then dry it with compressed air. Blow out all of the fuel and air passages in the main and upper body. **Caution:** *Never clean the jets or passages with a piece of wire or a drill bit, as they will be enlarged, causing the fuel and air metering rates to be upset.*

Inspection

Refer to illustrations 7.15, 7.18 and 7.19

14   Check the operation of the choke plunger. If it doesn't move smoothly, replace it, along with the return spring.

15   Check the tapered portion of the pilot screw for wear or damage **(see illustration)**. Replace the pilot screw if necessary.

16   Check the carburetor body, float chamber and vacuum chamber cover for cracks, distorted sealing surfaces and other damage. If any defects are found, replace the faulty component, although replacement of the entire carburetor will probably be necessary (check with your parts supplier for the availability of separate components).

17   Check the jet needle for straightness by rolling it on a flat surface (such as a piece of glass). Replace it if it's bent or if the tip is worn.

18   Check the needle jet and replace the carburetor if it's worn or damaged **(see illustration)**.

19   Check the tip of the fuel inlet valve needle. If it has grooves or scratches in it, it must be replaced. Push in on the rod in the other end of the needle, then release it - if it doesn't spring back, replace the

when installing the screw. Now remove the pilot screw along with its spring, washer and O-ring.

11   The choke plunger can be removed by unscrewing the nut that retains it to the carburetor body **(see illustrations)** if the choke shaft has been removed (see Step 2).

Cleaning

Caution: *Use only a carburetor cleaning solution that is safe for use with plastic parts (be sure to read the label on the container).*

12   Submerge the metal components in the carburetor cleaner for

7.11a Unscrew the choke plunger cap with a socket . . .

7.11b . . . and take out the spring and plunger

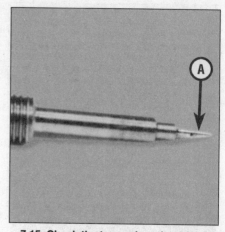

7.15 Check the tapered portion of the pilot screw for wear or damage

7.18 Check the piston insert and the needle jet for wear or damage

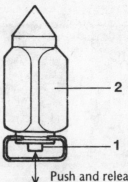
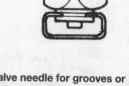
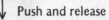

Push and release

7.19 Check the tip of the fuel inlet valve needle for grooves or scratches - also make sure the rod in the end of the needle pops back out quickly after it's pushed in

1   *Rod*   3   *Groove in tip*
2   *Valve needle*

8.9 Measure float height with a vernier caliper or similar tool

8.14a Make sure the choke shaft engages all four plungers (arrows)

8.14b Be sure to reinstall the plastic washers on both sides of the shaft; no. 2 carburetor doesn't have a screw or washers

valve needle **(see illustration)**.

20　Check the O-rings on the float chamber and the drain plug (in the float chamber). Replace them if they're damaged.

21　Operate the throttle shaft to make sure the throttle butterfly valve opens and closes smoothly. If it doesn't, replace the carburetor.

22　Check the floats for damage. This will usually be apparent by the presence of fuel inside one of the floats. If the floats are damaged, they must be replaced.

23　Check the diaphragm for splits, holes and general deterioration. Holding it up to a light will help to reveal problems of this nature.

24　Insert the vacuum piston in the carburetor body and see that it moves up-and-down smoothly. Check the surface of the piston for wear. If it's worn excessively or doesn't move smoothly in the bore, replace the carburetor.

8 Carburetors - reassembly and float height adjustment

Refer to illustrations 8.9, 8.14a and 8.14b

Caution: *When installing the jets, be careful not to over-tighten them - they're made of soft material and can strip or shear easily.*

Note: *When reassembling the carburetors, be sure to use the new O-rings, gaskets and other parts supplied in the rebuild kit.*

1　If the choke plunger was removed, install it in its bore, followed by its spring and nut. Tighten the nut securely and install the cap.

2　Install the pilot screw (if removed) along with its spring, washer and O-ring, turning it in until it seats lightly. Now, turn the screw out the number of turns that was previously recorded. If you're working on a US model, install a new metal plug in the hole over the screw. Apply a little bonding agent around the circumference of the plug after it has been seated.

3　Install the pilot jet, tightening it securely.

4　Install the needle jet holder/air bleed pipe, tightening it securely.

5　Install the main jet into the needle jet holder/air bleed pipe, tightening it securely.

6　Drop the jet needle down into its hole in the vacuum piston and install the spring seat over the needle. Make sure the spring seat doesn't cover the hole at the bottom of the vacuum piston - reposition it if necessary.

7　Install the diaphragm/vacuum piston assembly into the carburetor body. Lower the spring into the piston. Seat the bead of the diaphragm into the groove in the top of the carburetor body, making sure the diaphragm isn't distorted or kinked. This is not always an easy task. If the diaphragm seems too large in diameter and doesn't want to seat in the groove, place the vacuum chamber cover over the carburetor

diaphragm, insert your finger into the throat of the carburetor and push up on the vacuum piston. Push down gently on the vacuum chamber cover - it should drop into place, indicating the diaphragm has seated in its groove.

8　Install the vacuum chamber cover, tightening the screws securely. If you're working on the no. 3 carburetor, don't forget to install the dowel and choke cable bracket **(see illustration 7.3b)**.

9　Invert the carburetor. Attach the fuel inlet valve needle to the float. Set the float into position in the carburetor, making sure the valve needle seats correctly. Install the float pivot pin. To check the float height, hold the carburetor so the float hangs down, then tilt it back until the valve needle is just seated (the rod in the end of the valve shouldn't be compressed). Measure the distance from the float chamber gasket surface to the top of the float **(see illustration)** and compare your measurement to the float height listed in this Chapter's Specifications. If it isn't as specified, carefully bend the tang that contacts the valve needle up or down until the float height is correct.

10　Install the O-ring into the groove in the float chamber. Place the float chamber on the carburetor and install the screws, tightening them securely.

11　If the carburetors were separated, install new O-rings on the fuel and vent fittings. Lubricate the O-rings on the fittings with a light film of oil and install them into their respective holes, making sure they seat completely **(see illustration 7.2h)**.

12　Position the coil springs between the carburetors, gently push the carburetors together, then make sure the throttle linkages are correctly engaged. Check the fuel and vent fittings to make sure they engage properly also.

13　Install the lower mounting plate and install the screws, but don't tighten them completely yet. Set the carburetors on a sheet of glass, then align them with a straightedge placed along the edges of the bores. When the centerlines of the carburetors are all in horizontal and vertical alignment, tighten the mounting plate screws securely.

14　Install the choke lever, making sure it engages correctly with all the choke plungers **(see illustration)**. Position a plastic washer on each side of the choke lever, except on the no. 2 carburetor **(see illustration)** and install the screws, tightening them securely. Install the lever return spring **(see illustration 7.2a)**, then make sure the choke mechanism operates smoothly.

15　Install the throttle linkage springs **(see illustration 7.2g)**. Visually synchronize the throttle butterfly valves, turning the adjusting screws on the throttle linkage, if necessary, to equalize the clearance between the butterfly valve and throttle bore of each carburetor. Check to ensure the throttle operates smoothly.

16　If they were removed, install the throttle stop screw, throttle cable bracket and the air cleaner housing intake fittings.

4

9.2a Loosen the float chamber drain screw

9   Carburetors - fuel level adjustment

Refer to illustrations 9.2a, 9.2b and 9.5

Warning: *Gasoline (petrol) is extremely flammable, so take extra precautions when you work on any part of the fuel system. Don't smoke or allow open flames or bare light bulbs near the work area, and don't work in a garage where a natural gas-type appliance (such as a water heater or clothes dryer) with a pilot light is present. Since gasoline is carcinogenic, wear latex gloves when there's a possibility of being exposed to fuel, and, if you spill any fuel on your skin, rinse it off immediately with soap and water. Mop up any spills immediately and do not store fuel-soaked rags where they could ignite. When you perform any kind of work on the fuel system, wear safety glasses and have a fire extinguisher suitable for a class B type fire (flammable liquids) on hand.*

1   Remove the fuel tank (see Section 2) and the air filter housing (see Section 4). Connect an auxiliary fuel tank to the carburetors with a suitable length of hose, then support the motorcycle in an upright position.

2   Attach Kawasaki service tool no. 57001-1017 to the drain fitting on the bottom of one of the carburetor float chambers (all four will be checked) **(see illustrations)**. This is a clear plastic tube graduated in millimeters. An alternative is to use a length of clear plastic tubing and an accurate ruler. Hold the graduated tube (or the free end of the clear plastic tube) against the carburetor body, as shown in the accompanying illustration. If the Kawasaki tool is being used, raise the zero mark to a point several millimeters above the bottom edge of the carburetor main body. If a piece of clear plastic tubing is being used, make a mark on the tubing at a point several millimeters above the bottom edge of the carburetor main body.

3   Unscrew the drain screw at the bottom of the float chamber a couple of turns, then let fuel flow into the tube. Wait for the fuel level to stabilize, then slowly lower the tube until the zero mark is level with the fuel level mark on the carburetor body. **Note:** *Don't lower the zero mark below the bottom edge of the carburetor then bring it back up - the reading won't be accurate.*

4   Measure the distance between the mark and top of the fuel level in the tube or gauge. This distance is the fuel level - write it down on a piece of paper, screw in the drain screw, shut off the fuel flow, then move on to the next carburetor and check it the same way.

5   Compare your fuel level readings to the value listed in this Chapter's Specifications. If the fuel level in any carburetor is not correct, remove the float chamber and bend the tang up or down (see Section 8), as necessary, then recheck the fuel level. Measure the float height with the carburetor tilted so that the tang on the float just touches the needle rod in the float valve **(see illustration)**. *Bending the tang up increases the float height and lowers the fuel level - bending it down decreases the float height and raises the fuel level.*

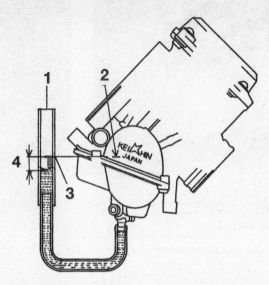

9.2b The fuel level measuring tool is attached like this

1	Fuel level gauge (part no. 57001-1017)	3	Top line
2	Mark	4	Fuel level

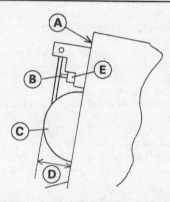

9.5 Make sure you measure the float height with the carburetor tilted so that the tang on the float is just barely touching the needle rod in the float valve

1	Float bowl mating surfaces	3	Float
		4	Float height
2	Needle rod	5	Float valve

10   Throttle cables and grip - removal, installation and adjustment

Throttle cables

Removal

Refer to illustrations 10.3a, 10.3b and 10.4

1   Remove the fuel tank (see Section 2).

2   Loosen the accelerator cable lockwheel and screw the cable adjuster in.

3   Remove the cable/switch housing screws **(see illustration)** and remove the front and rear halves of the housing **(see illustration)**.

4   Rotate the ends of the cables to align with the slots in the throttle grip pulley, then detach the cables from the pulley **(see illustration)**.

5   Detach the accelerator cable, its guide and the decelerator cable from the cable/switch housing.

6   Loosen the throttle cable adjusters to create slack in the cables,

10.3a Remove the screws from the front half of the throttle housing/switch assembly . . .

10.3b . . . and take the rear half off the handlebar

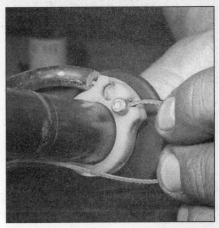

10.4 Disconnect the cables from the throttle pulley

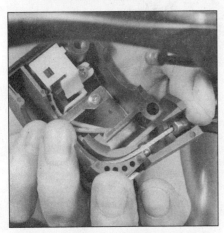

10.12 Slide the decelerator cable into its slot in the housing

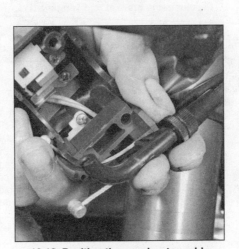

10.13 Position the accelerator cable guide in the housing

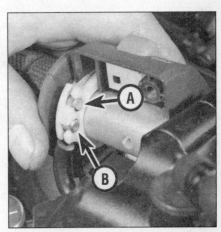

10.14 Engage the decelerator cable (A) and accelerator cable (B) with the throttle pulley

then detach the cables from the throttle pulley **(see illustrations 5.7a, 5.7b and 5.7c)**.

7   Remove the cables, noting how they are routed.

Installation

Refer to illustrations 10.12, 10.13, 10.14 and 10.15

8   Installation is basically the reverse of removal. Make sure the cables are routed properly. Make sure they don't interfere with any other components and aren't kinked or bent sharply.

9   Lubricate the end of the accelerator cable with multi-purpose grease and connect it to the throttle pulley at the carburetor. Pass the inner cable through the slot in the bracket, then seat the cable housing in the bracket.

10   Repeat the previous step to connect the decelerator cable.

11   Route the decelerator cable around the backside of the handlebar and connect it to the rear hole in the throttle grip pulley.

12   Seat the decelerator cable in the throttle housing groove **(see illustration)**.

13   Push the accelerator cable guide into place, making sure the notched portion is correctly engaged with the housing **(see illustration)**.

14   From the front side of the handlebar, connect the accelerator cable to the forward hole in the throttle grip pulley. Connect the decelerator cable to the rearward hole **(see illustration)**.

15   Install the front half of the cable/switch housing, making sure the locating pin engages with the hole in the handlebar **(see illustration)**. If necessary, rotate the housing back and forth, until the locating pin

drops into the hole and the housing halves mate together. Install the screws and tighten them securely.

Adjustment

16   Follow the procedure outlined in Chapter 1, *Throttle operation/grip freeplay - check and adjustment*, to adjust the cables.

10.15 Make sure the locating pin (A) engages the hole (B) in the handlebar; if it doesn't, you won't be able to screw the switch housing halves back together

4

11.2a Loosen the locknut (A), and back off the adjuster nut (B) to put some slack in the choke cable

11.2b Pull the choke cable housing free of the bracket and slide the cable through the slot in the bracket to disengage it

11.3a Remove the choke cable/switch housing screws . . .

17   Turn the handlebars back and forth to make sure the cables don't cause the steering to bind.

18   Install the fuel tank.

19   With the engine idling, turn the handlebars through their full travel (full left lock to full right lock) and note whether idle speed increases. If it does, the cables are routed incorrectly. Correct this dangerous condition before riding the bike.

Throttle grip

Removal

20   Follow Steps 2 through 4 to detach the upper ends of the throttle cables from the throttle grip pulley.

21   Remove the grip end weight and slide the throttle grip off the handlebar.

Installation

22   Clean the handlebar and apply a light coat of multi-purpose grease.

23   Push the throttle grip on. Install the grip end weight and tighten the screw securely.

24   Attach the cables following Steps 11 through 15, then adjust the cables following the procedure outlined in Chapter 1, *Throttle operation/grip freeplay - check and adjustment.*

11   Choke cable - removal, installation and adjustment

Removal

Refer to illustrations 11.2a, 11.2b, 11.3a and 11.3b

1   Remove the seat and fuel tank (see Section 2).

2   Loosen the choke cable adjuster **(see illustration)**. Pull the choke cable housing out of its mounting bracket at the carburetor assembly, then pass the cable through the opening in the bracket **(see illustration)**. Detach the cable end from the choke lever.

3   Remove the two screws securing the choke cable/switch housing halves to the left handlebar **(see illustration)**. Pull the front half of the housing off and separate the choke cable from the lever **(see illustration)**.

4   Remove the cable, noting how it's routed.

Installation

Refer to illustration 11.5

5   Route the cable into position. Connect the upper end of the cable to the choke lever. Make sure the cable guide seats properly in the housing **(see illustration)**. Place the housing up against the handlebar, making sure the pin in the housing fits into the hole in the handlebar. Install the screws, tightening them securely.

6   Connect the lower end of the cable to the choke lever. Pull back

11.3b . . . separate the housing halves and disengage the cable from the lever

11.5 When installing the choke cable, lever and cable guide, make sure everything is installed in their half of the switch housing before installing the housing halves on the handlebar

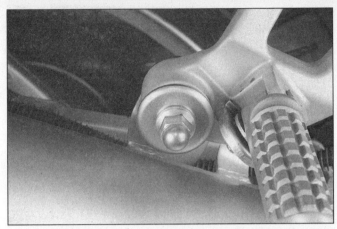

13.4 To detach a muffler from the frame, remove this bolt, washer and nut; inspect the two rubber bushings for cracks and tears and replace them if they're damaged

13.5 Loosen the muffler-to-exhaust pipe clamp bolt

on the cable casing and connect it to the bracket on the no. 3 carburetor.

Adjustment

7   Check the freeplay at the choke plunger lever on the carburetor assembly. It should move about two to three millimeters (1/8-inch).
8   If the freeplay isn't as specified, follow the cable to its mid-line adjuster above the engine valve cover (it resembles the throttle cable adjusters). Loosen the cable adjusting locknut and turn the adjusting nut in or out, as necessary, until the freeplay at the lever is correct. Tighten the locknut.
9   Install the fuel tank and all of the other components that were previously removed.

12 Idle fuel/air mixture adjustment - general information

1   Due to the increased emphasis on controlling motorcycle exhaust emissions, certain governmental regulations have been formulated which directly affect the carburetion of this machine. In order to comply with the regulations, the carburetors on some models have a metal sealing plug pressed into the hole over the pilot screw (which controls the idle fuel/air mixture) on each carburetor, so they can't be tampered with. These should only be removed in the event of a complete carburetor overhaul, and even then the screws should be returned to their original settings. The pilot screws on other models are

accessible, but the use of an exhaust gas analyzer is the only accurate way to adjust the idle fuel/air mixture and be sure the machine doesn't exceed the emissions regulations.
2   If the engine runs extremely rough at idle or continually stalls, and if a carburetor overhaul does not cure the problem, take the motorcycle to a Kawasaki dealer service department or other repair shop equipped with an exhaust gas analyzer. They will be able to properly adjust the idle fuel/air mixture to achieve a smooth idle and restore low speed performance.

13 Exhaust system - removal and installation

Refer to illustrations 13.4, 13.5, 13.6, 13.7, 13.8a, 13.8b and 13.8c
1   Remove the lower fairing (see Chapter 8).
2   Drain the coolant (see Chapter 1).
3   Remove the radiator and oil cooler (see Chapter 3).
4   Remove the muffler mounting bolts and nuts **(see illustration)**.
5   Loosen the clamps which attach the mufflers to the exhaust pipe **(see illustration)**, slide the clamps back, and pull the mufflers to the rear to disengage them from the exhaust pipe.
6   Remove the two bolts which attach the exhaust pipe to the underside of the bike **(see illustration)**.
7   Remove the exhaust pipe nuts and slide the holders off the mounting studs **(see illustration)**. If the split keepers didn't come off with the holders, remove them from the pipes.

4

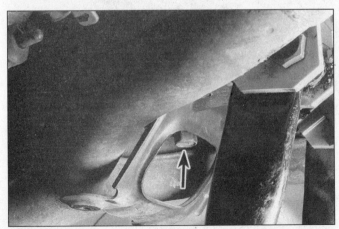

13.6 To detach the exhaust pipe from the underside of the bike, remove these two bolts (arrow); inspect the rubber bushing with each bolt and replace it if it's cracked or torn (only one bolt visible in this photo)

13.7 To detach the exhaust pipe from the cylinder head, remove these eight nuts (arrows) (not all nut are visible in this photo)

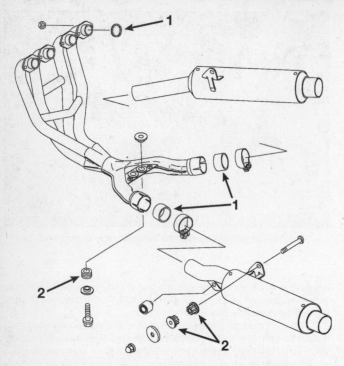

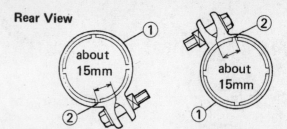

13.8b On earlier models with slits in the exhaust pipes, install the clamps in relation to the slits as shown:

    1   Clamps   *2   Slits*

13.8a An exploded view of the exhaust system

1   Always replace the exhaust pipe-to-muffler gaskets and the exhaust header gaskets
2   Replace the rubber bushings for the muffler mounting bolts and the exhaust mounting bolts as necessary

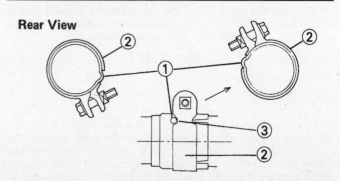

13.8c On later models with projections on the exhaust pipes, install the clamps so the groove fits the projection on the exhaust pipe as shown:

    1   Projection   *3   Groove*
    2   Clamps

8   Installation is the reverse of removal **(see illustration)**, but be sure to install a new gasket at the connection point between the mufflers and the exhaust pipe, and make sure the clamps are properly positioned **(see illustrations)**.

Chapter 5   Ignition system

Contents

Specifications

5

Ignition coil

Primary resistance .... 2.3 to 3.5 ohms
Secondary resistance .... 12.0 to 18.0 k-ohms
Arcing distance .... 6 mm (1/64-inch) or more

Pickup coil

Air gap .... 0.4 to 0.6 mm (0.016 to 0.024 inch)
Resistance .... 380 to 570 ohms

Ignition timing

D models
California models .... From 7.5° BTDC @ 1300 rpm to 40° BTDC @ 3000 rpm
All other models .... From 12.5° BTDC @ 1050 rpm to 40° BTDC @ 3000 rpm
E models
California models .... From 5° BTDC @ 1300 rpm to 35° BTDC @ 5000 rpm
All other models .... From 12.5° BTDC @ 1050 rpm to 35° BTDC @ 5000 rpm

Torque specifications

Alternator cover bolts .... 8.8 Nm (78 in-lbs)
Pickup coil cover bolts .... 8.8 Nm (78 in-lbs)
Timing rotor Allen bolt .... 25 Nm (18 ft-lbs)

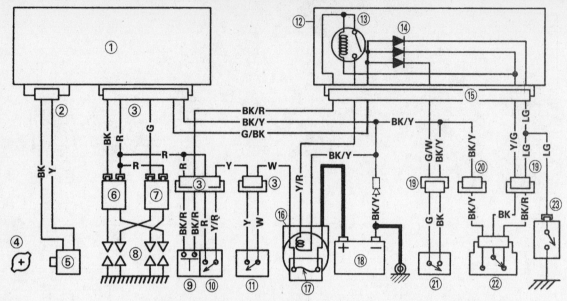

1.1a Ignition system circuit (U.S. and Canadian D models)

1	IC igniter	9	Starter button	17	Main (30A) fuse
2	4-pin connector	10	Engine stop switch	18	Battery
3	6-pin connector	11	Ignition switch	19	2-pin connector
4	Timing rotor	12	Junction box	20	9-pin connector
5	Pickup coil	13	Starter circuit relay	21	Sidestand switch
6	Ignition coil (nos. 1 and 4 cylinders)	14	Diodes	22	Starter lockout switch
7	Ignition coil (nos. 2 and 3 cylinders)	15	10-pin connector	23	Neutral switch
8	Spark plugs	16	Starter relay		

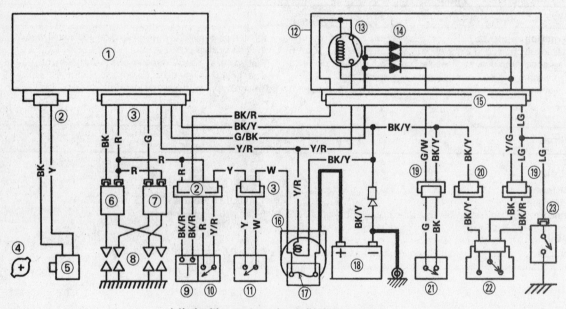

1.1b Ignition system circuit (U.K. D models)

1	IC igniter	9	Starter button	17	Main (30A) fuse
2	4-pin connector	10	Engine stop switch	18	Battery
3	6-pin connector	11	Ignition switch	19	2-pin connector
4	Timing rotor	12	Junction box	20	9-pin connector
5	Pickup coil	13	Starter circuit relay	21	Sidestand switch
6	Ignition coil (nos. 1 and 4 cylinders)	14	Diodes	22	Starter lockout switch
7	Ignition coil (nos. 2 and 3 cylinders)	15	10-pin connector	23	Neutral switch
8	Spark plugs	16	Starter relay		

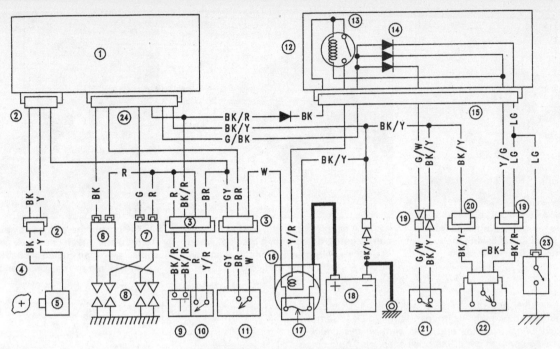

1.1c Ignition system circuit (all E models)

1	IC igniter	9	Starter button	17	Main (30A) fuse
2	4-pin connector	10	Engine stop switch	18	Battery
3	6-pin connector	11	Ignition switch	19	2-pin connector
4	Timing rotor	12	Junction box	20	9-pin connector
5	Pickup coil	13	Starter circuit relay	21	Sidestand switch
6	Ignition coil (nos. 1 and 4 cylinders)	14	Diodes	22	Starter lockout switch
7	Ignition coil (nos. 2 and 3 cylinders)	15	10-pin connector	23	Neutral switch
8	Spark plugs	16	Starter relay	24	8-pin connector

1 General information

Refer to illustrations 1.1a, 1.1b and 1.1c

This motorcycle is equipped with a battery-operated, fully-transistorized, breakerless ignition system **(see illustrations)**. The system consists of the following components:

Pickup coils
IC igniter unit
Battery and fuse
Ignition coils
Spark plugs
Stop and main (key) switches
Primary and secondary circuit wiring

The transistorized ignition system functions on the same principle as a conventional DC ignition system with the pickup unit and igniter performing the tasks normally associated with the breaker points and mechanical advance system. As a result, adjustment and maintenance of ignition components is eliminated (with the exception of spark plug replacement).

Because of their nature, the individual ignition system components can be checked but not repaired. If ignition system troubles occur, and the faulty component can be isolated, the only cure for the problem is to replace the part with a new one. Keep in mind that most electrical parts, once purchased, can't be returned. To avoid unnecessary expense, make very sure the faulty component has been positively identified before buying a replacement part.

2 Ignition system - check

Warning: *Because of the very high voltage generated by the ignition system, extreme care should be taken when these checks are performed.*

2.3 With the wire attached, ground (earth) a spark plug to the engine and operate the starter - bright blue sparks should be visible

1   If the ignition system is the suspected cause of poor engine performance or failure to start, a number of checks can be made to isolate the problem.
2   Make sure the ignition stop switch is in the Run or On position.

Engine will not start

Refer to illustrations 2.3 and 2.5

3   Remove the fuel tank (see Chapter 4). Disconnect one of the spark plug wires, connect the wire to a spare spark plug and lay the plug on the engine with the threads contacting the engine. If necessary, hold the spark plug with an insulated tool **(see illustration)**.

2.5 Unscrew the spark plug caps from the plug wires and measure their resistance with an ohmmeter

2.13 A simple spark gap testing fixture can be constructed from a block of wood, two nails, a large alligator clip, a screw and a piece of wire

2.14 Connect the tester to a good ground (earth) and attach one of the spark plug wires - when the engine is cranked, sparks should jump the gap between the nails

Crank the engine over and make sure a well-defined, blue spark occurs between the spark plug electrodes. **Warning:** *Don't remove one of the spark plugs from the engine to perform this check - atomized fuel being pumped out of the open spark plug hole could ignite, causing severe injury!*

4   If no spark occurs, the following checks should be made:

5   Unscrew a spark plug cap from a plug wire and check the cap resistance with an ohmmeter **(see illustration)**. If the resistance is infinite, replace it with a new one. Repeat this check on the remaining plug caps.

6   Make sure all electrical connectors are clean and tight. Check all wires for shorts, opens and correct installation.

7   Check the battery voltage with a voltmeter and the specific gravity with a hydrometer (see Chapter 1). If the voltage is less than 12-volts or if the specific gravity is low, recharge the battery.

8   Check the ignition fuse and the fuse connections. If the fuse is blown, replace it with a new one; if the connections are loose or corroded, clean or repair them.

9   Refer to Section 3 and check the ignition coil primary and secondary resistance.

10   Refer to Section 4 and check the pickup coil resistance.

11   If the preceding checks produce positive results but there is still no spark at the plug, remove the IC igniter and have it checked by a Kawasaki dealer service department or other repair shop equipped with the special tester required.

Engine starts but misfires

Refer to illustrations 2.13 and 2.14

12   If the engine starts but misfires, make the following checks before deciding that the ignition system is at fault.

13   The ignition system must be able to produce a spark across a seven millimeter (1/4-inch) gap (minimum). A simple test fixture **(see illustration)** can be constructed to make sure the minimum spark gap can be jumped. Make sure the fixture electrodes are positioned seven millimeters apart.

14   Connect one of the spark plug wires to the protruding test fixture electrode, then attach the fixture's alligator clip to a good engine ground **(see illustration)**.

15   Crank the engine over (it will probably start and run on the remaining cylinders) and see if well-defined, blue sparks occur between the test fixture electrodes. If the minimum spark gap test is positive, the ignition coil for that cylinder (and its companion cylinder) is functioning properly. Repeat the check on one of the spark plug wires that is connected to the other coil. If the spark will not jump the gap during either test, or if it is weak (orange colored), refer to Paragraphs 5 through 11 of this Section and perform the component checks described.

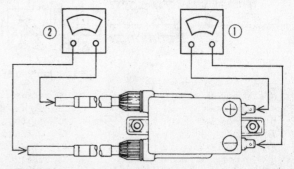

3.4 To check the resistance of the primary windings, connect the leads of the ohmmeter to the primary terminals (1); to check the resistance of the secondary (high tension) windings, attach the leads of the ohmmeter to the spark plug wires of that coil (2)

3   Ignition coils - check, removal and installation

Check

Refer to illustration 3.4

1   In order to determine conclusively that the ignition coils are defective, they should be tested by an authorized Kawasaki dealer service department which is equipped with the special electrical tester required for this check.

2   However, the coils can be checked visually (for cracks and other damage) and the primary and secondary coil resistances can be measured with an ohmmeter. If the coils are undamaged, and if the resistances are as specified, they are probably capable of proper operation.

3   To check the coils for physical damage, they must be removed (see Step 9). To check the resistances, simply remove the fuel tank (see Chapter 4), unplug the primary circuit electrical connectors from the coil(s) and remove the spark plug wires from the plugs that are connected to the coil being checked. Mark the locations of all wires before disconnecting them.

4   To check the coil primary resistance, attach one ohmmeter lead to one of the primary terminals and the other ohmmeter lead to the other primary terminal **(see illustration)**.

5   Place the ohmmeter selector switch in the Rx1 position and compare the measured resistance to the value listed in this Chapter's Specifications.

6   If the coil primary resistance is as specified, check the coil secondary resistance by disconnecting the meter leads from the primary terminals and attaching them to the spark plug wire terminals **(see illustration 3.4)**.

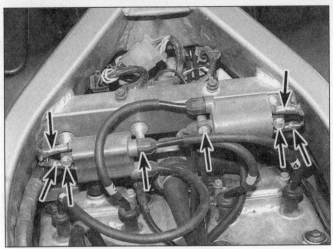

3.10a To remove an ignition coil from a D model, remove the mounting bolts (arrows), label the positive primary lead and unplug the primary leads (arrows)

3.10b To remove an ignition coil from an E model, remove the mounting bolts (arrows), label the positive primary lead and unplug the primary leads (arrows)

4.2a Unplug the pickup coil connector from the IC igniter (D models)

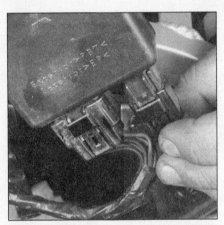

4.2b Unplug the pickup coil connector from the 2-pin connector located underneath the IC igniter (E models)

4.3 Measure the resistance across the two pickup coil terminals and compare your reading to the resistance range listed in this Chapter's Specifications

7   Place the ohmmeter selector switch in the Rx100 position and compare the measured resistance to the values listed in this Chapter's Specifications.

8   If the resistances are not as specified, unscrew the spark plug wire retainers from the coil, detach the wires and check the resistance again. If it is now within specifications, one or both of the wires are bad. If it's still not as specified, the coil is probably defective and should be replaced with a new one.

Removal and installation

Refer to illustrations 3.10a and 3.10b

9   Remove the fuel tank (see Chapter 4), then disconnect the spark plug wires from the plugs. Label them with tape to aid in reinstallation.

10   Support the coil with one hand, remove the coil mounting bolts **(see illustrations)**, and remove the coil from its bracket. Label the positive primary terminal on the coil **(see illustration)** to ensure that the primary leads aren't accidentally switched during reassembly. If you're removing both coils, it's also a good idea to label the coils with the cylinder numbers to which they're connected.

11   Installation is the reverse of removal. If a new coil is being installed, unscrew the spark plug wire terminals from the coil, pull the wires out and transfer them to the new coil. Make sure the primary circuit electrical connectors are attached to the proper terminals. Just in case you forgot to mark the wires, the black and red wires connect to the no. 1 and 4 ignition coil (red to positive, black to negative) and the red and green wires attach to the no. 2 and 3 coil (red to positive, green to negative).

4   Pickup coils - check, removal and installation

Check

Refer to illustrations 4.2a, 4.2b, 4.3 and 4.4

1   On D models, remove the seat (see Chapter 8). On E models, remove the right side cover (see Chapter 8).

2   On D models, remove the IC igniter **(see illustration)** from its "holster." On E models, unbolt the IC igniter (see Section 6). The pickup coil electrical lead consists of two wires (black wire and yellow wire) that exit the pickup coil cover on the right end of the crankshaft and are routed along the right side of the bike back to the igniter. Unplug the connector from the bottom of the igniter **(see illustration)**. The pickup coil connector is the smaller of the two multi-pin connectors on the bottom of the igniter (if it doesn't have a black wire and a yellow wire, you've got the wrong connector!).

3   Probe the terminals in the pickup coil connector with an ohmmeter **(see illustration)** and compare the resistance reading with the range of resistance listed in this Chapter's Specifications.

4   Set the ohmmeter on the highest resistance range. Measure the resistance between a good ground and each terminal in the pickup coil

5

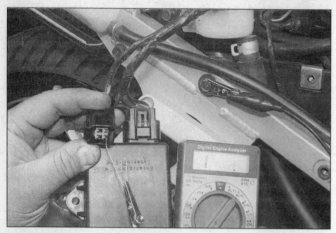

4.4 Measure the resistance between each pickup coil terminal and ground

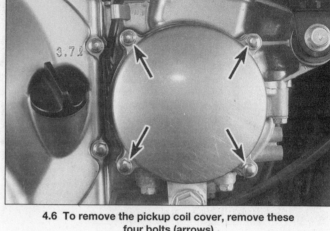

4.6 To remove the pickup coil cover, remove these four bolts (arrows)

4.7 To remove the pickup coil, remove these two screws (arrows), pull the grommet (arrow) for the electrical leads out of its notch in the case and trace the leads back to the pickup coil connector at the IC igniter

5.2 Hold the timing rotor with a wrench and remove the Allen bolt

connector **(see illustration)**. The meter should indicate infinite resistance.

5   If the pickup coil fails either of the above tests, it must be replaced.

Removal

Refer to illustrations 4.6 and 4.7

6   Remove the screws that secure the pickup coil cover to the engine case **(see illustration)** and detach the cover from the engine.

7   Unscrew the pickup coil mounting screws **(see illustration)** and remove the pickup coil. Note how the pickup coil wires are routed to insure proper rerouting of the new wires. Follow the wires back to the IC igniter and unplug the connector.

Installation

8   Install the new pickup coil unit and tighten the screws securely. Apply silicone sealant to the grommet for the electrical leads and push the grommet into its notch in the case.

9   Apply silicone sealant to the "split-line" of the crankcase halves, then install the pickup coil cover. Make sure the cover is installed with the "UP" mark facing upward. Tighten the cover bolts to the torque listed in this Chapter's Specifications.

10   Route the electrical lead exactly the same way it was routed before.

11   Plug in the electrical connector, install the IC igniter and install the seat (D models) or side cover (E models) and seat.

5   Timing rotor - removal and installation

Refer to illustrations 5.2 and 5.4

1   Refer to Section 4 and remove the pick-up coil cover.

2   Hold the timing rotor with a wrench on its hex and remove the Allen bolt **(see illustration)**.

3   Take the timing rotor off the crankshaft.

4   Installation is the reverse of the removal steps, with the following additions:

   a) Align the timing rotor notch with the pin on the end of the crankshaft **(see illustration)**.

   b) Hold the timing rotor hex with the same wrench used during removal and tighten the Allen bolt to the torque listed in this Chapter's Specifications.

6   IC igniter - removal, check and installation

Removal

Refer to illustration 6.2

1   Remove the right side cover (see Chapter 8).

2   Unbolt the igniter **(see illustration)** and unplug the electrical connectors.

5.4 Align the notch in the timing rotor with the pin on the crankshaft (arrows)

6.2 To detach the IC igniter, remove these two bolts (arrows), then pull the igniter out and unplug the multi-pin electrical connectors

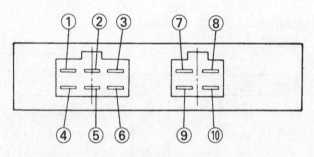

6.3a Terminal guide for the IC igniter (D models)

	Tester (+) Lead Connection					
Termi-nal No.	1	2	3	4	5	6
1		∞	∞	∞	∞	∞
2	∞		∞	∞	∞	∞
3	12 – 40	∞		12 – 40	7.6 – 14.0	4 – 10
4	∞	∞	∞		∞	∞
5	33 – 102	∞	7.6 – 14.0	33 – 102		17 – 35
6	2 – 4	∞	3.4 – 7.0	2 – 5	12 – 23	

(Tester (–) Lead Connection is the row label)

6.3b Resistance table for the IC igniter (D models) (all values given in k-ohms)

	Tester (+) Lead Connection			
Terminal Number	7	8	9	10
7		∞	∞	∞
8	∞		∞	33 – 60
9	∞	∞		∞
10	∞	32 – 60	∞	

(Tester (–) Lead Connection is the row label)

6.3c Resistance table for IC the igniter (D models) (all values given in k-ohms)

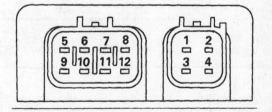

6.3d Terminal guide for the IC igniter (E models)

Check

Refer to illustrations 6.3a, 6.3b, 6.3c, 6.3d, 6.3e and 6.3f

3   According to Kawasaki, a special tester is required to accurately measure the resistance values across the various terminals of the IC igniter. However, if you have a high-impedance (10 meg-ohm) digital multimeter, you can test the igniter yourself. **Caution:** *Using an analog meter without 10 meg-ohm internal circuitry will produce inaccurate results and damage the IC igniter.* Referring to the accompanying resistance tables and terminal guides **(see illustrations)**, measure the resistance at the specified terminals and compare your measurements to the values listed in the resistance table for your model. If the igniter

5

		Tester (+) Lead Connection					
	Terminal	1	2	3	4	5	6
Tester (−) Lead Connection	1	−	∞	∞	∞	−	−
	2	∞	−	0.08 ~ 0.18	36 ~ 78	−	−
	3	∞	0.08 ~ 0.18	−	36 ~ 78	−	−
	4	∞	32 ~ 78	32 ~ 78	−	−	−
	5	−	−	−	−	−	∞
	6	−	−	−	−	32 ~ 132	−
	7	−	−	−	−	∞	∞
	8	−	−	−	−	6.5 ~ 16	6.5 ~ 16
	9	−	−	−	−	∞	∞
	10	−	−	−	−	18 ~ 42	18 ~ 42
	11	−	−	−	−	∞	∞
	12	−	−	−	−	1.9 ~ 5	2.3 ~ 6

6.3e Resistance table for the IC igniter (E models) (all values given in k-ohms)

		Tester (+) Lead Connection					
	Terminal	7	8	9	10	11	12
Tester (−) Lead Connection	1	−	−	−	−	−	−
	2	−	−	−	−	−	−
	3	−	−	−	−	−	−
	4	−	−	−	−	−	−
	5	∞	∞	∞	∞	∞	∞
	6	∞	28 ~ 60	32 ~ 132	40 ~ 96	∞	19 ~48
	7	−	∞	∞	∞	∞	∞
	8	∞	−	6.5 ~ 16	7.5 ~ 17	∞	3.3 ~ 6.6
	9	∞	∞	−	∞	∞	∞
	10	∞	7.5 ~ 17	18 ~ 43	−	∞	12 ~ 32
	11	∞	∞	∞	∞	−	∞
	12	∞	2.3 ~ 6	1.9 ~ 5	11 ~ 22	∞	−

6.3f Resistance table for the IC igniter (E models) (all values given in k-ohms)

fails any test, replace it. If you're in any doubt about the accuracy of your readings, or if you don't have a high-impedance digital multimeter, take the unit to a Kawasaki dealer service department or other repair shop equipped with the special tester.

Installation

4   Plug in the electrical connectors, place the igniter in position, install the mounting bolts and tighten them securely.
6   Install the side cover (see Chapter 8).

Chapter 6
Steering and suspension

Contents

Specifications

Front fork

Spring free length
  D models
    Standard .... 415 mm (16-23/64 inches)
    Minimum .... 407 mm (16-1/32 inches)
  E models
    Standard .... 283.6 mm (11-11/64 inches)
    Minimum .... 278 mm (10-61/64 inches)

Rear shock absorber

Gas pressure (D models) .... 980 to 1280 kPa (10 to 13 kg/cm², 142 to 185 psi)
Spring preload setting
  D models
    Standard .... Spring free length minus 8 mm (0.3152 inch)
    Usable range .... Spring free length minus 8 to 17 mm (0.3152 to 0.6698 inch)
  E models
    Standard .... Spring free length minus 15 mm (.0591 inch)
    Usable range .... Spring free length minus 15 to 24 mm (0.0591 to 0.9456 inch)

Torque specifications

Front forks
  Oil drain bolt (D models only) .... 88 Nm (65 ft-lbs)
  Front axle pinch bolt .... 20 Nm (14.5 ft-lbs)
Rear shock absorber
  Upper and lower bolts/nuts... 59 Nm (43 ft-lbs)
  Coil spring preload adjuster lock ring .... 88 Nm (65 ft-lbs)
  Tie-rod bolts/nuts... 59 Nm (43 ft-lbs)
Steering head
  Steering stem head nut
    D models .... 39 Nm (29 ft-lbs)
    E models .... 49 Nm (36 ft-lbs)
  Steering stem adjuster nut .... 4.9 Nm (43 in-lbs) or hand tighten
  Triple clamp/fork tube pinch bolts (all)................................... 20 Nm (14.5 ft-lbs)
  Handlebar-to-upper triple clamp bolts
    D models .... 20 Nm (14.5 ft-lbs)
    E models .... 23 Nm (16.5 ft-lbs)
Swingarm pivot bolt/nut .... 88 Nm (65 ft-lbs)

2.1a To get to the handlebar bolts, pry out these two caps with a small screwdriver

2.1b You'll need an Allen bit to remove the handlebar bolts

3.7a To detach the fork tube from the bike, remove the upper triple clamp bolt (arrow) . . .

1   General information

The front forks are a conventional coil-spring, hydraulically-damped telescopic type, designed to run at atmospheric pressure (i.e. they're not pressurized).

The rear suspension consists of a single nitrogen-charged shock absorber/coil spring assembly, a rocker arm, two tie-rods and a square-section aluminum swingarm. The shock absorber has an adjuster knob at the bottom which allows three rebound damping settings. Setting 1, which provides weak damping force, is for light loads, good roads and/or low speeds; setting 3, which produces the strongest damping force, is for heavy loads, bad roads and/or high speed. The coil spring preload can be adjusted by loosening a locknut and turning an adjusting nut at the upper end of the shock/coil assembly; the range of adjustment - from soft to hard - compresses the spring from 8 mm (no preload) to 17 mm (maximum preload).

2   Handlebars - removal and installation

Refer to illustrations 2.1a and 2.1b

1   The handlebars are individual assemblies that slip over the tops of the fork tubes, each being retained to the steering head by two Allen-head bolts. If the handlebars must be removed for access to other components, such as the forks or the steering head, simply pry out the caps, remove the bolts and slip the handlebar(s) off the fork tubes **(see illustrations)**. It isn't necessary to disconnect the cables, wires or hoses, but it is a good idea to support the assembly with a piece of

wire or rope, to avoid unnecessary strain on the cables, wires and (on the right side) the brake hose.
2   If the handlebars are to be removed completely, refer to Chapter 9 for the master cylinder removal procedure, Chapter 4 for the throttle grip removal procedure and Chapter 9 for the switch removal procedure.
3   Check the handlebars for cracks and distortion and replace them if any undesirable conditions are found. When installing the handlebars, tighten the bolts to the torque listed in this Chapter's Specifications.

3   Forks - removal and installation

Removal

Refer to illustrations 3.7a and 3.7b

1   Set the bike on its centerstand.
2   Remove the handlebars (see Section 2). Support them so the cables, wires and brake hose aren't strained or kinked.
3   Remove the small horn access panel from the upper fairing **(see illustration 6.20 in Chapter 8)**. (Removing this panel provides access to the lower triple clamp bolts.)
4   Unbolt the brake calipers (see Chapter 7) and hang them with pieces of wire or rope.
5   Disconnect the speedometer cable and remove the front wheel (see Chapter 7).
6   Remove the front fender/mudguard (see Chapter 8).
7   Loosen the fork upper and lower triple clamp bolts **(see illustrations)**, then slide the fork tubes down, using a twisting motion.

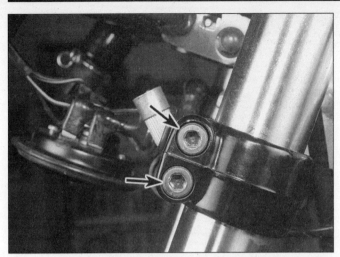

3.7b ... and the lower triple clamps bolts (arrows) (the bodywork has been removed for clarity - it isn't actually necessary to remove the fairing to get to the lower clamp bolts; simply remove the small horn access panel on the underside of the upper fairing)

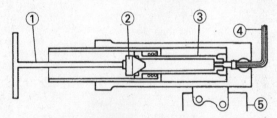

4.5b This is the setup you'll need if the slider-to-piston cylinder bolt is really tight:

1   Cylinder holder handle (Kawasaki tool no. 57001-183)
2   Cylinder holder adapter (Kawasaki tool no. 57001-1057)
3   Piston cylinder unit
4   Allen wrench

Installation

8   Slide each fork leg into the lower and upper triple clamps and snug the triple clamp bolts, but don't torque them yet. Pull each tube up until it's protruding the specified amount about the upper triple clamp, then tighten the triple clamp bolts tightly enough to hold the tubes in place. Do NOT torque any of the triple clamp bolts until the front wheel is installed.
9   Install the front fender/mudguard (see Chapter 8).
10   Install the front wheel (see Chapter 7).
11   Tighten the clamp bolts to the torque listed in this Chapter's Specifications.
12   The remainder of installation is the reverse of removal. Be sure to tighten all fasteners to the specification listed in the Chapter in which that particular component is covered.
13   Pump the front brake lever several times to bring the pads into contact with the discs.

4   Forks - disassembly, inspection and reassembly

Disassembly

Refer to illustrations 4.5a, 4.5b, 4.5c, 4.6, 4.7, 4.8, 4.9, 4.11a, 4.11b and 4.11c
Note: *Work on one fork leg at a time to avoid mixing up the parts.*
1   On D models, you can drain the fork oil (see Chapter 1) before removing the forks. On E models, there are no drain screws in the fork legs, so you can't drain the fork oil until the fork is removed from the bike.

4.5a If the bolt isn't too tight, you'll be able to remove it with an Allen wrench

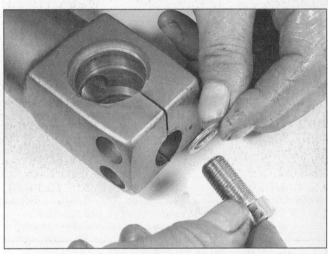

4.5c Be sure to remove and discard the old sealing washer; sometimes, this washer sticks to the lower end of the outer fork tube, then you forget about it during reassembly

2   Remove the forks (see Section 3).
3   Place the fork leg in a bench vise (clamp the vise jaws onto the brake caliper bosses on the slider; do not clamp onto the friction surface of the fork tube itself) and remove the top plug, spacer, washer and spring (see Section 29 in Chapter 1).
4   Pour out the fork oil, if you haven't already drained it.
5   Place the fork leg back in the bench vise again. To finish disassembling the fork, you must remove the large Allen bolt in the bottom of the slider. This bolt attaches the piston cylinder unit to the slider (the outer fork tube). Sometimes (if you're lucky), this step can be as easy as inserting an Allen key into the bolt and unscrewing it **(see illustration)**. More often (if you're not), the bolt is too tight and the piston cylinder unit turns when you try to loosen the bolt. If this happens, the usual next step is to use an air tool, if you have it. If not, have an assistant push the inner fork tube firmly into the slider; compressing the fork spring is often sufficient to lock the piston cylinder into place while the bolt is loosened. If that doesn't work, try compressing the fork spring *and* loosening the bolt with your air tool. And if that doesn't work? Borrow or buy the special Kawasaki holder and adapter (tool no. 57001-183 and no. 57001-1057) or a suitable equivalent **(see illustration)**, or have a dealer service department loosen the bolt. When removing the Allen bolt, retrieve the old copper sealing washer **(see illustration)** and discard it. This washer must be replaced when the fork is reassembled.

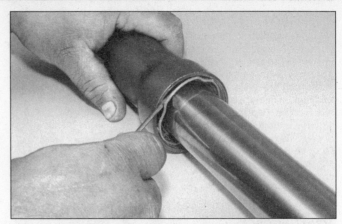

4.6 Pry the dust seal from the outer fork tube with a small screwdriver and slide it up the tube, out of the way; if you plan to reuse the dust seal, make sure you don't slide it over rust spots or scratches on the fork tube, or you will ruin it

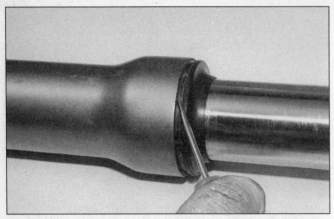

4.7 Pry the retainer ring out of the outer fork tube with a small screwdriver; do not distort this ring any more than necessary or you will have to use a new ring during reassembly

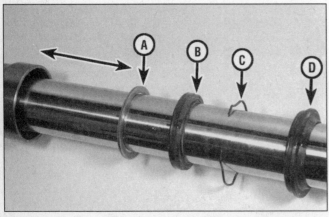

4.8 Grasp the inner and outer fork tubes, and pull them in opposite directions with a few sharp jerks (like a slide hammer) - they will separate easily; the washer (A), oil seal (B), retaining ring (C) and dust seal (D) will come off with the inner tube

4.9 Invert the inner fork tube and remove the piston cylinder unit and spring

6   Pry the dust seal from the outer tube (**see illustration**).
7   Pry the retaining ring from its groove in the outer tube (**see illustration**). Remove the ring.
8   To separate the inner and outer fork tubes, hold the outer tube and yank the inner tube upward repeatedly (like a slide hammer); the outer tube bushing on the inner fork tube will pop loose the washer and seal from the outer tube (**see illustration**).
9   Slide the seal and washer off the inner tube. Invert the tube and remove the piston cylinder unit (**see illustration**).

10   Invert the outer tube and retrieve the damper rod base - the small conical-shaped aluminum piece that's in the bottom of the outer fork tube below the piston cylinder unit (**see illustration 4.5b**).
11   There are two guide bushings at the lower end of the inner fork tube (**see illustration**). You need not remove either bushing unless it appears worn or scratched. If it's necessary to replace the inner tube guide bushing (the one that doesn't slide up and down, on the bottom of the inner tube), pry it apart at the slit and slide it off; the outer tube guide bushing can then be removed (**see illustrations**).

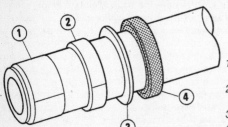

1 Inner tube guide bushing
2 Outer tube guide bushing
3 Washer
4 Seal

4.11a There are two bushings on the lower end of the inner fork tube: A (smaller) inner tube guide bushing and a (larger) outer tube guide bushing; the outer bushing slides freely up and down the fork tube but the inner bushing fits tightly to a slightly smaller diameter end of the tube, and is seated against a shoulder

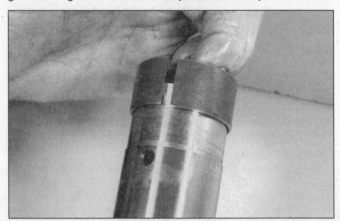

4.11b To remove the inner tube guide bushing from the inner fork tube, pry it apart at the slit and slide it off

Inspection

12 Clean all parts in solvent and blow them dry with compressed air, if available. Check the inner and outer fork tubes, the guide bushings and the damper rod for score marks, scratches, flaking of the chrome and excessive or abnormal wear. Look for dents in the tubes and replace them if any are found. Check the fork seal seat for nicks, gouges and scratches. If damage is evident, leaks will occur around the seal-to-outer tube junction. Replace worn or defective parts with new ones.

13 Have the fork inner tube checked for runout at a dealer service department or other repair shop. **Warning:** *If it is bent, it should not be straightened; replace it with a new one.*

14 Measure the overall length of the long spring and check it for cracks and other damage. Compare the length to the minimum length listed in this Chapter's Specifications. If it's defective or sagged, replace both fork springs with new ones. Never replace only one spring.

Reassembly

Refer to illustrations 4.15a, 4.15b, 4.15c, 4.15d, 4.15e, 4.15f, 4.15g and 4.15h

15 Reassembly is basically the reverse of disassembly **(see illustration)**, with the following special instructions:

   a) *To seat the large bushing in the outer fork tube, place the old bushing against the new bushing after the tubes are assembled.*

4.11c The outer tube guide bushing can now be removed by simply sliding it off

Make sure that, when installed, the split in the new bushing faces to one side - not to the front or rear - of the fork tube, then tap against the washer with a fork seal driver (Kawasaki tool no. 57001-1340 or a suitable equivalent) **(see illustrations)**.

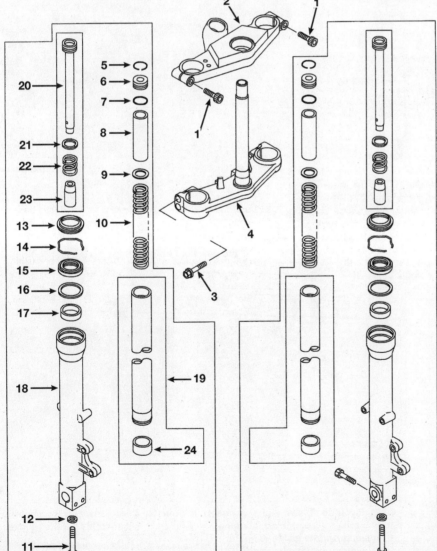

4.15a An exploded view of the front suspension assembly:

  1   *Upper triple clamp pinch bolt*
  2   *Upper triple clamp*
  3   *Lower triple clamp pinch bolt*
  4   *Lower triple clamp*
  5   *Retaining ring*
  6   *Top plug*
  7   *O-ring*
  8   *Spacer*
  9   *Washer (spring seat)*
 10 *Spring*
 11 *Piston cylinder unit bolt*
 12 *Sealing washer*
 13 *Dust seal*
 14 *Retaining ring*
 15 *Seal*
 16 *Washer*
 17 *Outer tube guide bushing*
 18 *Slider (outer fork tube)*
 19 *Inner fork tube*
 20 *Piston cylinder unit*
 21 *Washer*
 22 *Spring*
 23 *Cylinder base*
 24 *Inner tube guide bushing*

6

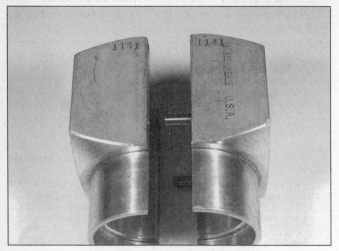

4.15b . . . Using a split-type seal driver (this is a Kent-Moore, but any suitable equivalent will work), . . .

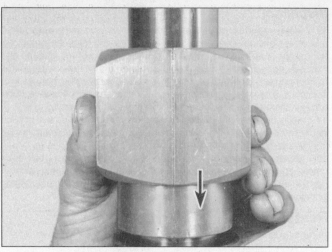

4.15c . . . tap down gently and repeatedly to seat the bushings; make sure the inner tube guide bushing (shown) is seated firmly against the shoulder

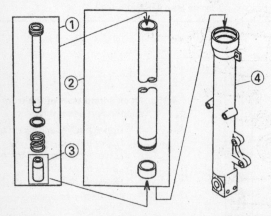

4.14d When installing the piston cylinder unit (1) into the inner fork tube (2), make sure you attach the cylinder base (3) to the lower end of the piston cylinder unit (the cylinder base will fit in the inner tube, but it won't go through the bottom end of the tube - it must, therefore, be installed after the cylinder unit has been installed into the tube); then flip the outer fork tube (4) upside down and insert the piston cylinder unit, fork tube and cylinder base into the fork tube as a single assembly

4.15e Wrap the top of the fork tube with tape to prevent the lip on the new seal from damage during installation

4.15f Using the same driver you used to install the bushings, tap the seal into place until it seats in the outer fork tube (one half of the driver has been removed for clarity)

4.15g If you don't have a bushing/seal driver tool, PVC plumbing fittings of the appropriate inside diameter work just fine as drivers

4.15h Compress the retaining ring and fit it securely into its groove

b) *When reassembling and installing the piston cylinder unit, install the piston cylinder unit into the fork tube, then insert the lower end of the unit (the damper rod) into the cylinder base* **(see illustration)**. *You can't install the cylinder base through the fork tube! Then invert the outer fork tube (axle end up), insert the reassembled fork tube, piston cylinder unit and cylinder base into the outer fork tube and install the damper rod bolt. Use a new sealing washer on the damper rod bolt. Apply non-permanent thread locking agent to the threads and tighten the bolt to the torque listed in this Chapter's Specifications.*

c) *Wrap the end of the inner fork tube with tape to protect the oil seal while it's installed* **(see illustration)**. *Drive in the seal with the same tool used to install the bushing, then install the retaining ring and make sure it's securely seated in its groove* **(see illustrations)**.

d) *Install the dust seal and make sure it's securely seated in the outer fork tube.*

5   Steering stem and bearings - removal, inspection and installation

Removal

Refer to illustrations 5.3, 5.4, 5.8, 5.9a, 5.9b and 5.11

1   If the steering head bearing check/adjustment (see Chapter 1) does not remedy excessive play or roughness in the steering head bearings, the entire front end must be disassembled and the bearings and races replaced with new ones.
2   Remove the fuel tank (see Chapter 4).
3   On D models, remove the steering stem nut cover **(see illustration)**.
4   Remove the steering stem head nut **(see illustration)** and washer, loosen the upper triple clamp-to-fork tube pinch bolts, then lift

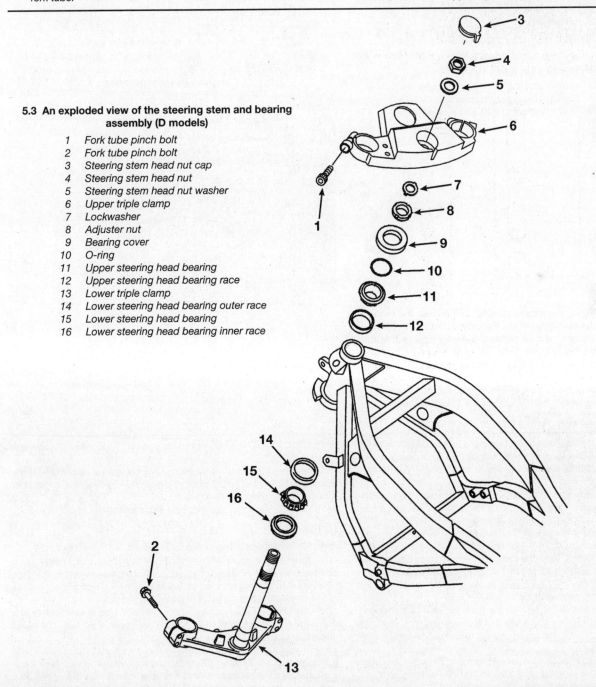

5.3 An exploded view of the steering stem and bearing assembly (D models)

1   *Fork tube pinch bolt*
2   *Fork tube pinch bolt*
3   *Steering stem head nut cap*
4   *Steering stem head nut*
5   *Steering stem head nut washer*
6   *Upper triple clamp*
7   *Lockwasher*
8   *Adjuster nut*
9   *Bearing cover*
10 *O-ring*
11 *Upper steering head bearing*
12 *Upper steering head bearing race*
13 *Lower triple clamp*
14 *Lower steering head bearing outer race*
15 *Lower steering head bearing*
16 *Lower steering head bearing inner race*

6

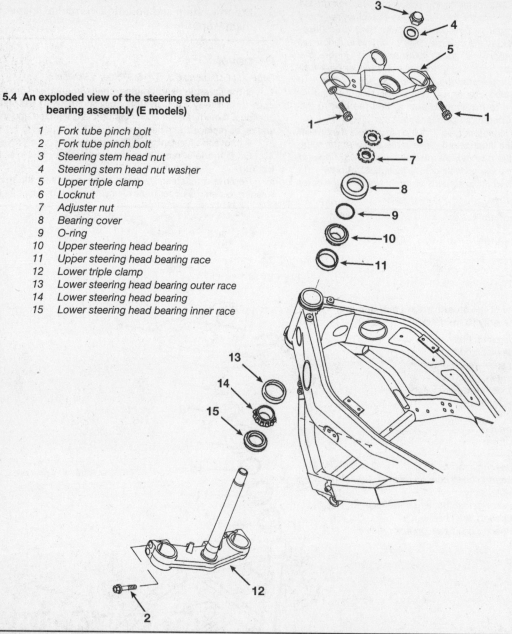

5.4 An exploded view of the steering stem and bearing assembly (E models)

1   *Fork tube pinch bolt*
2   *Fork tube pinch bolt*
3   *Steering stem head nut*
4   *Steering stem head nut washer*
5   *Upper triple clamp*
6   *Locknut*
7   *Adjuster nut*
8   *Bearing cover*
9   *O-ring*
10   *Upper steering head bearing*
11   *Upper steering head bearing race*
12   *Lower triple clamp*
13   *Lower steering head bearing outer race*
14   *Lower steering head bearing*
15   *Lower steering head bearing inner race*

off the upper triple clamp (sometimes called the fork bridge or crown). Unless you plan to replace the upper triple clamp, it isn't necessary to remove the handlebars - just set the upper triple clamp aside with everything attached.

5   If there's any strain on the electrical leads between the ignition main (key) switch and the main harness, unplug the electrical connectors for the main switch (see Chapter 9).

6   Unbolt the brake hose union (the metal pipe that serves as the junction between the hose from the master cylinder and the two hoses to the front brake calipers) from the lower triple clamp (see Chapter 7). It isn't necessary to disconnect the hydraulic hoses, but make sure no strain is placed on them.

7   Remove the front forks (see Section 3).

8   On D models, remove the lockwasher from the stem adjuster nut **(see illustration)**. (E models don't use this lockwasher; they use two identical castellated nuts - the upper one is the locknut and the lower one is the adjuster nut.)

9   Using a spanner wrench (C-spanner), remove the stem adjuster nut (D models) or the locknut and adjuster nut (E models), and the bearing cover **(see illustrations)**, while supporting the lower triple

clamp (so that it doesn't fall out of the steering head when the adjuster nut is removed).

10   Remove the steering stem/lower triple clamp assembly. If it's stuck, gently tap on the top of the steering stem with a plastic mallet or a hammer and a wood block.

11   Remove the upper bearing **(see illustration)**.

Inspection

Refer to illustrations 5.14a, 5.14b, 5.14c, 5.16, 5.17, 5.20 and 5.21

12   Clean all the parts with solvent and dry them thoroughly, using compressed air, if available. If you do use compressed air, don't let the bearings spin as they're dried - it could ruin them. Wipe the old grease out of the frame steering head and bearing races.

13   Examine the races in the steering head for cracks, dents, and pits. If even the slightest amount of wear or damage is evident, the races should be replaced with new ones.

14   To remove the races, drive them out of the steering head with Kawasaki tool no. 57001-1107 or a hammer and drift punch **(see illustrations)**. A slide hammer with the proper internal-jaw puller will also work. Since the races are an interference fit in the frame, installation will

5.8 On D models, lift the lockwasher off the steering stem (E models don't use this lockwasher, they use a locknut identical to the adjuster nut) . . .

5.9a . . . remove the adjuster nut with a spanner wrench (C-spanner) . . .

5.9b . . . and lift off the nut and bearing cover

5.11 Lift the upper steering head bearing out of the steering head

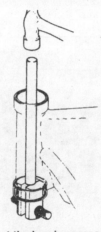

5.14a Drive out the bearing races with the special Kawasaki tool (no. 57001-1107) or a similar tool . . .

5.14b . . . or insert a drift from above to drive out the race

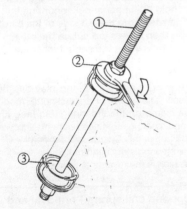

5.14c Kawasaki's special tools for pressing the outer races into the steering head

1 Driver press shaft (tool no. 57001-1075
2 Driver (tool no. 57001-1106)
3 Driver (tool no. 57001-1076)

5.16 Remove the lower bearing and grease seal from the steering stem only if they're to be replaced; the wider side of the grease seal goes down

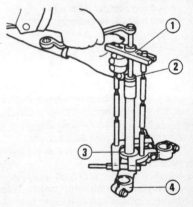

5.17 Kawasaki's special tools for removing the lower bearing and grease seal

1 Bearing puller (tool no. 57001-158)
2 Adapter (tool no. 57001-137)
3 Lower bearing
4 Steering stem

be easier if the new races are left overnight in a refrigerator. This will cause them to contract and slip into place in the frame with very little effort. When installing the races, use Kawasaki press shaft no. 57001-1075 and drivers no. 57001-1106 and 57001-1076 **(see illustration)**, or tap them gently into place with a hammer and punch or a large socket. Do not strike the bearing surface or the race will be damaged.

15   Check the bearings for wear. Look for cracks, dents, and pits in the races and flat spots on the bearings. Replace any defective parts with new ones. If a new bearing is required, replace both of them as a set.

16   Check the grease seal under the lower bearing and replace it with a new one if necessary **(see illustration)**.

17   To remove the lower bearing and grease seal from the steering stem, use a bearing puller (Kawasaki tool no. 57001-158) combined with adapter no. 57001-317 **(see illustration)**. A bearing puller, which

5.20 Work the grease completely into the rollers

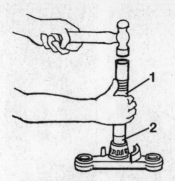

5.21 Drive the lower bearing onto the steering stem with the special Kawasaki tools (or use a piece of tubing with the same diameter as the bearing inner race)

1   *Stem bearing driver (tool no. 57001-137*
2   *Adapter (tool no. 1074)*

5.22a Install the upper bearing and the O-ring

5.22b Install the bearing cover and tighten the adjuster nut until all play has been removed from the steering head bearings

5.23 Install the lockwasher (D models, shown), making sure it engages the notches in the nut; or install the locknut (E models, not shown) and tighten it snugly to prevent the adjuster nut from turning

6.3 Using a socket on a long extension inserted through the hole in the frame, hold the upper shock mounting bolt (arrow) from the left side of the bike, then loosen the nut on the other side using the same technique

can be rented, will also work. Don't remove this bearing unless it, or the grease seal underneath, must be replaced. Removal will damage the grease seal, so replace it whenever the bearing is removed.
18   Inspect the steering stem/lower triple clamp for cracks and other damage. Do not attempt to repair any steering components. Replace them with new parts if defects are found.
19   Check the O-ring under the bearing cover - if it's worn or deteriorated, replace it.
20   Pack the bearings with high-quality grease (preferably a moly-based grease) **(see illustration)**. Coat the outer races with grease also.
21   Install the grease seal and lower bearing onto the steering stem. Drive the lower bearing onto the steering stem using Kawasaki stem bearing driver no. 57001-137 and adapter no. 57001-1074 **(see illustration)**. If you don't have access to these tools, a section of pipe with a diameter the same as the inner race of the bearing can be used. Drive the bearing on until it's fully seated.

Installation

Refer to illustrations 5. 22a, 5.22b and 5.23
22   Insert the steering stem/lower triple clamp into the steering head. Install the upper bearing, O-ring, bearing cover and adjuster nut **(see illustrations)**. Using the spanner wrench (C-spanner), tighten the adjuster nut while moving the lower triple clamp back and forth. Continue to tighten the nut, 1/8-turn at a time, until all play has been removed from the steering head bearings. However, don't overtighten the adjuster nut, or the steering will be too firm and the new bearings

and/or races will wear out prematurely.
23   Once the adjuster nut is tight and all bearing play has been removed, install the lockwasher (D models), or the locknut (E models), then install the upper triple clamp on the steering stem **(see illustration)**. Install the washer and steering stem head nut and tighten the stem head nut to the torque listed in this Chapter's Specifications.
24   On D models, install the steering stem head nut cap.
25   The remainder of installation is the reverse of removal.

6   Rear shock absorber and coil spring - removal and installation

Refer to illustrations 6.3 and 6.4
Warning: *Do not attempt to disassemble this shock absorber. It is nitrogen-charged under high pressure. Improper disassembly could result in serious injury. Instead, take the shock to a dealer service department with the proper equipment to do the job.*
1   Set the bike on its centerstand.
2   Remove the side covers (see Chapter 8).
3   Loosen the shock absorber upper nut **(see illustration)**. Don't remove it yet.
4   Remove the shock absorber lower nut and bolt and the tie-rod lower nut and bolt **(see illustration)**.
5   Remove the upper nut and bolt. Pull the tie-rods back and lower the shock absorber from the bike.

6.4 To disconnect the lower end of the rear shock absorber from the bike, remove the shock-to-rocker arm nut and bolt (1) and the rocker arm-to-tie rod nut and bolt (2). The upper end of the tie-rods are connected to the swingarm by a bolt and nut (3) (although it isn't necessary to remove the bolt for shock absorber removal)

7.5 Inspect the needle bearings inside the rocker arm (shown) and the swingarm (not shown) for wear and damage - if they look dry, discolored or dirty, remove and wash them, then have a better look

6   Installation is the reverse of the removal procedure. Tighten the shock absorber and tie-rod nuts/bolts to the torque values listed in this Chapter's Specifications.

7   Rear suspension linkage - removal, check and installation

Removal

Refer to illustration 7.4

1   Set the bike on its centerstand.
2   Remove the nut and bolt that attach the shock absorber and the tie-rods to the rocker arm (see illustration 6.4).
3   Remove the nut and bolt that attach the tie-rods to the swingarm (see illustration 6.4) and remove the tie-rods.
4   Remove the nut and bolt that attach the rocker arm to the frame (see illustration).

Check

Refer to illustrations 7.5, 7.6a, 7.6b, 7.6c, 7.7, 7.9, 7.10 and 7.11

5   Inspect the bearings and sleeves (see illustration) with a flashlight.

7.4 Remove the nut and bolt which attach the rocker arm to the frame (arrow)

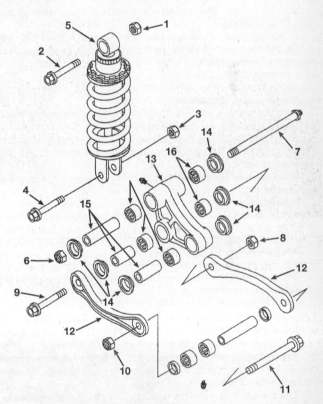

7.6a An exploded view of the suspension linkage assembly:

1 Upper shock bolt nut	9 Tie rod-to-rocker arm bolt
2 Upper shock bolt	
3 Lower shock bolt nut	10 Tie rod-to-swingarm bolt nut
4 Lower shock bolt	
5 Shock absorber/coil spring assembly	11 Tie rod-to-swingarm bolt
6 Rocker arm pivot bolt nut	12 Tie rods
	13 Rocker arm
7 Rocker arm pivot bolt	14 Dust seals
8 Tie rod-to-rocker arm bolt nut	15 Sleeves
	16 Needle bearings

6   If the bearings or the sleeves look dry, dirty or worn, push out the sleeves and pry off the grease seals (see illustrations).
7   Remove the needle bearings out of the rocker arm and swingarm with an oil seal/bearing remover tool (Kawasaki tool no. 57001-1058 or

6

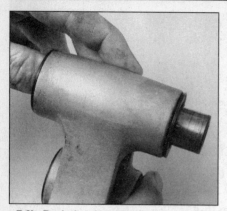

7.6b Push the sleeves out of the rocker arm (shown) and the swingarm (not shown)

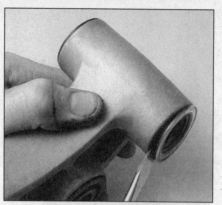

7.6c Pry out the dust seals from the rocker arm (shown) and the swingarm (not shown)

7.7 If you don't have access to a Kawasaki oil seal and bearing remover set, knock out the old needle bearings with a hammer and punch

a suitable equivalent). They can also be driven out with a hammer and punch **(see illustration)**.

8 Thoroughly wash all parts in clean solvent, then inspect both the sleeves and the bearings for dryness, discoloration, excessive wear and general deterioration. If either the sleeves or the bearings are worn, replace them as a set.

9 Apply a thin coat of moly-based grease to the sleeves before installing them **(see illustration)**.

10 Pack the bearings with moly-based grease before installing them. You'll need a bearing driver set (Kawasaki tool no. 57001-1129 or a suitable equivalent) to install the bearings. Or, install new bearing sets by driving them in with a hammer and a socket of the appropriate size **(see illustration)**.

11 Install the dust seals on either end of each sleeve and bearing set **(see illustration)**.

12 Installation is otherwise the reverse of removal. Tighten all fasteners to the torque listed in this Chapter's Specifications.

8 Swingarm bearings - check

1 Remove the rear wheel (see Chapter 7), then remove the rear shock absorber (see Section 6).

2 Grasp the rear of the swingarm with one hand and place your other hand at the junction of the swingarm and the frame. Try to move the rear of the swingarm from side-to-side. Any wear (play) in the bearings should be felt as movement between the swingarm and the

7.9 Be sure to coat the sleeves with moly-based grease before installing them

frame at the front. The swingarm will actually be felt to move forward and backward at the front (not from side-to-side). If any play is noted, the bearings should be replaced with new ones (see Section 10).

3 Next, move the swingarm up and down through its full travel. It should move freely, without any binding or rough spots. If it does not move freely, refer to Section 10 for servicing procedures.

7.10 If you don't have access to a Kawasaki bearing driver set, drive the new needle bearings into the rocker arm (shown) or the swingarm (not shown) with a socket that just fits into the bore of the rocker arm

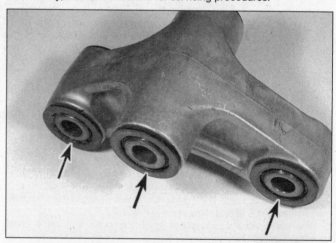

7.11 Be sure to install new dust seals (arrows); make sure the seals are properly seated as shown - flush with the ends of the sleeves - or the rocker arm won't fit between the frame bracket or the tie rods

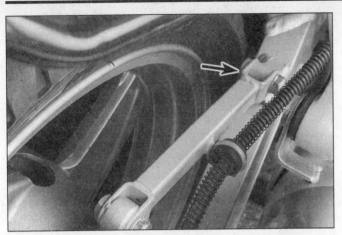

9.3 To disconnect the torque arm from the swingarm, remove this nut (arrow) and bolt

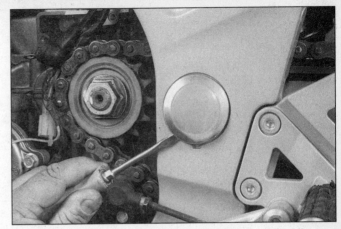

9.4 Pry off this protective cap on the left side of the bike and loosen the nut underneath

9   Swingarm - removal and installation

Refer to illustrations 9.3 and 9.4

1   Raise the bike and set it on its centerstand.
2   Remove the rear wheel (see Chapter 7).
3   Detach the torque arm from the swingarm **(see illustration)**. Support the rear brake caliper and torque arm with a piece of rope or wire - don't let them hang by the brake hose.
4   Remove the swingarm pivot nut **(see illustration)**. Don't remove the pivot bolt yet.
5   Detach the tie-rods and the shock absorber from the rocker arm (see Section 7). Support the swingarm while doing this.
6   Pry off the cap on the other side of the frame, support the swingarm and pull out the pivot bolt. Remove the swingarm. If necessary, remove the bolts and detach the tie-rods from the swingarm.

7   Check the pivot bearings in the swingarm for dryness or deterioration. If they're in need of lubrication or replacement, refer to Section 10.
8   Installation is the reverse of removal. Be sure the bearing seals are in position before installing the pivot shaft. Tighten the pivot shaft nut and the shock absorber and tie-rod lower mounting bolts/nuts to the torque values listed in this Chapter's Specifications. Adjust the chain as described in Chapter 1.

10   Swingarm bearings - replacement

Refer to illustrations 10.2a, 10.2b, 10.3a, 10.3b and 10.6

1   Remove the swingarm (see Section 9).
2   Slide out the sleeve **(see illustrations)**.

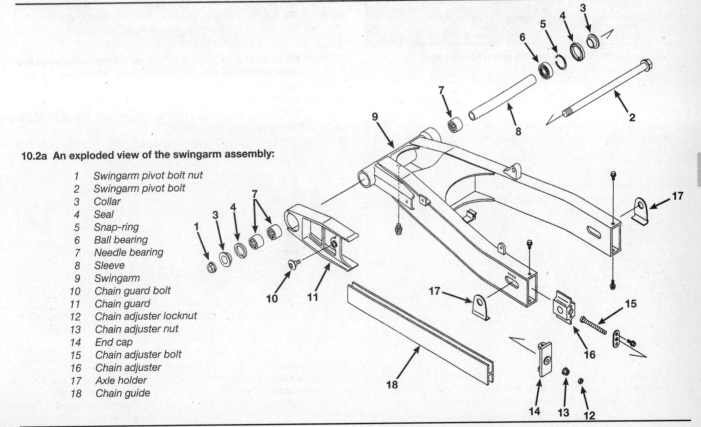

10.2a An exploded view of the swingarm assembly:

1   Swingarm pivot bolt nut
2   Swingarm pivot bolt
3   Collar
4   Seal
5   Snap-ring
6   Ball bearing
7   Needle bearing
8   Sleeve
9   Swingarm
10   Chain guard bolt
11   Chain guard
12   Chain adjuster locknut
13   Chain adjuster nut
14   End cap
15   Chain adjuster bolt
16   Chain adjuster
17   Axle holder
18   Chain guide

6

10.2b Slide the sleeve out of the front of the swingarm

10.3a Remove the collar(s) from the grease seal(s)

10.3b Pry out the seals with a screwdriver

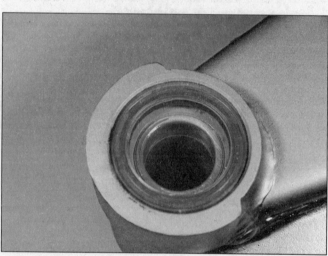

10.6 Make sure the seal faces are flush with the pivot boss of the swingarm as shown before installing the collars

3   Remove the collars and pry out the seals **(see illustrations)**.
4   To remove the ball bearing from the right end of the swingarm, remove the snap-ring **(see illustration 10.2a)**.
5   Refer to Section 7, Steps 7 through 10 for the bearing service

procedures.
6   Make sure the new seal faces are flush with the side of the swingarm as shown **(see illustration)**.
7   Install the swingarm (see Section 9).

Chapter 7
Brakes, wheels, tires and final drive

Contents

Specifications

Brakes

Brake fluid type	See Chapter 1
Brake lever freeplay	Non-adjustable
Brake pad minimum thickness	See Chapter 1

Disc thickness
  D models
    Front
      Standard .... 4.3 to 4.6 mm (0.1694 to 0.1812 inch)
      Minimum* .... 4.0 mm (0.1576 inch)
    Rear
      Standard .... 5.8 to 6.1 mm (0.2285 to 0.2403 inch)
      Minimum* .... 5.5 mm (0.2167 inch)
  E models
    Front
      Standard .... 3.8 to 4.2 mm (0.1497 to 0.1655 inch)
      Minimum* .... 3.5 mm (0.1379 inch)
    Rear
      Standard .... 5.8 to 6.1 mm (0.2285 to 0.2403 inch)
      Minimum* .... 5.0 mm (0.197 inch)

Refer to marks stamped into the disc (they supersede information printed here)

Disc runout (front and rear, all models)
  Standard .... 0.2 mm or less (0.0079 inch)
  Minimum .... 0.3 mm (0.0118 inch)

Final drive

Rear sprocket runout
  Standard .... 0.4 mm (0.0158 inch) or less
  Maximum .... 0.5 mm (0.020 inch)

Wheels and tires

Wheel runout	
Axial (side-to-side)	0.5 mm (0.020 inch)
Radial (out-of-round)	0.8 mm (0.031 inch)
Rear axle runout	
Standard	0.05 mm (0.0020 inch)
Service limit	0.2 mm (0.0079 inch)
Tire pressures	See Chapter 1
Tire sizes	
D models	
Front	120/60 VR17-V250 Dunlop K510F; 120/60 ZR17 Metzeler ME Front Comp K; 120/60 ZR17 Pirelli MP7 Sport; 110/70 V17-V250 Metzeler ME1 Front Racing
Rear	160/60 VR17-V250 Dunlop K510; 160/60 ZR17 Metzeler ME1 Comp K; 160/60 ZR17 Pirelli MP7 Sport; 160/60 VB17 Metzeler ME1 Comp K
E models	
Front	120/60 ZR17 Michelin A59; 120/60 ZR17 Bridgestone Battlax BT-50F Radial; 120/60 ZR17 Dunlop K510F
Rear	160/60 ZR17 Michelin M59; 160/60 ZR17 Bridgestone Battlax BT-50R Radial G; 160/60 ZR17 Dunlop D202G

Torque specifications

Axle nut (front and rear)	
D models	88 Nm (65 ft-lbs)
E models	110 Nm (80 ft-lbs)
Brake caliper bleeder screw	7.8 Nm (69 in-lbs)
Brake hose banjo bolts	25 Nm (18 ft-lbs)
Brake disc-to-wheel bolts	23 Nm (16.5 ft-lbs)
Front axle clamp bolts	20 Nm (14.5 ft-lbs)
Front caliper bolts	
Upper bolt	34 Nm (25 ft-lbs)
Lower bolt	21 Nm (15 ft-lbs)
Master cylinder mounting bolts	
Front	9.8 Nm (87 in-lbs)
Rear	23 Nm (16.5 ft-lbs)

1   General information

The models covered by this manual are equipped with hydraulic disc brakes on the front and rear. All models employ dual-piston front calipers. D models employ dual-piston rear calipers as well; E models use single-piston rear calipers.

All models are equipped with cast aluminum wheels, which require very little maintenance and allow tubeless tires to be used. **Caution:** *Disc brake components rarely require disassembly. Do not disassemble components unless absolutely necessary. If any hydraulic brake line connection in the system is loosened, the entire system should be disassembled, drained, cleaned and then properly filled and bled upon reassembly. Do not use solvents on internal brake components. Solvents will cause seals to swell and distort. Use only clean brake fluid or alcohol for cleaning. Use care when working with brake fluid as it can injure your eyes and it will damage painted surfaces and plastic parts.*

2   Brake caliper - removal, overhaul and installation

Warning: *If a front caliper indicates the need for an overhaul (usually due to leaking fluid or sticky operation), BOTH front calipers should be overhauled and all old brake fluid flushed from the system. Also, the dust created by the brake system may contain asbestos, which is harmful to your health. Never blow it out with compressed air and don't inhale any of it. An approved filtering mask should be worn when working on the brakes. Do not, under any circumstances, use petroleum-based solvents to clean brake parts. Use brake cleaner or denatured alcohol only!*
Note: *If you are removing the caliper only to remove the front or rear wheel or to replace or inspect the rear brake pads, don't disconnect the hose from the caliper.*

Removal

Front caliper

Refer to illustrations 2.2a and 2.2b

1   Support the bike securely upright. **Note:** *If you're planning to disassemble the caliper, read through the overhaul procedure, paying particular attention to the steps involved in removing the pistons with compressed air. If you don't have access to an air compressor, you can use the bike's hydraulic system to force the pistons out instead. To do this, remove the pads and pump the brake lever. If one piston comes out before the others, push it back into its bore and hold it in with a C-clamp while pumping the brake lever to remove the remaining pistons.*

2   **Note:** *Remember, if you're just removing the caliper to remove the front wheel, ignore this step.* Disconnect the brake hose from the caliper. Remove the brake hose banjo fitting bolt and separate the hose from the caliper **(see illustrations)**. Discard the sealing washers. Plug the fitting or wrap a plastic bag tightly around it to prevent excessive fluid loss and contamination.

3   Unscrew the caliper mounting bolts **(see illustration 2.2a)**. Lift off the caliper, being careful not to strain or twist the brake hose if it's still connected.

Rear caliper

Refer to illustrations 2.4a, 2.4b and 2.7

4   If you're removing the rear caliper but leaving the brake hose connected, detach the brake hose from the clip on the torque arm **(see illustrations)**.

5   **Note:** *If you're only removing the caliper to replace brake pads or remove the wheel, ignore this step.* Disconnect the brake hose from the caliper. Remove the brake hose banjo fitting bolt and separate the hose from the caliper **(see illustration 2.2b)**. Discard the sealing washers. Plug the fitting or wrap a plastic bag tightly around it to

2.2a To remove a front caliper, unscrew and disconnect the threaded ferrule (arrow) on the end of the speedometer cable (left caliper only), then remove the two big caliper-to-slider mounting bolts (arrows); if you're going to overhaul the caliper, also unscrew the banjo bolt (arrow) that connects the brake hose to the caliper (don't unscrew this bolt if you're only replacing the brake pads)

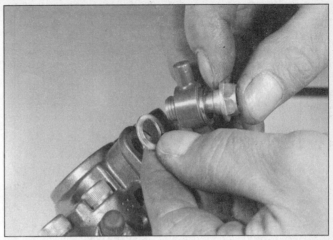

2.2b When you separate the hose from the front caliper, remove and discard the copper sealing washers on each side of the banjo fitting; always use new sealing washers when reattaching a brake hose to a caliper

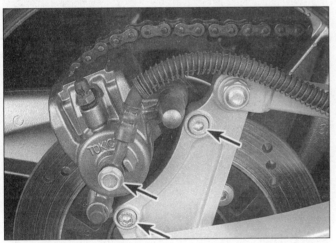

2.4a To remove a rear caliper, remove these two caliper-to-hanger Allen bolts (arrows); if you're going to overhaul the caliper, also unscrew the banjo bolt (arrow) connecting the rear brake hose to the caliper (don't unscrew this bolt if you're only replacing the brake pads, however) (single-piston E model caliper shown; dual-piston caliper similar)

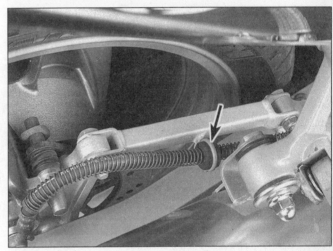

2.4b Separate the brake hose from its clip on the torque arm

prevent excessive fluid loss and contamination.

6 Unscrew the caliper mounting bolts (see illustration 2.4a) and, if you're planning to overhaul the caliper, remove the caliper from the hanger. If you're removing the caliper to replace the brake pads rather than overhaul the caliper, read the next Step before removing the caliper from the disc.

7 If you're planning to simply replace the brake pads (rather than overhaul the caliper), pivot the caliper back and up slightly (to allow the clamp to clear the sprocket) and place a C-clamp on the caliper as shown (see illustration). Position the clamp so that the pad on the end of the screw is seated directly against the back of the inner brake pad. When you tighten the clamp, it pushes the piston back into its bore so that the caliper can be installed back over the disc with the new (thicker) brake pads. Keep tightening the clamp until the piston bottoms out. **Note:** *This trick only works on E models with a single-piston rear caliper. On D models with dual-piston rear calipers, you'll have to manually depress the pistons after removing the caliper from the bike.* Once the piston is depressed, remove the caliper. Be careful not to strain or twist the brake hose if it's still connected.

2.7 If you're planning to replace the pads on an E model single-piston rear caliper, tilt the caliper back slightly and raise it up a little, then install a C-clamp as shown; when you tighten the clamp, it will push the caliper piston back into its bore so you can get the caliper to fit over the disc with the new pads

7

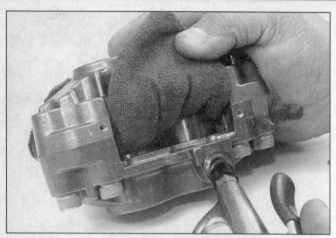

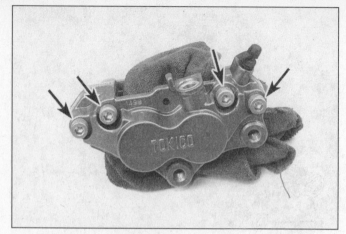

2.8 Place a couple of rags through the brake pad cavity to protect the pistons from damage and apply a small blast of compressed air to the brake hose inlet; this procedure is tricky on four-piston calipers, but remember: all you want to do is break the pistons loose so you can pull them out of their bores after the caliper halves are separated

2.9 To separate the caliper halves, remove these four Allen bolts (arrows)

Overhaul

Front caliper

Refer to illustrations 2.8, 2.9, 2.10, 2.11 and 2.15

8   Remove the brake pads and anti-rattle spring from the caliper (see Section 3). Clean the exterior of the caliper with rubbing alcohol or brake system cleaner. Shove a couple of shop rags through the caliper and pop the four pistons loose with a *small* burst of compressed air **(see illustration)**. **Warning:** *Do NOT stick your fingers in between the pistons when applying compressed air!*

9   Remove the four Allen bolts that hold the caliper halves together and separate the caliper **(see illustration)**.

10   If you were unsuccessful in loosening any of the pistons in Step 8, bolt a piece of wood at least 10 mm thick to the mating surface of each caliper half to prevent the piston(s) from flying out. The wood must block one of the fluid inlets. Use compressed air, directed into the other fluid inlet, to remove the piston(s). Use only enough air pressure to ease the piston(s) out of the bore. If a piston is blown out forcefully, even with the wood in place, it may be damaged. **Warning:** *Never place your fingers in front of the piston in an attempt to catch or protect it when applying compressed air, as serious injury could occur.* Carefully remove each piston from its bore **(see illustration)**.

11   Remove the piston seals **(see illustration)**, preferably with a wood or plastic tool. If you *do* use a metal tool - and use it carelessly -

you may cause bore damage. Note that there are two seals per piston bore: the upper seal is the dust seal and the lower seal is the piston seal. Also, be sure to remove the two small O-rings from the caliper half. They must be discarded and new ones used during reassembly.

12   Clean the pistons and the bores with rubbing alcohol, clean brake fluid or brake system cleaner and blow dry them with filtered, unlubricated compressed air. Inspect the surfaces of the pistons for nicks and burrs and loss of plating. Check the caliper bores, too. If surface defects are present, the caliper must be replaced. If the caliper is in bad shape, the master cylinder should also be checked.

13   Lubricate the piston (lower) seals with clean brake fluid and install them in their grooves in the caliper bore. Make sure they seat completely and aren't twisted.

14   Lubricate the dust (upper) seals with clean brake fluid and install them in their grooves, making sure they seat correctly.

15   Lubricate the pistons with clean brake fluid and install them into the caliper bores **(see illustration)**. Carefully position each piston square with the bore, then use your thumb to push the piston all the way in until it's bottomed out. Don't allow a piston to become cocked in the bore. If it does, don't try to force it - gently work it back out, square it with the bore, then push again with your thumb.

Rear caliper

Refer to illustrations 2.17a, 2.17b, 2.17c, 2.17d, 2.17e, 2.26, 2.27 and 2.28

Note: *The following overhaul procedure depicts an E model single-piston rear caliper, but the procedure for overhauling a D model*

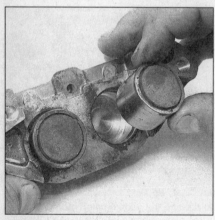

2.10 Remove the pistons from their bores

2.11 To avoid damage to the bore and the seal grooves, use a pencil - or some other plastic or wooden tool - to remove the dust seal and the piston seal

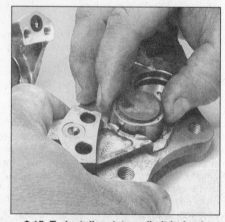

2.15 To install a piston, dip it in fresh brake fluid, align it so it's perpendicular to its bore, then push it straight into the bore with your thumbs

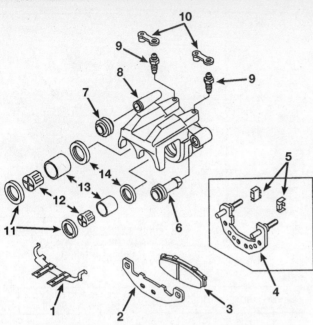

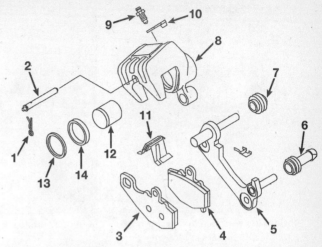

**2.17a An exploded view of the rear brake caliper assembly
(D models)**

1	Anti-rattle spring	8	Caliper
2	Inner brake pad	9	Caliper bleeder screw
3	Outer brake pad	10	Bleeder screw caps
4	Caliper bracket	11	Dust seals
5	Pad support clips	12	Piston inserts
6	Slider pin boot	13	Pistons
7	Slider pin boot	14	Piston seals

**2.17b An exploded view of the rear brake caliper assembly
(E models)**

1	Retaining pin clip	8	Caliper
2	Pad retaining pin	9	Bleeder screw
3	Inner brake pad	10	Bleeder screw cap
4	Outer brake pad	11	Anti-rattle spring
5	Caliper bracket	12	Piston
6	Slider pin boot	13	Dust seal
7	Slider pin boot	14	Piston seal

dual-piston caliper is essentially the same. If you have trouble with a two-piston caliper overhaul, refer to the accompanying exploded view of the D model rear caliper.

16 Remove the brake pads from the caliper (see Section 3, if necessary). Clean the exterior of the caliper with rubbing alcohol or brake system cleaner.

17 Remove the caliper bracket and the slider pin boots from the caliper **(see illustrations)**. Remove the anti-rattle spring **(see illustration)**.

18 Place a few rags between the piston(s) and the caliper frame to act as a cushion, then use compressed air, directed into the fluid inlet, to remove the piston(s) **(see illustration 2.8)**. Use only enough air pressure to ease the piston(s) out of the bore. If a piston is blown out, even with the cushion in place, it may be damaged. **Warning:** *Never place your fingers in front of the piston in an attempt to catch or protect*

it when applying compressed air, as serious injury could occur.

19 If compressed air isn't available, reconnect the caliper to the brake hose and pump the brake lever or pedal until the piston(s) are free.

20 Using a wood or plastic tool, remove the dust seal(s) **(see illustration 2.11)**. Metal tools may cause bore damage.

21 Using a wood or plastic tool, remove the piston seal(s) from the groove in the caliper bore.

22 Clean the piston(s) and the bore(s) with denatured alcohol, clean brake fluid or brake system cleaner and blow dry them with filtered, unlubricated compressed air. Inspect the surfaces of the piston(s) for nicks and burrs and loss of plating. Check the caliper bore(s), too. If surface defects are present, the caliper must be replaced. If the caliper is in bad shape, the master cylinder should also be checked.

23 Temporarily reinstall the caliper bracket. Make sure it slides smoothly in-and-out of the caliper. If it doesn't, check the slider pins for burrs or excessive wear. also check the slider pin bores in the caliper for wear and scoring. Replace the caliper bracket, the caliper, or both if necessary.

24 Lubricate the piston seal(s) with clean brake fluid and install it in its groove in the caliper bore. Make sure it isn't twisted and seats completely.

2.17c Pull the bracket out of the caliper . . .

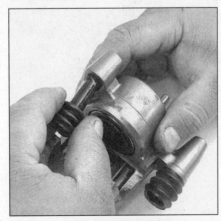

2.17d . . . and remove the slider pin boots

2.17e Remove the anti-rattle spring

7

2.26 Bottom the piston in the caliper bore - make sure it goes in straight

2.27 Install the slider pin boots

2.28 Apply a thin coat of the specified grease to the slider pins on the caliper bracket

25   Lubricate the dust seal(s) with clean brake fluid and install it in its groove, making sure it seats correctly.

26   Lubricate the piston(s) with clean brake fluid and install it into the caliper bore. Using your thumbs, push the piston all the way in **(see illustration)**, making sure it doesn't get cocked in the bore.

27   Install the slider pin boots **(see illustration)**.

28   Apply a thin coat of silicone grease designed for high-temperature brake applications to the slider pins on the caliper bracket **(see illustration)**. Install the caliper bracket to the caliper and seat the boots over the lips on the bracket.

Installation

29   Installation is the reverse of the removal steps, with the following additions:

a) *If you're installing a rear caliper, space the pads apart so the disc will fit between them.*

b) *Use new sealing washers on the brake hose fitting and position the protrusion on the fitting against the locating tab on the caliper (see illustration 2.2b).*

c) *Tighten the caliper mounting bolts and banjo fitting bolt to the torque listed in this Chapter's Specifications.*

d) *On rear calipers, tighten the torque arm bolt and nut to the torque listed in this Chapter's Specifications and install a new cotter pin.*

30   Fill the master cylinder with the recommended brake fluid (see Chapter 1) and bleed the system (see Section 8). Check for leaks.

31   Check the operation of the brakes carefully before riding the motorcycle.

3   Brake pads - replacement

Warning: *When replacing the front brake pads always replace the pads in BOTH calipers - never just on one side. Also, the dust created by the brake system may contain asbestos, which is harmful to your health. Never blow it out with compressed air and don't inhale any of it. An approved filtering mask should be worn when working on the brakes.*

1   Unbolt the caliper (see Section 2) and support it so that it's not hanging by the brake hose.

Front caliper

Refer to illustrations 3.2, 3.3a, 3.3b, 3.3c and 3.3d

2   Remove the pad cover **(see illustration)**.

3   Remove the clip from the pad pin, depress the pistons by wedging a pair of needle-nose pliers or some other suitable small hand tool between the old pads, and withdraw the pin **(see illustrations)**. Pull the pads out of the caliper opening **(see illustrations)**.

4   Refer to Chapter 1 and inspect the pads.

5   Check the condition of the brake discs (see Section 4). If they're in need of machining or replacement, follow the procedure in that Section to remove them. If they are okay, deglaze them with sandpaper or emery cloth, using a swirling motion.

6   Remove the cap from the master cylinder reservoir and siphon out some fluid. Push the pistons into the caliper again, this time as far as possible, while keeping an eye on the master cylinder reservoir fluid level to make sure it doesn't overflow. If you can't depress the pistons

3.2 To get at the pads on either front caliper, remove the pad cover screws (arrows) and the cover

3.3a To remove the brake pads, pull out the retaining pin clip . . .

3.3b . . . insert a pair of pliers between the pads and twist the head of the pliers to depress the pads back into their bores . . .

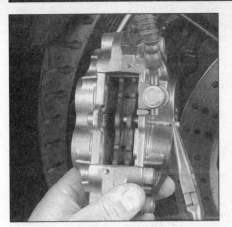

3.3c . . . remove the retaining pin . . .

3.3d . . . and remove the brake pads

3.10a Before removing the pads from the rear caliper, remove this retaining pin clip . . .

with thumb pressure, try pushing them down with a pair of pliers or some other small tool. If the pistons stick, remove the caliper and overhaul it as described in Section 2.

7   Install the new pads, the retaining pin and the clip. Install the pad cover.

8   Operate the brake lever or pedal several times to bring the pads into contact with the disc. Check the operation of the brakes carefully before riding the motorcycle.

Rear caliper

Refer to illustrations 3.10a, 3.10b, 3.11a, 3.11b and 3.15

Note: *The following pad replacement procedure depicts an E model single-piston rear caliper, but the procedure for changing pads on a D model dual-piston caliper is essentially the same. If you have trouble with pad replacement on a two-piston caliper, refer to the exploded view of the D model rear caliper in Section 2.*

9   Remove the caliper (see Section 2).

10   Remove the clip from the pad retaining pin and pull out the pin **(see illustrations)**.

11   Pull the pads out of the caliper **(see illustrations)**.

12   Refer to Chapter 1 and inspect the pads.

13   Check the condition of the brake discs (see Section 4). If they're in need of machining or replacement, follow the procedure in that Section to remove them. If they are okay, deglaze them with sandpaper or emery cloth, using a swirling motion.

14   Remove the cap from the master cylinder reservoir and siphon out some fluid. Push the pistons into the caliper as far as possible,

3.10b . . . then pull out this pin

while checking the master cylinder reservoir to make sure it doesn't overflow. If you can't depress the pistons with thumb pressure, try using a C-clamp. If the pistons stick, remove the caliper and overhaul it as described in Section 2.

15   Install the new pads **(see illustration)**, retaining pin and clip.

16   Install the caliper (see Section 2).

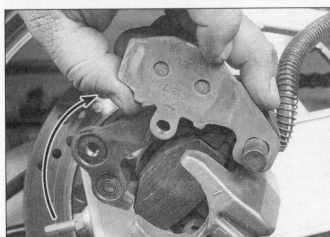

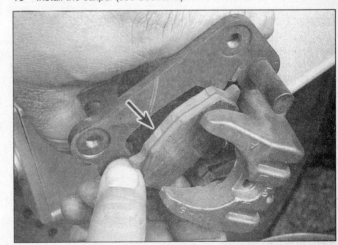

3.11a To remove the inner pad from the rear caliper, pivot the free end up, then slide the pad off the pin

3.11b To remove the outer pad from the rear caliper, push down on the pad (at the spot indicated by the arrow) and pull the upper edge out from under the caliper bracket

7

3.15 When installing the new outer pad (the one that fits against the piston), make sure it's properly engaged with the caliper bracket as shown (caliper assembly removed for clarity)

4.3 Set up a dial indicator as shown, with the probe touching the surface of the disc, and turn the wheel to measure runout

4.4a Use a micrometer to measure the thickness of the disc at several points

4.4b The minimum thickness is stamped into the disc; the directional arrow points in the forward rotating direction of the wheel (if the arrow points the other way on a dual-disc setup, the disc is on the wrong side of the wheel)

---

4   Brake disc(s) - inspection, removal and installation

Inspection

Refer to illustrations 4.3, 4.4a and 4.4b

1   Set the bike on its centerstand.

2   Visually inspect the surface of the disc(s) for score marks and other damage. Light scratches are normal after use and won't affect brake operation, but deep grooves and heavy score marks will reduce braking efficiency and accelerate pad wear. If the discs are badly grooved they must be machined or replaced.

3   To check disc runout, mount a dial indicator to a fork leg or the swing-arm, with the plunger on the indicator touching the surface of the disc about 1/2-inch from the outer edge **(see illustration)**. Slowly turn the wheel (if you're checking the front discs, have an assistant sit on the seat to raise the front wheel off the ground) and watch the indicator needle, comparing your reading with the limit listed in this Chapter's Specifications. If the runout is greater than allowed, check the hub bearings for play (see Chapter 1). If the bearings are worn, replace them and repeat this check. If the disc runout is still excessive, it will have to be replaced.

4   The disc must not be machined or allowed to wear down to a thickness less than the minimum allowable thickness, listed in this Chapter's Specifications. The thickness of the disc can be checked

with a micrometer **(see illustration)**. If the thickness of the disc is less than the minimum allowable, it must be replaced. The minimum thickness is also stamped into the disc **(see illustration)**.

Removal

Refer to illustration 4.6

5   Remove the wheel (front wheel, see Section 11; rear wheel, see Section 12). **Caution:** *Don't lay the wheel down and allow it to rest on one of the discs - the disc could become warped. Set the wheel on wood blocks so the disc doesn't support the weight of the wheel.*

6   Mark the relationship of the disc to the wheel, so it can be installed in the same position. Remove the Allen head bolts that retain the disc to the wheel **(see illustration)**. Loosen the bolts a little at a time, in a criss-cross pattern, to avoid distorting the disc.

7   Take note of any paper shims that may be present where the disc mates to the wheel. If there are any, mark their position and be sure to include them when installing the disc.

Installation

8   Position the disc on the wheel, aligning the previously applied matchmarks (if you're reinstalling the original disc). Make sure the arrow (stamped on the disc) marking the direction of rotation is pointing in the proper direction.

4.6 Remove the Allen bolts to detach the disc from the wheel

5.4 Loosen the banjo bolt at the master cylinder and disconnect the brake hose; discard both sealing washers - always use new washers when reattaching the banjo fitting

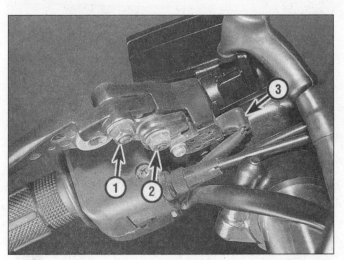

5.5 To remove the brake lever, remove the pivot nut (1) and pull out the pivot bolt; to remove the brake lever and lever adjuster as a single assembly, remove the other nut (2) instead and pull out the adjuster bolt; unplug the electrical connectors (3) from the brake light switch

5.6 To detach the master cylinder from the handlebar, remove these two Allen bolts (arrows)

9   Apply a non-hardening thread locking compound to the threads of the bolts. Install the bolts, tightening them a little at a time, in a criss-cross pattern, until the torque listed in this Chapter's Specifications is reached. Clean off all grease from the brake disc(s) using acetone or brake system cleaner.

10   Install the wheel.

11   Operate the brake lever or pedal several times to bring the pads into contact with the disc. Check the operation of the brakes carefully before riding the motorcycle.

5   Master cylinder (front) - removal, overhaul and installation

1   If the master cylinder is leaking fluid, or if the lever does not produce a firm feel when the brake is applied, and bleeding the brakes does not help, master cylinder overhaul is recommended. Before disassembling the master cylinder, read through the entire procedure and make sure that you have the correct rebuild kit. Also, you will need some new, clean brake fluid of the recommended type, some clean rags and internal snap-ring pliers. **Note:** *To prevent damage to the*

paint from spilled brake fluid, always cover the gas tank when working on the master cylinder.

2   **Caution:** *Disassembly, overhaul and reassembly of the brake master cylinder must be done in a spotlessly clean work area to avoid contamination and possible failure of the brake hydraulic system components.*

Removal

Refer to illustrations 5.4, 5.5 and 5.6

3   Loosen, but do not remove, the screws holding the reservoir cover in place.

4   Pull back the rubber boot, loosen the banjo fitting bolt **(see illustration)** and separate the brake hose from the master cylinder. Wrap the end of the hose in a clean rag and suspend the hose in an upright position or bend it down carefully and place the open end in a clean container. The objective is to prevent excess loss of brake fluid, fluid spills and system contamination.

5   Remove the locknut from the underside of the lever pivot bolt, then unscrew the bolt **(see illustration)**.

6   Remove the master cylinder mounting bolts **(see illustration)** and separate the master cylinder from the handlebar. **Caution:** *Do not tip the master cylinder upside down or brake fluid will run out.*

7   Disconnect the electrical connectors from the brake light switch **(see illustration 5.5)**.

7

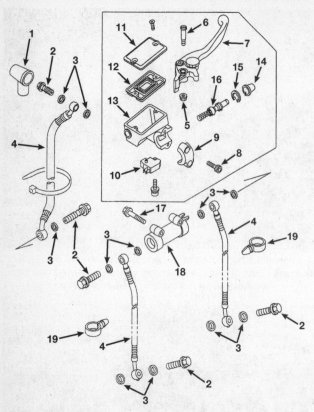

5.9a An exploded view of the front master cylinder and brake hose assembly

1	Rubber boot	11	Reservoir cap
2	Banjo bolt	12	Diaphragm
3	Sealing washers	13	Master cylinder body
4	Brake hose	14	Dust boot
5	Nut	15	Snap-ring
6	Brake lever pivot bolt	16	Piston assembly
7	Brake lever	17	Junction bolt
8	Clamp bolt	18	Junction
9	Clamp shell	19	Brake hose retainer
10	Brake light switch		

Overhaul

Refer to illustrations 5.9a, 5.9b, 5.10a, 5.10b and 5.12

8   Detach the top cover and the rubber diaphragm, then drain the brake fluid into a suitable container. Wipe any remaining fluid out of the reservoir with a clean rag.

9   Carefully remove the rubber dust boot from the end of the piston **(see illustrations)**.

10   Using snap-ring pliers, remove the snap-ring **(see illustrations)** and slide out the piston, the cup seals and the spring. Lay the parts out in the proper order to prevent confusion during reassembly.

11   Clean all of the parts with brake system cleaner (available at auto parts stores), rubbing alcohol or clean brake fluid. **Caution:** *Do not, under any circumstances, use a petroleum-based solvent to clean brake parts. If compressed air is available, use it to dry the parts thoroughly (make sure it's filtered and unlubricated). Check the master cylinder bore for corrosion, scratches, nicks and score marks. If damage is evident, the master cylinder must be replaced with a new one. If the master cylinder is in poor condition, then the calipers should be checked as well.*

12   Remove the old cup seals from the piston and spring and install the new ones. Make sure the lips face away from the lever end of the piston **(see illustration)**. If a new piston is included in the rebuild kit, use it regardless of the condition of the old one.

13   Before reassembling the master cylinder, soak the piston and the rubber cup seals in clean brake fluid for ten or fifteen minutes.

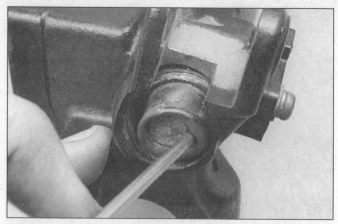

5.9b Remove the rubber boot from the end of the master cylinder piston . . .

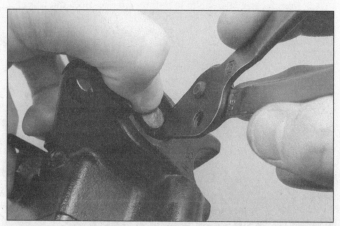

5.10a . . . then depress the piston and remove the snap-ring with a pair of snap-ring pliers

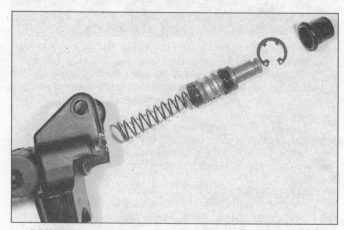

5.10b When you remove the internal parts from the master cylinder, lay them out as shown (even if you're planning to install new parts) so you'll install the new parts in the correct sequence and orientation

Lubricate the master cylinder bore with clean brake fluid, then carefully insert the piston and related parts in the reverse order of disassembly. Make sure the lips on the cup seals do not turn inside out when they are slipped into the bore.

14   Depress the piston, then install the snap-ring (make sure the snap-ring is properly seated in the groove with the sharp edge facing out). Install the rubber dust boot (make sure the lip is seated properly in the piston groove).

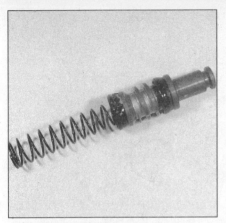

5.12 Make sure the lips of the cups face in the proper direction

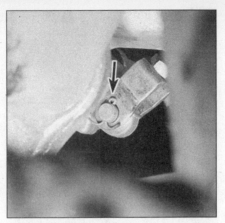

6.4 Remove this cotter pin (arrow) and remove the clevis pin that attaches the rear master cylinder clevis to the rear brake pushrod

6.5 To detach the rear master cylinder from its mounting bracket, remove these two Allen bolts (arrows)

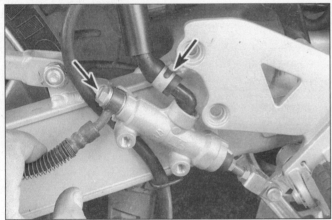

6.6 After separating the rear master cylinder from its mounting bracket, loosen the hose clamp (arrow) and detach the reservoir hose, then unscrew the banjo bolt (arrow) and disconnect the high pressure hose; discard the sealing washers and use new ones when you install the master cylinder assembly (E model shown; D model similar)

6.8a Remove the snap-ring that secures the fluid inlet fitting

Installation

15 Attach the master cylinder to the handlebar and tighten the bolts to the torque listed in this Chapter's Specifications. The arrow and the word "UP" on the master cylinder clamp should be pointing up and readable. Install the brake lever and tighten the pivot bolt locknut.

16 Connect the brake hose to the master cylinder, using new sealing washers. Tighten the banjo fitting bolt to the torque listed in this Chapter's Specifications.

17 Reattach the brake light switch leads.

18 Bleed the air from the system (see Section 8).

6 Master cylinder (rear) - removal, overhaul and installation

1 If the master cylinder is leaking fluid, or if the pedal does not produce a firm feel when the brake is applied, and bleeding the brakes does not help, master cylinder overhaul is recommended. Before disassembling the master cylinder, read through the entire procedure and make sure that you have the correct rebuild kit. Also, you will need some new, clean brake fluid of the recommended type, some clean rags and internal snap-ring pliers.

2 **Caution:** *Disassembly, overhaul and reassembly of the brake master cylinder must be done in a spotlessly clean work area to avoid contamination and possible failure of the brake hydraulic system components.*

Removal

Refer to illustrations 6.4, 6.5 and 6.6

3 Set the bike on its centerstand. Remove the right side cover (see Chapter 8).

4 Remove the cotter pin from the clevis pin on the master cylinder pushrod **(see illustration)**. Remove the clevis pin.

5 Remove the two master cylinder mounting bolts **(see illustration)** and detach the cylinder from the bracket.

6 Have a container and some rags ready to catch spilling brake fluid. Using a pair of pliers, slide the clamp up the fluid feed hose and detach the hose from the master cylinder **(see illustration)**. Direct the end of the hose into the container, unscrew the cap on the master cylinder reservoir and allow the fluid to drain.

7 Using a six-point box-end wrench, unscrew the banjo fitting bolt from the top of the master cylinder **(see illustration 6.6)**. Discard the sealing washers on either side of the fitting.

Overhaul

Refer to illustrations 6.8a, 6.8b, 6.9a, 6.9b, 6.10a, 6.10b and 6.12

8 Using a pair of snap-ring pliers, remove the snap-ring from the fluid inlet fitting **(see illustration)** and detach the fitting from the master cylinder. Remove the O-ring from the bore **(see illustration)**.

7

6.8b Remove the O-ring from the
bore and discard it

6.9a Hold the clevis with a pair of pliers
and loosen the locknut

6.9b Remove the dust boot from
the pushrod

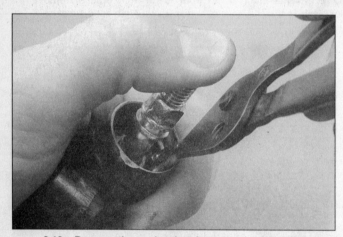

6.10a Depress the pushrod and remove the snap-ring
from the cylinder bore

9   Hold the clevis with a pair of pliers and loosen the locknut **(see illustration)**. Carefully remove the rubber dust boot from the pushrod **(see illustration)**.

10   Depress the pushrod and, using snap-ring pliers, remove the snap-ring **(see illustrations)**. Slide out the piston, the cup seal and spring. Lay the parts out in the proper order to prevent confusion during reassembly.

11   Clean all of the parts with brake system cleaner (available at auto parts stores), isopropyl alcohol or clean brake fluid. **Caution:** *Do not, under any circumstances, use a petroleum-based solvent to clean brake parts.* If compressed air is available, use it to dry the parts thoroughly (make sure it's filtered and unlubricated). Check the master cylinder bore for corrosion, scratches, nicks and score marks. If damage is evident, the master cylinder must be replaced with a new one. If the master cylinder is in poor condition, then the caliper should be checked as well.

12   Remove the old cup seals from the piston and spring and install the new ones. Make sure the lips face away from the pushrod end of the piston **(see illustration)**. If a new piston is included in the rebuild kit, use it regardless of the condition of the old one.

13   Before reassembling the master cylinder, soak the piston and the rubber cup seals in clean brake fluid for ten or fifteen minutes. Lubricate the master cylinder bore with clean brake fluid, then carefully insert the parts in the reverse order of disassembly. Make sure the lips on the cup seals do not turn inside out when they are slipped into the bore.

14   Lubricate the end of the pushrod with silicone grease designed for brake applications, and install the pushrod and stop washer into the cylinder bore. Depress the pushrod, then install the snap-ring (make sure the snap-ring is properly seated in the groove with the sharp edge facing out). Install the rubber dust boot (make sure the lip is seated

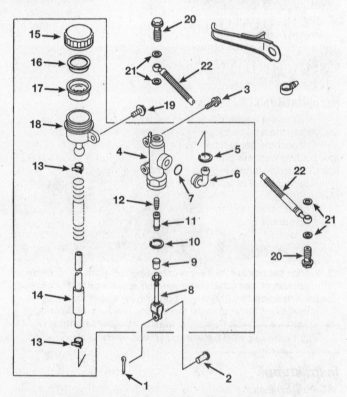

6.10b An exploded view of the rear brake reservoir and master
cylinder assembly (D model shown, E model similar)

1	Cotter pin	12	Spring
2	Clevis pin	13	Hose clamp
3	Master cylinder mounting	14	Brake hose
	bolt (2)	15	Reservoir cap
4	Rear master cylinder	16	Diaphragm retainer
5	Snap-ring	17	Diaphragm
6	Elbow fitting	18	Reservoir
7	O-ring	19	Reservoir mounting bolt
8	Clevis/pushrod assembly	20	Banjo bolt
9	Dust boot	21	Sealing washers
10	Snap-ring	22	Brake hose
11	Piston/cup assembly		

properly in the groove in the piston stop nut).

15   Install the clevis on the end of the pushrod, adjust the brake pedal height (see Chapter 1), then tighten the locknut.

16   Install the feed hose fitting, using a new O-ring. Install the snap-ring, making sure it seats properly in its groove.

6.12 Make sure the lips of the cups (arrow) face away from the pushrod end of the piston

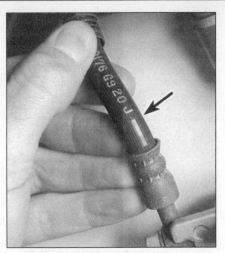

7.2 Flex the brake hoses and check for cracks, bulges and leaking fluid

8.7 All you need to bleed the brakes are a box wrench, a short section of clear tubing and a clear container half-filled with brake fluid. Warning: *If you use a beverage container, throw it away immediately after the bleeding procedure so nobody accidentally drinks from it.*

Installation

17 Position the master cylinder on the frame bracket, install the bolts and tighten them to the torque listed in this Chapter's Specifications.

18 Connect the banjo fitting to the top of the master cylinder, using new sealing washers on each side of the fitting. Tighten the banjo fitting bolt to the torque listed in this Chapter's Specifications.

19 Connect the fluid feed hose to the inlet fitting and install the hose clamp.

20 Connect the clevis to the brake pedal and secure the clevis pin with a new cotter pin.

21 Fill the fluid reservoir with the specified fluid (see Chapter 1) and bleed the system following the procedure in Section 8. Install the side cover.

22 Check the position of the brake pedal (see Chapter 1) and adjust it if necessary. Check the operation of the brakes carefully before riding the motorcycle.

7 Brake hoses and lines - inspection and replacement

Inspection

Refer to illustration 7.2

1 Once a week, or if the motorcycle is used less frequently, before every ride, check the condition of the brake hoses and fittings.

2 Twist and flex the rubber hoses **(see illustration)** while looking for cracks, bulges and seeping fluid. Check extra carefully around the areas where the hoses connect with the banjo fittings, as these are common areas for hose failure.

3 Inspect the metal lines connected to the banjo fittings. If the plating on the lines is chipped or scratched, the lines may rust. If the lines are rusted, scratched or cracked, replace them.

Replacement

4 Most brake hoses have banjo fittings on each end of the hose **(front brakes, see illustration 5.9a; rear brake hoses, see illustration 6.10b)**. Cover the surrounding area with plenty of rags and unscrew the banjo bolts on either end of the hose. If a threaded fitting is used instead of a banjo bolt, use a flare nut wrench to loosen it. Detach the hose from any clips that may be present and remove the hose.

5 Position the new hose, making sure it isn't twisted or otherwise strained, between the two components. Make sure the metal tube portion of the banjo fitting is located between the casting protrusions on the component it's connected to, if equipped. Install the banjo bolts, using new sealing washers on both sides of the fittings, and tighten them to the torque listed in this Chapter's Specifications. If a threaded fitting is used instead of a banjo bolt, tighten it securely, again using a flare nut wrench.

6 Flush the old brake fluid from the system, refill the system with the recommended fluid (see Chapter 1) and bleed the air from the system (see Section 8). Check the operation of the brakes carefully before riding the motorcycle.

8 Brake system bleeding

Refer to illustration 8.7

1 Bleeding the brake is simply the process of removing all the air bubbles from the brake fluid reservoir, the lines and the brake caliper. Bleeding is necessary whenever a brake system hydraulic connection is loosened, when a component or hose is replaced, or when the master cylinder or caliper is overhauled. Leaks in the system may also allow air to enter, but leaking brake fluid will reveal their presence and warn you of the need for repair.

2 To bleed the brake, you will need some new, clean brake fluid of the recommended type (see Chapter 1), a length of clear vinyl or plastic tubing, a small container partially filled with clean brake fluid, some rags and a wrench to fit the brake caliper bleeder valve.

3 Cover the gas tank and other painted components to prevent damage in the event that brake fluid is spilled.

4 Remove the reservoir cap or cover and slowly pump the brake lever or pedal a few times, until no air bubbles can be seen floating up from the holes at the bottom of the reservoir. Doing this bleeds the air from the master cylinder end of the line. Reinstall the reservoir cap or cover.

5 Attach one end of the clear vinyl or plastic tubing to the brake caliper bleeder valve and submerge the other end in the brake fluid in the container.

6 Remove the reservoir cap or cover and check the fluid level. Do not allow the fluid level to drop below the lower mark during the bleeding process.

7 Slowly pump the brake lever or pedal three or four times and hold it while opening the caliper bleeder valve **(see illustration)**. When the valve is opened, brake fluid will flow out of the caliper into the clear tubing and the lever will move toward the handlebar or the pedal will move down.

8 Retighten the bleeder valve, then release the brake lever or pedal gradually. Repeat the process until no air bubbles are visible in the brake fluid leaving the caliper and the lever or pedal is firm when

7

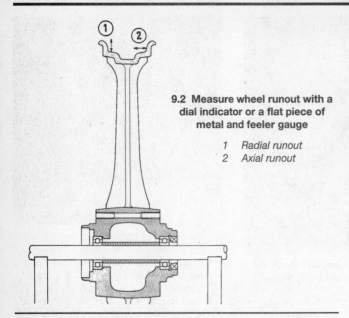

9.2 Measure wheel runout with a dial indicator or a flat piece of metal and feeler gauge

1   *Radial runout*
2   *Axial runout*

11.1 Prop up the front end of the bike by placing a jack under the engine as shown; be sure to use a block of wood to protect the oil pan

applied. **Note:** *The rear calipers on D models have two bleeder valves - air must be bled from both, one after the other. Remember to add fluid to the reservoir as the level drops.* Use only new, clean brake fluid of the recommended type. Never reuse the fluid lost during bleeding.

9   If you're bleeding the front brakes, repeat this procedure to the other caliper. Be sure to check the fluid level in the master cylinder reservoir frequently.

10   Replace the reservoir cover, wipe up any spilled brake fluid and check the entire system for leaks. **Note:** *If bleeding is difficult, it may be necessary to let the brake fluid in the system stabilize for a few hours (it may be aerated). Repeat the bleeding procedure when the tiny bubbles in the system have settled out.*

9   Wheels - inspection and repair

Refer to illustration 9.2

1   Place the motorcycle on the centerstand, then clean the wheels thoroughly to remove mud and dirt that may interfere with the inspection procedure or mask defects. Make a general check of the wheels and tires as described in Chapter 1.

2   With the motorcycle on the centerstand and the wheel in the air, attach a dial indicator to the fork slider or the swingarm and position the stem against the side of the rim **(see illustration)**. Spin the wheel slowly and check the side-to-side (axial) runout of the rim, then compare your readings with the value listed in this Chapter's Specifications. In order to accurately check radial runout with the dial indicator, the wheel would have to be removed from the machine and the tire removed from the wheel. With the axle clamped in a vise, the wheel can be rotated to check the runout.

3   An easier, though slightly less accurate, method is to attach a stiff wire pointer to the fork slider or the swingarm and position the end a fraction of an inch from the wheel (where the wheel and tire join). If the wheel is true, the distance from the pointer to the rim will be constant as the wheel is rotated. Repeat the procedure to check the runout of the rear wheel. **Note:** *If wheel runout is excessive, refer to the appropriate Section in this Chapter and check the wheel bearings very carefully before replacing the wheel.*

4   The wheels should also be visually inspected for cracks, flat spots on the rim and other damage. Since tubeless tires are involved, look very closely for dents in the area where the tire bead contacts the rim. Dents in this area may prevent complete sealing of the tire against the rim, which leads to deflation of the tire over a period of time.

5   If damage is evident, or if runout in either direction is excessive, the wheel will have to be replaced with a new one. Never attempt to repair a damaged cast aluminum wheel.

10   Wheels - alignment check

1   Misalignment of the wheels, which may be due to a cocked rear wheel or a bent frame or triple clamps, can cause strange and possibly serious handling problems. If the frame or triple clamps are at fault, repair by a frame specialist or replacement with new parts are the only alternatives.

2   To check the alignment you will need an assistant, a length of string or a perfectly straight piece of wood and a ruler graduated in 1/64 inch increments. A plumb bob or other suitable weight will also be required.

3   Place the motorcycle on the centerstand, then measure the width of both tires at their widest points. Subtract the smaller measurement from the larger measurement, then divide the difference by two. The result is the amount of offset that should exist between the front and rear tires on both sides.

4   If a string is used, have your assistant hold one end of it about half way between the floor and the rear axle, touching the rear sidewall of the tire.

5   Run the other end of the string forward and pull it tight so that it is roughly parallel to the floor. Slowly bring the string into contact with the front sidewall of the rear tire, then turn the front wheel until it is parallel with the string. Measure the distance from the front tire sidewall to the string.

6   Repeat the procedure on the other side of the motorcycle. The distance from the front tire sidewall to the string should be equal on both sides.

7   As was previously pointed out, a perfectly straight length of wood may be substituted for the string. The procedure is the same.

8   If the distance between the string and tire is greater on one side, or if the rear wheel appears to be cocked, refer to Chapter 6, *Swingarm bearings - check*, and make sure the swingarm is tight.

9   If the front-to-back alignment is correct, the wheels still may be out of alignment vertically.

10   Using the plumb bob, or other suitable weight, and a length of string, check the rear wheel to make sure it is vertical. To do this, hold the string against the tire upper sidewall and allow the weight to settle just off the floor. When the string touches both the upper and lower tire sidewalls and is perfectly straight, the wheel is vertical. If it is not, place thin spacers under one leg of the centerstand.

11   Once the rear wheel is vertical, check the front wheel in the same manner. If both wheels are not perfectly vertical, the frame and/or major suspension components are bent.

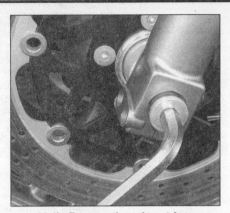

11.4a Loosen the axle clamp bolts (arrows) on both sliders (outer fork tubes) (left slider shown, right identical)

11.4b Remove the axle nut from the left slider

11.5a Pull out the axle from the right side

11.5b If the axle is difficult to remove, drive it out from the left side with a hammer and punch

12.7 Remove the wheel, allowing the chain to rest on the swingarm

11 Wheel (front)- removal and installation

Removal

Refer to illustrations 11.1, 11.4a, 11.4b, 11.5a and 11.5b

1   Remove the lower portion of the fairing (see Chapter 8). Place the motorcycle on the centerstand, then raise the front wheel off the ground by placing a floor jack, with a wood block on the jack head, under the engine **(see illustration)**.

2   Disconnect the speedometer cable **(see illustration 2.2a)** from the drive unit.

3   Remove the brake calipers (see Section 2) and support them with a piece of wire. Don't disconnect the brake hoses from the calipers.

4   Loosen the axle clamp bolts on both sliders **(see illustration)**, then unscrew the axle nut **(see illustration)**.

5   Support the wheel, pull out the axle from the right side **(see illustration)** and carefully lower the wheel. If the axle is stuck, drive it out from the left side with a hammer and punch **(see illustration)**. Don't lose the spacer that fits into the right side of the hub. **Caution:** *Don't lay the wheel down and allow it to rest on one of the discs - the disc could become warped. Set the wheel on wood blocks so the disc doesn't support the weight of the wheel.* If the axle is corroded, remove the corrosion with fine emery cloth. **Note:** *Do not operate the front brake lever with the wheel removed.*

6   Check the condition of the wheel bearings (see Section 13).

Installation

7   Installation is the reverse of removal. Apply a thin coat of grease to the seal lip, then slide the collar into the right side of the hub.

Position the speedometer drive unit in place in the left side of the hub, then slide the wheel into place. Make sure the notches in the speedometer drive housing line up with the lugs in the wheel.

8   Slip the axle into place, then tighten the axle nut to the torque listed in this Chapter's Specifications. Tighten the axle clamp bolts to the torque listed in this Chapter's Specifications.

9   Install the brake calipers (see Section 2).

10   Apply the front brake, pump the forks up and down several times and check for binding and proper brake operation.

12 Wheel (rear) - removal and installation

Removal

Refer to illustrations 12.7 and 12.8

1   Set the bike on its centerstand.

2   Remove the chain guard (see Section 15).

3   Loosen the torque link nut **(see illustration 11.7 in Chapter 1)**.

4   Remove the cotter pin from the axle nut **(see illustration 11.8 in Chapter 1)** and remove the nut.

5   Loosen the chain adjusting bolt locknuts **(see illustration 11.9 in Chapter 1)** and fully loosen both adjusting bolts.

6   Push the rear wheel as far forward as possible. Lift the top of the chain up off the rear sprocket and pull it to the left while rotating the wheel backwards. This will disengage the chain from the sprocket. **Warning:** *Don't let your fingers slip between the chain and the sprocket.*

7   Support the wheel and slide out the axle. Lower the wheel and remove it from the swingarm **(see illustration)**, being careful not to lose the spacers on either side of the hub. If the axle is stuck or difficult

7

to remove, drive it out with a plastic hammer. **Caution:** *Don't lay the wheel down and allow it to rest on the disc or the sprocket - they could become warped. Set the wheel on wood blocks so the disc or the sprocket doesn't support the weight of the wheel. Do not operate the brake pedal with the wheel removed.*

8   Before installing the wheel, check the axle for straightness. If the axle is corroded, first remove the corrosion with fine emery cloth. Set the axle on V-blocks and check it for runout using a dial indicator **(see illustration)**. If the axle exceeds the maximum allowable runout limit listed in this Chapter's Specifications, it must be replaced.

9   Check the condition of the wheel bearings (see Section 13).

Installation

10   Apply a thin coat of grease to the seal lips, then slide the spacers into their proper positions on the sides of the hub.

11   Slide the wheel into place, making sure the brake disc slides

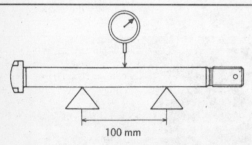

12.8 Check the axle for runout with a dial indicator and a set of V-blocks

between the brake pads. If it doesn't, spread the pads apart with a piece of wood.

12   Pull the chain up over the sprocket, raise the wheel and install the axle and axle nut. Don't tighten the axle nut at this time.

13   Adjust the chain slack (see Chapter 1) and tighten the adjuster locknuts.

14   Tighten the axle nut to the torque listed in this Chapter's Specifications. Install a new cotter pin, tightening the axle nut an additional amount, if necessary, to align the hole in the axle with the castellations on the nut.

15   Tighten the torque link nut to the torque listed in the Chapter 6 Specifications.

16   Check the operation of the brakes carefully before riding the motorcycle.

---

13   Wheel and rear coupling bearings - inspection and maintenance

---

Front wheel bearings

Refer to illustrations 13.3a, 13.3b, 13.4a, 13.4b, 13.4c, 13.5, 13.8, 13.9, 13.10 and 13.11

1   Support the bike securely and remove the front wheel (see Section 11).

2   Set the wheel on blocks so as not to allow the weight of the wheel to rest on the brake disc.

3   From the left side of the wheel, remove the snap-ring securing the speedometer drive and remove the speedometer drive from the hub **(see illustrations)**.

13.3a Lift the speedometer drive unit out of the wheel and remove the snap-ring that secures the speedometer drive (arrows) . . .

13.3b . . . then remove the drive

13.4a Lift the spacer out of the wheel

13.4b A screwdriver can be used to pry out the grease seal if you don't have a removal tool like this one

13.4c Remove the snap-ring from the right side of the wheel

13.5 Once the snap-rings have been removed, drive the bearings from the hub with a brass drift and a hammer

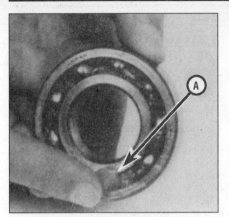

13.8 Press grease into the open side of the bearing (A) until it's full

13.9 With the bearing in position, install the snap-ring and make sure it's securely seated in its groove

13.10 Install the speedometer drive and secure it with the snap-ring

4   Remove the spacer and pry out the grease seal from the right side of the wheel **(see illustrations)**. Remove the bearing snap-ring from beneath the grease seal **(see illustration)**.

5   Using a metal rod (preferably a brass drift punch) inserted through the center of the hub bearing, tap evenly around the inner race of the opposite bearing to drive it from the hub **(see illustration)**. The bearing spacer will also come out.

6   Lay the wheel on its other side and remove the remaining bearing using the same technique.

7   If the bearings are open on one or both sides, clean them with a high flash-point solvent (one which won't leave any residue), blow

13.11 Apply a coat of grease to the lip of the seal

them dry with compressed air (don't let the bearings spin as you dry them) and apply a few drops of oil to the bearing. On all bearings (open or sealed), hold the outer race of the bearing and rotate the inner race - if the bearing doesn't turn smoothly, has rough spots or is noisy, replace it with a new one.

8   If an open bearing checks out okay and will be reused, wash it in solvent once again and dry it, then pack the bearing from the open side with high-quality bearing grease **(see illustration)**.

9   Thoroughly clean the hub area of the wheel. Install the right side bearing into its recess in the hub, with the marked or shielded side facing out. Using a bearing driver or a socket large enough to contact the outer race of the bearing, drive it in until the snap-ring groove is visible and install the snap-ring **(see illustration)**.

10   Turn the wheel over and install the bearing spacer and left side bearing, driving the bearing into place as described in Step 10, then install the speedometer drive and the snap-ring **(see illustration)**.

11   Coat the lip of a new grease seal with grease **(see illustration)**.

12   Install the grease seal on the right side of the wheel; it should go in with thumb pressure but if not, use a seal driver, large socket or a flat piece of wood to drive it into place.

13   Clean off all grease from the brake discs using acetone or brake system cleaner. Install the wheel (see Section 11).

Rear coupling bearing

Refer to illustrations 13.15a, 13.15b, 13.16, 13.17, 13.18 and 13.23

14   Refer to Section 12 and remove the rear wheel. Lay the wheel on its brake disc side, supported on blocks so its weight doesn't rest on the brake disc.

15   Lift off the spacer and rear wheel coupling **(see illustrations)**.

16   Pry out the grease seal **(see illustration 13.4b)** and remove the snap-ring from the sprocket side of the coupling **(see illustration)**.

13.15a Remove the spacer . . .

13.15b . . . and lift the coupling out of the wheel

13.16 Remove the snap-ring after the grease seal has been removed

7

13.17 Lift out the coupling collar

13.18 Drive out the coupling bearing only if it will be replaced; removal requires driving against the inner race, which may damage the bearing

13.23 Press in the new grease seal

13.31a Apply a coat of grease to the inside of the spacer . . .

13.31b . . . and install the spacer in the hub

17 Turn the wheel over and remove the coupling collar from the other side of the hub **(see illustration)**.

18 Drive the bearing out of the coupling with a bearing driver or drift punch **(see illustration)**.

19 If the bearings are open on one or both sides, clean the bearing with a high flash-point solvent (one which won't leave any residue), blow it dry with compressed air (don't let the bearing spin as you dry it) and apply a few drops of oil to the bearing. On all bearings (open or sealed), hold the outer race of the bearing and rotate the inner race - if the bearing doesn't turn smoothly, has rough spots or is noisy, replace it with a new one.

20 If the bearing checks out okay and will be reused, wash it in solvent once again and dry it, then pack the bearing from the open side with high-quality bearing grease **(see illustration 13.8)**.

21 Drive the bearing into the coupling with a bearing driver or socket that bears against the outer race of the bearing.

22 Install the snap-ring to secure the bearing, making sure it fits securely in its groove. Install the collar on the other side of the coupling.

23 Coat the lip of a new grease seal with grease and install it on top of the snap-ring **(see illustration)**. It should go in with thumb pressure, but if not, tap it in with a hammer and socket, bearing driver or flat piece of wood. Install the coupling and spacer in the wheel and install the wheel (see Section 12).

Rear wheel bearings

Refer to illustrations 13.31a, 13.31b and 13.33

24 Pry out the grease seal on the brake disc side of the wheel **(see**

illustration 13.4b)**.

25 Remove the snap-ring from beneath the grease seal with snap-ring pliers **(see illustration 13.4c)**.

26 Using a metal rod (preferably a brass drift punch) inserted through the center of the hub bearing, tap evenly around the inner race of the opposite bearing to drive it from the hub **(see illustration 13.5)**. The bearing spacer will also come out.

27 Lay the wheel on its other side and remove the remaining bearing using the same technique.

28 Clean the bearings with a high flash-point solvent (one which won't leave any residue) and blow them dry with compressed air (don't let the bearing spin as you dry them). Apply a few drops of oil to the bearing. Hold the outer race of the bearing and rotate the inner race - if the bearing doesn't turn smoothly, has rough spots or is noisy, replace it with a new one.

29 If the bearing checks out okay and will be reused, wash it in solvent once again and dry it, then pack the bearing from the open side with high-quality bearing grease **(see illustration 13.8)**.

30 Thoroughly clean the hub area of the wheel. Install the bearing into the recess in the hub, with the marked or shielded side facing out. Using a bearing driver or a socket large enough to contact the outer race of the bearing, drive it in until the snap-ring groove is visible. Install the snap-ring **(see illustration 13.9)**.

31 Turn the wheel over. Apply a coat of multi-purpose grease to the inside of the spacer **(see illustration)** and install it in the hub **(see illustration)**.

32 Pack the remaining bearing from the open side with grease **(see illustration 13.8)**, then install it in the hub, driving the bearing in with a

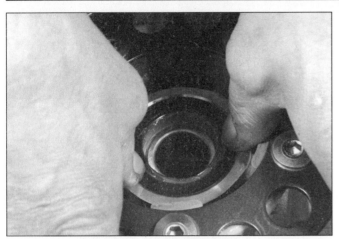

13.33 Press the seal into the hub with your thumbs

15.1 Mark the relationship of the shift lever to the shift shaft before loosening the pinch bolt (arrow A) and removing the lever, then remove the bolts (arrows) and detach the sprocket cover

16.4 Measure rear sprocket runout with a dial indicator and compare your measurements to the runout listed in this Chapter's Specifications; try to position the dial indicator so that the probe is as close to the outer circumference of the sprocket as possible

socket or bearing driver large enough to contact the outer race of the bearing.

33 Install a new grease seal. It should go in with thumb pressure **(see illustration)**, but if not, use a seal driver, large socket or a flat piece of wood to drive it into place.

34 Press a little grease into the bearing in the rear wheel coupling. Install the coupling to the wheel, making sure the coupling collar is located in the inside of the inner race (between the wheel and the coupling) **(see illustration 13.17)**.

35 Clean off all grease from the brake discs using acetone or brake system cleaner. Install the wheel.

14 Tubeless tires - general information

1 Tubeless tires are used as standard equipment on this motorcycle. They are generally safer than tube-type tires but if problems do occur they require special repair techniques.

2 The force required to break the seal between the rim and the bead of the tire is substantial, and is usually beyond the capabilities of an individual working with normal tire irons.

3 Also, repair of the punctured tire and replacement on the wheel rim requires special tools, skills and experience that the average do-it-yourselfer lacks.

4 For these reasons, if a puncture or flat occurs with a tubeless tire, the wheel should be removed from the motorcycle and taken to a dealer service department or a motorcycle repair shop for repair or replacement of the tire.

15 Drive chain - removal, cleaning and installation

Removal

Refer to illustration 15.1

1 Mark the relationship of the shift lever to the shift shaft **(see illustration)**. Remove the shift lever pinch bolt and slide the lever off the shaft.

2 Remove the bolts securing the engine sprocket cover to the engine case and remove the sprocket cover.

3 Remove the rear wheel (see Section 12).

4 Lift the chain off the engine sprocket.

5 Detach the swingarm from the frame (see Chapter 6). Pull the swingarm back far enough to allow the chain to slip between the frame and the front of the swingarm.

Cleaning

6 Soak the chain in kerosene or diesel fuel for approximately five or six minutes. **Caution:** *Don't use gasoline or other cleaning fluids. Remove the chain, wipe it off then blow dry it with compressed air immediately. The entire process shouldn't take longer than ten minutes - if it does, the O-rings in the chain rollers could be damaged.*

Installation

7 Installation is the reverse of the removal procedure. Tighten the suspension fasteners to the torque listed in the Chapter 6 Specifications. Tighten the engine sprocket cover bolts and the rear axle nut to the torque listed in this Chapter's Specifications.

8 Connect the shift lever to the shift shaft, lining up the marks. If it's installed correctly, the link rod should be parallel to the shift pedal.

9 Lubricate the chain (see Chapter 1).

16 Sprockets - check and replacement

Refer to illustrations 16.4, 16.6a, 16.6b and 16.9

1 Set the bike on its centerstand.

2 Whenever the drive chain is inspected, the sprockets should be inspected also. If you are replacing the chain, replace the sprockets as well. Likewise, if the sprockets are in need of replacement, install a new chain also.

3 Remove the engine sprocket cover (see Section 15).

4 Attach a dial indicator to the swingarm, with the plunger of the indicator touching the sprocket near its outer diameter **(see illustration)**. Turn the wheel and measure the runout. If the runout exceeds the maximum runout listed in this Chapter's Specifications, replace the rear sprocket. As stated before, it's a good idea to replace the chain

7

16.6a To remove the countershaft sprocket, flatten the
folded-up sides of the lockwasher . . .

16.6b . . . and loosen the sprocket nut with the transmission
in first gear and someone applying firm pressure
to the rear brake pedal

16.9 When removing the countershaft sprocket, be sure to note
the difference between the outer and inner faces; the inner face
(not visible) has a raised hub - when installing the countershaft
sprocket, this hub must face toward the engine case

17.3 To remove the rubber coupling damper, simply pull
it out of the wheel

and the sprockets as a set. However, if the components are relatively
new or in good condition, but the sprocket is warped, you may be able
to get away with just replacing the rear sprocket.

5   Check the wear pattern on the sprockets **(see illustration 11.5 in
Chapter 1)**. If the sprocket teeth are worn excessively, replace the
chain and sprockets.

6   If you're planning to remove the countershaft sprocket, place the
transmission in first gear, flatten the folded edges of the lockwasher
(see illustration), then have an assistant apply the rear brake while
you loosen the sprocket nut **(see illustration)**.

7   Remove the rear wheel (see Chapter 7).

8   To replace the rear sprocket, unscrew the nuts holding it to the
wheel coupling and lift the sprocket off. When installing the sprocket,
apply a non-hardening thread locking compound to the threads of the
studs. Tighten the nuts to the torque listed in this Chapter's Specifications. Also, check the condition of the rubber damper under the rear
wheel coupling (see Section 17).

9   Remove the sprocket retaining nut and pull the countershaft
sprocket and chain off the shaft **(see illustration)**, then separate the
sprocket from the chain.

10   When installing the engine sprocket, make sure the raised hub

faces toward the engine case. Install a new lockwasher, apply a non-
hardening thread locking compound to the threads on the end of the
countershaft, then tighten the nut to the torque listed in this Chapter's
Specifications.

11   Install the engine sprocket cover and shift lever (see Section 15).

17   Coupling/rubber damper (rear wheel) - check and replacement

Refer to illustration 17.3

1   Remove the rear wheel (see Chapter 7).

2   Lift the spacer and rear sprocket/rear wheel coupling from the
wheel **(see illustrations 13.15a and 13.15b)**.

3   Lift the rubber damper **(see illustration)** from the wheel and
check it for cracks, hardening and general deterioration. Replace it
with a new one if necessary.

4   Checking and replacement procedures for the coupling bearing
are in Section 13.

5   Installation is the reverse of the removal procedure.

TIRE CHANGING SEQUENCE - TUBELESS TIRES

Deflate tire. After releasing beads, push tire bead into well of rim at point opposite valve. Insert lever next to valve and work bead over edge of rim.

Use two levers to work bead over edge of rim. Note use of rim protectors.

When first bead is clear, remove tire as shown.

Before installing, ensure that tire is suitable for wheel. Take note of any sidewall markings such as direction of rotation arrows.

Work first bead over the rim flange.

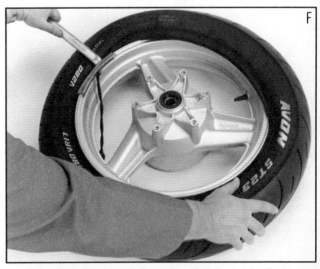

Use a tire lever to work the second bead over rim flange.

Notes

Chapter 8
Fairing, bodywork and frame

Contents

1 General information

Body parts

Refer to illustrations 1.1a through 1.1e

Many service and repair operations on these motorcycles require removal of the fairing and/or other body parts. This Chapter covers the removal and installation of these parts **(see illustrations)**.
If the fairing or any other body part is damaged, it must be repaired or replaced. But the plastic used to construct the fairing and body parts cannot be repaired using conventional repair techniques. Some shops specialize in "plastic welding", so it's a good idea to check with local shops before discarding the damaged part.

If you decide to replace the damaged body part, first try to find a used part at a motorcycle salvage yard. If you're successful, the part should be half as much as a new part. If the used part needs to be repainted to match your bike's colors, get an estimate on what it will cost to have it repainted, then compare the price for the used part plus

the cost of painting it with the retail price for the same new (already painted) part. And don't try to swap D model body parts with E model body parts. They're NOT interchangeable!

Frames

The two models covered by this manual use similar, but slightly different, frame designs. Both are square-section aluminum tubing, but D models have a detachable subframe, while E models use a one-piece design. Like the bodywork, the two frames are NOT interchangeable.

In the event that the bike is involved in a major accident, the frame may be damaged. If so, check with your local dealer and find out whether someone in your area specializes in frame straightening. This is a highly specialized craft and there aren't many shops which can perform this job, but it's often considerably less expensive to have the old frame straightened than it is to buy a new frame. And if the work is done by a reputable shop, the straightened frame will be as good as new.

8

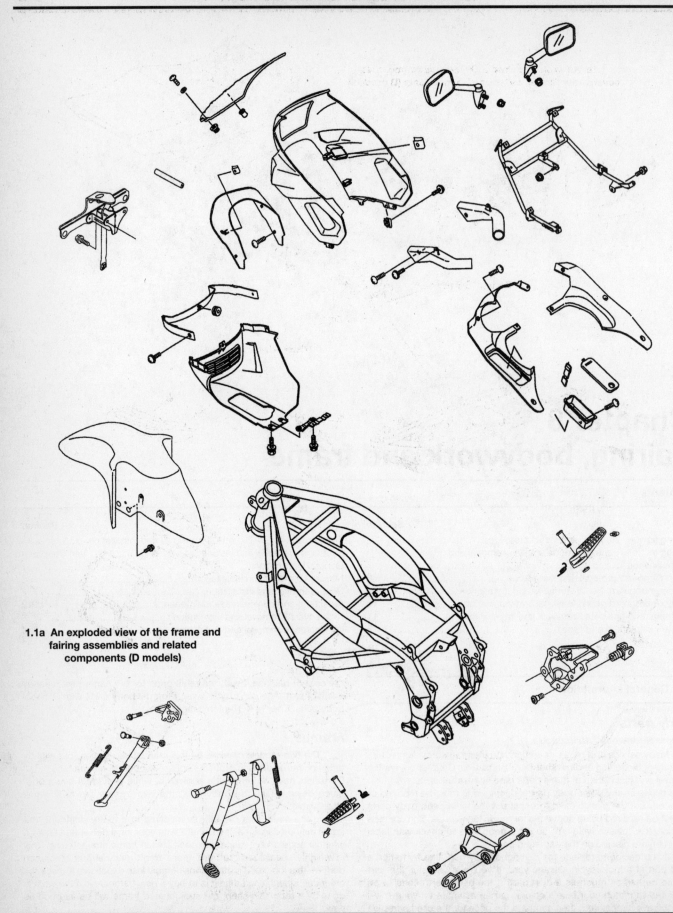

1.1a An exploded view of the frame and fairing assemblies and related components (D models)

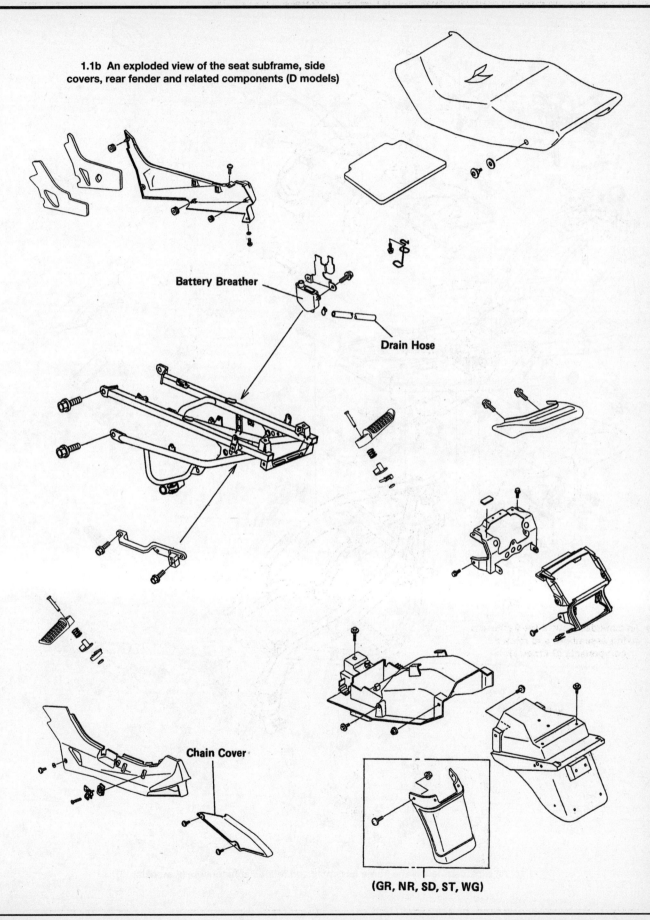

1.1b An exploded view of the seat subframe, side covers, rear fender and related components (D models)

Battery Breather

Drain Hose

Chain Cover

(GR, NR, SD, ST, WG)

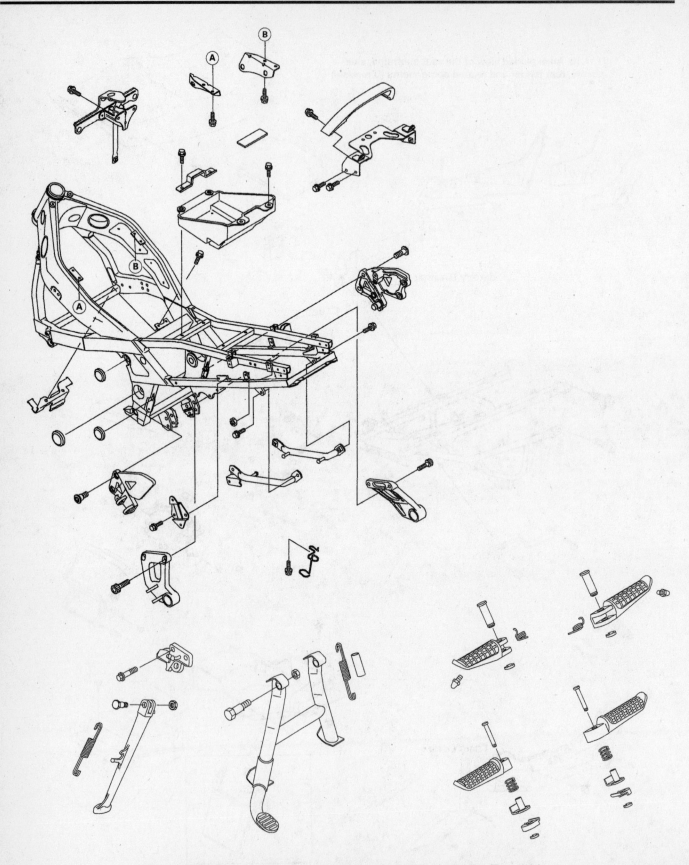

1.1c An exploded view of the frame assembly and related components (E models)

1.1d An exploded view of the fairing assembly and related hardware (E models)

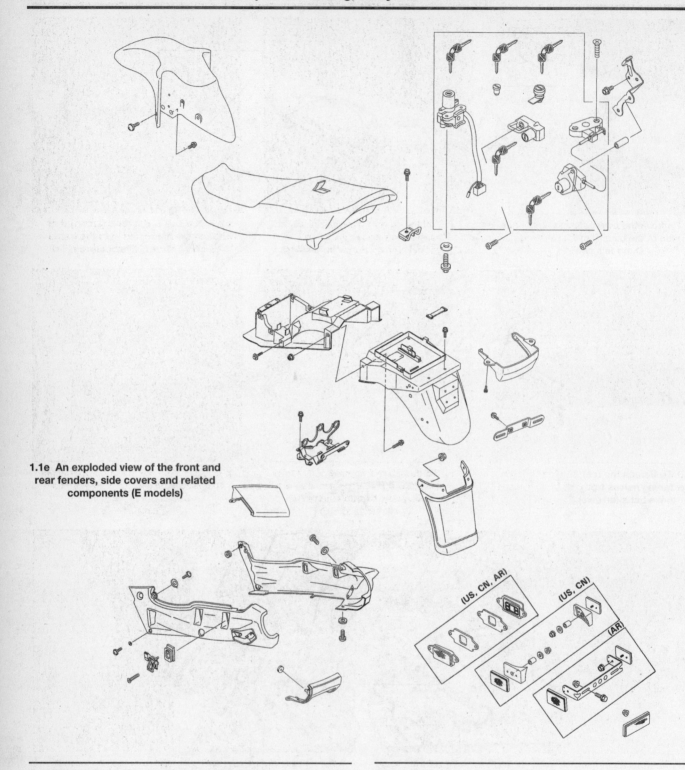

1.1e An exploded view of the front and rear fenders, side covers and related components (E models)

---

2   Fairing (lower) - removal and installation

D models

1   Set the bike on its centerstand.
2   Remove the reflector and the cover screws **(see illustration 2.7)**.
3   Pull the cover forward to clear the tabs and remove the cover **(see illustration 2.8)**.
4   Remove the lower fairing screws and bolts **(see illustration 2.9)**.
5   Carefully maneuver the fairing out from under the bike.
6   Installation is the reverse of removal.

E models

Refer to illustrations 2.7, 2.8, 2.9, 2.10, 2.11, 2.12 and 2.13
7   Remove the cover screws **(see illustration)**.
8   Pull the cover forward to clear the tabs **(see illustration)** and remove the cover.
9   Remove the screws that attach the lower fairing to the frame **(see illustration)**.
10   Remove the bolts that attach the lower fairing to the bracket under the exhaust pipe **(see illustration)**.
11   Remove the bolts that attach the lower fairing to the bracket

2.7 Remove the cover screws from each side of the bike (E model shown, D models similar)

2.8 Pull the cover forward to clear the tabs and remove the cover (E model shown, D models similar)

2.9 Remove the screws (arrow) that attach the lower fairing to the frame (E model shown, D models similar)

2.10 To detach the rear ends of the two lower fairing halves from the bike, remove these bolts (arrows) (E models)

2.11 To detach the forward ends of the two lower fairing halves from the bike, remove these two bolts (arrows) (E models)

2.12 To detach the lower fairing halves from the front piece, remove these three screws (arrows)

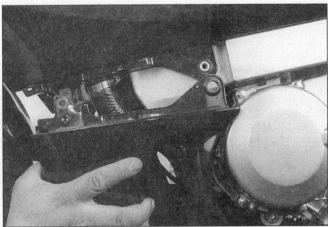

2.13 Carefully maneuver the lower fairing assembly off the bike; and don't forget that the tabs for the lower fairing halves are installed on top of the tabs for the fairing middle panels as shown (E models)

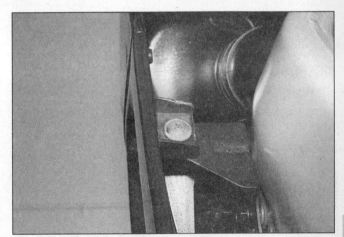

3.2 To detach the trailing edge of the middle fairing panel, remove this screw

behind the front wheel **(see illustration)**.
12   Remove the three screws from the front piece of the lower fairing **(see illustration)**.
13   Carefully maneuver the lower fairing out from under the bike **(see illustration)**.
14   Installation is the reverse of removal.

3   Fairing (middle) panels (E models only) - removal and installation

Refer to illustrations 3.2 and 3.3
1   Remove the lower fairing (see Section 2).
2   Remove the retaining screw from the back of the panel **(see illustration)**.

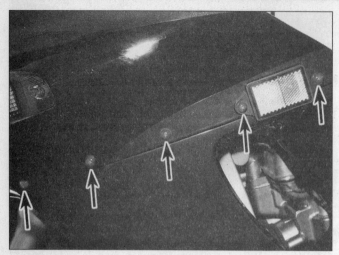

3.3 To detach the upper edge of the fairing middle panel on E models, remove these five screws (arrows) and the reflector

4.1 To detach the windscreen from the upper fairing, remove these screws (arrows) (E model shown, D models similar)

4.2a To detach the instrument cluster trim panel from the upper fairing on a D model, remove this screw . . .

4.2b . . . and this screw, both on the left side . . .

4.2c . . . remove this screw below the instrument cluster . . .

3   Remove the screws (five on each side) that attach the middle fairing panels to the upper fairing **(see illustration)**.
4   Remove the middle fairing panels.
5   Installation is the reverse of removal.

4.2d . . . and remove these screws (arrows) from the right side; the cluster trim panel can then be removed in two parts

4   Windscreen - removal and installation

Refer to illustrations 4.1, 4.2a, 4.2b, 4.2c, 4.2d, 4.2e and 4.2f
1   Remove the screws securing the windscreen to the fairing **(see illustration)**.
2   Remove the screws that attach the trim panel surrounding the instrument cluster **(see illustrations)**. Remove the panel and the windscreen together **(see illustration)**. (While it's not impossible to remove the windscreen by itself - without removing the trim panel - the upper fairing and the trim panel grip the windscreen so tightly that it's very difficult to remove the old windscreen, or install a new one, without damaging it.)
3   Installation is the reverse of the removal procedure. Be sure each screw has a plastic washer under its head. Tighten the screws securely, but be careful not to overtighten them, as the windshield might crack.

5   Mirrors - removal and installation

Refer to illustration 5.1
1   Remove the nuts from the two mirror mounting studs **(see illustration)**.
2   Remove the mirror
3   Installation is the reverse of removal.

4.2e To detach the instrument cluster trim panel from the upper fairing on an E model, remove this retaining screw (arrow) and the other screw, in the same location, below the right end of the panel (E models)

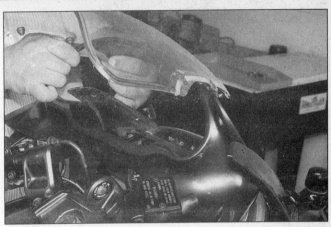

4.2f Remove the windscreen and the instrument cluster trim panel together, then separate them (E model shown)

5.1 To detach either mirror from the upper fairing, remove these two nuts (arrows) (E model shown, D models similar)

6.12a To remove the left trim panel on E models, remove these screws (arrows)

6   Fairing (upper) - removal and installation

D models

1   Set the bike on its centerstand.
2   Remove the lower fairing (see Section 2).
3   Remove the left and right trim panels **(see illustrations 4.2a, 4.2b, 4.2c and 4.2d)**.
4   Remove the windscreen (see Section 4).
5   Remove the rear view mirrors (see Section 5)
6   Unplug the electrical connectors for the headlight and turn signals.
7   Remove the cooling duct screws (located up inside the cooling ducts on either side of the upper fairing).
8   Carefully pull the fairing forward and off the bike **(see illustration 1.1a)**. It may be necessary to spread the lower sides of the fairing to clear the frame as you do this.
9   Installation is the reverse of removal.

E models

Refer to illustrations 6.12a, 6.12b, 6.16 and 6.17

10   Set the bike on its centerstand.
11   Remove the lower fairing (see Section 2).
12   Remove the left and right trim panels between the fairing and the tank **(see illustrations)**.
13   Remove the windscreen and the instrument cluster trim panel

(see illustrations 4.2e and 4.2f).
14   Remove the rear view mirrors (see Section 5).
15   Remove the rear fairing mounting screws **(see illustration 3.2)**.

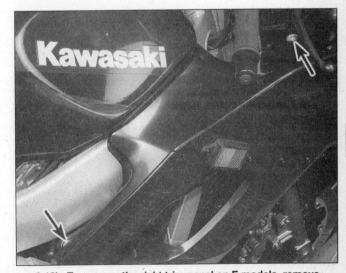

6.12b To remove the right trim panel on E models, remove these screws (arrows)

8

6.16 Loosen this hose clamp, slide it back and detach the hose from the ram air duct (left duct assembly shown, right duct identical; upper fairing removed for clarity) (E models)

6.17 Unplug the electrical connectors for the headlight and turn signals (arrows) (E models)

7.1 To remove the seat from a D model, remove the bolt from each side of the seat

16 Loosen the hose clamps for the ram air ducts, slide them back and detach the ducts from the rubber hose **(see illustration)**.
17 Unplug the electrical connectors for the headlight and the turn signals **(see illustration)**.
18 Remove the upper fairing assembly.
19 Installation is the reverse of removal.

Brake junction pipe/horn access panel

20 The small access panel underneath the upper fairing allows access to the brake crossover pipe (see Chapter 7) and the horn (see Chapter 9). To remove this panel, simply remove the four retaining screws. Installation is the reverse of removal.

---

7   Seat - removal and installation

D models

Refer to illustration 7.1
1 Remove the seat bolts **(see illustration)**.
2 Pull the seat up and to the rear.
3 Installation is the reverse of removal.

E models

4 Insert the key into the seat lock and turn it to the left to release the seat latch located underneath the rear edge of the seat.
5 To remove the seat, lift up the rear edge and pull the seat to the rear.
6 Installation is the reverse of removal. Place the seat in position, push it forward until the tang under the forward part of the seat and the two side tangs are properly engaged with their respective brackets on the frame, then push down firmly on the seat until you hear a clicking sound, which indicates the rear latch is locked into place.

---

8   Side covers - removal and installation

Refer to illustrations 8.2, 8.3a, 8.3b, 8.3c, 8.3d, 8.3e and 8.3f
1 Remove the seat (see Section 7).
2 Remove the grab rail **(see illustration)**.
3 Remove the side cover retaining screws and unplug the electrical connector for the turn signal **(see illustrations)**.
4 Remove the side cover from the bike with care. The forward end of the side cover has a plastic "stopper" that engages a rubber

8.2 To remove the grab rail, remove these two bolts (arrows) (E model shown, D models similar)

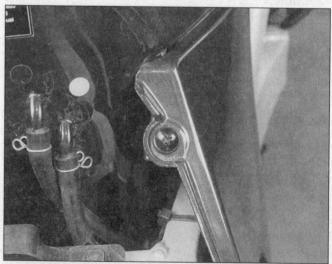

8.3a To detach the side cover, remove this screw at the front of the cover . . .

8.3b ...this screw on the side of the cover ...

8.3c ...these two screws (don't lose the cargo hooks!) ...

grommet on the fuel tank. You'll have to apply a little extra force to pull the stopper out of the grommet, but be careful! This stopper will easily break off if the side cover is bent at too sharp an angle during removal.

5   Installation is the reverse of the removal procedure.

9   Fender/mudguard (front) - removal and installation

Refer to illustrations 9.4 and 9.5

1   Set the bike on its centerstand.

2   Disconnect the speedometer from the speedometer drive and pull the cable though the retainer.

3   Detach the retainers that secure the brake hoses to the fender.

4   Remove the four inner fender retaining bolts (two on each side) from inside the fender **(see illustration)**.

5   Remove the two outer fender retaining screws from the fender **(see illustration)**.

6   Remove the fender by pulling it forward, between the fork legs.

7   Installation is the reverse of removal.

8.3d ...this screw (arrow), which is located underneath the tail light ...

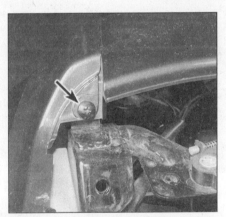

8.3e ...and this screw at the inner end of the panel (arrow)

8.3f Before removing the side cover on E models, unplug the electrical connector for the turn signal light

9.4 To remove the front fender, remove the two inner bolts on each side (arrows)

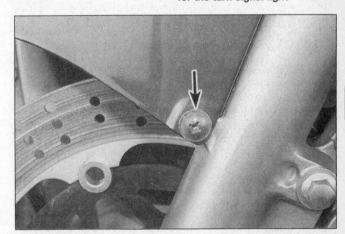

9.5 Remove the fender retaining screws from each side

8

11.1 Pry off the C-clip and push out the pivot pin to detach the footpeg from the bracket

11.3 Unscrew the shift lever pivot bolt from the left footpeg bracket

11.9 To remove the right footpeg and bracket from the frame, remove these two Allen head bolts

10 Fender/mudguard (rear) - removal and installation

Note: *All models use a two-piece rear fender. The rear section can be removed separately; removal of the front section, however, requires that the rear section be removed first.*

D models

Rear section

1   Set the bike on its centerstand.
2   Remove the seat (see Section 7).
3   Remove the side covers (see Section 8)
4   Remove the coolant reservoir (see Chapter 3).
5   Remove the rear section retaining bolts and nuts **(see illustration 1.1b)**.
6   Remove the rear section of the rear fender **(see illustration 1.1b)**.
7   Installation is the reverse of removal.

Front section

8   Remove the rear section of the rear fender (see Steps 1 through 5).
9   Unplug the electrical connectors for the brake light, tail light and turn signal lights (see Chapter 9).
10   Detach the starter relay and the turn signal relay and lay them aside, or unplug and remove them (see Chapter 9).
11   Remove the junction box (see Chapter 9).
12   Remove the igniter (see Chapter 5).
13   Remove the battery breather.
14   Detach the reservoir for the rear brake master cylinder (see Chapter 7).
15   Remove the battery (see Chapter 1).
16   Remove the front section retaining bolts **(see illustration 1.1b)**.
17   Remove the lower tie-rod bolt from the rear shock absorber (see Chapter 6). (This allows you to lower the rear wheel.)
18   Remove the front section of the rear fender by pulling it to the rear, over the top of the lowered rear wheel.
19   Installation is the reverse of removal. If you can't remember the routing for a hose, refer to the cable, wire and hose routing schematics which accompany Chapter 2.

E models

Rear section

20   Set the bike on its centerstand.
21   Remove the seat (see Section 7).
22   Remove the side covers (see Section 8).
23   On California models, remove the evaporative canister (see Chapter 1).
24   Remove the tool pouch.

25   Remove the coolant reservoir (see Chapter 3).
26   Remove the tail light bracket (see Chapter 9).
27   Remove the rear and side reflectors from the rear fender.
28   Remove the rear section retaining bolts **(see illustration 1.1e)**.
29   Remove the rear section.
30   Installation is the reverse of removal.

Front section

31   Remove the rear section (see Steps 20 through 29).
32   Remove the battery (see Chapter 1).
33   Remove the fuel pump, starter and turn signal relays (see Chapter 9).
34   Detach the reservoir for the rear brake master cylinder (see Chapter 7).
35   Remove the IC igniter (see Chapter 5).
36   Remove the front section retaining bolts **(see illustration 1.1e)**.
37   Remove the front section.
38   Installation is the reverse of removal.

11 Footpegs and brackets - removal and installation

Rider's left side

Refer to illustrations 11.1 and 11.3

1   If it's only necessary to detach the footpeg from the bracket, pry the C-clip off the pivot pin **(see illustration)**, slide out the pin and detach the footpeg from the bracket. Be careful not to lose the spring. Installation is the reverse of removal, but be sure to install the spring correctly.
2   If it's necessary to remove the entire bracket from the frame, mark the relationship of the shift lever to the shift shaft **(see illustration 15.1 in Chapter 7)**, then remove the clamp bolt. Slide the lever off the shaft.
3   Unscrew the shift lever pivot bolt **(see illustration)** and the bracket-to-frame bolt and separate the footpeg and bracket from the frame.
4   Installation is the basically the reverse of removal. Apply a thin coat of grease to the shift pedal pivot bolt, and be sure to line up the matchmarks on the shift lever and shift shaft. The link rod should be parallel to the shift pedal.

Rider's right side

Refer to illustration 11.9

5   If it's only necessary to detach the footpeg from the bracket, pry the C-clip off the pivot pin **(see illustration 11.1)**, slide out the pin and detach the footpeg from the bracket. Be careful not to lose the spring. Installation is the reverse of removal, but be sure to install the spring correctly.
6   If it's necessary to remove the entire bracket from the frame,

11.12 To remove either passenger footpeg bracket, remove the two Allen head bolts

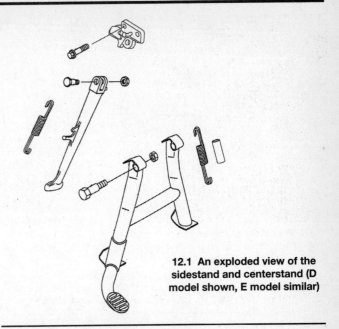

12.1 An exploded view of the sidestand and centerstand (D model shown, E model similar)

unplug the electrical connector for the rear brake light switch (see Chapter 9).

7   Remove the cotter pin from the clevis pin that attaches the brake pedal to the master cylinder, then remove the clevis pin (see Chapter 9).

8   Unbolt the master cylinder from the bracket (see Chapter 9).

9   Remove the Allen-head bolts that secure the bracket to the frame **(see illustration)**, then detach the footpeg and bracket.

10   Installation is the reverse of removal.

Passenger footpegs and brackets (either side)

Refer to illustration 11.12

11   If it's only necessary to detach the footpeg from the bracket, pry the C-clip off the pivot pin **(see illustration 4.1)**, slide out the pin and detach the footpeg from the bracket. Be careful not to lose the spring. Installation is the reverse of removal, but be sure to install the spring correctly.

12   If it's necessary to remove the entire bracket, unscrew the two Allen head bolts **(see illustration)** and detach the bracket from the frame.

13   Installation is the reverse of removal.

12 Sidestand and centerstand - maintenance

Refer to illustration 12.1

1   The centerstand **(see illustration)** pivots on two bolts attached to the frame. Periodically, remove the pivot bolts and grease them thoroughly to avoid excessive wear.

2   Make sure the return spring is in good condition. A broken or weak spring is an obvious safety hazard.

3   The sidestand **(see illustration 12.1)** is attached to a bracket bolted to the frame. An extension spring anchored to the bracket ensures that the stand is held in the retracted position.

4   Make sure the pivot bolt is tight and the extension spring is in good condition and not overstretched. An accident is almost certain to occur if the stand extends while the machine is in motion.

13 Frame - inspection and repair

1   The frame should not require attention unless accident damage has occurred. In most cases, frame replacement is the only satisfactory remedy for such damage. A few frame specialists have the jigs and other equipment necessary for straightening the frame to the required standard of accuracy, but even then there is no simple way of assessing to what extent the frame may have been overstressed.

2   After the machine has accumulated a lot of miles, the frame should be examined closely for signs of cracking or splitting at the welded joints. Rust corrosion can also cause weakness at these joints. Loose engine mount bolts can cause ovaling or fracturing of the mounting tabs. Minor damage can often be repaired by welding, depending on the extent and nature of the damage.

3   Remember that a frame which is out of alignment will cause handling problems. If misalignment is suspected as the result of an accident, it will be necessary to strip the machine completely so the frame can be thoroughly checked.

14 Frame rear section (D models only) - removal and installation

1   Remove the seat.

2   Remove the side covers (see Chapter 8).

3   Remove the rear fender/mudguard (see Section 10).

4   Detach any wiring harness clamps or other components which may interfere with removal of the frame rear section.

5   Unscrew the bolts and detach the frame rear section **(see illustration 1.1b)**.

6   If you're replacing the frame rear section, unbolt the passenger footpeg brackets, the seat lock and the helmet lock and install them on the new rear section.

7   Installation is the reverse of removal procedure. Be sure to tighten the bolts securely.

8

Notes

Chapter 9
Electrical system

Contents

Specifications

Battery

Type	12 volt, 12Ah (amp hours)
Specific gravity	
Fully charged	1.280 at 68-degrees F
Minimum	1.260 at 68-degrees F
Charging rate (E models)	
Standard charge	1.2 amps for 5 to 10 hours
Quick charge	5.0 amps for 1 hour

Charging system

Charging voltage	
Regulator/rectifier output voltage	14 to 15 volts
Alternator output voltage	45 volts
Stator coil resistance	0.2 to 0.6 ohms

9

Starter motor

Brush length
    Standard .... 11.6 to 12.4 mm (0.4570 to 0.4886 inch)
    Minimum .... 8.5 mm (0.3349 inch)
Commutator diameter
    Standard .... 27.8 to 28.1 mm (1.0953 inches)
    Minimum .... 27 mm (1.0638 inches)

Circuit fuse ratings

Accessory fuse 10A
Fan fuse 10A
Headlight fuse 10A
Main fuse 30A
Tail light 10A

Torque specifications

Alternator rotor bolt .... 78 Nm (58 ft-lbs)
Alternator stator bolts .... 12 Nm (104 in-lbs)
Alternator cover bolts .... 8.8 Nm (78 in-lbs)
Oil pressure sending unit .... 15 Nm (132 in-lbs)
Neutral switch .... 15 Nm (132 in-lbs)

1   General information

The machines covered by this manual are equipped with a 12-volt electrical system. The components include a crankshaft-mounted permanent magnet alternator and a solid state voltage regulator/rectifier unit.

The regulator maintains the charging system output within the specified range to prevent overcharging. The rectifier converts the AC output of the alternator to DC current to power the lights and other components and to charge the battery.

The alternator consists of a multi-coil stator (bolted to the left-hand engine case) and a permanent magnet rotor.

An electric starter is mounted to the engine case behind the cylinder block. The starting system includes the motor, the battery, the solenoid, the starter circuit relay (part of the junction box) and the various wires and switches. If the engine STOP switch and the main key switch are both in the On position, the circuit relay allows the starter motor to operate only if the transmission is in Neutral (Neutral switch on) or the clutch lever is pulled to the handlebar (clutch switch on) and the sidestand is up (sidestand switch on).

Note: *Keep in mind that electrical parts, once purchased, can't be returned. To avoid unnecessary expense, make very sure the faulty component has been positively identified before buying a replacement part.*

2   Electrical troubleshooting

A typical electrical circuit consists of an electrical component, the switches, relays, etc. related to that component and the wiring and connectors that hook the component to both the battery and the frame. To aid in locating a problem in any electrical circuit, complete wiring diagrams of each model are included at the end of this Chapter.

Before tackling any troublesome electrical circuit, first study the appropriate diagrams thoroughly to get a complete picture of what makes up that individual circuit. Trouble spots, for instance, can often be narrowed down by noting if other components related to that circuit are operating properly or not. If several components or circuits fail at one time, chances are the fault lies in the fuse or ground connection, as several circuits often are routed through the same fuse and ground connections.

Electrical problems often stem from simple causes, such as loose or corroded connections or a blown fuse. Prior to any electrical troubleshooting, always visually check the condition of the fuse, wires and connections in the problem circuit.

If testing instruments are going to be utilized, use the diagrams to plan where you will make the necessary connections in order to accurately pinpoint the trouble spot.

The basic tools needed for electrical troubleshooting include a test light or voltmeter, a continuity tester (which includes a bulb, battery and set of test leads) and a jumper wire, preferably with a circuit breaker incorporated, which can be used to bypass electrical components. Specific checks described later in this Chapter may also require an ammeter or ohmmeter.

Voltage checks should be performed if a circuit is not functioning properly. Connect one lead of a test light or voltmeter to either the negative battery terminal or a known good ground. Connect the other lead to a connector in the circuit being tested, preferably nearest to the battery or fuse. If the bulb lights, voltage is reaching that point, which means the part of the circuit between that connector and the battery is problem-free. Continue checking the remainder of the circuit in the same manner. When you reach a point where no voltage is present, the problem lies between there and the last good test point. Most of the time the problem is due to a loose connection. Keep in mind that some circuits only receive voltage when the ignition key is in the On position.

One method of finding short circuits is to remove the fuse and connect a test light or voltmeter in its place to the fuse terminals. There should be no load in the circuit. Move the wiring harness from side-to-side while watching the test light. If the bulb lights, there is a short to ground somewhere in that area, probably where insulation has rubbed off a wire. The same test can be performed on other components in the circuit, including the switch.

A ground check should be done to see if a component is grounded properly. Disconnect the battery and connect one lead of a self-powered test light (such as a continuity tester) to a known good ground. Connect the other lead to the wire or ground connection being tested. If the bulb lights, the ground is good. If the bulb does not light, the ground is not good.

A continuity check is performed to see if a circuit, section of circuit or individual component is capable of passing electricity through it. Disconnect the battery and connect one lead of a self-powered test light (such as a continuity tester) to one end of the circuit being tested and the other lead to the other end of the circuit. If the bulb lights, there is continuity, which means the circuit is passing electricity through it properly. Switches can be checked in the same way.

Remember that all electrical circuits are designed to conduct electricity from the battery, through the wires, switches, relays, etc. to the electrical component (light bulb, motor, etc.). From there it is directed to the frame (ground) where it is passed back to the battery. Electrical problems are basically an interruption in the flow of electricity from the battery or back to it.

3   Battery - inspection and maintenance

1   Most battery damage is caused by heat, vibration, and/or low electrolyte levels, so keep the battery securely mounted, check the electrolyte level frequently and make sure the charging system is functioning properly.

2   Refer to Chapter 1 for electrolyte level and specific gravity checking procedures.

3   Check around the base inside of the battery for sediment, which is the result of sulfation caused by low electrolyte levels. These deposits will cause internal short circuits, which can quickly discharge the battery. Look for cracks in the case and replace the battery if either of these conditions is found.

4   Check the battery terminals and cable ends for tightness and corrosion. If corrosion is evident, remove the cables from the battery and clean the terminals and cable ends with a wire brush or knife and emery paper. Reconnect the cables and apply a thin coat of petroleum jelly to the connections to slow further corrosion.

5   The battery case should be kept clean to prevent current leakage, which can discharge the battery over a period of time (especially when it sits unused). Wash the outside of the case with a solution of baking soda

and water. Do not get any baking soda solution in the battery cells. Rinse the battery thoroughly, then dry it.

6   If acid has been spilled on the frame or battery box, neutralize it with the baking soda and water solution, dry it thoroughly, then touch up any damaged paint. Make sure the battery vent tube is directed away from the frame and is not kinked or pinched.

7   If the motorcycle sits unused for long periods of time, disconnect the cables from the battery terminals and charge the battery once a month (see Section 4).

4   Battery - charging

Conventional batteries (D models)

Caution: *The following procedure applies to the conventional motorcycle battery used in D models. It does NOT apply to the maintenance-free battery used in E models. If, after checking a maintenance-free battery's state of charge, you decide to charge it, follow the manufacturer's instructions shown on the battery's label. If there are no instructions on the battery itself, follow the procedure below beginning with Step 10.*

1   If the machine sits idle for extended periods or if the charging system malfunctions, the battery can be charged from an external source.

2   To properly charge the battery, you will need a charger of the correct rating, a hydrometer, a clean rag and a syringe for adding distilled water to the battery cells.

3   The maximum charging rate for any battery is 1/10 of the rated amp/hour capacity. As an example, the maximum charging rate for the 14 amp/hour battery would be 1.4 amps. If the battery is charged at a higher rate, it could be damaged.

4   Do not allow the battery to be subjected to a so-called quick charge (high rate of charge over a short period of time) unless you are prepared to buy a new battery.

5   When charging the battery, always remove it from the machine and be sure to check the electrolyte level before hooking up the charger. Add distilled water to any cells that are low.

6   Loosen the cell caps, hook up the battery charger leads (red to positive, black to negative), cover the top of the battery with a clean rag, then, and only then, plug in the battery charger. **Warning:** *Remember, the gas escaping from a charging battery is explosive, so keep open flames and sparks well away from the area. Also, the electrolyte is extremely corrosive and will damage anything it comes in contact with.*

7   Allow the battery to charge until the specific gravity is as specified (refer to Chapter 1 for specific gravity checking procedures). The

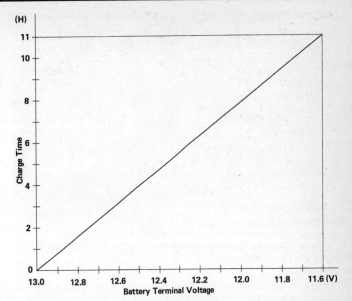

4.13 Battery charge time table (maintenance-free batteries)

charger must be unplugged and disconnected from the battery when making specific gravity checks. If the battery overheats or gases excessively, the charging rate is too high. Either disconnect the charger or lower the charging rate to prevent damage to the battery.

8   If one or more of the cells do not show an increase in specific gravity after a long slow charge, or if the battery as a whole does not seem to want to take a charge, it is time for a new battery.

9   When the battery is fully charged, unplug the charger first, then disconnect the leads from the battery. Install the cell caps and wipe any electrolyte off the outside of the battery case.

Maintenance-free batteries (E models)

Refer to illustration 4.13

10   Charging the maintenance-free battery used on these models requires a digital voltmeter and a variable-voltage charger with a built-in ammeter.

11   When charging the battery, always remove it from the machine and be sure to check the electrolyte level by looking through the translucent battery case before hooking up the charger. If the electrolyte level is low, the battery must be discarded; never remove the sealing plug to add water.

12   Disconnect the battery cables (negative cable first), then connect a digital voltmeter between the battery terminals and measure the voltage.

13   If terminal voltage is 12.6 volts or higher, the battery is fully charged. If it's lower, recharge the battery. Refer to the accompanying illustration and this Chapter's Specifications for charging rate and time **(see illustration)**.

14   A quick charge can be used in an emergency, provided the maximum charge rates and times are not exceeded (exceeding the maximum rate or time may ruin the battery). A quick charge should always be followed as soon as possible by a charge at the standard rate and time.

15   Hook up the battery charger leads (positive lead to battery positive terminal, negative lead to battery negative terminal), then, and only then, plug in the battery charger. **Warning:** *The hydrogen gas escaping from a charging battery is explosive, so keep open flames and sparks well away from the area. Also, the electrolyte is extremely corrosive and will damage anything it comes in contact with.*

16   Start charging at a high voltage setting (no more than 25 volts) and watch the ammeter for about 5 minutes. If the charging current doesn't increase, replace the battery with a new one.

17   When the charging current increases beyond the specified

9

5.1a To get at the fuses inside the junction box, remove the plastic cover by pulling up on either end

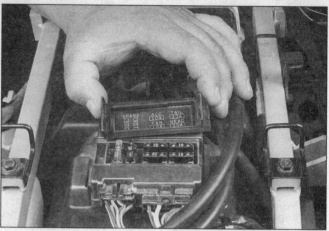

5.1b This junction box is on an E model, but the box on D models has a similar layout and is in almost the same location, under the seat, on top of the rear fender/mudguard (note the fuse guide inside the cover)

maximum, reduce the charging voltage to reduce the charging current to the rate listed in this Chapter's Specifications. Do this periodically as the battery charges.

18   Allow the battery to charge for the specified time listed in this Chapter's Specifications. If the battery overheats or gases excessively, the charging rate is too high. Either disconnect the charger or lower the charging rate to prevent damage to the battery.

19   After the specified time, unplug the charger first, then disconnect the leads from the battery.

20   Wait 30 minutes, then measure voltage between the battery terminals. If it's 12.6 volts or higher, the battery is fully charged. If it's between 12.0 and 12.6 volts, charge the battery again (refer to this Chapter's Specifications and illustration 4.13 for charge rate and time). If it's less than 12.0 volts, it's time for a new battery.

21   When the battery is fully charged, unplug the charger first, then disconnect the leads from the battery. Wipe off the outside of the battery case and install the battery in the bike.

5   Fuses - check and replacement

Refer to illustrations 5.1a, 5.1b and 5.3

1   The fuses are located under the seat, in the junction box. The fuses are protected by a plastic cover **(see illustration)** which snaps on and off. The junction box **(see illustration)** contains fuses which protect the fan, main, headlight, tail light and accessory circuit wiring and components from damage caused by short circuits. It also contains a couple of spare 10A fuses for roadside repairs.

2   If you have a test light, the fuses can be checked without removing them. Turn the ignition to the On position, connect one end of the test light to a good ground, then probe each terminal on top of the fuse. If the fuse is good, there will be voltage available at both terminals. If the fuse is blown, there will only be voltage present at one

of the terminals.

3   The fuses can be removed and checked visually. If you can't pull the fuse out with your fingertips, use a pair of needle-nose pliers. A blown fuse is easily identified by a break in the element **(see illustration)**.

4   If a fuse blows, be sure to check the wiring harnesses very carefully for evidence of a short circuit. Look for bare wires and chafed, melted or burned insulation. If a fuse is replaced before the cause is located, the new fuse will blow immediately.

5   Never, under any circumstances, use a higher rated fuse or bridge the fuse block terminals, as damage to the electrical system could result.

6   Occasionally a fuse will blow or cause an open circuit for no obvious reason. Corrosion of the fuse ends and fuse block terminals may occur and cause poor fuse contact. If this happens, remove the corrosion with a wire brush or emery paper, then spray the fuse end and terminals with electrical contact cleaner.

6   Junction box - check

1   Aside from serving as the fuse block, the junction box also houses two relays - the starter circuit relay (not the starter solenoid) and the headlight relay. Neither of these relays is replaceable individually. If either relay fails, the junction box must be replaced.

2   In addition to the relay checks, the fuse circuits and diode circuits should be checked also, to rule out the possibility of an open circuit

Fuse Circuit Inspection

Meter Connection	Meter Reading (Ω)
1 – 2	0
*1 – 3B	0
6 – 7	0
6 – 17	0
1 – 7	∞
*8 – 17	∞

(*) : US, Canada Models only

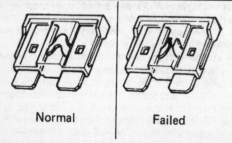

Normal   Failed

5.3 A blown fuse can be identified by a broken element - be sure to replace a blown fuse with one of the same amperage rating

6.4a Using an ohmmeter, check the continuity between the indicated terminals

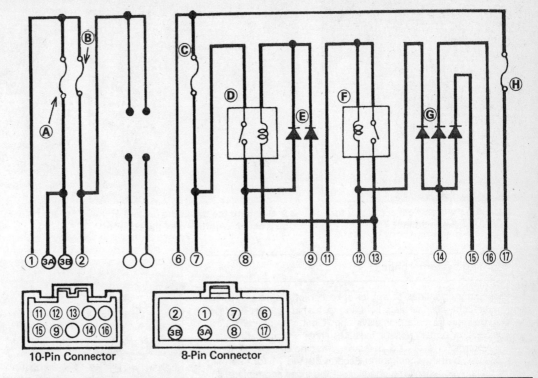

6.4b Junction box circuit (all models)

a   10 amp accessory fuse
b   10 amp fan fuse
c   10 amp headlight fuse
d   Headlight relay
e   Diodes
f   Starter circuit relay
g   Diodes for interlock circuit
h   10 amp taillight fuse

10-Pin Connector

8-Pin Connector

condition or blown diode within the junction block as the cause of an electrical problem. Schematics of the junction box can be found in the wiring diagrams at the end of this Chapter.

Fuse circuit check

Refer to illustrations 6.4a and 6.4b

3   Remove the junction box by sliding it out of its holder. Unplug the electrical connectors from the box.
4   If the terminals are dirty or bent, clean and straighten them. Using the accompanying table as a guide, check the continuity across the indicated terminals with an ohmmeter - some should have no resistance and others should have infinite resistance **(see illustration)**.
5   If the resistance values are not as specified, replace the junction box.

Diode circuit check

6   Remove the junction box by sliding it out of its holder. Unplug the electrical connectors from the box.
7   Using an ohmmeter, check the resistance across the following pairs of terminals, then write down the readings.
Here are the terminal pairs to be checked:

  13 and 8 (US and Canadian models only)
  13 and 9 (US and Canadian models only)
  12 and 14
  15 and 14
  16 and 14

8   Now, reverse the ohmmeter leads and check the resistances again, writing down the readings. The resistances should be low in one direction and more than ten times as much in the other direction. If the readings for any pair of terminals are low or high in both directions, a diode is defective and the junction box must be replaced.

Relay checks

Refer to illustration 6.10

9   Remove the junction box by sliding it out of its holder. Unplug the electrical connectors from the box.
10   Using an ohmmeter, check the conductivity across the terminals

Relay Circuit Inspection
(with the battery disconnected)

	Meter Connection	Meter Reading (Ω)
Headlight Relay	*7 – 8	∞
	*7 – 13	∞
Starter Relay	11 – 13	∞
	12 – 13	∞

Relay Circuit Inspection
(with the battery connected)

	Meter Connection	Battery Connection + –	Meter Reading (Ω)
Headlight Relay	*7 – 8	*9 – 13	0
Starter Relay	11 – 13	11 – 12	0

(*) : US, Canada Models only

6.10 With the junction box unplugged, there should be infinite resistance between the indicated terminals and no resistance (continuity) when battery voltage is applied

indicated in the accompanying table **(see illustration)**. Then, energize each relay by applying battery voltage across the indicated terminals and check the conductivity across the corresponding terminals shown on the table.
11   If the junction box fails any of these tests, it must be replaced.

9

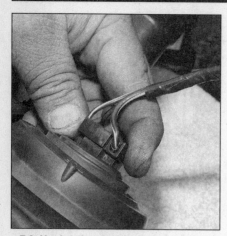

7.2 Unplug the electrical connector for the headlight

8.2 Grasping the tab at the bottom of the dust cover, carefully peel the cover off

8.3a To unlock the bulb holder, release the wire retainer . . .

7 Lighting system - check

1   The battery provides power for operation of the headlight, tail light, brake light, license plate light and instrument cluster lights. If none of the lights operate, always check battery voltage before proceeding. Low battery voltage indicates either a faulty battery, low battery electrolyte level or a defective charging system. Refer to Chapter 1 for battery checks and Section 30 and 31 for charging system tests. Also, check the condition of the fuses and replace any blown fuses with new ones.

Headlight

Refer to illustration 7.2

2   If the headlight is out with the engine running (US and Canadian models) or with the lighting switch in the On position (UK models), check the fuse first with the key On (see Section 5), then unplug the electrical connector for the headlight **(see illustration)** and use jumper wires to connect the bulb directly to the battery terminals. If the light comes on, the problem lies in the wiring or one of the switches in the circuit. Refer to Sections 20 and 21 for the switch testing procedures, and also the wiring diagrams at the end of this Chapter.

3   US and Canadian models have a headlight relay in the junction box (see Section 6). On these models, the headlight doesn't come on when the ignition switch is first turned on, but comes on when the starter button is pressed and stays on until the ignition is turned off. If the engine stalls, the light goes out, and stays off while the starter is operated, to prevent excessive strain on the battery).

Tail light/license plate lights

4   If the tail light fails to work, or isn't as bright as it should be, check the bulbs (there are two) and the bulb terminals first, then check for battery voltage at the red wire in the tail light. If voltage is present, check the ground circuit for an open or a poor connection. Check the license plate light the same way.

5   If no voltage is indicated, check the wiring between the tail light or license plate light and the main (key) switch, then check the switch itself.

Brake lights

6   See Section 14 for the brake light circuit checking procedure.

Neutral indicator light

7   If the neutral light fails to operate when the transmission is in Neutral, check the fuses and the bulb (see Section 18 for bulb removal procedures). If the bulb and fuses are in good condition, check for battery voltage at the light green wire attached to the neutral switch on the left side of the engine. If battery voltage is present, refer to

8.3b . . . then remove the bulb holder from its socket

Section 23 for the neutral switch check and replacement procedures.

8   If no voltage is indicated, check the brown wire between the junction box and the bulb, and the light green wire between the junction box and the switch and between the switch and the bulb for open circuits and poor connections.

Oil pressure warning light

9   See Section 19 for the oil pressure warning light circuit check.

8 Headlight bulb - replacement

Refer to illustrations 8.2, 8.3a and 8.3b

1   Remove the upper fairing (see Chapter 8).

2   Remove the dust cover from the headlight **(see illustration)**.

3   Lift up the retaining clip and swing it out of the way **(see illustration)**. Remove the bulb holder **(see illustration)**.

4   When installing the new bulb, reverse the removal procedure. Be sure not to touch the bulb with your fingers - oil from your skin will cause the bulb to overheat and fail prematurely. If you do touch the bulb, wipe it off with a clean rag dampened with rubbing alcohol.

5   The parking (or city) light on UK models is positioned in the base of the headlight unit. Peel back the rubber dust cover and pull the bulb holder out of the grommet in the headlight. Twist the bulb counterclockwise to release it.

9.2 To remove the headlight assembly from the fairing, remove these four bolts (arrows)

10.4 To adjust the headlight horizontally, turn the adjuster screw with a Phillips screwdriver (left arrow); to adjust the headlight vertically, turn the adjuster knob (right arrow)

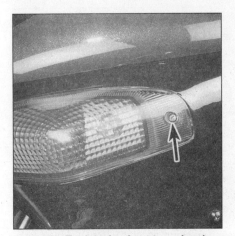

11.1a To detach a front turn signal assembly from the upper fairing, remove this screw (arrow) (E model shown, D models similar)

11.1b To detach a rear turn signal lens from the side cover, remove this screw (E model shown; on D models the rear turn signal assemblies are mounted on short stalks)

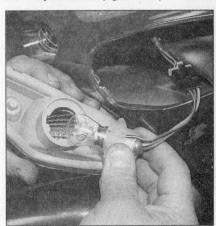

11.2a To remove a bulb holder from the front turn signal assembly, turn it counterclockwise and pull out; to remove the bulb from the holder, push it into the holder, turn it counterclockwise and pull it out

9 Headlight assembly - removal and installation

Refer to illustration 9.2

1   Remove the upper fairing (see Chapter 8).
2   Remove the screws holding the headlight assembly to the fairing **(see illustration)**. Separate the headlight assembly from the fairing.
3   Installation is the reverse of removal. Be sure to adjust the headlight aim (see Section 10).

10 Headlight aim - check and adjustment

Refer to illustration 10.4

1   An improperly adjusted headlight may cause problems for oncoming traffic or provide poor, unsafe illumination of the road ahead. Before adjusting the headlight, be sure to consult with local traffic laws and regulations.
2   The headlight beam can be adjusted both vertically and horizontally. Before performing the adjustment, make sure the fuel tank has at least a half tank of gas, and have an assistant sit on the seat.
3   Remove the trim panel around the instrument cluster and unbolt the cluster (see Section 15). It isn't necessary to unplug anything; but

pulling the cluster back slightly will give you enough room to reach the horizontal and vertical headlight adjusters.
4   Insert a Phillips screwdriver into the horizontal adjuster guide **(see illustration)**, then turn the adjuster as necessary to center the beam.
5   To adjust the vertical position of the beam, turn the adjuster knob **(see illustration 10.4)**, located at the lower right corner of the headlight assembly, to raise or lower the beam.
6   Install the instrument cluster and trim panel.

11 Turn signal and tail light bulbs - replacement

Turn signal bulbs

Refer to illustrations 11.1a, 11.1b, 11.2a and 11.2b

1   If you're replacing a front turn signal bulb, remove the retaining screw from the lens **(see illustration)** and pull out the turn signal assembly. If you're replacing a rear turn signal bulb, remove the lens retaining screw **(see illustration)** and remove the lens.
2   To remove a front turn signal bulb, remove the bulb holder **(see illustration)**, then remove the bulb from the holder by pushing the bulb in and turning it counterclockwise. Rear turn signal bulbs can be removed from the holder without removing the holder from the turn

11.2b To remove a bulb from a rear turn signal bulb holder, push it in into the holder, turn it counterclockwise and pull it out

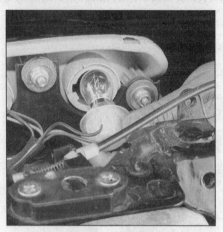

11.5 To replace a tail light/brake light bulb, push in and turn counterclockwise, then pull out

11.9 To remove the license plate light lens, remove these screws (arrows)

signal assembly **(see illustration)**. Check the socket terminal for corrosion and clean them if necessary. Line up the pins on the new bulb with the slots in the socket, push in and turn the bulb clockwise until it locks in place. **Note:** *The pins on the bulb are offset so it can only be installed one way. It is a good idea to use a paper towel or dry cloth when handling the new bulb to prevent injury if the bulb should break and to increase bulb life.*

3   Position the lens on the turn signal housing and install the screw. Be careful not to overtighten it.

Tail light/brake light bulbs

Refer to illustration 11.5

Note: *There are actually two tail light/brake light bulbs. They're both replaced the same way.*

4   Remove the seat (see Chapter 8).

5   Turn the bulb holder counterclockwise **(see illustration)** until it stops, then pull straight out to remove it from the tail light housing. The bulb can be removed from its holder by turning it counterclockwise and pulling straight out.

6   Check the socket terminal for corrosion and clean it if necessary. Line up the pins on the new bulb with the slots in the socket, push in and turn the bulb clockwise until it locks in place. **Note:** *The pins on the bulb are offset so it can only be installed one way. It is a good idea to use a paper towel or dry cloth when handling the new bulb to increase bulb life and to prevent injury if the bulb breaks.*

7   Make sure the rubber gaskets are in place and in good condition, then line up the tabs on the holder with the slots in the housing and push the holder into the mounting hole. Turn it clockwise until it stops to lock it in place. **Note:** *The tabs and slots are two different sizes so the holders can only be installed one way.*

8   Install the seat.

License plate light bulb

Refer to illustration 11.9

9   Remove the license plate lens retaining screws **(see illustration)**.

10   Turn the bulb counterclockwise until it stops, then pull straight out to remove it from the housing.

11   Installation is the reverse of removal. Be sure to install the lens so that the "TOP" mark on the lens faces up. And don't overtighten the lens retaining screws.

12   Turn signal assemblies - removal and installation

Front turn signals

1   Remove the lens retaining screw **(see illustration 11.1a)**.

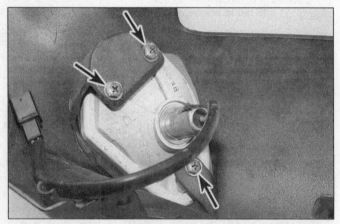

12.5 To remove a rear turn signal assembly from a side cover, remove these three screws (arrows)

2   Remove the bulb holder from the turn signal assembly **(see illustration 11.2a)**.

3   Installation is the reverse of removal.

Rear turn signals

Refer to illustration 12.5

4   Remove the side cover (see Chapter 8).

5   Remove the turn signal assembly retaining screws **(see illustration)**.

6   Installation is the reverse of removal.

13   Turn signal circuit - check and component replacement

Check

Refer to illustration 13.3

1   The battery provides power for operation of the signal lights, so if they don't operate, always check the battery voltage and specific gravity first. Low battery voltage indicates either a faulty battery, low electrolyte level or a defective charging system. Refer to Chapter 1 for battery checks and Sections 30 and 31 for charging system tests. Also, check the fuses (see Section 5).

2   Most turn signal problems are the result of a burned out bulb or corroded socket, particularly when the turn signals function properly in one direction, but fail to flash in the other direction. Check the bulbs

13.3 The turn signal relay (flasher) is located on the left side of the bike behind the side cover just behind (D models) or ahead of (E models) the battery (E model shown)

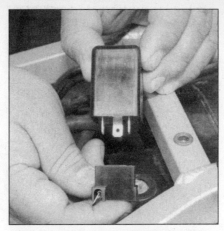

13.8 To replace a turn signal relay, lift up the relay assembly to free it from its rubber mounting, then unplug the relay from the base (E model shown, D models similar)

14.6 To replace the front brake light switch, simply unplug the two electrical connectors (arrow) from the spade connectors on the switch, then remove the switch retaining screw (arrow)

and the sockets (see Section 11).

3   If the bulbs and sockets check out okay, remove the left side cover (see Chapter 8), turn the ignition switch to On and check for voltage at the turn signal relay **(see illustration)**. There should be battery voltage at both the orange/green wire, which brings voltage from the ignition switch to the relay, and at the orange wire, which delivers voltage from the relay to the turn signal switch.

4   If there's no power at the orange/green wire, check the wire back to the ignition switch. If the orange/green wire is okay, check the ignition switch itself (see Section 20).

5   If there's no voltage at the orange wire, check the orange wire back to the turn signal switch. If the orange wire is okay, check the turn signal switch itself (see Section 21).

6   Activate the turn signal switch in both directions and verify that there's voltage at the black/yellow wire at the relay. There should be voltage in this wire when the left or the right turn signals are activated. If there's no voltage when the switch is activated in either direction, replace the relay.

Replacement

Refer to illustration 13.8

7   Remove the left side cover, if you haven't already done so (see Chapter 8).

8   Simply detach the relay assembly from its rubber mounting and unplug the relay from the base **(see illustration)**.

9   Installation is the reverse of removal.

14   Brake light switches - check and replacement

Circuit check

Note: *The following circuit check applies to either the front or rear brake light circuits.*

1   Before checking any electrical circuit, check the fuses (see Section 5).

2   Using a test light connected to a good ground, check for voltage to the brown wire at the brake light switch. If there's no voltage present, check the brown wire between the switch and the junction box (see the wiring diagrams at the end of this Chapter).

3   If voltage is available at the brown wire between the brake light switch and the junction box, touch the probe of the test light to the other terminal of the front or rear brake light switch, then pull the front brake lever or depress the rear brake pedal. The test light should come on.

4   If the test light doesn't come on, replace the front or rear brake

light switch.

5   If the test light does come on, check the wiring between the switch and the brake lights (see the wiring diagrams at the end of this Chapter).

Switch replacement

Front brake lever switch

Refer to illustration 14.6

6   Unplug the electrical connectors from the switch **(see illustration)**.

7   Remove the mounting screw **(see illustration 14.6)** and detach the switch from the master cylinder.

8   Installation is the reverse of removal procedure.

Rear brake pedal switch

Refer to illustrations 14.10, 14.11 and 14.12

9   Trace the electrical leads (brown and blue/red on D models; brown and blue on E models) from the top of the switch to the electrical connector (below the fuel sensor relay and fuel level warning light relay on D models; below the IC igniter on E models) and unplug the connector. (On E models, you'll have to unbolt the IC igniter to reach the connector.)

10   Disengage the switch return spring from the brake pedal return spring **(see illustration)**. (The switch return spring is the little spring; the brake pedal return spring is the bigger spring.)

14.10 Disengage the lower end of the rear brake light switch spring from the brake pedal spring

9

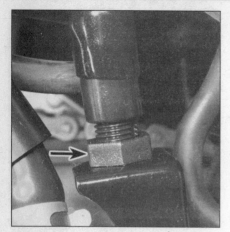

14.11 To remove the rear brake light switch, back off the adjuster nut (arrow) and unscrew the switch from its bracket

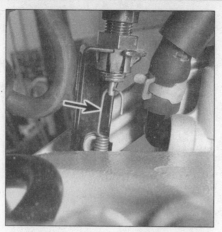

14.12 When installing the rear brake light switch, make sure the upper end of the switch spring (arrow) is properly engaged with the switch plunger

15.2a Unplug the electrical connector for the instrument cluster

15.2b Unscrew the threaded ferrule and disconnect the speedometer cable from the speedometer

15.3 Remove the instrument cluster mounting bolts (arrow) (left bolt shown, right bolt in same location under right end of cluster)

11   Loosen the adjuster nut **(see illustration)** and unscrew the switch.

12   Installation is the reverse of removal. Make sure the switch spring is properly engaged with the switch plunger **(see illustration)**.

13   Adjust the switch (see Chapter 1, Section 6).

15   Instrument cluster - removal and installation

Refer to illustrations 15.2a, 15.2b, 15.3 and 15.4

1   Remove the windscreen and the instrument cluster trim panel (see Chapter 8).

2   Unplug the electrical connectors from the cluster harness and detach the speedometer cable from the speedometer **(see illustrations)**.

3   Remove the instrument cluster mounting bolts **(see illustration)** and detach the cluster from the upper fairing mount.

4   If you're replacing the old instrument cluster, remove the cluster mounting bracket **(see illustration)** and transfer it to the new cluster. Be sure to replace the three cluster-to-bracket bushings if they're cracked or torn.

5   Installation is the reverse of removal.

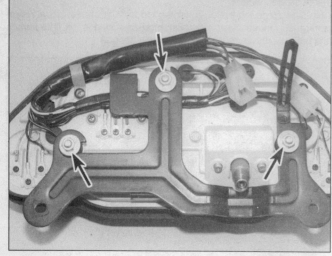

15.4 To remove the mounting bracket from the old cluster, remove these three bolts (arrows) and washers; be sure to inspect the three bushings and, if they're torn or cracked, replace them

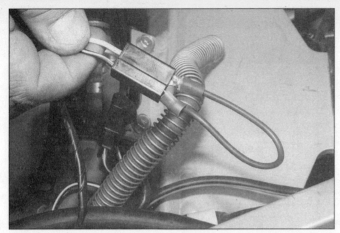

16.2 To test the fuel gauge, bridge the two terminals of the female (wire-harness) side of the electrical connector for the fuel level sensor and verify that the gauge needle jumps to the Full mark when the ignition key is turned on

16.5a Before removing the cover from the instrument cluster, unscrew the trip reset knob

16 Meters and gauges - check and replacement

Fuel gauge (E models)

Refer to illustrations 16.2, 16.5a and 16.5b

1   To check the operation of the fuel gauge, remove the fuel tank (see Chapter 4).

2   Turn the ignition switch to the On position. Using a jumper wire, bridge the terminals of the female side of the fuel level sensor connector (the wiring harness side - not the wires that lead back to the fuel tank) **(see illustration)**. If the fuel level gauge is working properly, the needle will swing past the full mark on the gauge. **Caution:** *Don't leave the wire grounded longer than necessary to perform this check. If you do, the gauge could be damaged. With the wire disconnected, the needle should fall to the empty mark.*

3   If the gauge doesn't respond as described, either the wiring is defective or the gauge itself is malfunctioning. If the gauge does pass the above test, the fuel level sensor is defective (see Section 17).

4   If it's necessary to replace the gauge, remove the instrument cluster (see Section 15). Remove the fasteners that secure the cluster mounting bracket to the cluster **(see illustration 15.4)** and detach the bracket.

5   Unscrew the trip reset knob **(see illustration)**. Remove the three screws that secure the instrument cluster cover **(see illustration)**. Detach the cover. **Caution:** *When the cluster cover is removed, always store the cluster with the gauges facing up or in a horizontal position - never in a face-down position, which could damage the unit.*

6   Mark the positions of the wires and remove the three small screws that secure the gauge to the cluster housing **(see illustration 16.5b)**.

7   Detach the gauge from the housing, being careful not to disturb the other components.

8   Installation is the reverse of the removal procedure.

Temperature gauge

9   Refer to Chapter 3 for the temperature gauge checking procedure. It's part of the *Coolant temperature sensor and gauge - check and replacement* procedure.

10   The procedure for replacing the coolant temperature gauge is exactly the same as for the fuel level gauge, except that the gauge is on the other end of the instrument cluster. See Steps 4 through 8.

Tachometer and speedometer

11   Special instruments are required to properly check the operation of these meters. Take the instrument cluster to a Kawasaki dealer service department or other qualified repair shop for diagnosis.

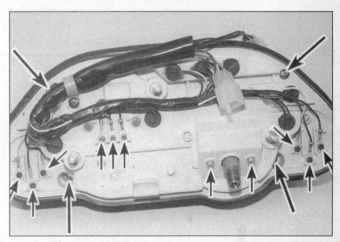

16.5b To remove the cover from the instrument cluster, remove these four screws (large arrows); to remove the fuel level gauge, the coolant temperature gauge, the speedometer or the tachometer, label the leads to that gauge (except for the speedometer) and remove the gauge retaining screws (small arrows)

12   The replacement procedure for either of these meters is also essentially the same as the fuel level gauge replacement procedure. Follow Steps 4 through 8.

17 Fuel level system - check and component replacement

D models

Refer to illustration 17.1

1   D models have a low fuel warning system **(see illustration on next page)**. When the ignition switch is turned on, the low fuel level warning lights should flash (indicating that the bulbs are okay), then go out. If the fuel level is low, the lights should continue to flash until fuel is added. If the system doesn't function properly, inspect it as follows.

Warning system inspection

2   If the warning lights don't flash when the ignition switch is turned on, check the warning light bulbs, the oil pressure switch, the rectifier and the wiring.

3   If the warning lights don't flash when the engine runs and the fuel level is low, check the fuel level warning light.

9

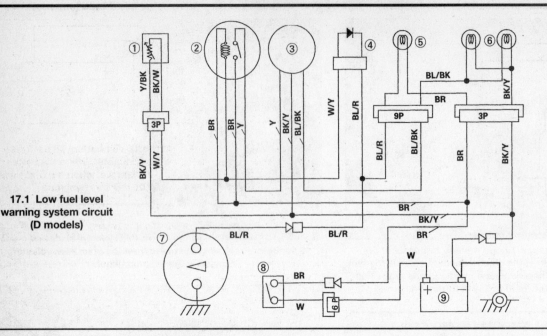

17.1 Low fuel level warning system circuit (D models)

a) If the warning light is operating okay, replace the fuel level sensor.
b) If the warning light is not operating properly, check the warning system wiring.
c) If the wiring is okay, check the fuel level sensor relay.
d) If the fuel level sensor is okay, check the fuel level warning light relay.

4 If the fuel level isn't low, but the warning lights remain on, check the warning system wiring. If the wiring is okay, check the fuel level warning light relay or replace the fuel level sensor.

5 If the warning lights go on and off intermittently, check the following:

a) Verify that the fuel level is not low.
b) Verify that the wiring is not shorting out against other parts.
c) Verify that battery charging voltage is adequate.

If the fuel level is not, the battery isn't shorting out and battery charging voltage is okay, replace the fuel level sensor.

Fuel level warning light operation

Refer to illustration 17.6

6 Remove the fuel tank (see Chapter 4) and locate the fuel level sensor connector **(see illustration)**. Turn the ignition switch on, then unplug the fuel level sensor connector. The fuel level warning lights should go off when the connector is unplugged. Now short the

connector wires - the warning lights should flash. If the lights operate as described, replace the fuel level sensor.

Fuel level warning light relay check

Refer to illustrations 17.8 and 17.9

7 Remove the right side cover (see Chapter 8).
8 Remove the fuel level warning light relay **(see illustration)**.
9 Connect a 12-volt battery and two 3-watt bulbs as indicated **(see illustration)**, and count how many times the lights flash for one minute. If the relay is operating properly, they should flash between 140 and 200 times a minute.
10 If the warning lights don't operate as described, replace the relay.

Fuel level sensor relay check

Refer to illustration 17.13

11 Remove the right side cover (see Chapter 8).
12 Remove the fuel level sensor relay **(see illustration 17.8)**.
13 Hook up an ohmmeter and 12-volt battery as shown **(see illustration)**. Flip the resistance range knob on the ohmmeter to the 1-ohm scale. When the battery is connected, there should be zero resistance; when the battery is disconnected, there should be infinite resistance.
14 If the relay doesn't operate as described, replace it.

17.6 Unplug the two-pin electrical connector (A) for the low fuel level sensor (D models)

17.8 Fuel level sensor relay (A) and fuel level warning light relay (B) (D models)

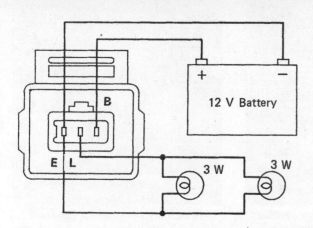

17.9 Connect a 12-volt battery and two 3-watt bulbs as indicated, and count how many times the lights flash for one minute; if the relay is operating properly, they should flash between 140 and 200 times a minute (D models)

Rectifier check

Refer to illustration 17.16

Note: *This device, which is part of the low fuel level warning system on D models, is actually a diode. "Rectifier" is Kawasaki's term.*

15   Remove the upper inner trim panels (between the upper fairing and the fuel tank) and the windscreen (see Chapter 8).

16   Pull the rectifier **(see illustration)** out of the main wiring harness.

17   Zero your ohmmeter and hook it up to each terminal of the rectifier and check the resistance in both directions. Resistance should be low in one direction and more than 10 times as much in the other direction.

18   If your ohmmeter indicates high or low resistance in both directions, replace the rectifier.

E models

Refer to illustrations 17.20 and 17.21

Warning: *Gasoline (petrol) is extremely flammable, so take extra precautions when you work on any part of the fuel system. Don't smoke or allow open flames or bare light bulbs near the work area, and don't work in a garage where a natural gas-type appliance (such as a water*

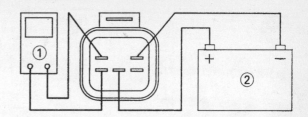

17.13 Hook up an ohmmeter (1) and 12-volt battery (2) as shown and select the 1-ohm scale on your ohmmeter. When the battery is connected, there should be zero resistance; when the battery is disconnected, there should be infinite resistance

heater or clothes dryer) with a pilot light is present. Since gasoline is carcinogenic, wear latex gloves when there's a possibility of being exposed to fuel, and, if you spill any fuel on your skin, rinse it off immediately with soap and water. Mop up any spills immediately and do not store fuel-soaked rags where they could ignite. When you perform any kind of work on the fuel system, wear safety glasses and have a fire extinguisher suitable for a class B type fire (flammable liquids) on hand.

19   Remove the fuel tank (see Chapter 4). Drain the fuel into an approved fuel container.

20   Remove the sending unit mounting bolts **(see illustration)** and remove the sending unit from the tank.

21   Using an ohmmeter, measure the resistance across the terminals of the sensor electrical connector **(see illustration)**. With the float in the full position, the resistance should be low (around 3 to 4 ohms); with the float in the empty position, the resistance should be high (about 100 to 110 ohms).

22   If the sensor is okay, check the wiring between the sensor and the fuel level gauge (see the wiring diagrams at the end of this Chapter). If the wiring is okay, check the gauge itself (see Section 16).

23   If the sensor fails either test, replace it. Be sure to tighten the bolts securely, but don't overtighten them.

18   Instrument and warning light bulbs - replacement

Refer to illustrations 18.2a and 18.2b

1   Remove the instrument cluster (see Section 15).

2   To replace a bulb, pull the appropriate rubber socket out of the

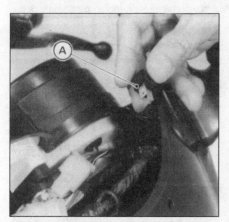

17.16 The low fuel level warning system "rectifier" (A) is located inside the upper left corner of the upper fairing; you'll have to remove the windscreen to get at it

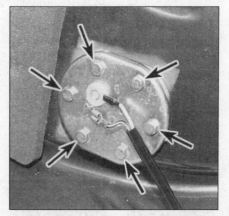

17.20 To remove the fuel level sensor from the fuel tank, remove these six bolts (arrows) and carefully pull the sensor assembly out - be extremely careful not to bend or damage the sensor arm or float

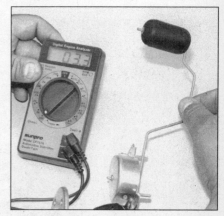

17.21 Measure the resistance of the fuel level sensor at the empty and full positions, note the indicated readings and compare them to the specified resistance. At the full position you should see about 3 to 4 ohms; at the empty position you should see about 100 to 110 ohms

9

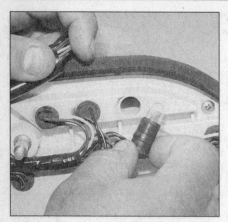

18.2a To remove a bulb holder from the instrument, simply pull the holder straight out

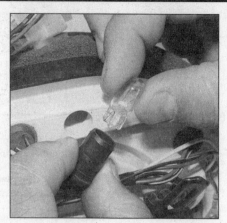

18.2b To remove a bulb from a holder, simply pull the bulb straight out

19.2a The oil pressure sending unit (arrow) is located on the left side of the engine, right in front of the water pump

back of the instrument cluster housing **(see illustration)**, then pull the bulb out of the socket **(see illustration)**. If the socket contacts are dirty or corroded, they should be scraped clean and sprayed with electrical contact cleaner before new bulbs are installed.

3   Carefully push the new bulb into position, then push the socket into the cluster housing.

19 Oil pressure sending unit - check and replacement

Refer to illustration 19.2a and 19.2b

1   If the oil pressure warning light fails to operate properly, check the oil level and make sure it is correct.

2   If the oil level is correct, disconnect the wire from the oil pressure sending unit **(see illustration)**. Turn on the ignition main (key) switch on and ground the end of the wire **(see illustration)**. If the light comes on, the oil pressure sending unit is defective and must be replaced with a new one (only after draining the engine oil).

3   If the light does not come on, check the oil pressure warning light bulb, the wiring between the oil pressure sending unit and the light, and between the light and the junction box (see the wiring diagrams at the end of this Chapter).

4   To replace the sending unit, drain the engine oil (see Chapter 1) and unscrew the sending unit from the case. Wrap the threads of the new sending unit with Teflon tape or apply a thin coat of sealant on them, then screw the unit into its hole and tighten it to the torque listed

in this Chapter's Specifications.

5   Fill the crankcase with the recommended type and amount of oil (see Chapter 1) and check for leaks.

20 Ignition main (key) switch - check and replacement

Check

Refer to illustrations 20.2, 20.3a and 20.3b

1   Remove the fuel tank (see Chapter 4).

2   Unplug the switch electrical connector **(see illustration)**.

3   Using an ohmmeter, check the continuity of the terminal pairs indicated in the ignition switch continuity table **(see illustrations)**. Continuity should exist between the terminals connected by a solid line when the switch is in the indicated position.

4   If the switch fails any of the tests, replace it.

Replacement

Refer to illustrations 20.7

5   Remove the fuel tank (see Chapter 4) and unplug the switch electrical connector, if you haven't already done so.

6   Remove the instrument cluster (see Section 15). Remove the upper triple clamp (see Chapter 6) and flip it over.

7   The switch is attached to the upper clamp with two shear-head bolts **(see illustration)**. Using a hammer and a sharp punch, knock the

19.2b To check the oil pressure sending unit, disconnect the wire, turn on the ignition main (key) switch and ground the end of the wire; if the light comes on, the oil pressure sending unit is defective and must be replaced

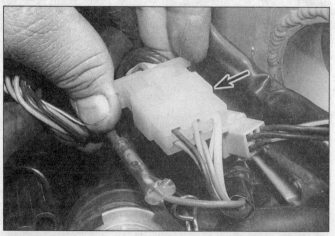

20.2 Unplug the electrical connector (arrow) for the ignition main (key) switch (to get at this connector, you'll have to remove the fuel tank)

IGNITION SWITCH CONNECTIONS						
	Ignition	Battery	Ignition	Tail1	Tail2	Battery	Tail3
Color	BR	W	Y	BL	R	W/BK	O/G
OFF, LOCK							
ON	⊙—⊙—⊙		⊙—⊙		⊙—⊙	
P		⊙—⊙			⊙—⊙	

20.3a Continuity table for the ignition main (key) switch terminals
(US and Canadian models)

IGNITION SWITCH CONNECTIONS					
	Ignition	Battery	Ignition	Tail1	Tail2
Color	BR	W	Y	BL	R
OFF, LOCK					
ON	⊙—⊙—⊙		⊙—⊙	
P		⊙—⊙		⊙—⊙	

20.3b Continuity table for the ignition main (key) switch terminals
(UK models)

20.7 To detach the ignition main (key) switch, drill out these two
shear-head bolts (arrows)

shear-head bolts in a counterclockwise direction to unscrew them. If they're too tight and won't turn, carefully drill holes through the centers of the bolts and unscrew them using a screw extractor (E-Z out). If necessary, remove the fairing mount for better access to the bolts. Detach the switch from the upper clamp.

8   Hold the new switch in position and install the new shear-head bolts. Tighten the bolts until the heads break off.

9   The remainder of installation is the reverse of removal.

21 Handlebar switches - check

Refer to illustration 21.4

1   Generally speaking, the switches are reliable and trouble-free.

Most troubles, when they do occur, are caused by dirty or corroded contacts, but wear and breakage of internal parts is a possibility that should not be overlooked. If breakage does occur, the entire switch and related wiring harness will have to be replaced with a new one, since individual parts are not usually available.

2   The switches can be checked for continuity with an ohmmeter or a continuity test light. Always disconnect the battery ground cable, which will prevent the possibility of a short circuit, before making the checks.

3   Trace the wiring harness of the suspect switch and unplug the electrical connectors.

4   Using the ohmmeter or test light, check for continuity between the terminals of the switch harness with the switch in the various positions **(see illustration)**. Continuity should exist between the terminals connected by a solid line when the switch is in the indicated position.

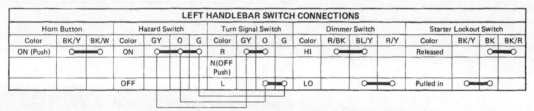

LEFT HANDLEBAR SWITCH CONNECTIONS															
Horn Button			Hazard Switch				Turn Signal Switch				Dimmer Switch				Starter Lockout Switch			
Color	BK/Y	BK/W	Color	GY	O	G	Color	GY	O	G	Color	R/BK	BL/Y	R/Y	Color	BK/Y	BK	BK/R
ON (Push)	⊙—⊙		ON	⊙—⊙—⊙			R	⊙—⊙			HI	⊙—⊙			Released	⊙—⊙	
							N(OFF Push)										
			OFF				L		⊙—⊙		LO		⊙—⊙		Pulled in	⊙—⊙	

US/Canadian models

RIGHT HANDLEBAR SWTICH CONNECTIONS							
Engine Stop Switch			Starter Button			Front Brake Light Switch		
Color	Y/R	R	Color	BK/R	BK/R	Color	BK	BK
OFF			PUSH	⊙—⊙		Released		
RUN	⊙—⊙		Released			Pulled in	⊙—⊙	

US/Canadian models

LEFT HANDLEBAR SWITCH CONNECTIONS															
Horn Button			Passing Button			Turn Signal Switch				Dimmer Switch				Starter Lockout Switch			
Color	BK/Y	BK/W	Color	R/BK	BR	Color	GY	O	G	Color	R/BK	BL/Y	R/Y	Color	BK/Y	BK	BK/R
Released			Released			R	⊙—⊙			HI	⊙—⊙			Released		⊙—⊙	
ON (PUSH)	⊙—⊙		ON (PUSH)	⊙—⊙		N (OFF, PUSH)										
						L		⊙—⊙		LO		⊙—⊙		PULL	⊙—⊙	

UK models

RIGHT HANDLEBAR SWITCH CONNECTIONS												
Engine Stop Switch			Starter Button			Headlight Switch					Front Brake Light Switch		
Color	Y/R	R	Color	BK/R	BK/R	Color	R/W	R/BL	BL	BL/Y	Color	BK	BK
OFF						OFF					Released		
RUN	⊙—⊙		PUSH	⊙—⊙		O					Pulled in	⊙—⊙	
			Released			ON	⊙—⊙		⊙—⊙				

UK models

21.4 Continuity tables for the handlebar switches

23.3a The neutral switch (arrow) is located on the left side of the engine, just behind the water pump and below the countershaft sprocket (you'll have to remove the sprocket cover to get at it); the connector (arrow) and the other two leads (the black/yellow wire and the green/white wire) are for the sidestand switch

23.3b To check the neutral switch, unplug the light green wire from the switch and hook up one lead of an ohmmeter to the switch and the other lead to ground; when the transmission is in neutral, there should be zero resistance; in any other gear position, there should be infinite resistance (note that the sprocket cover is installed in this photo; that's because you can actually unplug the neutral switch without removing the cover - it's located just above the bottom edge of the cover)

5   If the continuity check indicates a problem, refer to Section 22, disassemble the switch and spray the switch contacts with electrical contact cleaner. If they're accessible, the contacts can be scraped clean with a knife or polished with crocus cloth. If switch components are damaged or broken, it will be obvious when the switch is disassembled.

22 Handlebar switches - removal and installation

1   The handlebar switches are composed of two halves that clamp around the bars. They are easily removed for cleaning or inspection by taking out the clamp screws and pulling the switch halves away from the handlebars.
2   To completely remove the switches, the electrical connectors in the wiring harness should be unplugged. The right side switch must be separated from the throttle cables, also.
3   When installing the switches, make sure the wiring harnesses are properly routed to avoid pinching or stretching the wires.

23 Neutral switch - check and replacement

Check

Refer to illustrations 23.3a and 23.3b

1   Mark the position of the shift lever to the shift lever shaft (see Chapter 7, Section 15). Remove the shift lever pinch bolt and slide the lever off the shaft.
2   If you don't know what the neutral switch looks like or where it is, remove the bolts securing the engine sprocket cover to the engine case (see Chapter 7, Section 15). Slide off the sprocket cover. (If you do know where the switch is located, it's not absolutely necessary to remove the sprocket cover, because you can reach up under the bottom edge of the cover, unplug the lead and test the switch without actually removing the cover.
3   Disconnect the wire from the neutral switch **(see illustration)**. Connect one lead of an ohmmeter to a good ground and the other lead to the post on the switch **(see illustration)**.
4   When the transmission is in neutral, the ohmmeter should indicate zero resistance; in any other gear, the ohmmeter should indicate infinite resistance.
5   If the switch doesn't check out as described, replace it.

Replacement

6   Unscrew the neutral switch from the case.
7   Wrap the threads of the new switch with Teflon tape or apply a thin coat of RTV sealant to them. Install the switch in the case and tighten it to the torque listed in this Chapter's Specifications.

24 Sidestand switch - check and replacement

Check

Refer to illustration 24.3

1   Mark the position of the shift lever to the shift lever shaft (see Chapter 7, Section 15). Remove the shift lever pinch bolt and slide the lever off the shaft.
2   Remove the bolts securing the engine sprocket cover to the engine case (see Chapter 8, Section 15). Slide the sprocket cover off.
3   Follow the wiring harness from the sidestand switch to the connector **(see illustration 23.3a)**, then unplug the connector. Connect the leads of an ohmmeter to the terminals of the switch side of the connector **(see illustration)**. With the sidestand in its retracted (up) position, there should be continuity (zero resistance) through the switch; with the sidestand down, there should be no continuity (infinite resistance).
4   If the switch fails either of these tests, replace it.

Replacement

Refer to illustration 24.6

5   Unplug the switch electrical connector, if you haven't already done so (see Steps 1, 2 and 3).
6   Remove the two Phillips head retaining screws **(see illustration)** and remove the switch.
7   Installation is the reverse of removal.

25 Horn - check, replacement and adjustment

Check

1   On D models, remove the lower fairing (see Chapter 8) the horns

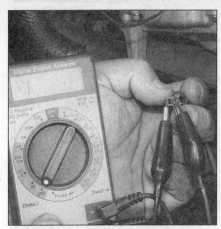

24.3 To check the sidestand switch, unplug the connector, hook up an ohmmeter to the terminals on the switch side of the connector and watch what happens when you raise and lower the stand - when the stand is retracted, there should be continuity; when the stand is down, there should be no continuity

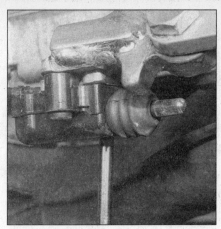

24.6 The sidestand switch is secured by two screws

25.5 To replace the horn on an E model, unplug the electrical connectors (1), remove the two horn bracket mounting bolts (2), remove the horn mounting nut (3), install a new horn on the bracket, install the bracket on the bike and reattach the electrical connectors; the small screw (4) is for adjusting the horn's tone (upper fairing removed for clarity)

26.2 The starter relay is located on the left side of the bike, behind the left side cover; to remove the relay, remove the two terminal nuts (arrows) and unplug the electrical connector (arrow)

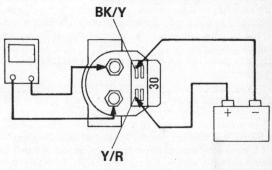

26.3 To test the starter relay, hook up an ohmmeter to the battery and starter terminals as shown, then hook up jumper cables between a 12-volt battery and the control terminals as shown: Negative terminal to the black/yellow wire terminal; positive terminal to the yellow/red wire terminal. When the cable from the positive battery terminal is touched to the black/yellow wire terminal, the relay should click and the ohmmeter should indicate zero resistance

are mounted on brackets at the lower corners of the radiator. On E models, remove the small panel from the underside of the upper fairing (E models only have one horn).

2   Unplug the electrical connectors from the horn. Using two jumper wires, apply battery voltage directly to the terminals on the horn. If the horn sounds, check the horn switch (see Section 21) and the wiring between the switch and the horn (see the wiring diagrams at the end of this Chapter).

3   If the horn doesn't sound, replace it. If it makes noise, but sounds "sick", try adjusting the tone as described below.

Replacement

Refer to illustration 25.5

4   On D models, remove the lower fairing (see Chapter 8). On E models, remove the access panel from the upper fairing.

5   Unbolt the horn bracket from the frame **(see illustration)** and detach the electrical connectors.

6   Unbolt the horn from the bracket and transfer the bracket to the new horn.

7   Installation is the reverse of removal.

Adjustment

8   Loosen the locknut on the adjustment screw **(see illustration 25.5)**. Have an assistant operate the horn. Turn the adjustment screw in or out until the tone is satisfactory. Tighten the locknut.

26   Starter relay - check and replacement

Check

Refer to illustration 26.2

1   Remove the left side cover (see Chapter 8). Disconnect the cable from the negative terminal of the battery.

2   Disconnect the battery positive cable and the starter wire from the terminals on the starter relay **(see illustration)**. **Caution:** *Don't let the battery positive cable make contact with anything, as it would be a direct short to ground.*

3   Connect the leads of an ohmmeter to the terminals of the starter relay **(see illustration)**. Hook up a jumper cable between the negative

9

27.3 To remove the starter motor, slide back the rubber dust boot (arrow), remove the terminal nut and disconnect the cable from the terminal, then remove the two starter mounting bolts (arrows)

27.6 Inspect this O-ring on the starter; if it's cracked or torn, replace it

28.2a Before taking anything apart, mark the relationship of the end covers to the armature housing to ensure that they're reassembled in the same relationship to each other

terminal of a 12-volt battery and the black/yellow wire terminal on the starter relay as shown. Hook up another jumper cable to the positive terminal of the 12-volt battery. When you touch this cable to the yellow/red wire terminal as shown, the relay should click and the ohmmeter should indicate zero resistance (0 ohms). When the cable is disconnected from the yellow/red wire terminal, the ohmmeter should indicate infinite resistance.

4   If the relay clicks but the ohmmeter doesn't indicate zero ohms, replace the relay.

5   If the relay doesn't click, it may be defective or there may be a problem in the starter circuit. To determine which, disconnect the electrical connector from the relay and connect a voltmeter or 12-volt test lamp between the terminals of the black/yellow and yellow/red wires in the wiring harness. Press the starter button again - the voltmeter should indicate approximately 12 volts or the test lamp should light.

a) *If the voltmeter indicates 12 volts or the test lamp lights, the circuit is good. Replace the relay.*

b) *If the voltmeter indicates no voltage or the test lamp stays out, check all wiring connections in the starter circuit (refer to the Wiring diagrams at the end of this book). Also test the starter circuit relay in the junction box, the starter lockout switch, starter switch (button), engine stop switch and ignition switch.*

Replacement

6   Disconnect the cable from the negative terminal of the battery.

7   Detach the battery positive cable, the starter cable and two-wire electrical connector from the relay **(see illustration 26.2)**.

8   To disengage the relay from its two plastic mounting tabs on the front section of the rear fender, simply lift it straight up.

9   Installation is the reverse of removal. Reconnect the negative battery cable after all the other electrical connections are made.

27   Starter motor - removal and installation

Removal

Refer to illustration 27.3 and 27.6

1   Disconnect the cable from the negative terminal of the battery.

2   Remove the fuel tank and the carburetors (see Chapter 4).

3   Remove the nut retaining the starter wire to the starter **(see illustration)**.

4   Remove the starter mounting bolts **(see illustration 27.3)**.

5   Lift the inner end of the starter up a little bit, slide the starter

toward the right side of the engine case, then lift it out once it's disengaged from the starter ring gear.

6   Check the condition of the O-ring on the end of the starter **(see illustration)** and replace it if necessary.

Installation

7   Remove any corrosion or dirt from the mounting lugs on the starter and the mounting points on the crankcase.

8   Apply a little engine oil to the O-ring. Installation is otherwise the reverse of removal.

28   Starter motor - disassembly, inspection and reassembly

1   Remove the starter motor (see Section 27).

Disassembly

Refer to illustrations 28.2a, 28.2b, 28.4 and 28.5

2   Mark the relationship of both end covers to the armature housing. Remove the two long screws and detach both end covers **(see illustration)**. Make sure you don't damage the brushes when disengaging the armature from the rear end cover. The brush plate must remain with the rear end cover when the cover is being separated from the armature (the electrical lead for one of the brushes is attached to the terminal bolt in the end cover) **(see illustration)**. However, the brushes are spring-loaded, and push against the commutator, so one of the brushes might become "cocked" in its holder as you're separating the armature from the end cover. If this happens, using force to pull out the armature can damage a brush or its wire. So if you feel any resistance, stop and look at what's catching; don't just try to pull the armature, rear end cover and brush plate apart by force!

3   Pull the armature out of the housing, toward the pinion gear side.

4   Lift the brush plate off the rear end cover **(see illustration)**.

5   Remove the nut from the terminal bolt, push the terminal bolt through the end cover and remove the bolt and positive brush assembly **(see illustration)**.

Inspection

Refer to illustrations 28.6, 28.7, 28.8a, 28.8b, 28.9 and 28.10

6   The parts of the starter motor that will most likely require attention are the brushes. Measure the length of the brushes and compare the results to the brush length listed in this Chapter's Specifications **(see illustration)**. If either of the brushes is worn beyond the specified

28.2b Carefully separate the rear end cover and the armature housing; if either brush digs into the commutator, stop! The commutator may be slightly cocked. Make sure it's perpendicular to the brush plate and carefully continue to pull it through the plate

28.4 Remove the brush plate from the end cover

28.5 Remove the nut from the terminal bolt, push the terminal bolt through the end cover and remove the terminal bolt/positive brush assembly

limits, replace the brush plate and terminal bolt (remember: one brush is attached to the brush plate and the other brush is attached to the terminal bolt; however, both brushes must be replaced even if only one brush is excessively worn). If the brushes are not worn excessively, cracked, chipped, or otherwise damaged, they may be reused.

7   Inspect the commutator for scoring, scratches and discoloration. The commutator can be cleaned and polished with crocus cloth, but do not use sandpaper or emery paper. After cleaning, wipe away any residue with a cloth soaked in an electrical system cleaner or denatured alcohol. Measure the commutator diameter **(see illustration)** and compare it to the diameter listed in this Chapter's Specifications. If it is less than the service limit, the motor must be replaced with a new one.

8   Using an ohmmeter or a continuity test light, check for continuity between the commutator bars **(see illustration)**. Continuity should exist between each bar and all of the others. Also, check for continuity between the commutator bars and the armature shaft **(see illustration)**. There should be no continuity between the commutator and the shaft. If the checks indicate otherwise, the armature is defective.

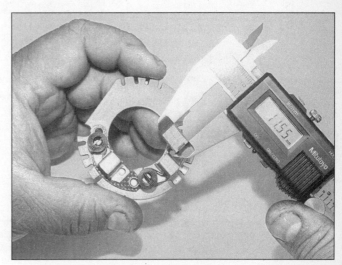

28.6 Measure the length of the brushes and compare the length of the shortest brush with the length listed in this Chapter's Specifications

28.7 Check the commutator for cracks and discoloring, then measure the diameter and compare it with the minimum diameter listed in this Chapter's Specifications

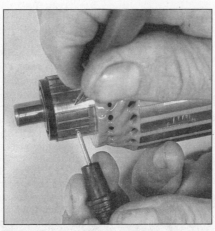

28.8a There should be continuity between the commutator bars

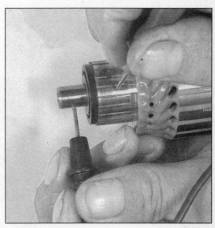

28.8b There should be no continuity between the commutator bars and the armature shaft

9

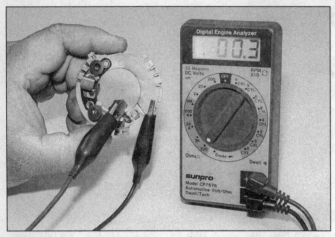

28.9 There should be virtually no resistance between the negative brush and the brush plate

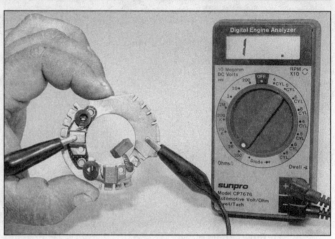

28.10 There should be no continuity between the brush plate holders and the brush plate

28.12a Install the terminal bolt in the rear end cover

28.12b Make sure that the O-ring and insulator are installed in this order, with the O-ring first, then the insulator, then the nut

28.13a The easiest way to get the commutator back through the brush plate without damaging the brushes is to push the brushes into their holders with the side of the commutator while simultaneously sliding the commutator through the plate

28.13b Don't forget to install this washer on the commutator shaft before inserting the shaft into its bushing in the rear end cover

9   Using the 1-ohm scale of your ohmmeter, check for continuity between the brush plate and the negative brush (see illustration). (The negative brush is the one attached to the brush plate.) The meter should indicate close to zero resistance (0 ohms). If it doesn't, the positive brush plate has an open and must be replaced. Now check for continuity between the positive brush and the terminal bolt. Again, the meter should indicate near zero resistance. If either reading indicates higher resistance, the brush lead has an open. Replace the brush plate and terminal bolt assemblies.

10   Using the highest range on the ohmmeter, measure the resistance between the brush holders and the brush plate (see illustration), then measure the resistance between the terminal bolt and the negative brush holder, between the terminal bolt and the end cover, and between the terminal bolt and the brush plate. All four readings should indicate infinite resistance. If any of these readings indicates less than infinite resistance, replace the brush plate and/or the terminal bolt.

11   Check the starter pinion gear for worn, cracked, chipped and broken teeth. If the gear is damaged or worn, replace the starter motor.

Reassembly

Refer to illustrations 28.12a, 28.12b, 28.13a, 28.13b and 28.13c

12   Install the positive brush/terminal bolt assembly (see illustration); make sure the O-ring, insulator and washer are installed on the

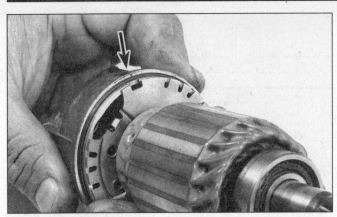

28.13c Make sure the notch in the brush plate is aligned with the notch in the armature housing as shown

terminal bolt in the correct sequence **(see illustration)**. Tighten the terminal nut securely.

13   Position the brush plate next to the rear end cover and insert the positive brush into its holder, then carefully (*very* carefully!) push the brushes into their holders with the side of the commutator and work the commutator through the brush plate as shown **(see illustration)**. Make sure you don't force anything or you could easily damage one or both of the brushes. Slip the washer over the end of the commutator shaft **(see illustration)** and insert the shaft into its bushing in the rear end cover **(see illustration)**.

14   Slide the housing over the armature.

15   Install the pinion end cover, align the previously applied matchmarks, install the two long screws and tighten them securely.

Starter clutch check and replacement

Refer to illustrations 28.16, 28.17, 28.18 and 28.19

16   Remove the alternator cover **(see illustration)**. It's not necessary to unplug the electrical connector for the alternator stator coil, but don't hang the alternator cover by these three wires or you will damage the charging system.

17   Remove the starter idler gear and bushing **(see illustration)**. Inspect the bushing and the gear teeth on the idler gear. If either part is excessively worn, replace it.

18   Turn the starter clutch gear by hand **(see illustration)**. The starter clutch gear should turn clockwise freely, but should not turn counterclockwise.

19   If the starter clutch doesn't operate as described, or if it's noisy, replace the one-way clutch assembly. Remove the alternator rotor (see

28.16 To remove/replace the starter idler gear, starter clutch or alternator, remove these bolts (arrows) and remove this cover from the left side of the engine

28.17 Remove the starter motor idler gear and bushing and inspect both for excessive wear

28.18 To check the starter clutch, verify that it won't turn in a counterclockwise direction, but freewheels in a clockwise direction; if the starter clutch doesn't operate as described, replace it

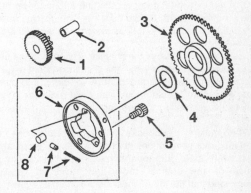

28.19 An exploded view of the starter clutch assembly

1 *Starter motor idler gear*	5 *One-way clutch bolt (3)*
2 *Idler gear bushing*	6 *One-way clutch*
3 *Starter clutch ring gear*	7 *Spring assembly (3)*
4 *Thrust washer*	8 *Roller (3)*

9

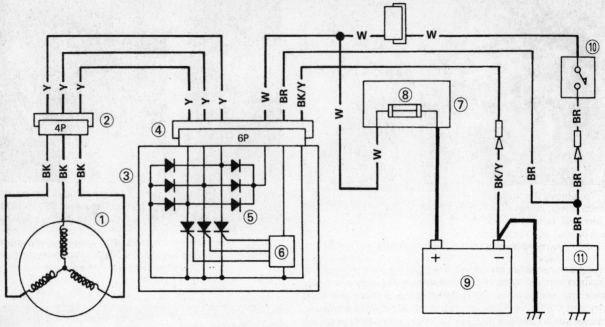

29.1 The charging system circuit

1	Alternator	5	Rectifier
2	Stator coil connector	6	Regulator
3	Regulator/rectifier	7	Starter relay
4	Rectifier/regulator connector		

8	Main (30A) fuse
9	Battery
10	Ignition switch
11	Load

Section 32) and unbolt the one-way clutch from the backside of the rotor **(see illustration)**. Inspect the teeth on the starter ring gear; if they're excessively worn, replace the starter ring gear.

20   Installation is the reverse of removal.

29   Charging system testing - general information and precautions

Refer to illustration 29.1

1   If the performance of the charging system **(see illustration)** is suspect, the system as a whole should be checked first, followed by testing of the individual components (the alternator and the voltage regulator/rectifier). **Note:** *Before beginning the checks, make sure the battery is fully charged and that all system connections are clean and tight.*

2   Checking the output of the charging system and the performance of the various components within the charging system requires the use of special electrical test equipment. A voltmeter and ammeter or a multimeter are the absolute minimum tools required. In addition, an ohmmeter is generally required for checking the remainder of the system.

3   When making the checks, follow the procedures carefully to prevent incorrect connections or short circuits, as irreparable damage to electrical system components may result if short circuits occur. Because of the special tools and expertise required, it is recommended that the job of checking the charging system be left to a dealer service department or a reputable motorcycle repair shop.

30   Charging system - output test

Caution: *Never disconnect the battery cables from the battery while the engine is running. If the battery is disconnected, the alternator and*

regulator/rectifier will be damaged.

1   To check the charging system output, you will need a voltmeter or a multimeter with a voltmeter function.

2   The battery must be fully charged (charge it from an external source if necessary) and the engine must be at normal operating temperature to obtain an accurate reading.

3   Attach the positive (red) voltmeter lead to the positive (+) battery terminal and the negative (black) lead to the battery negative (-) terminal. the voltmeter selector switch (if so equipped) must be in a DC volt range greater than 15 volts.

4   Start the engine.

5   The charging system output should be 14.5 ± 0.5 volts at 4000 or more rpm.

6   If the output is as specified, the alternator is functioning properly. If the charging system as a whole is not performing as it should, refer to Section 33 and check the voltage regulator/rectifier.

7   Low voltage output may be the result of damaged windings in the alternator stator coils, loss of magnetism in the alternator rotor, defective regulator/rectifier or wiring problems. Make sure all electrical connections are clean and tight, then refer to Section 31 and check the alternator stator coil windings and leads for continuity.

31   Alternator stator coil - continuity test

1   If charging system output is low or non-existent, the alternator stator coil windings and leads should be checked for proper continuity. The test can be made with the stator in place on the machine.

2   Trace the three black wires from the alternator/starter clutch cover, behind the water pump and up to the three-terminal connector above the transmission area, near the left side of the frame. This is the electrical connector for the stator coil (the three wires on the main wiring harness side of this connector should all be yellow - if they're not, you've got the wrong connector!).

3   Unplug the stator coil electrical connector.

32.3 To remove the stator coil from the alternator cover, remove these three Allen bolts (arrows), remove the clamp retaining bolt (arrow) and remove the wiring harness clamp

32.4 You'll need Kawasaki's special flywheel holder (A) (tool no. 57001-1313), or a similar tool, to remove the bolt (C) from the alternator rotor (B)

32.5 You'll need Kawasaki's special rotor puller (A) (tool no. 57001-1216) and flywheel puller (B) (tool no. 57001-1223), or an equivalent setup, to remove the alternator rotor from the crankshaft

4   Using an ohmmeter, check for continuity between each of the wires coming from the stator coil. Continuity should exist between any one wire and each of the others (Kawasaki actually specifies a resistance of 0.2 to 0.6 ohms, but the stator coil resistance of our project bike was 0.7 ohms, and it was working fine, so take this specification with a grain of salt!).
5   Check for continuity between each of the wires and the engine. No continuity should exist between any of the wires and the case.
6   If there is no continuity between any two of the wires, or if there is continuity between the wires and an engine ground, an open circuit or a short exists within the stator coils. Replace the stator coil (see Section 32).

32 Alternator - removal and installation

Removal

Refer to illustrations 32.3, 32.4 and 32.5
1   Disconnect the cable from the negative terminal of the battery.
2   Remove the lower fairing.
3   Remove the alternator cover **(see illustration 28.16)**. Trace the three black wires from the alternator/starter clutch cover, behind the water pump and up to the three-terminal connector above the transmission area, near the left side of the frame. This is the electrical connector for the stator coil (the three wires on the main wiring harness side of this connector should all be yellow - if they're not, you've got the wrong connector!). Unplug this connector. Remove the Allen bolt and wiring harness clamp from inside the alternator cover **(see illustration)**. Remove the three Allen bolts which attach the stator to the alternator cover and remove the stator.
4   Prevent the alternator rotor from turning by holding it with Kawasaki tool no. 57001-1313 or a similar tool. Remove the rotor bolt **(see illustration)**.
5   Hold the rotor from turning again, and using Kawasaki tool nos. 57001-1216 and 57001-1223, or an equivalent tool, remove the rotor from the crankshaft **(see illustration)**.

Installation

Refer to illustration 32.6
6   Clean the tapered end of the crankshaft, the alternator rotor bolt, the threads in the crankshaft and the tapered portion of the rotor **(see illustration)** with an oil-less cleaning solvent such as acetone or brake system cleaner.
7   Install the rotor, washer and bolt. Make sure the chamfer on the washer faces out. Prevent the rotor from turning using the method described in Step 4, and tighten the rotor bolt to the torque listed in

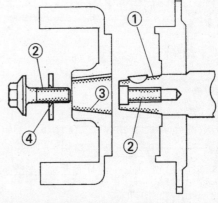

32.6 Before installing the alternator rotor on the crankshaft, clean the indicated areas with an oil-less solvent such as acetone or brake system cleaner

1   *Tapered end of crankshaft*
2   *Threaded portion of rotor bolt and hole in crankshaft*
3   *Tapered portion of rotor*
4   *Note that the chamfered side of the washer faces out*

this Chapter's Specifications.
8   Place the stator coil in position on the inside of the alternator cover, install the bolts and tighten them to the torque listed in this Chapter's Specifications. Route the wiring harness just as it was before and install the wiring harness clamp. Tighten the clamp bolt securely. Apply silicone sealant to the rubber grommet for the stator coil leads and push the grommet into its slot in the alternator cover. Apply silicone sealant to the "split-line" for the crankcase halves, make sure the starter clutch idler gear and bushing are still properly positioned (see Section 28), then install the alternator cover and tighten the cover bolts to the torque listed in this Chapter's Specifications. Route the stator coil wiring behind the water pump, then plug it into the main wiring harness electrical connector.
9   Install the lower fairing (see Chapter 8).
10   Connect the cable to the negative terminal of the battery.

33 Voltage rectifier/regulator - check and replacement

Refer to illustration 33.2
1   Remove the seat and the right side cover (D models) or the left

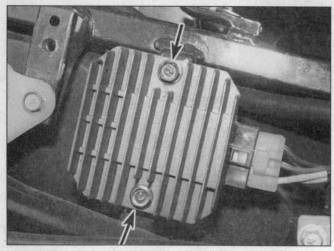

33.2 The rectifier/regulator is located on the right side of the frame on D models; to remove it, simply remove these two bolts (arrows) and unplug the electrical connector - on E models it's on the left side of the frame

No.	Connections		Reading	Meter Range
	Meter (+) to	Meter (−) to		
1	Y1			
2	Y2	W	∞	
3	Y3			
4	Y1			
5	Y2	BK/Y		× 10 Ω
6	Y3		1/2 scale	or
7		Y1		× 100 Ω
8	W	Y2		
9		Y3		
10		Y1		
11	BK/Y	Y2	∞	
12		Y3		

33.3a Continuity table for testing the rectifier

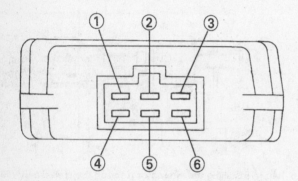

33.3b Terminal guide for the rectifier tests

1	White lead	4	Yellow lead
2	Brown lead	5	Yellow lead
3	Black/yellow lead	6	Yellow lead

side cover (E models) (see Chapter 8).
2   Remove the two bolts securing the regulator/rectifier to its bracket **(see illustrations)**, then unplug the electrical connector.

Rectifier check

Refer to illustrations 33.3a and 33.3b
3   Using an ohmmeter, check the resistance across the terminals indicated in the accompanying table **(see illustrations)**. If the meter readings are not as specified, replace the regulator/rectifier.

Regulator check

Refer to illustrations 33.4, 33.5 and 33.6
4   Hook up a 12-volt battery and test light as shown, with a terminal for one of the yellow leads connected to the positive terminal of the battery, and a test light in series between the terminal for the

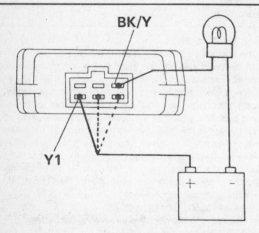

33.4 Hook up a 12-volt battery and test light as shown, with a terminal for one of the yellow leads connected to the positive terminal of the battery, and a test light in series between the terminal for the black/yellow wire and the negative battery terminal - the bulb should NOT come on yet.

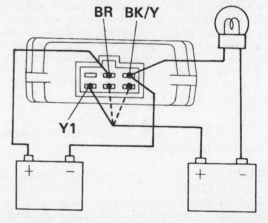

33.5 Hook up a second 12-volt battery by connecting the terminal for the brown lead to the positive battery terminal and the terminal for the black/yellow lead to the negative battery terminal - the bulb should still not come on.

black/yellow wire and the negative battery terminal **(see illustration)**. The bulb should NOT come on yet. **Caution:** *Do NOT use an ammeter instead of a test light! The test light in this testing circuit functions as an indicator and as a current limiter to protect the regulator/rectifier from excessive current.*

5   Now hook up a second 12-volt battery by connecting the terminal for the brown lead to the positive battery terminal and the terminal for the black/yellow lead to the negative battery terminal **(see illustration)**. The bulb should *still* not come on.

6   Connect a third 12-volt battery in series to the second battery **(see illustration)** and BRIEFLY connect the terminal for the brown lead to the battery positive terminal and the terminal for the black/yellow lead to the battery negative terminal. This applies 24 volts to the regulator and the bulb should now come on and stay on, briefly, until the bulb circuit is opened.

7   Repeat this entire test (Steps 4, 5 and 6) at the terminals for the other two yellow leads.

8   If the bulb doesn't light as described during the third step for all three yellow leads, the regulator is defective. Replace the rectifier/regulator unit.

9   These checks, combined with the charging system output test described in Section 30 and the alternator stator coil test outlined in Section 31, should diagnose most charging system problems. If the voltage regulator/rectifier passes the tests described above, and the stator coil passes the test in Section 31, have the charging system checked by a dealer service department or other repair shop (or substitute a known good rectifier/regulator unit and recheck the charging system).

34 Wiring diagrams

Prior to troubleshooting a circuit, check the fuses to make sure

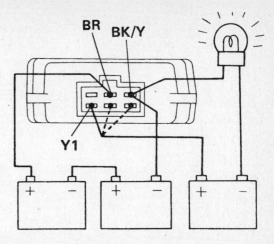

33.6 Connect a third 12-volt battery in series to the second battery and *briefly* connect the terminal for the brown lead to the battery positive terminal and the terminal for the black/yellow lead to the battery negative terminal (this applies 24 volts to the regulator) - the bulb should now come on and stay on, briefly, until the bulb circuit is opened.

they're in good condition. Make sure the battery is fully charged and check the cable connections.

When checking a circuit, make sure all connectors are clean, with no broken or loose terminals or wires. When unplugging a connector, don't pull on the wires - pull only on the connector housings themselves.

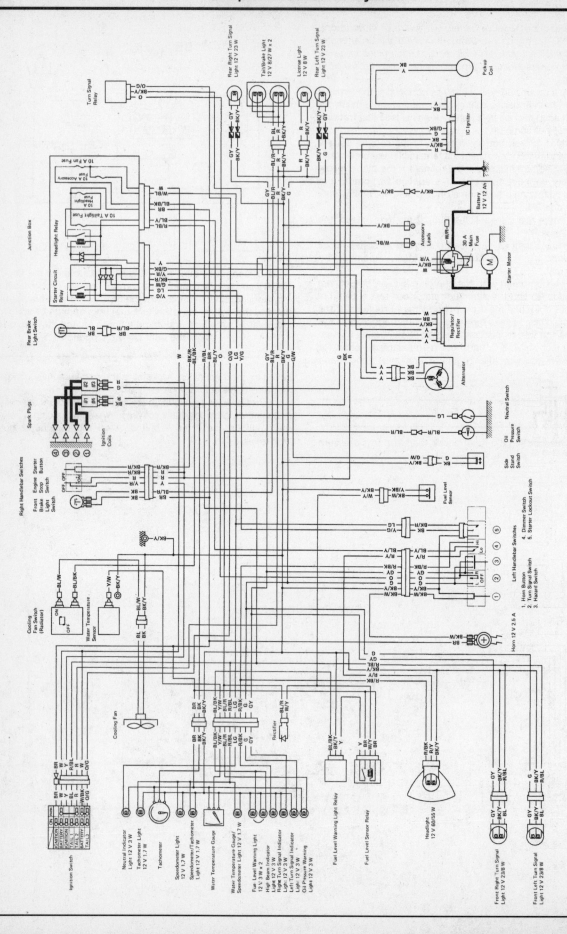

Wiring diagram for D models (US and Canada)

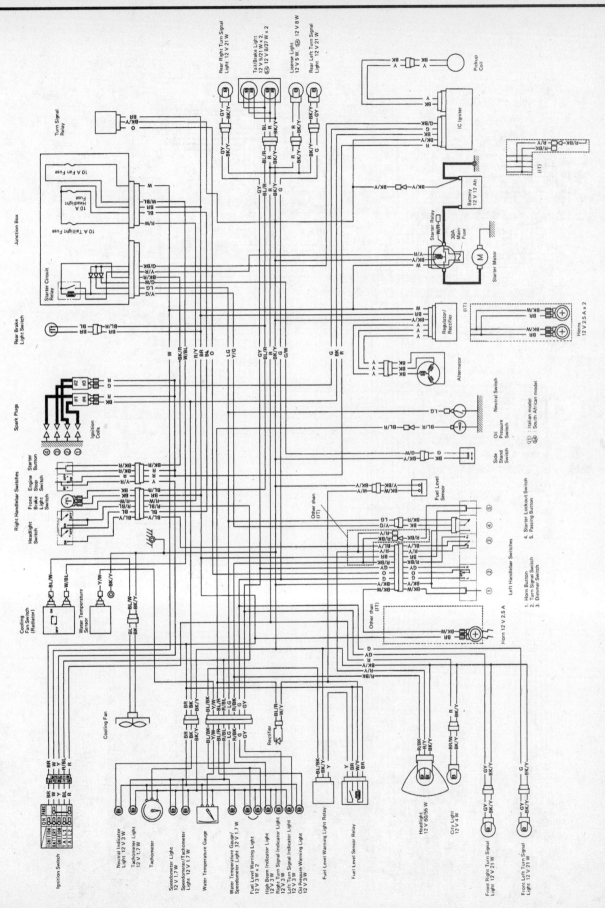

Wiring diagram for D models (U.K.)

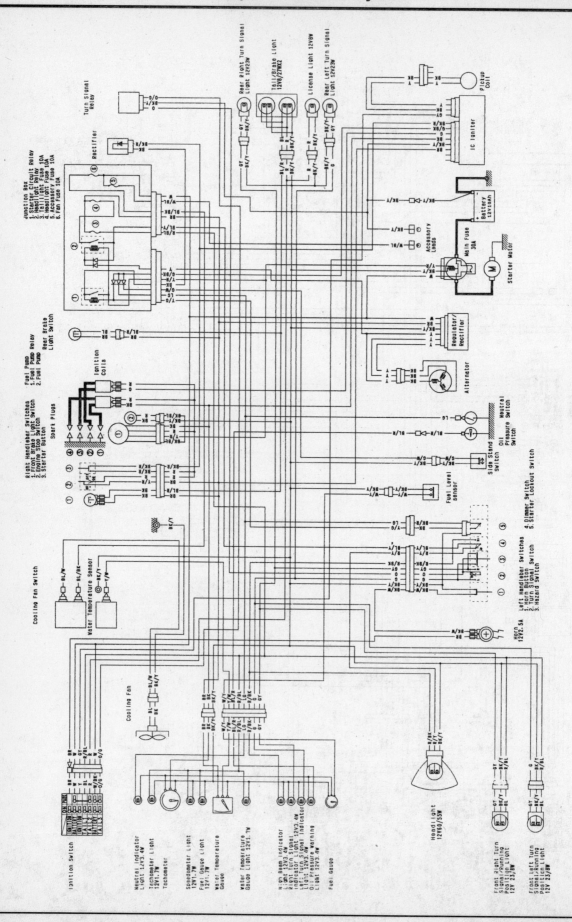

Wiring diagram for E models (US and Canada)

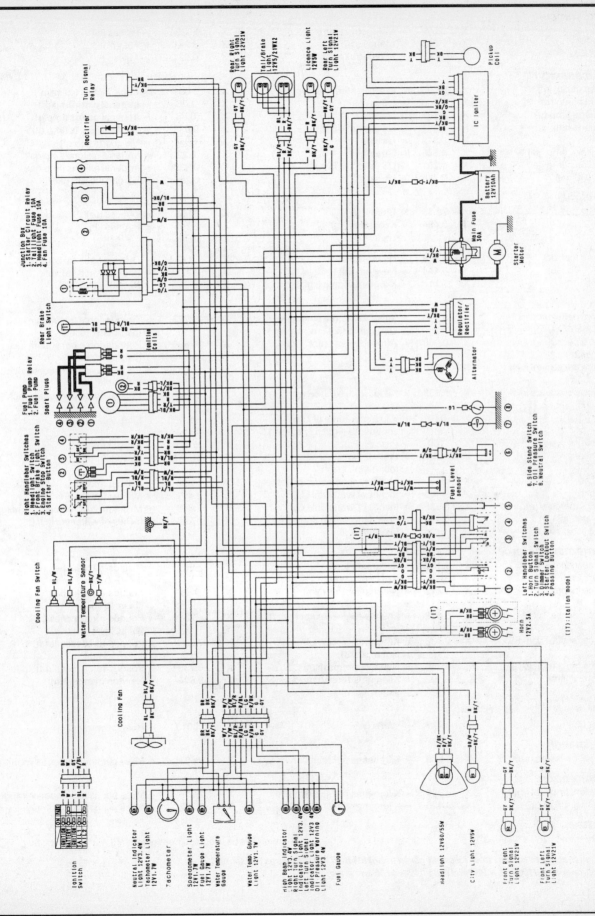

Wiring diagram for E models (U.K.)

Conversion factors

Length (distance)

Inches (in)	X	25.4	= Millimetres (mm)		X	0.0394	= Inches (in)
Feet (ft)	X	0.305	= Metres (m)		X	3.281	= Feet (ft)
Miles	X	1.609	= Kilometres (km)		X	0.621	= Miles

Volume (capacity)

Cubic inches (cu in; in^3)	X	16.387	= Cubic centimetres (cc; cm^3)		X	0.061	= Cubic inches (cu in; in^3)
Imperial pints (Imp pt)	X	0.568	= Litres (l)		X	1.76	= Imperial pints (Imp pt)
Imperial quarts (Imp qt)	X	1.137	= Litres (l)		X	0.88	= Imperial quarts (Imp qt)
Imperial quarts (Imp qt)	X	1.201	= US quarts (US qt)		X	0.833	= Imperial quarts (Imp qt)
US quarts (US qt)	X	0.946	= Litres (l)		X	1.057	= US quarts (US qt)
Imperial gallons (Imp gal)	X	4.546	= Litres (l)		X	0.22	= Imperial gallons (Imp gal)
Imperial gallons (Imp gal)	X	1.201	= US gallons (US gal)		X	0.833	= Imperial gallons (Imp gal)
US gallons (US gal)	X	3.785	= Litres (l)		X	0.264	= US gallons (US gal)

Mass (weight)

Ounces (oz)	X	28.35	= Grams (g)		X	0.035	= Ounces (oz)
Pounds (lb)	X	0.454	= Kilograms (kg)		X	2.205	= Pounds (lb)

Force

Ounces-force (ozf; oz)	X	0.278	= Newtons (N)		X	3.6	= Ounces-force (ozf; oz)
Pounds-force (lbf; lb)	X	4.448	= Newtons (N)		X	0.225	= Pounds-force (lbf; lb)
Newtons (N)	X	0.1	= Kilograms-force (kgf; kg)		X	9.81	= Newtons (N)

Pressure

Pounds-force per square inch (psi; lbf/in^2; lb/in^2)	X	0.070	= Kilograms-force per square centimetre (kgf/cm^2; kg/cm^2)		X	14.223	= Pounds-force per square inch (psi; lbf/in^2; lb/in^2)
Pounds-force per square inch (psi; lbf/in^2; lb/in^2)	X	0.068	= Atmospheres (atm)		X	14.696	= Pounds-force per square inch (psi; lbf/in^2; lb/in^2)
Pounds-force per square inch (psi; lbf/in^2; lb/in^2)	X	0.069	= Bars		X	14.5	= Pounds-force per square inch (psi; lbf/in^2; lb/in^2)
Pounds-force per square inch (psi; lbf/in^2; lb/in^2)	X	6.895	= Kilopascals (kPa)		X	0.145	= Pounds-force per square inch (psi; lbf/in^2; lb/in^2)
Kilopascals (kPa)	X	0.01	= Kilograms-force per square centimetre (kgf/cm^2; kg/cm^2)		X	98.1	= Kilopascals (kPa)
Millibar (mbar)	X	100	= Pascals (Pa)		X	0.01	= Millibar (mbar)
Millibar (mbar)	X	0.0145	= Pounds-force per square inch (psi; lbf/in^2; lb/in^2)		X	68.947	= Millibar (mbar)
Millibar (mbar)	X	0.75	= Millimetres of mercury (mmHg)		X	1.333	= Millibar (mbar)
Millibar (mbar)	X	0.401	= Inches of water (inH$_2$O)		X	2.491	= Millibar (mbar)
Millimetres of mercury (mmHg)	X	0.535	= Inches of water (inH$_2$O)		X	1.868	= Millimetres of mercury (mmHg)
Inches of water (inH$_2$O)	X	0.036	= Pounds-force per square inch (psi; lbf/in^2; lb/in^2)		X	27.68	= Inches of water (inH$_2$O)

Torque (moment of force)

Pounds-force inches (lbf in; lb in)	X	1.152	= Kilograms-force centimetre (kgf cm; kg cm)		X	0.868	= Pounds-force inches (lbf in; lb in)
Pounds-force inches (lbf in; lb in)	X	0.113	= Newton metres (Nm)		X	8.85	= Pounds-force inches (lbf in; lb in)
Pounds-force inches (lbf in; lb in)	X	0.083	= Pounds-force feet (lbf ft; lb ft)		X	12	= Pounds-force inches (lbf in; lb in)
Pounds-force feet (lbf ft; lb ft)	X	0.138	= Kilograms-force metres (kgf m; kg m)		X	7.233	= Pounds-force feet (lbf ft; lb ft)
Pounds-force feet (lbf ft; lb ft)	X	1.356	= Newton metres (Nm)		X	0.738	= Pounds-force feet (lbf ft; lb ft)
Newton metres (Nm)	X	0.102	= Kilograms-force metres (kgf m; kg m)		X	9.804	= Newton metres (Nm)

Power

Horsepower (hp)	X	745.7	= Watts (W)		X	0.0013	= Horsepower (hp)

Velocity (speed)

Miles per hour (miles/hr; mph)	X	1.609	= Kilometres per hour (km/hr; kph)		X	0.621	= Miles per hour (miles/hr; mph)

Fuel consumption

Miles per gallon, Imperial (mpg)	X	0.354	= Kilometres per litre (km/l)		X	2.825	= Miles per gallon, Imperial (mpg)
Miles per gallon, US (mpg)	X	0.425	= Kilometres per litre (km/l)		X	2.352	= Miles per gallon, US (mpg)

Temperature

Degrees Fahrenheit = (°C x 1.8) + 32

Degrees Celsius (Degrees Centigrade; °C) = (°F – 32) x 0.56

It is common practice to convert from miles per gallon (mpg) to litres/100 kilometres (l/100km), where mpg (Imperial) x l/100 km = 282 and mpg (US) x l/100 km = 235

Index